I0254775

The Binary

The Mend, Holistic Healing Through Channelled Entities: channelled by Lucy Dumouchelle through the entity Michael, High Beings, Angels.
Healing From The Farside: channelled by Lucy Dumouchelle through High Beings and the Ancient Entities: Master Twag, Quan Yin, Hu Li.

First Edition print and ebook

Published by Mountaintop Healing Publishing, Inc
P.O. Box 193
Lantzville, B.C.
Canada V0R 2H0

email: mountaintophealingpublishing@shaw.ca

ISBN [print version]: 978-0-9879355-8-8
ISBN [ebook version]: 978-0-9879355-8-8

Imprints: Mountaintop Healing Publishing

Covers courtesy of Tara Cook.
Charts courtesy of Tara Cook.
Graphic illustrations and paintings courtesy of Tara Cook.

Dedication

Man's existence has always been torn between war and peace.
Souls, these volumes give an agenda separate from.
The agenda is the healing of mankind.
It is the aim of each individual to be as well as they may be.
We proclaim unto humanity
that humanity combined requires a mutual agenda,
not singular, Soul.
We place this before you.
The way to heal the spirit will give unto thee all that is necessary.
Reach from your human self unto the Soul of your being
which then may reach into the Spirit of all that is.
For you are merely a fragment of all that is.
This we say unto you.
Gathered together are Souls who have made it possible
that these words might come to be.
They are six.

Tara Cook
Joanne Drummond
Lucy Dumouchelle
Kitty Lloyd
Grace Piontkovsky
Roman Piontkovsky

The medium and compilers of the present volume were under strict instruction to record all transmissions by mechanical means and not to change any detail in the transcription without verification from the source of the message. This we have done.

THE BINARY

Table of Contents

THE MEND

Holistic Healing Through Channelled Entities

Dedication		7
Preface		8
Table of Contents		9
Chart, Path Between Farside and Earth		11
Introduction		12
Chapter One	Time To Heal	34
	Pillar of Light	40
	Eye of Beholding	46
	Healing Vibration	53
	Earth Mend	70
	Visions	84
Chapter Two	Be in the Day	
	Purpose of Humanity	117
	Presence	135
	Acceptance	146
	Stillness	157
	Field	167
	Vibration	178
Chapter Three	Teach Humanity	
	Existence	198
	Eye	213
	Farside	230
	Aliens	241
	Angels	252
	Transition	261
Chapter Four	Blend Your Energy	272
	Oneness of Humanity	273
	Tranquility	296

Chart, The Realm Beyond		310
Chapter Five	The Ultimate Solution	311
	One Thousand Years	314
	Implosion	319
	Cauldron	326
Painting, Entering In To The Cauldron		329
Appendix A	equation of T	330
Appendix B	Daily East Ritual	331
Appendix C	Book List	332
Endnotes		754

HEALING
From The Farside

Dedication		337
Preface		338
Healing Chart		339
Introduction		340
Chapter One	Reiki	349
Chapter Two	Quan Yin	359
Chapter Three	Color	375
Chapter Four	Sound	403
	Mudras	417
Chapter Five	Vibration	569
	Mudras, Hu Li	600
	Mudras, Master Twag	628
Epilogue		727
Appendix A		753
Appendix B		754
Endnotes		758
Mudra Index		764

The Mend
Holistic Healing
Through
Channelled Entities

The Mend Holistic Healing Through Channelled Entities
Channelled by Lucy Dumouchelle through the Entity Michael, High Beings and Angels.

Publisher: Mountaintop Healing Publishing
P.O. Box 193
Lantzville, B. C.
Canada
V0R 2H0

email inquiries: mountaintophealingpublishing@shaw.ca

first revised edition
ISBN [ebook version]: 978-0-9948745-1-1
ISBN [print version] 978-0-9948745-0-4

Imprints: Mountaintop Healing Publishing Inc

Covers, Quan Yin's Earth and Heaven, original artwork courtesy of Tara Cook
Entering In To The Cauldron, original artwork courtesy of Tara Cook
Charts, courtesy of Tara Cook.

Dedication

Man's existence has always been torn between war and peace.
Souls, these volumes give an agenda separate from.
The agenda is the healing of mankind.
It is the aim of each individual to be as well as they may be.
We proclaim unto humanity
that humanity combined requires a mutual agenda,
not singular, Soul.
We place this before you.
The way to heal the spirit will give unto thee all that is necessary.
Reach from your human self unto the Soul of your being
which then may reach into the Spirit of all that is.
For you are merely a fragment of all that is.
This we say unto you.
Gathered together are Souls who have made it possible
that these words might come to be.
They are six.

Tara Cook
Joanne Drummond
Lucy Dumouchelle
Kitty Lloyd
Grace Piontkovsky
Roman Piontkovsky

The medium and compilers of the present volume were under strict instruction to record all transmissions by mechanical means and not to change any detail in the transcription without verification from the source of the message. This we have done.

Preface

Dear readers,

Within a sentence there often will be a word capitalized, yet that same word in another sentence will not be capitalized. The capitalized word is specific to the Farside, the uncapitalized word is specific to earth.

For example, humanity comes to earth armed with Truth. Capitalized Truth is an attribute of Creator that allows humanity upon earth to recognize and overcome negativity created by man.

Uncapitalized truth is a reference to earth conceptuality of the word, truth, a truism. An earth plane truth changes as wisdom, knowledge accumulates. What was truth for you as a child, more than likely changed as you matured. Capitalized Truth does not change, remains always true.

The Mend
Holistic Healing Through Channelled Entities
Table of Contents

Dedication		7
Preface		8
Chart, Path Between Farside and Earth		11
Introduction		12
Chapter One	Time To Heal	34
	Pillar of Light	40
	Eye of Beholding	46
	Healing Vibration	53
	Earth Mend	70
	Visions	84
Chapter Two	Be in the Day	
	Purpose of Humanity	117
	Presence	135
	Acceptance	146
	Stillness	157
	Field	167
	Vibration	178
Chapter Three	Teach Humanity	
	Existence	198
	Eye	213
	Farside	230
	Aliens	241
	Angels	252
	Transition	261
Chapter Four	Blend Your Energy	272
	Oneness of Humanity	273
	Tranquility	296
Chart, The Realm Beyond		310
Chapter Five	The Ultimate Solution	311
	One Thousand Years	314
	Implosion	319

	Cauldron	326
Painting, Entering In To The Cauldron		329
Appendix A	equation of T	330
Appendix B	Daily East Ritual	331
Appendix C	Book List	332
Endnotes		754

Path Between Farside and Earth

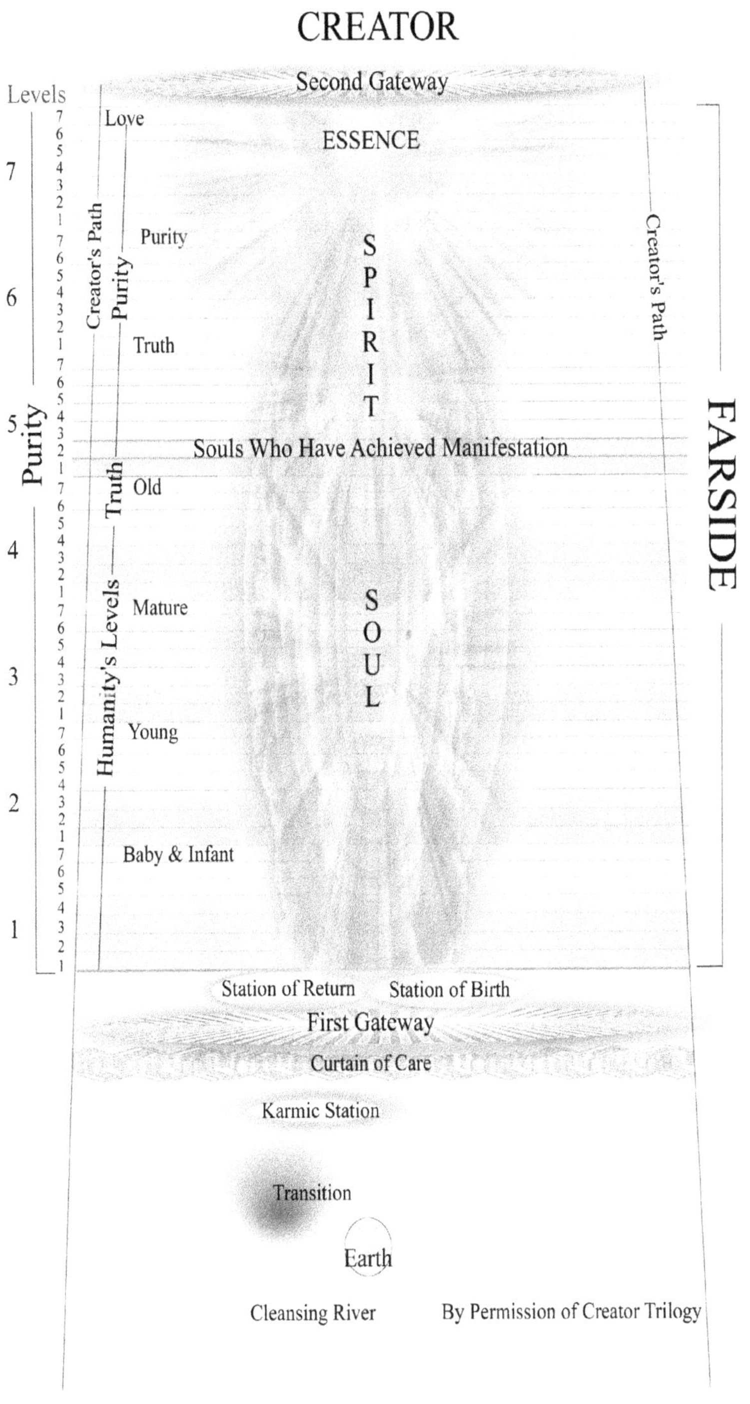

INTRODUCTION

1 Enter thou in to the knowing of who you are,
from whence you have come,
and why you have come.
Within these pages you will find many techniques,
many modalities, much information
and much to ponder.
Within these pages you will find healing for individuals,
using Energy of vibration, color, sound.
You will find information
on the movements of the hands and the fingers.
You will find information on the values of color,
the values of vibration and the values of sound.
And you will find much information
on the purpose of humanity[1]
on the purpose of mankind,
on the very existence of your being
and on the web of existences throughout many universes.
You will find information on the very Creator of your being.
You will find the very lineage of your being,
and you will find keys;
keys to healing, keys to your very existence,
not only upon the earth, but also beyond.
Open the doors, Souls of earth.
Use the keys provided within and enter forth in your oneness,
for you have within the very existence of your being,
the key to the very salvation[2] of humanity.
You will meet within these pages Jesu, Krishna,
Buddha, Mohammed.
You will come to know the great messages of Truth,
of Purity, of Agape Love, and ultimate compassion.
This we give unto you.

2 Enter in to the knowledge
of who you are and of whom you are.
Indeed, much of your earth is confused
by the many legends and writings
found in your holy texts,
confused by much of the teachings
that have come through orally down through the ages.

You are not of the earth,
    you are on the earth!
You are of Farside[3], you are of your Creator.
You have not evolved from animals.
You have not evolved from fish.
You have come unto the earth plane,
    and yet in the blink, less than the blink of an eye,
    you may enter in to the dimension
    of Farside from which you came.
Souls of earth,
    much of the learning that you have been taught,
    much of the learning that you read,
    have come through eons of time,
    and were given to humanity from High Beings.[4]
But humanity felt the necessity
    to interpret that which was given
    into a language, into a way,
    into a form that they interpreted
    would be more expressive
    to the beings at that historical time.
Hence the reason for much of the distortion that occurs.
Souls of earth, you are fed much.
Knowledge is given unto you in various places of learning,
    in various forms of learning, whether they be
    in an institution called school, college, university,
    whether they be in an institution called a church,
    or associated with a church.
In these covers we ask that you think for self,
    that you weigh the information given,
    that you hear with your heart, Soul, and mind
    that which you read.
It is given in all Purity, in all sincerity,
    and in all truthfulness of being.
This we say unto you.

3 We would have you understand that there is a covenant,
    not just between you and your Creator, but also with self,
    also with humanity, also with the Angels.
The covenant is not lightly entered in to.
The covenant is a sacred trust.
You have been entrusted

with a key to bringing forth the Angels from transition,
the Archangels in level four.
This is a sacred trust that you willingly accepted,
nay, indeed requested.
There is purpose in all things.
You have within you, Souls of earth, within that thrum,
all knowledge, consciousness of the sacred trust,
of the covenant.
You have only to use the eye to access the information.
We term it, for your understanding, a sacred trust,
for you to understand the weight of the undertaking
as your gift to your Creator.
The being that has been given the sacred trust
has an enormity of intellect,
an enormity of Purity,
an enormity of consciousness, awareness,
an enormity of stature, an enormity of level.
You have not just come
from the flesh and blood of your parents.
You have come from the consciousness
of the be all and the end all, the supreme.
That is your reality.
That is what holds the sacred trust of resolution, of solution.
Know ye, be secure in the knowledge that
you are the keeper of the sacred trust of your reality.

4 We would have you know the behavior of mankind
is closely guarded, closely watched,
watched in amazement.
Indeed humanity is amazing in its complexity of behavior.
Not even your greatest of machines called computers
could possibly devise the complexity of mankind,
the many variations of being,
the many dispersements of being.
Souls of earth, look at the pattern of mankind
and you will recognize this is no accident.
This was not haphazardly formed.
The intricacies of the human mind, of the human body,
could not be designed by the greatest of your minds,
or the greatest of your machines.
Indeed not.

Every minute portion of your outer being, your epidermis,
has reason, has purpose.
There are no extraneous parts of your body,
whether it be the epidermis that covers the skeleton
or the skeleton, the bones that comprise the skeleton,
the muscles and the sinew that hold it together in place,
the internal organs that facilitate the breathing,
and the flow of liquid throughout your being.
All has purpose!
Your colors, your shades of being have purpose.
Your ability to laugh has purpose.
Your ability to cry has purpose.
All your senses have purpose.
All the differences that are upon the face of mother earth,
that are within mankind, have purpose.
And the purpose is the learning field, always the learning field;
to bring mankind unto the purpose of their being,
the blending into oneness to bring forth
the most precious Blessed Angels and all Souls
caught in a hell of their making in transition.[5]
Honor, respect each minute portion of your being
and that of all mankind.
Understand the great almighty power of Creator
that brought forth all of the complexities of man.
Beloved Souls of earth, you are not just a blob of protoplasm.
Indeed not.
You have within a fragment of the Creator.
Remember this in your darkest moments,
remember this when you may see only difference.
Look beyond that difference into the Light[6]
that is within all mankind.
Your Creator Loves thee unconditionally
and would have you know the greatness of your being.

5 Greetings!
We have no time as in your earth time.
We have waiting.
We have expectation.
We have acceptance.
We do not have time.
We have no limitations,

except that to which we have not yet acceded to, risen to.
We watch always with interest, the antics,
and we glory in the Light and we glory in the laughter,
and, Souls, we admire the blessedness.
Even at your most contentious,
it provides us with hope for the future.
Odd that we have hope, and yet, we do.
We hope to attain another level
and we vociferously enter in to gaining that level.
If we were to decide to remain as we are,
hope would not enter in to the equation for us.
For we would be totally content and have no requirement
for any other adventure or experience.
Souls of earth, hopes are wonderful, but static.
Hopes should be as a light shining on your horizon
but one that you walk toward,
not one that you merely look upon
and expect to come to you at some unforeseen moment,
in, for some unforeseen play of life.
Indeed, walk toward your hopes.
Enter in to your dreams and make them a reality.
But understand a note of caution for your hopes and dreams,
understand, as you enter in to them,
you affect all beings, all humanity.
Be aware of that which you do.
Be aware of the effect of your actions upon mankind.
Be aware that you can, indeed, realize your hopes and dreams
and understand the consequences of those.
You are powerful beings, should you wish to be.
For, as in all things, it is choice,
and there is no judgment from our side unto your side.
When you enter in to, begin to realize that hope or dream,
there is an Energy attached.
All that you do is not separate from another.
All that you do affects each and every particle of humanity.
It is the action that brings about the effect.
And so, when the action is in negativity,
that energy becomes rampant among humanity.
When the action is in positive, is in goodness,
is in compassion and Love,
so, too, that Energy enters in to humanity.

6 We speak of the flame of being.
We speak of the fire within each being, within each Soul of earth.
There is the fire of consciousness.
The more you allow the consciousness to flower,
the more you are aware, the brighter the flame.
You are, Souls of earth, incandescent and yet you know it not.
You are the bud that may bloom
into the most gracious of flowers,
and yet you know it not.
For you denigrate your being
and you denigrate the being of others.
Look to the inner flame of being, not to the outer covering.
Judge not by color, judge not by form,
judge not by perfection, imperfection.
Judge not with your earth eyes.
Judge and you place a barrier between self and all others.
Know that the flame that burns within you
burns within all others,
and connects the consciousness of your being
to the consciousness of all mankind.
You have within a knowing, an intimate knowledge,
of the origin of this flame and yet you deny.
You deny that you are all one.
Particles, separate, indeed, to overcome and gather scars,
and yet one in your divinity.
Souls of earth, know that when you judge another,
you judge all others.
This we would have you ponder.

7 Souls of earth, you are bemused in your being
and we have, are bemused as we watch and listen
and note that what you do, that which you say,
that which is your intent.
How do we do this?
Your aura.
All auras are open to all other auras.
There is no hidden secret.
You are bemused by the actions of yourselves,
not so much the actions of other beings,
but of yourselves.
For you have a knowing within.

Even the baby Soul has a knowing within of negativity,[7]
has a knowing within of purpose,
and comes unto earth with the greatest of intent.
And yet, falls prey to negativity, falls prey to the ego,
the negative ego,
falls prey to the incitements of negativity,
despite the great intent.
And as you enter in to your daily activity
there is a portion of your being, the knower,
that is bemused by that which you do
in spite of the pureness of your intent.
There is no stigma attached to you.
There is gratitude and honor for that which you have done.
There is knowledge throughout the worlds
of your great valor as humanity,
the courage of your being with its intent, great intention.
And your entering in is looked upon with wonder
by worlds and worlds.
Fear not to pass from earth.
You will not be held in a hell.
There are not pitchforks.
There is no Satan or satanic beings to hold you captive.
You may transit through transition immediately
unto the Light, should you will it.
But if you will to punish self,
then you will, with your will create a hellish existence;
not forever, but until you can relinquish that need
and acknowledge the pureness of your being.
Know, each and every is welcome home again.
Enter thou into the knowledge
that you may leave at the karmic station,[8]
the burden you have shouldered of negativity,
and enter home prepared, if you choose,
to once again take up that burden and overcome.
Souls of earth, how great thou are.

8 We would have you know
the Farside celebrates the courage of humanity,
we celebrate the dedication,
the onward movement unto Creator of humanity.
There is no lowly Soul.

There are only Souls of Purity, of goodness, of Love,
entering bravely forth into the vale of negativity.
We see it as a triumphal entry in.
And we are grateful for each and every Soul
who enters in to complete the Writing on the Wall,[9]
the Akashic Record.[10]
Souls of earth, you enter in armed with Truth
and you are indeed armed with the glorious raiment.
And we celebrate not only your entering in,
we celebrate each moment of your struggle
of your existence upon the plane of earth.
We celebrate each overcoming, each step forward.
We celebrate even the red linears,[11]
for all has purpose, all has choice.
All is existent upon the earth plane by agreement,
the intention to bring forth the Angels
and all from transition.
What great glory!
We come forward with news
that will scintillate your being.
We would have you know to understand who you are
will bring unto you great peace and contentment.
For knowing who you arc,
beyond the illusion of the earth plane,
brings you understanding of all that occurs.
It brings unto you the knowledge of why,
for you are human upon the earth.
As human, you are enticed by the foibles of humanity,
you are enticed by the inveigling, innocuous Wilful Child.
Souls of earth, to understand why you are here
is to understand why you choose what you choose.
It gives you greater information on which to base your choices.
It does not preclude you making negative choices,
but it does enforce the ability of the mind,
the heart and the Soul
to examine the conclusion of a choice.
You become mindful in your choice, rather than mindless.
You fully understand with this awareness, with this knowledge.
You fully understand why you do what you do,
and the consequences of your choice,
and you see the scope beyond your own being.

You see the scope of the effects of your action upon humanity.
For, indeed you are individual, but you are humanity.
In your Oneness upon the Farside,
before you entered in to the earth plane,
you are Humanity as one united in purpose.
You come unto the earth, individual,
to grow in Purity for that purpose of humanity.
You come willingly,
and as a young Soul, as a baby Soul, as a mature Soul,
you have varying levels of Purity,
you have varying levels of understanding,
varying levels of knowledge.
Even as an aged Soul, the levels will vary from Soul to Soul,
depending upon the growth of your Purity.
When you have reached the level wherein you are fully human,
wherein you have learned all there is to learn as human,
you then have the opportunity to see beyond the illusion,
to know who you are and from whence you came,
and use this knowledge
in full awareness of the earth plane.
You will understand the Wilful Child.
You understand from whence came the Wilful Child,
and why the Wilful Child is here upon the earth plane.
You understand why you volunteered, asked to enter in.
You understand the full purpose of humanity.
and you understand the fullness
of possibilities of your being;
that you are a particle of Creator.
That becomes not a mere intellectual fact to your being,
but becomes a vibratory knowledge within your being,
and you shimmer with that knowledge
when you realize who you are.
We do not place the veil of illusion forced upon you.
You willingly choose the veil of illusion
so that you might grow in overcoming of negativity,
so that you might fully enter in to being human.
It is when you have accomplished this
that you see beyond the veils you have placed.
This, you will do; this humanity will do in their oneness.
In the thousand years of healing, each and every human
will come to know that which they are and why they are.

9 Souls of earth place value upon gold, upon minerals,
and we would have you know that you are crowned with
a worth more than all the gold of your earth.
You are crowned with the diadem of humanity.
Each and every mankind entered in,
enters in with the diadem of humanity,
enters in with the knowledge of their being,
their sacred self.
It is not hidden.
It is not a secret in a vault, in a heavenly vault.
Each and every Soul upon the earth is free,
is welcome, indeed to see the diadem,
to know upon the earth plane,
the diadem of humanity.
In your growth, in your speculations,
in your drive and in your need for gold,
we would have you understand, it is illusion.
You cannot hold on to a bar of gold as you pass from the earth.
Indeed not.
But indeed, Souls of earth,
you hold to the diadem of humanity,
great, wonderful, glorious worth.
Scramble not into the earth.
Dig not into the earth.
Pour no more toxins into the earth.
Sacrifice no more lives in a conquest of gold,
in the search for the illusory power of gold.
You have more power, within the diadem of humanity,
than you could conceive
of your earth billions and millions of gold.
You have the power to cleanse the earth,
to alleviate all anguish of every Soul.
You have within your being the power to stop the wind,
indeed, to start the wind.
And yet, you focus, you concentrate
on what is in the solids of earth to hold in your hand.
And we would have you release the illusory power,
the greed, the avarice, the focus down.
And understand, and turn to the sacred self,
the understanding of the humanity of your being,
the diadem that you are, the crown within the heavens,

heavens upon heavens upon heavens,
galaxies upon galaxies.
You are the crown.
Recognize, acknowledge, accept.

10 We come to speak with thee
to verify the most recent nudges from thy guides.
When Negativity, our dear brother Negativity,[12]
is recognized by you,
your awareness causes the recognition.
Your level of Purity allows instant recognition.
We verify, Souls, that it is necessary,
and it is of great gratitude
when you send that recognized Negativity to Creator.
We await with open arms to welcome our brother Negativity.
And, oh Souls, we are beyond grateful
that you have sent our brother to us.
Understand, each time you send our brother to us,
we learn a little more
and a welcoming chorus greets each thread.
It gladdens our hearts that thou hast begun
to be more particularly aware,
to be more particularly conscientious
in sending our brother to us.
We would verify that a whoosh, and the intent,
the loving intent to send our brother home to Creator,
is a part of your purpose
and welcoming is a part of our purpose.
You do not know how anxiously
we await each thread of negativity.
Beloveds, be aware of the immensity of your power.
It surprises us each time you find another way
to overcome negativity.
Ah, it is joyous here each time, each moment
that you recognize and send home negativity.
And know ye that when it is done with loving intent
and negativity is in the Flow,[13]
oh beloveds, the chorus of hallelujahs that arises!
Spread ye the word, Souls, spread ye the word:
"Send us our Brother."

11 We would speak with thee on the Will.
You have within your being, within your earth form,
that which you call will.
It has long been a premise of many religions
that your will is not your own,
that your will belongs to another.
Some teachings will tell you
your will belongs to your Creator,
Allah, God, Supreme Being.
Other teachings will tell you that Satan controls the will,
you have a saying "The devil made me do it."
We would have you understand,
that which you call will is beholden to no one.
That which you call will is primarily
that which is written on the wall.
That which you call will brings forth motion,
brings forth action,
which, indeed, is accountable to humanity;
but it always is within your control.
It is your will that makes choice.
It is your will that bombards you with options,
with many choices.
And that which you choose
has not been deemed or ordained by any other being
or power other than your own.
You, each and every beloved Soul of earth,
has accountability to all of humanity.
That which your will proposes to do affects all of humanity.
Your actions for goodness or for negativity
are not contained within your immediate space,
but like a pebble thrown into the ocean,
reverberate and spread to all of humanity.
We would have you know that the spiritual growth of mankind
is such that you are, each and every Soul,
able to understand your accountability.
It is this understanding, it is this level of growth,
that brings forth the Gathering Time.[14]
So be it.

12 We speak of perception.
Were you to perceive from the Farside fence,[15]

you would see the struggle of mankind.
You would perceive the great Light of some beings
who emit from their being great compassion and Love.
You come from the place you call heaven.
You come from the great Being
you call Creator, God, Yahweh, Allah.
You came unto this earth for a purpose,
a purpose of dedication, a purpose to gather scars.
Indeed, Souls, gather scars
that you might open the gate of transition
and show unto the beings beyond the gate, your scars.
Indeed it is reality.
They will perceive you.
They will perceive your Light and your scars
and know that they too have Light.
And you will hold out your arms and many will run toward you.
And the Angels will be there to lift these beings out of transition.
The first to perceive will be the Angels as they rise once more.
That, Souls of earth, is your true reality.
That is your true mission.
That is your true reason for being as human, as mankind.
Open your beings to the perception
of the great Love and compassion within you.
You do not have to reach for Love and compassion,
for you have within you, Agape Love,
worthy of the greatest, held within the very least.

13 Souls of earth, fear no spiral of being,
for each spiral of being has purpose,
has intent, has state, has field of energy.
The spiral of being may be equateable to a spiral of Energy.
The spiral is defined by choice.
That is always the parameter of any spiral of being.
Indeed, you may have spirals of negativity,
for you may have chosen to indulge in acts of negativity,
of depravity, of harm to self or others.
Even those spirals have purpose,
purpose of growth, purpose of containment;
a containment, that is open, not closed;
a containment that may lead to another spiral.
As you enter in to growth, as you choose an act of goodness,

you enter in to a different spiral.
All spirals are states of energy.
All spirals have parameter of choice,
for that will define the spiral of your being.
Acknowledge, recognize that you are a spiral
and recognize the choice is entirely yours,
and know that no containment holds you within.
It is not a jail, it is not a pit without a door.
Always there is the window of opportunity.
Always there is the Flow that is available,
always you are creations of glory.
Indeed, Souls of earth, you are creators of glory.

14 We would have you soar.
Indeed, not as the eagle.
Beyond where the eagle might go.
We would have you soar unto the Farside.
We would have you enter in to stay as long as you wish.
Be it a moment or an hour in your earth time,
we would have you enter in.
And we will greet you, Soul, and ask what would you do?
What would you see?
What would you read?
What would you learn?
And you will tell us.
And you will be guided to the place you wish to be.
It will not take long;
dimensional travel in your earth time is instantaneous.
You will not need to worry about translation,
for you will read and understand directly, conceptually
from the aura of the beings you meet.
If you travel through the gardens,
you will know intimately the Energy of each bud,
of each flower, of each tree.
All will be eager to impart to you who they are,
why they are, what they do, how they came to be.
If you travel into other worlds, the inhabitants
will be as eager to answer all your questions.
You have only to wonder
and the answer will be present to the level of your Purity.
You may enter in to great repositories of knowledge

where minute specific records are kept of all that occurs,
all that is shared upon Farside, even from other worlds.
You will know without communication that the creatures
you know upon earth are in various guises.
And when you meet the reality of their being
you will know their earth representation.
We invite you to soar into a voyage of discovery,
to understand the vastness
and the complexity of one of the web of existences.
You do not need to spend years in meditation,
years in a schooling facility.
You do not need to reach a certain age of wisdom,
for you have the ability to travel.
You enter earth with this ability.
You have only to access it to bring it forth,
for you have it within.
You have only to set your Soul free
from its binding to the earth,
and do so without fear that you will not return.
For indeed you will.
For you have set the time of your demise from the earth plane,
and you will not be demised before that earth time.
Fear not to enter in.
Fear not to explore your homeland.
Fear not to gather knowledge and return with knowledge
that you may share with others.
Fear not to take a respite from the throes of negativity.
Fear not,
for always about your being are your Angels, your guides.
You will not enter in alone.
Indeed, not.
Trust in the Holiness of your being.
Travel with the great eye of beholding,
and know you are assured of welcome home.

15 You have upon your planet a song, "Let it Be, Let it Be".
Indeed, let it Be.
Let acceptance Be.
Let Purity Be.
Let compassion Be.
Let Love Be.

In all things, in all activity, indeed, let it Be,
for you struggle unnecessarily.
You have attained the level required, agreed to,
to gather unto oneness, the oneness of your humanity.
All that we have spoken of:
Purity, Love, compassion, acceptance,
involve no struggle.
They are!
In your humanness, in the individual humanity of your being,
you struggle mightily with negativity to overcome.
You struggle not to create more negativity.
And we would tell you that you have at your fingertips,
nay, within the very electrons of your being,
you have that which Negativity hungers for:
Love, compassion, Purity, acceptance,
acceptance of the Wilful Child,
acceptance of the search of the Wilful Child,
acceptance of your participation in that search,
of your answer to that search.
For it is the note that is the welcome end of the search
within the negative void.
We are not speaking of beyond,
for indeed there is a further search,
but here in this blessed place is of which we speak.
Every moment that you emit from your being
Love, compassion, acceptance of another,
acceptance of the vagaries of all other beings,
each moment, you build great Purity.
You build compassion for the Wilful Child.
You build the building blocks of oneness,
wherein humanity will come unto its ultimate purpose.
Gather to you acceptance, Love, compassion and expel Purity.
Not expunge it,
expel unto all others.
Souls of earth, indeed you are coming unto oneness
and we bless your beings.

16 Mankind, you are fearless.
We, from the fence, see you as fearless.
All Farside knows of the fearlessness of humanity.
Souls of earth, before you choose,

indeed you have all free choice,
before you choose to enter in to the earth plane,
you understand every iota, every nuance,
every possibility of pain that you will endure,
that you will latch on to, that you will give unto another.
You understand the possibilities of pain
as well as you understand the possibilities of joy.
And yet, in your fearlessness, knowing what you will endure,
what you will overcome,
knowing that the illusion will be reality
during your time upon the earth;
in your great dedication to Creator and beyond,
you fearlessly enter in to negativity,
to the realm of negativity,
to where negativity reigns in many places unhindered.
And yet, you enter in time and time and time again.
Oh, how great thou art!
Souls of earth, we would have you understand,
you have been entering in
for millennia and millennia and millennia.
You have been entering in since before recorded time.
You have been entering in dedicated to the purpose of humanity,
and we would have you understand,
we would have you know without doubt,
that you have completed!
Indeed, you have completed!
It is only your doubt,
your refusal to recognize the oneness of mankind,
the oneness of your humanity,
that prevents the next stage of, not evolution,
development; the next stage
of dimensional development, change; of alteration.
And we speak not of individual
but of the oneness of man, of the humanity that you are,
the who you are, the very Soul of Creator,[16]
the very epitome of Creator
in your Truth, Love and Purity,
in your compassion.
For without such great compassion and Love
you would not be fearless in your entering in,
over and over and over.

Souls of earth, you have reached the pinnacle,
    but, in your illusion, you do not recognize the reality.
We would have you understand, be aware of, recognize,
    you have reached the pinnacle of humanity,
    Holy unto Holy![17]
Lift your beings in great choruses of hallelujah.
Lift your being in recognition of reaching the goal.
Raise your being so that you might raise the beings in transition
    and then unto the Cauldron, and then unto the beyond.
It only takes the acceptance of your humanity.

17 We would have you gaze upward at the sky,
    at the panoply before you, the vastness that you see,
    and know that that vastness is less
    than the minutest head of a pin
    in comparison to other dimensions,
    to other worlds that you may visit.
There are dimensions beyond dimension beyond dimension,
    and your eye gives you access.
You may visit the world of the Jinn.[18]
Souls of earth, your very purpose has become their purpose.
With the eye you may enter in to the world of the
    Gummerians.[19]
They are repository of great knowledge.
Of the Pleiadians[20] much knowledge has been given.
Understand, you have within your being,
    within the eye, within the aura,
    within the Soul of your being,
    a direct connection to the Farside.
You have the key to enter in.
The earth is not your home world.
You have all come from other worlds.
Understand, Souls of earth, the concept of alien,
    it is only alien to earth, not alien to each other,
    for you are all of one Energy.
This you will understand, using the eye.
We would gladly take your hand and assist your leaving behind
    the bindings that you have placed upon your being.
Take our hand and enter in with the eye
    and return with a greater sense of who you are,
    with a greater sense of your Creator.

18 We have made reference to Light Beings,[21]
and we would have you understand,
we are specific to what we will call twelve Light Beings.
You will come to understand you are all Light Beings,
in the sense, the broadest sense,
that you carry within you Light,
and that you emit Light,
and that your Light may Light upon another,
whether it be creature, nature or another being.
You carry within you, the memory of the Light Being
from which you came.
Indeed, this is not a contradiction,
for your Creator is a Light Being,
and eleven Light Beings lent unto one
their strength, their Energy, their solidarity,
and each of the twelve have given forth their Energy
in a reflection of their Being.
We have said you are Archangel, we have said you are Angel,
and, indeed, you are all of these.
For your understanding, we say to you,
these are reflections of your originator.
We say to you that you carry within the seed of your originator.
Each of the twelve is a tribe.
We are being simplistic for a very complex panoply of energies,
and yet we would give unto you
this most basic of understanding.
Each of you were entered forth; entered,
sounded forth in all your glory,
in all positive, in all Purity and Love,
and your Creator provided unto you, the armor of Truth.
You were not entered forth without agreement,
for you have the agreement of the Light Being
who gave of their Energy for the web of existence.
You have come unto earth for a purpose.
You have been entered forth in order
to return unto the fold the Wilful Child,
the Angels in transition.[22]
Your world is a fold.
Each of your reflections are a fold.
Existence is fold upon fold upon fold upon fold.
This your science already knows in theory,

and folded space will become clear to your science
with the equation[23] evolving.
Souls of earth, you are not minuscule in stature.
You are, indeed,
given the great panoply of existences in minute portion,
but as in all things, in all existences, every portion,
no matter its minuteness,
has a part to play in the web of existences.
Your part, Souls of earth, in the play of time and space,
is of great, monumental proportions
though you are minute.
That which you will do; the implosion, the Thousand Years,
will enfold space, will begin a new day.
And you will, it will come to be;
you will reunite with the Being that entered you forth.

19 Souls of earth, we would have you shout hallelujah,
in recognition of your great accomplishments,
in recognition of your glory,
of a paean of glory to your Creator.
Paean!
Hallelujah, hallelujah, for your journey is nearly ended.
Hallelujah, for the gates, and it is plural,
the gates will soon be opened.
Not by aliens, not by the Angels,
not even by your Creator, but by you, humanity.
You will open the gates,
the gate of transition and the Second Gateway.
The First Gateway will be opened by the Angels
in recognition and in preparation
for when you open the gate of transition.
Triad, Soul.
Hallelujah!
Hallelujah, as you welcome Souls
caught in agony for thousands of years.
Hallelujah, as you welcome particles of being
and watch the particles coalesce into oneness.
Hallelujah, as you reach unto the Angels.
Hallelujah, as you freely travel beyond the First Gateway
and back unto the earth.
Hallelujah, as the earth is cleansed of negativity.

Hallelujah, as the earth is healed.
Hallelujah, as the Wilful Child alters its being.
Hallelujah, as Creator's Soul becomes whole in its Divinity.
Hallelujah, Souls of earth, will be sung
    by worlds upon worlds upon worlds,
    when you enter in, open the gate of transition,
    and begin the process of return.
Hallelujah! Hallelujah! Hallelujah!
The Angels in a mighty chorus sing
    and you will hear the reverberation
    of their Sound and Color unto your being.
You will hear the gratitude, the fellowship,
    you will hear the hope of knowing.
So be it.

20 Souls of earth, brevity.
You have such a word, brevity.
It encompasses much in its conceptuality,
    brevity: terseness, shortness, conciseness.
And, you wonder, where is the brevity in what we have taught?
Why is it so extensive?
Why does it seem to repeat itself now and then?
Why do the teachings seem so complex,
    and yet, in a moment,
    you come across a simple teaching.
We would have you understand,
    that each being that places their eyes to read,
    their ears to hear the channelling,
    will interpret according to the subsets of their brain,
    will interpret according to their mind's level.
The overall concept will be similar from being to being,
    but within each individual being
    they will see very differently,
    and they will hear very differently.
Some will accept the surface of a sentence.
Others will see the myriad of meanings within the sentence.
There are sentences that we have given during the channelling
    that could be studied for months,
    that would lead to a chain of thoughts and learning
    that would take months,
    and these will be dissected

and attacked by scholars and matched.
The channelling is for all humanity, and therefore
the complexity that you see is, in actuality, a simplicity.
For without the complexity that you see,
it would only be apparent to a very few beings
what the meaning is of a sentence or a passage.
We would suggest and we would ask,
as you delve into the learning present,
that you do so with the knowledge
that you will receive teachings for your individual being,
as will all others who read, who hear the words given.
These words were not chosen lightly,
they are exact in their meaning, they are precise.
We would ask that you read within the context of the passage
and then dissect, if you will, each sentence or a few.
Reading within the context will give you the full lesson,
for each passage is within itself a lesson.
It is not the whole paragraph, it is the whole passage.
It is not the whole chapter that is the lesson,
it is each passage within that chapter.
Read with the heart and the mind and the Soul,
read with the triad to gain full perspective,
to gain the fullness of meaning, of intent, of lesson.
You will come back again and again
to a particular sentence or passage that will have meaning
for your heart, for your mind, indeed, for your body.
And this is as it should be.
Each would have their own relationship with the passages.
Indeed, Soul, a relationship.
And you will come to find this as you delve into the volume.

Chapter One
TIME TO HEAL

21 We speak of layers.
You will understand, Souls of earth, your earth has layers,
the very soil has layers.
The very mind of your being has layers of awareness.
The very Soul of your being has layers of Purity.
The very flesh of your being has layers: skin, cell, bone, blood.
There is upon your earth no one thing that is single layered,
all has a multiplicity, even your aura has layers.
Even the Farside has layers and we speak of Energy.
Energy is not one dimensional, not one layered.
Energy has a multiplicity of being.
Energy is not one dimensional,
it is indeed multidimensional,
whether upon the earth or upon the Farside,
or whether in the earth, or earth itself.
Each and every being upon this earth is multidimensional
and has multidimensional energies.
You think of yourself contained in your flesh
and blood and bone.
Indeed, you are not one dimensional,
nor is your universe one dimensional.
You have layers, dimensions within dimensions,
a complexity that would astound your scientists.
A complexity your science will discover
has a basic simplicity to it,
that simplicity is the Flow of Energy from Creator.
We would have you understand
there is no limit to the dimensions of being,
except that which you choose.
You place limitation.
Creator places no limitation.
Your galaxy places no limitation.
Only you place limitation upon your being.
And when you place limitations upon your being,
you snuff out the possibilities open to you.
You become fragile in your being.
You have clung to the illusion, to the one dimensional illusion.
Souls of earth, you have great power.

Fear not the power,
for your power lies in the healing of mankind,
in the healing of all the creatures upon your earth,
in the healing of the very sky above your being,
in the healing of the very waters of your earth,
in the healing of the Souls
caught in transition and beyond.
Recognize the multidimensional Essence[24] of your being.
Recognize all possibilities are yours to explore,
to become aware of, to be.
Recognize who you are and enter in
to the multidimensional possibilities of your being.

22 We would have you understand three battles.
First two Battles fought upon the Farside.
Not battles with weapons, indeed not!
The First Battle fought with Love, the second with Purity,
your battle, Souls of earth, you are armed with Truth.
The First Battle,[25] the Farside, Angels armed with Love,
brought forth to enter in and
by virtue of unconditional Love,
cease the pain of the split.
It was not to be.
The Second Battle,[26] Purity;
the Angels, world to world, absorbing the sleep,
the inertness caused by the Wilful Child,
and placing within the Cleansing River,[27] the Negativity.
And entering in again and again and again
until there were those Angels who were overburdened,
and fearing to contaminate Creator,
placed the curtain of care.[28]
Soul, we speak very simply of a great magnitude of events,
only to place in a perspective for you.
Humanity volunteered to go on to the earth
and fight the third[29] and final battle with Truth,
the very ability to attract, recognize,
and overcome negativity.
The very scars of your being that you have gained,
through overcoming negativity,
will show unto the Angels in transition
that it is possible to overcome and not taint Creator.

They will see in the oneness of humanity,
the very Soul of their Creator,
and they will rush forward into
the arms of their brethren.
Souls of earth, you are indeed an armada,
the armada of humanity, Creator's Armada.
And Melchezidec is the being who placed forth the call
to all the worlds, and you, humanity, answered the call
and entered in and then out unto the earth,
time and time and time and time and time again.
How great you are!
We would have you know
you have the strength to enter in to oneness,
to complete the battle.
You need not, Souls of earth, continue.
Hear what we say!
Recognize the battle is won; it only needs your recognition,
your acquiescence,
your agreement to enter in to oneness.

23 We bring unto you greetings
from what we call, for your understanding, the Farside.
The Farside is merely a step away.
It is a dimensional step away.
You will understand, you may make this step only in Purity,
for negativity is not allowed.
There is no negativity here.
There is only one place where the Wilful Child,
the negativity abounds, and that is upon the earth.
And this is no accident,
for as you know, there are no accidents,
there are no coincidences.
All has reason for being.
We would have you understand,
you have given, as a gift unto your Creator,
these lifetimes that you spend here in growth,
overcoming the negativity that you create.
Negativity is not created by your Creator
nor by some phantom being called Satan.
No, Soul, you take the Energy and distort it,
and it becomes negativity,

and you come back lifetime after lifetime
to take that negativity you created,
and offer it back as you overcome,
unto your Creator who then may alter.
Why do you do this, Souls?
Why do you do this time after time
when you know you are particled from Creator,
that in each and every, every being,
you have a particle of Creator.
Indeed, you do.
Even the most heinous, in earth terms,
of a being is a particle of Creator.
And all are as they grow in Purity and bring back unto Creator
this Energy of the Wilful Child;
all gathering together in a oneness,
a oneness that will reclaim the planet.
You have this power.
Your Creator will not interfere with that which you do,
for that was your agreement.
You said unto Creator:
You are a being of total Love and Truth and Purity
and your Love will not allow you
to force the Wilful Child to return.
Allow us to become your Soul.
Allow us, Creator, to enter in to the vale of tears
and reclaim the Energy for you."
And so it was that you entered in, and particled of Creator,
were brought unto the earth by the Angels.
Each and every being upon the earth
volunteered of your own free will, to come unto earth,
and choose between negative and positive.
You have forgotten, Souls of earth, that which you came to do.
You have lost your purpose.
And we bring unto you a reminder of your purpose to overcome
negativity, to Love each and every other,
to know there is in reality no other;
that you are all one being called humanity,
that you are all brothers and sisters.
That there are no barriers of race or color or creed or sex,
except those that you have created,
that becomes negativity, a distortion of Energy.

Hear ye, Souls, hear ye of your Angelic being and your purpose
and know that you are blest and blessed.
Know you have purpose, each and every being;
no action, however minuscule, has ever wasted.
You have before you all opportunity to save your planet,
to heal all the beings that are here,
that have come to support you.
Think you the rock has no feeling?
The rock has Soul.
The snake has Soul.
The tree has Soul.
You, humanity, are the caretakers and you have forgotten.
Recall who you are.
Recall your purpose and know you never walk alone,
that always, with you, your Angels step before you,
your brethren Angels.
Hasten to Love one another.
Hasten, Soul, heal the earth
and by healing the earth, you heal self.

24 Remorse, Souls of earth, remorse!
You spend much time in remorse and it is unnecessary.
It is what you would term a waste of your time.
Remorse for what?
Rather, invest in the reparation.
Rather, invest the Energy in goodness.
Once you have recognized that your action
caused harm to self or another,
falling into remorse becomes negative,
for then you are caught within that action constantly.
The mind worries at it, as a dog gnaws at a bone.
Remorse serves one purpose; it is offered as gift unto Creator.
Is it necessary to mea culpa?
Indeed not.
Is it necessary to berate self for an action?
Indeed not.
For you have then compounded
the initial negative action with another negative.
And two negatives do not make a positive.
When you have committed an action of harm, recognize,
and where possible, repair.

Recognize that there are no accidents.
You did not accidentally harm self or another.
You harmed for a reason.
You harmed for an opportunity to learn to grow,
to utter forth from your being, goodness,
not more negativity.
It is not necessary to punish self or others.
Your Creator has no punishment within.
Your Creator is incapable because of the Love He holds for all,
of even considering a punishment.
It is not within the mentality, the language of your Creator.
It does not exist as a possibility.
The possibilities of your Creator are Truth, Love, and Purity,
and you have within
all possibilities of Truth, Love and Purity.
There is no requirement for remorse
or punishment of any deed.
Recognize the Holiness of your being.
Recognize the pure Soul of self.
Recognize you are of Creator.
You are in essence born of Love, unconditional Love.
And you may bear that Love, and you may give out that Love,
for it is your birthright.
The blessed Souls are not insignificant.
When you came to the earth plane,
you voluntarily shouldered great responsibility
for the power that dwells within thee.
You are not powerless.
You are not a helpless frail being.
You are not a being of insignificance.
No Soul is insignificant.
All Souls hold great power.
We would ask that this power be focused to heal;
to heal the land, to heal thy brother, thy sister,
thy child, thy mother, thy father, thy neighbor, thyself.
All are connected.
All are one in their birth.
All are one in their being.
All are one in thy creation.
Know that thy being is of Creator.
You come from Creator.

How can you be powerless?
Use thy power to heal.

Pillar of Light

25 We would speak of Energy.
Upon your earth you equate energy with electricity,
with electrons, with nuclei, with ions, with atoms.
The Energy that is contained within each being has within it,
to equate to your earth knowledge,
a spark that may be ignited to a flame, a violet flame.
That spark is indeed within your Soul, reflected in your aura
and connected to the Pillar of Light,[30] a triad.
The Energy of your being is that of your Creator.
You understand that the Energy of your being
is given movement by the Great One.[31]
You understand that the Energy of your being
is given enlightenment by Godhead, all triad.
The electricity of your earth, when it is activated,
whoever, whatever touches it is affected by it.
The electricity, the Energy within your being,
when turned on, affects all that it touches.
It does not remain within your being.
It flows freely when you ignite the flame of your high self.
In that instant you heal.
In an instant,
you touch and you heal,
for that charge has entered out from you unto another.
You may with the eye place your being across the world
and it will be the same effect.
Souls of earth, you cannot once you have ignited your Soul,
contain your healing compassion unto one another.
When you enter in to this choice,
know ye the responsibility you have accepted.
Know ye, you do not require to be a Holy man or woman,
a priest or Rabbi.
It is not necessary.
All have this possibility.
And so, when you choose,
be alert to the choice of your being.

You are hallowed beings.
The Energy you may access is hallowed.
Use the triad of your being to heal one another,
to heal that earth who cries in piteous pain.
Beloveds, you have awaiting you the violet flame of healing.
Ignite it, Soul, in your Love and compassion.

26 We would have you understand the entering in,
the passing unto another dimensional reality.
We would explain that your being is compressed
unto a very minute form,
and you enter in to what your scientists think of
as the gravity well of a black hole.
But we would tell you, there is not gravity,
there is a deep magnetic pull that pulls you in,
and as you are pulled in from one end,
from your earth end,
you come out another end,
and it is as if you expand exponentially
from the minuteness that you were.
This is not, Soul, over a long period of time;
this happens in less than your instant upon the earth.
It is simply a process and we would have you understand
that you must dispense with fear, for fear is negative,
and in your negativity you are bound to the earth.
The science involved in this corridor
that you enter in to and out of,
to enter in again, will be unravelled in this century.
Quicker than you can imagine science will discover
the key to unravelling
what you may think of as time travel,
and indeed, Soul, it is time and space travel.
And indeed, it is possible without gravity,
this we would have your science understand.
The enormity of the energies available in your cosmos
are beyond the comprehension of the earth mind.
This is not to denigrate the capacity of the earth mind,
merely to give you a comparison
of the volatility of the energies with which you deal.
And as enormous as these energies are, Soul,
you may access with your Energy

all other Energy within your Yawn.
In the vibration of your Energy
is the linkage to all other energies.
You see yourself as separate, as minute, and yet you are not!
Indeed, you are particles,
but you are not separate from the other energies,
unless you will it to be.
You see your Energy as finite,
and we would have you understand you have access
to an unending well of Energy.
Your aura, your Pillar of Light is not a finite well
that you may drain to nothingness; indeed not,
for it is connected to the well of Energy of all energies.
You underestimate your possibilities,
and we would have you understand the greatness
of your Soul consciousness, of who you are.
You have the possibility to stand
with the greatest that you are aware of,
and the even greater that you are not yet aware of.
Mankind is not small in stature, mankind has great stature.
All Farside is aware of mankind, and welcomes mankind.
Fear not to drain your Energy well,
fear not to share it with another,
fear not to give forth from your well.
Fear not, Souls of earth, the expansion of your being.
Share thy Light grant solace unto another,
grant healing unto another,
grant unto Mother earth healing
from that which plagues her being.
You can, Souls of earth.
It is your choice.

27 We speak of Light, the rays that continuously
form a spiral, a ring about your being.
Light is not static.
Indeed, it is filled with Energy.
The Light that you see, the Light you do not see,
except with the eye, filled with Energy.
It is Energy, this Light;
the streaming rays always around your being, available.
As your Angels are always about your being,

so is the Light.
Not forced unto you, indeed not,
but available for you to reach out,
to allow it to enter in to heal self
and allowing it to enter in to heal unto others.
For each being upon the earth has this potential to heal
with Light Energy, self and others.
And not, simply, when we say others,
are we referring not only to humanity;
for you may heal all manner of creature,
all manner of form.
All matter may be healed, may be altered,
even unto the earth itself.
The rays of Light dance constantly,
they do not rest, they are peripatetic in their being.
For the Light, these rays of which we speak,
are not simply Energy,
as you think of energy upon your earth.
They are imbued with Love, Agape Love.
They are imbued with a kaleidoscope of the Prism,[32]
of the Crystal Cave.
They are imbued with Truth, with Purity,
indeed with ecstasy, wisdom and enlightenment.
The Light rays are from the Triad;[33]
Creator, Godhead and Great One;
they have all the attributes of the Triad.
These Light rays are only a minuscule portion of the Triad.
We do not say that to denigrate the Lights,
we would only have you understand,
in your earth being you could not fathom
the expansiveness of the Light rays of the Triad.
Even within the eye, to visualize, to understand the fullness,
you have not the ability.
This is not to say you are not deserving, indeed not,
but this is to say that what you see with your eye
upon the earth plane, when you see the aura
and you see the Light dance,
has been muted for your visual acuity.
As your Purity, as your enlightenment increases,
you begin to see more and more
of the depth of the rays of Light,

for they are not one dimensional,
they are multidimensional.
And you, humanity, may energize your being,
may capture this Energy,
this God given, this Divine Energy, for in your Purity,
you may indeed allow the rays to enter in,
and you may direct them.
These rays of Light alter matter, alter the mind,
alter mental, what you call mental illness,
mental disability.
It alters physical illness, physical disability, it alters thought.
Not as if you were the magician, but it may alter
with the permission of the Soul,
for there is always choice.
You must connect the Energy of self to the other,
to another being, human,
to the animal, to the earth, for they alter,
and in the connection you may discern their willingness
to accept the alteration of matter.
And you will know, Souls of earth, whether or not you have,
permission to alter.
For seeing with the eye
and making a connection of Energy to Energy,
you understand that which can be
and that which cannot be.
And you will not therefore misuse or misjudge
the power of the Light rays.
It is impossible.

28 Souls of earth, on those days
when you feel immured in despair,
in pain, alone, drenched with negativity,
we ask that you pause a moment.
Place your hands outward, palms up in supplication,
not to your god, but to your high self,
to your Pillar of Light.
Do not place the fingers tightly together.
Leave them loose and extend your hands in this position
to the full extension of your arms.
And know as you do without doubt
that you are embracing your Pillar of Light.

That you may now hold on to that Light
and bring it in toward your being.
Move your hands, Soul.
Bring it in.
Deep breath, breathe it in.
Place it over your body as if you were showering with water,
Cup your hands, move it over your being,
allow the Light to enter in.
Bathe your being, bathe your face, your arms,
your body in the Light.
Know it is there and you will feel within moments
a lifting a lifting of the intensity of the pain,
a lifting of the despair, of the aloneness.
You will know you are not alone.
You will begin to be able to cope
with the negativity that you have embraced.
It will allow you the opportunity to pause and make your choice,
to release the negativity, to embrace the joy of being.
You will feel a pressure,
you will feel the Light around your being,
for the Light indeed has substance;
it has form, it has matter.
And you may choose to bring that unto your earth being,
to embrace the beauty of the Light,
the goodness of your Soul,
to find compassion in the Light for self,
so that you may then choose the joy of being.
Enter out that Light unto others.
You have all possibilities of Light.
Harken, Soul, to who you are.
Fear not your Light.
Enter it unto thee.
For as in all things you have that choice and all possibility.

29 We would have you place your hands together slowly,
and make a hole.
Some would call it a crater.
Some would call it a cauldron.
It is the shape
that enables your being to cradle the being of another.
You may from a distance, place the Energy of a being

within the cradle of your hands, within the form
And as you cradle the Energy of the being,
you may soothe the being,
as if you held close to you a babe in your arms;
you have the same effect upon that being.
This is efficacious for the being
who is of a distance from you, and has troubled spirit.
The cradling, holding the Energy of the being
within the sacred chakras of your palms,
allows the being to have care about it.
It is similar to the placing of the golden thread of care;
but it deepens the relationship of the Energy to the Soul.
Care placed about a being does not
remove the strife from the being,
but it does give pause
so that no other negativity will enter in
while the being struggles to overcome.
The cradle allows the being to be content in that moment,
to have a relaxation,
which then allows for the contemplation of choice.
You are cradling the Energy of the being,
not the physical form of the being,
and with the Energy of your palms
you enhance that being.
Understand, Souls of earth, you are not removing
any of the choice from that being,
you are enhancing the ability of that being to choose.
You are providing non judgmental compassion unto another.
Hold the Energy until you feel relief,
for that is how the being will feel,
and then place the right hand over the left,
hold for the count of three, move your hands upwards
and release the Energy of the being.

Eye of Beholding

30 We speak of rainbow Energy,
we speak of the energetic colors of the rainbow.
We speak, not of your cloud rainbow in your sky, your earth sky,
we speak of the rainbow of the Prism.

We would have you understand
that each color of the Prism carries Energy.
This Energy may be used to heal.
It may be used to repair the limb,
to seal the scar, to staunch the flow of blood;
to heal the sores,
the crusts that build with the various skin diseases;
to heal the maimed limb; to heal the injured mind;
to heal the spine and all the diseases that affect the spine.
This Energy of the Prism may be used by you, humanity.
Indeed for you have a connection to the Prism.
That connection is the triad of Soul, Spirit, and Essence.
Your Essence, direct connection to the Prism,
your Spirit, direct connection to the Essence
and your Soul, direct connection to Spirit.
Indeed, you have this potential, this capability.
And we say potential,
for it is your choice to connect to Spirit through the eye.
Go inward and find Spirit.
Reach unto Spirit and know that your Spirit,
although upon the Farside, is always available unto you.
Hasten then.
Connect with Spirit and then connect with Essence.
And with the power of the triad enter unto the Prism,
for it is hallowed ground.
It is hallowed halls of Energy of humanity.
It is Purity.
Indeed, Souls of earth, Purity.
It is Truth.
It is Love, Creator Love, Agape Love.
You, who see yourself as insignificant, as powerless,
may reach unto the Crystal Cave,
may reach the Prism of healing of color,
of sound, of vibration.
For the Crystal Cave is also a triad, sound, color, vibration;
a powerful combination, Creator healing power.
This is the power available unto you.
In the goodness, in the Purity of your being,
in the fullness of Love
you may connect through the eye
and behold the rainbow, behold Humanity.

Indeed, behold the very Soul of Creator.
Hitherto, you have thought of yourself
as separated from your Creator.
That is illusion.
For indeed you are not separated.
The connection exists in your reality.
Always the Angels sing
in a great chorus of sound unto the Crystal Cave.
And they sing in a great chorus unto humanity.
For therein lays the key to that which is lost and will be found.
Harken to the knowledge of the rainbow of healing.
Enter ye in and bring comfort, surcease,
healing unto all of humanity,
unto the very earth that you tread.
One being joined in a triad with another being
joined in a triad, with another being joined in a triad.
Oh, Souls of earth, recall your drive for oneness
and know that all great healings
utter forth from the oneness of humanity.
Enter in.
Use the great eye, the connector of your being.

31 We would have you understand
positive and negative energy have an effect,
not only upon self but upon other beings.
When sending forth positive, we would use the analogy
of placing loving arms of comfort
and soothing to another being.
You do not have to visualize such happening.
It will automatically occur.
The being will be bathed in Purity.
They will feel comforted without a visible representation.
They will sense their body, the cells of their body.
Their mind will sense the Energy and hold it to themselves.
With negative energy, it is as if you were poking sharp jabs
into the aura, into the Energy of the other being.
Negativity is a powerful energy.
Never discount the power of negative thought.
Understand, a young, a baby Soul
does not yet have the memories,
you would call it experience,

the memories to understand how to grapple
with negativity and release it.
And so they are very vulnerable, more so than the old Soul,
the mature Soul who has the memories
and knows the effects.
Now understand, when we say memories, we speak of past lives.
And though you may not recall individual lives,
they are within your being.
They are available,
all that you have learned in past lives
is available unto you.
You see yourself as coming unto earth unarmed,
unknowing, vulnerable, totally vulnerable.
And yet, you are not totally vulnerable.
You have a background to call upon.
And how would you do this, Souls of earth?
You would do it with the eye.
Indeed the eye may read all the memories
that you have struggled to gain.
The eye can read all the experiences.
The eye can read even unto the beings
that were with you in experiences.
The eye can read the Writing on the Wall
for this life or lives to come.
Indeed, the eye can bring unto your being, great awareness
of all that you have done through other lifetimes.
This is a great aid to understanding
why you are as you are in this lifetime;
why you are with this mate, why you had these parents,
why you have these friends, why you have this teacher.
If you wish to delve into why, use the eye and you will know,
your questions will be answered.
And for those who are of aged Soul, you may also look further
unto the Akashic Record and read humanity.
For upon the Farside
there are no secrets to the level of your Purity.
There are no locked tomes.
There are no locked halls of learning.
Your humanity, your eye, is your entrance in.

32 We speak of the equality of dark and light.

Indeed equal, for could you discern dark without light?
Could you discern light without dark?
The contrast is ultimately a necessity.
Dark and light in your universe
 is a reflection of all other universes.
All has dark and light.
Even in your own teachings,
 upon your earth plane, your many religions,
 your many sciences, delve into contrast,
 to teach, to learn, to experiment.
And we would have you not contain dark and light,
 simply as that which is only the contrast.
You will understand dark and light
 exists only within two dimensions,
 as all must operate in two dimensions.
When you add the third dimension, when you add the eye
 then you see beyond dark and light.
You see the myriad of dimensions that are possible.
Your science is beginning to understand.
They have found within dark many dimensions.
They have found within light many dimensions,
 and we tell you beyond dark and light
 there are other dimensions.
But these other dimensions are a reality only glimpsed,
 only explored by the eye of your being,
 by the very consciousness of your Soul.
Indeed, Souls of earth, you limit yourselves
 when you do not accept the presence of the third eye.
You limit yourselves when you do not use the third eye
 to explore, to know, to be.
You have the potential to enter in to other dimensions of being.
You have the potential to enter in to galaxies,
 to planets without a spacesuit, without a space vehicle
 that must surround your fragile humanity.
You have a space vehicle, the third eye, indeed!
And it requires no metal, it requires no suit,
 and it can carry your consciousness
 beyond the earth plane.
This, Souls of earth, you have as a gift from Creator.
It is not given only to a few, it is given to all,
 but only a few reach unto that consciousness.

There will come a day
when it will be commonplace to use the eye to travel.
Indeed your science would help show the way
when they solve the equation.

33 You have before you all possibilities,
and you know it not.
We speak of the possibilities of travel,
of traveling without vehicle, without container,
we would have you know you may,
using the great eye of beholding.
Allowing the great eye to open,
to carry the consciousness of your being,
the Soul consciousness of your being,
you may visit those galaxies
your telescopes have discovered and beyond.
You may enter in to the Farside.
You may enter in to worlds and worlds and worlds.
You do not require a space vehicle to explore,
for you may do so with the eye.
You may explore as your great explorers
of your earth did for thousands of years.
You may explore new worlds, new to man,
and bring back knowledge of your explorations,
knowledge of worlds unknown to man.
It is not the purpose of the eye of beholding
to accumulate material wealth or riches;
nothing so paltry.
The eye of beholding is Holy Energy
of far greater value than earth matter, material goods.
You may travel, singly, individually,
or you may travel with another or even in group,
all linked together exploring the same worlds,
and bringing back unto the earth
that which they have discovered and learned:
knowledge of beings they meet,
interchanging learning, ideas,
what you would call upon your earth, a symposium.
Indeed, this will become commonplace.
It will not be the rare occurrence.
There will be many who travel this way,

who allow the Soul Energy to leave the earth constraints
and enter in to what you would term, freedom,
no barrier, no barriers of vehicles.
Enter thou into the knowledge that you have as yet
untapped possibilities,
that your enter in will in effect be entering out,
for you would leave the plane of earth.
You have, Souls of earth, within the very tips of your fingers,
an access to worlds and worlds and worlds
of knowledge and discovery, of beings.
Hasten to discover,
hasten to open your being to all possibilities.
Souls of earth, you have before you great opportunities,
great adventures, mountains to climb, rivers to ford,
streams to cross, valleys to discover,
but they are not physical earth that we speak of.
We speak of your Soul being.
We speak of that which is aura.
We speak of that which contains
the potential of healing with Sound and Color.
We speak of that connection
from the third eye unto thy sacred self.
Within each being there is this potential to attain,
to become the high Energy of sacred self,
and to direct with your intent the power of that healing
unto self or unto the well being of another,
even unto the flora and fauna and earth itself.
You speak, Souls of earth, of the Savior.
You speak of God, of Allah.
You speak of Buddha, Krishna.
You pray to these beings.
You make of them deities
and you call upon them to bless, to heal,
when you may do that which you ask them to do!
The healing that would come from Jesu
may come from your sacred self.
But you place barriers
and barriers refute your connection to Creator.
The barriers refute the ability, the potential to heal.
The barriers push away the Light of your Creator.
Pull it toward you!

Allow that Light to enter in.
Allow that Light to be as if you were breathing.
The Light!
Allow it to become as breath upon your being.
Acceptance.
Begin with acceptance and acknowledgment
of the Holy triad of your being: Soul, Spirit, Essence.

Healing Vibration

34 We would have you understand the need of vibration,
not your needs, nor the needs of mankind,
but the need of vibration.
For all is predicated upon vibration.
There is not one iota of existence
that is not predicated upon vibration.
For without vibration, you have non existence,
you have no thing.
Even naught has vibration.
Even within the void is a vibration.
Your whole being, individual and as humanity, has vibration.
All that you see, all that is illusion,
is predicated upon vibration.
Left to itself it does not grow, it lies fallow.
But give it Energy and the vibration increases,
increases to another level of vibration,
increases the distance that it travels.
Vibration, Souls of earth, has breadth and width
and height and depth.
It has form.
You may touch vibration with the eye.
Vibration carries sound and color.
It is as the wire that carries your electricity upon the earth,
to give you a simplistic understanding.
The Pillar of Light that you are is vibration.
The earth upon which you are is vibration.
The Farside is vibration.
The dome is vibration.
The Zero,[34] implosion, vibration; a triad for your science.

35 Frequencies are the earth terminology
for vibrational echo.
Frequencies are natural within all upon the earth,
but they may also be manufactured
by mankind, by your science.
They may also be augmented by modalities of science,
by machines,
by various permutations of light and sound.
Many of your scientists experiment
with these various permutations.
Much of the experimentation is devoted
to instruments of destruction
as is common upon your earth.
It is the role of negativity.
But out of destruction, out of intent for destruction,
may come construction
and lead, although through devious paths,
to new discoveries of how
frequencies work within the earth plane.
You are aware that much of humanity learns through negativity.
Have no judgment, Souls.
For judgment has a frequency also.
Recall, we stated, "All upon the earth has frequency."
That includes thought and emotion.
But understand the difference.
The thought, the frequency of the thought,
is a very low vibrational echo
constrained within the parameters of the earth mind.
It is why it is called fleeting thought many times.
Emotion gives energy, impetus to the thought,
allowing the frequency to alter
and to leave the immediate vicinity of the mind.
The depth, the length, the breath of the frequency
depends on the emotion involved.
For all emotion is vibrational.
The emotions that cause pain and harm to self,
class them as negative, indeed have an impact.
Their impact, their frequency,
enters in to the vibrational modality
of any within the vicinity of the bearer of that emotion.
You cannot enter in to the vicinity

    of a person enthralled with hate
    without feeling the frequency of that hatred.
It is almost palpable,
    it is so strong in its need to destruct.
You cannot enter in to the space of a being deep in sorrow
    without feeling the frequency of that sorrow.
It touches a chord within thee.
And how you respond
    will depend upon the frequency of your being.
If you are in the modality of goodness, of Purity,
    the frequency of your response
    will gentle the frequency of the negative emotion,
    altering it, so that its effect is ameliorated,
    and allows the being giving forth that negative emotion
    the opportunity to adjust the frequency,
    to alter it within self.
When you enter the vicinity of a being giving forth,
    emitting the frequency of Love,
    and we speak not of carnal love,
    you become enveloped in the warmth of that Love.
That too is palpable.
All emotions of goodness put in motion a frequency
    that vibrates beyond the vicinity of the aura of the being,
    and enters in to the other of all upon the earth plane,
    and as a vibrational echo, enters forth unto the Farside.
The vibrational echo of the negative emotion,
    its frequency is such that it cannot enter
    beyond the curtain of care.
It cannot lift.
It is seen as color, as sound by Farside and beyond,
    but it may not enter beyond the curtain.
Souls of earth, you are the harp.
You have strings of being called emotion.
When plucked they give forth a frequency,
    a vibration, a sound.
Know that as you pluck the harp of your being,
    others hear and feel your sound.
Your frequency is not denoted by another being
    and impressed upon you,
    it is the choice of your being.
Your harp may be in accord and play a melody of Love,

or it may be out of tune, discordant,
and caught in the throes of negativity.
It is choice.

36 You have sound constantly about your being.
There is no silence upon your earth,
externally; the only silence you will find is in the eye.
You are constantly inundated with sound, and we speak
not only of sound that you hear with earth ears,
but we speak of sound you are not each conscious of
with your earth hearing.
The very gnat has sound.
Indeed, the very light upon your earth has sound!
All that exists upon your earth has a form of sound,
and you are constantly in the midst of sound.
You learn to differentiate sounds that you hear with the ears.
You learn to discern from whence the sounds come,
and from whom the sounds come.
And we would have you understand
that the very skin of your being absorbs sound.
All creatures of your earth absorb sound,
with the ear and with the very skin that covers.
Indeed, you are constantly,
consciously or unconsciously, absorbing sound.
Many creatures upon your earth
are maimed by the sounds of machineries,
by the sound of detectors, by the sounds of explosions,
You cannot, even if you cover your ears,
stop sound on its course from entering in to your being,
for it enters the very pores.
When you are exposed to constant explosions,
sounds that are not melodious and harmonic,
the very cells of your being alter.
The very cells of your brain alter.
We would have you understand sound can harm or it can help.
We would have you aware of the effect sound has
upon the human body
and that of the creatures of your earth.
The discordancy, the sound of negativity;
harmony, the sound of positive, of goodness.
You may, Souls of earth, balance the discordancy with positive,

and it is choice, as in all things.
As you make your choice,
be aware of the effects of your choice,
know that you alter the very brain cells of a babe
with raucous sounds, with your explosions.

37 We speak of harmony.
You will understand there are many Souls upon your earth
who can not stand within their very being, harmony.
There are Souls who thrive on chaos.
There are Souls who thrive in a cacophonous environment,
who enliven their being with chaos,
who have yet not allowed the conception of compassion
to enter unto their earth being, who thrive on negativity,
who see no other option in their lives except chaos,
negativity and cacophony.
Do not judge these beings.
Do not place upon them harsh judgments, for indeed
we would have you understand these beings are Holy,
they have come unto the earth plane Holy,
pure in their Souls,
and yet have taken on the guise of negativity.
They are chaotic in their being, they show no compassion,
and yet we say unto you, do not judge,
for you were as they.
Because their being is chaotic does not mean
they are baby or young Souls,
and we would have you
withhold judgment upon these beings.
Place upon them compassion, place upon them Love,
place upon them the very Purity of your being
but withhold judgment.
There are many beings upon your earth who relish harmony,
who thrust from their being
any semblance of disharmony.
They try to blank from their being
any knowledge of disharmony
that would disturb their being.
Understand, disharmony is within their individual judgment,
for what may be disharmonious to one
may not be disharmonious to another.

These beings attempt to hide from all pain.
These beings may attempt to do so
through drugs of different sorts,
through gaiety of many varieties,
through the accumulation of material goods;
many ways.
And their growth becomes stifled,
for they refuse to enter fully into life,
and instead hide as well as they may from life.
For life holds both harmony and disharmony.
Life to its fullest embraces all that there is, without judgment.
The highest form of compassion is unconditional Love,
and by the very nature of that state of being,
of unconditional Love,
there is no judgment, for all is as it is.
As you strive for oneness,
understand it is the very compassion within your being
that brings forth the oneness of humanity.
As you accept who you are,
as you recognize the very Holiness of your being,
compassion flowers into oneness.

38 Beloved earth Souls, many of you have
at the ends of your members, digits.
Many activities, many things can be done with these digits
when in proper working order.
One can play chords, one can care for another,
one can hug another,
one may caress another being,
one may make food for another,
one may make clothing for another.
Many and varied are the uses of these digits.
We would urge that you use the digits in works of care,
in works of goodness for one another,
that you use them to work toward that ultimate end,
that ultimate aim of recognizing
that grace within each Soul is as your grace.
There are many graces upon the earth plain.
There is the grace of caring, of stewardship.
There is the grace of comfort.
There is the grace of drying the tears of another.

There is the grace of being, of be
and there is the grace of the joining of auras, of healing.
Each Soul, all of mankind, may choose these graces.
And we would have you know
that when mankind does choose these graces
a joyous, wondrous moment that will be!
Enter in, Souls, enter in!

39 Understand the power of the circle.
Any being placed in the circle
feels an immediate benefit to their well being.
We would explain.
The circle sets up, for your understanding,
a cycle of Energy that becomes a spiral reaching upward
to your higher consciousness.
In turn, that higher consciousness enters in to
the being placed in the circle,
for that is your intent, to heal that being,
to provide wellness to that being;
and so the high consciousness enters in.
Your Energy from the high self enters in
and affects the cells of the being,
altering the mutated cells back unto their perfect shape,
their perfect form of wellness.
Understand, Souls, what you do is not inconsequential.
Each being, the earth,
is the recipient of your blessed Energy
when you have the intent to place in the circle.
We would have you understand the part
that intent plays in wellness.
For if a being is determined to be ill,
determined not to let go of their identity of unwellness,
it will be retained.
The intent to bring forth wellness forms a triad
with the blessed Energy and the high consciousness.
All the being needs to do is to accept and healing is instant.

40 We would have you place about a rainbow of color.
A rainbow that has a vibrancy.
It is not pale.
The colors have depths, the colors are alive with Energy,

sparkling in their electricity.
A red goes first about your being
and then a blue and then yellow
and then the green and then a purple
and then the brown.
Indeed, brown.
And black, indeed black.
Souls of earth, you understand
that the representation of the rainbow
that you see upon your earth
is the very palest of comparison
to the rainbows of the Farside,
to the rainbows of color that surround your being.
Color is available always to your aura.
You do not have to search for it.
The eye knows exactly where it is.
But understand, even on the earth plane
to place these colors about your being
visually or physically
will remind you of who you are.
They will be as a warm, comforting cloak
on a cold wintery day,
for indeed, they will give out a warmth.
They have an electricity to them,
not one that is harmful to your being,
but one full of Energy.
It is power that we speak of in color.
It is power that we speak of in the sound of color.
It is power that we speak of in the vibration of color.
Indeed, upon your earth it is minute
in comparison to that which you may reach with the eye.
This rainbow is a harmony.
There is not within these colors that is contradictory.
There is not a discord within these colors, for they harmonize,
and if you but hear with the eye,
you would hear a chord of great beauty.
And when others are gathered,
more than one Soul are gathered,
and place the colors about their being,
you have an orchestra with the potential of a symphony.
Indeed, for the colors do not hold themselves only to you.

The Energy is not held only to you.
The Energy is impossible to still.
It needs movement.
It vibrates beyond your physical self, it vibrates,
and you may reach unto others
and combine the power of the colors of the rainbows,
of the individual rainbows.
They connect.
And in that connection,
you have exceeded the power of the individual rainbow.
You may heal beings not even present in the same space.
Distance is of no consequence
when you have combined the rainbows of color.
For the sound and vibration will reach unto those beings
no matter what space they are in.
You have, Souls of earth,
such great potential and you know it not.
We urge you to gather together to make healing connections
using the power of the rainbows.
It is a gift from one to the other.
It is a prelude to the oneness that you strive for.
It is a prelude
to the oneness that is the purpose of your being.

41 We would teach on the sacred chakra within the palm.
There will come a time when all will understand chakras
in scientific terminology, in scientific equation,
and with scientific proof
of their existence within the earth plane.
The Holy chakra in the palm of the hand is most efficacious
to treat any and all disease, dis ease, infirmity,
mental, emotional, physical.
It is not limited.
This chakra found in the palms of the hands, colored white,
indeed, contains the colors of all the chakras
that are familiar to your Souls, to your beings of earth.
When placed outward, the palm placed toward another being
whether, man, plant, or animal,
is as a beam of sunlight but with
many times the power of that sun, muted for earth use.
When using the sacred chakra, your whole being vibrates,

not just the palm, the whole being of your earth self,
vibrates as it transmits from the palm
the White Light from your Pillar of Light.
The aura of your being vibrates in intensity to heal,
to physically alter cells of the being,
to physically alter the perception of the being,
to lift despair, depression.
The sacred chakra does not heal without permission.
Always the Soul of the other being
must have agreement for the healing to occur.
When healing and using the sacred chakra,
you may place directly upon the wound or disease,
but it is not necessary.
It is only necessary to visualize with the eye the healing.
Understand you work, in your earth terms,
you work with a triad;
the eye, the aura, the Pillar of Light,
and you place it forward with the sacred chakra.
The vibration is necessary to gain momentum,
to gather speed in hastening that Energy unto another.
Even were you to use the healing for self,
you require the vibration,
you require the momentum, the motion.
contain, embrace, all the colors
of the iridescent Crystal Cave.
Once the momentum carries it forward,
the Soul of the being to be healed, will attract,
will embrace, will imbibe the colors that it requires
to heal flesh or mind, body, spirit.
And as you vibrate in wellness,
so too will you send that vibration.
The left hand is no less than the right hand.
For the sacred chakras of both are equal.
Both working in tandem.
All upon your earth gives and receives.
It is no less with the sacred self;
all in spiral of being,
all in circle of being.

42 We would have you cup your hands, make a bowl.
Look at your hands, Soul.

You see them with your earth eyes as empty,
and yet were you to look at your hands with the eye
you would see swirling Energy, you would see color.
You would see movement
and you would hear the chakras
in the palms of your hands.
You would see the meridians.
We would have you understand the golden ball of Energy
that you build with your eye, with your Spirit and Soul,
has form, has texture.
It is not illusionary.
With your earth eyes, indeed, it may seem illusionary.
But with the eye it is not.
It has a reality, it has form, it has substance.
And this golden ball of Energy,
has a connection unto the very Soul of Creator.
And you may use this golden ball to heal.
You may splash its Energy upon self.
You may make the motion
as you would with water splashing on your face.
Only you are splashing Energy
that permeates the most minute cell of your being,
that permeates your flesh and blood and bone.
And you may, with permission,
share the golden ball of Light with another being.
That they might heal,
that you might lift their spirits,
that you might remind them
of their connection to Creator.
Souls of earth, you ask; "How does
this golden ball of Energy come to be?"
We would advise you of a technique to assist you
in the formation of this Energy.

Step 1:
Begin in a comfortable position,
in a quiet, calm state of being
and if possible, your feet are flat upon the ground
or pointing toward the ground.

Step 2:

With your head upright, place your hands palm up.
The fingers held close together,
the thumbs held close to the flesh of the forefingers.
Close your eyes.

Step 3:
Cupping your hands, place the left palm above the right palm,
and hold for the count of three.

Step 4:
Cupping your hands, place the right palm above the left palm,
and hold for the count of three.

Step 5:
Maintaining the hands cupped,
move your hands apart, just slightly.
And at that point you will begin to feel a heaviness,
a tingling around the top of your head,
around the third eye.

Step 6:
Repeat three times, left over right,
hold for the count of three
and then the right over left,
hold for the count of three.

Step 7:
Move your hands apart,
bringing them up in front of the third eye.
At this point, the hands will be touching only
along the outer edges of the smallest finger.
Hold this position for the count of twelve while
breathing gently in and gently out, .

Step 8:
Move your hands cupped as a bowl, waiting to receive,
to in front of your heart chakra,

Step 9:
Lift your head upward, lift the eye up
and ask for the connection

to the golden ball of Energy.
You will feel it start to build within your palms,
you will feel a weight.
Yes, the Energy has weight.
You would think, if you opened your earth eyes,
that you would see a form that has substance.
And yet, we tell you, using the eye you will know it;
form and substance,
you will see the whirling, vibrant Energy
of the golden healing that is available to you.
Practice daily until
you feel the weight is almost too much to hold.
And you then know, Soul,
that you have indeed, ready for healing,
this Energy connection unto your Creator.
Know that you hold within your chakras
sacred Energy with great powers of healing

43 Beloved Souls of earth, humanity,
we would have you understand
that scars can be healed, lesions can be closed.
Laceration of babes are done in hell, not abnormal.
If thou would but cast negativity from thee,
the power you hold
is beyond any of your comprehension!
You have the ability to heal.
You have the ability to unmaim the maimed.
You have the power, the awesome power of your Purity.
Reach, reach up unto where thou canst hold unto.
Form thyself in Purity.
Inform thy being in Purity.
Know that one touch of your Purity
can heal the land, can heal the child.
A touch of your Purity can heal thyself.
A touch of thy Purity cleanses the waters.
Heal the poor, the frail,
the whale caught in the toxins of the oceans.
It need not be.
We would have you know, you have the power to heal.
You have the power to cleanse.
Reach and use that awesome power.

Reach!
Everyone reach!
Lift thy arms high!
Lift thy eye high!
Feel your being a power!
Feel thy Purity!
Within thy being is the will.
Release the will!
Come into thy Purity.
Come into thy Holiness.
Spew from thee all the negativity.
Drench yourself only in Purity.
And drench the land with that Purity.
It is up to you, Soul, and you, Soul;
and you, Soul; and you, Soul.
Your Creator awaits.
All Farside awaits.

44 We would place a blessing upon each
and we would ask that you accept.
We thank you for this opportunity
and we would ask you to remind your beings
that you may also place blessings one upon another,
that you may place blessing upon large numbers.
It need not be one to one.
It may be one to thousands, for you have all capability,
all the power,
all the Love potentially in your being of Creator.
Oh Souls, how blessed art thou that you may be as Creator!
We see thee in your Holiness and we weep for your despair.
We weep that you take not the Wilful Child
and embrace and still the being, but instead,
you willfully use the Energy
to create negativity upon your planet,
upon your brothers and sisters as you smite them,
as you maim them.
Yea, negativity is growth.
This we do not dispute but we would remind you
there is no more need to continue to create negativity.
We would hasten you to understand
your Holiness, your levels of Purity.

We would hasten you to begin the Gathering
to bring our blessed home.
Yea, you have the power, you have the Love,
you have the Purity to enter in, to show,
to remove your cloak,
and show the scars of your being,
and bring forth those tortured Souls
home into the waiting arms of the Angels.
The Energy of Negativity is not negative.
It is what is done with the Energy
that may cause you to become earth negativity,
bringing forth harm, not goodness.
There is a difference between embracing negativity
and holding to it.
Beloved Souls,
we would give you a succinct defining of embracing.
Embracing the beloved brother, the Wilful,
it is the acknowledgment of a wayward son.
It is not the condoning of action but it is the understanding,
the compassion given to the wayward one,
to the Wilful Child,
an understanding of the concept of embracing,
of the concept of the purpose of your being,
of the purpose of humanity.
In all its guises,
the Wilful Child is no more nor less an Energy
as you are Energy.
You are akin!
We long to bring the Wilful Child home
as we long to bring our beloved brethren,
once more unto the fold of our being.
And in this, beloved humanity, you are key,
and we thank you, honor you
and await the day of glory, of return of all.

45 We teach on Energy.
We would have you understand,
we speak not only of a few,
but we speak of all humanity,
each and every mankind,
from the very youngest to the most aged.

We speak of the Energy integral,
implicit at the command of every being.
Know that the Energy at your command
may be wielded in negative or in the positive manner.
Just as your electricity has a negative and positive charge
so do you, Souls of earth.
Each has a different ability, a different propensity.
The negative flows counterclockwise.
The positive flows clockwise.
The negative, when wielded with the intent of harm,
when wielded with the negative ego,
is indeed harmful.
But positive, when the intent is to heal,
becomes connected to a greater electricity of being,
to a greater Energy of being,
one that may alter matter in a positive.
The negative also alters matter and it too is powerful,
for it feeds upon the negative energy of others,
it grows, it expands, it is puissant.
The positive charge, the Purity of intent,
the Purity of your being unhindered by negativity,
is also puissant, and it too expands and grows
in the presence of other like Purity,
or greater Purity.
The energy of negativity corrodes the being.
The Purity, the Energy of Purity enhances in many ways,
enhances the power of a being,
enhances the wellness, enhances the healing.
It repairs; it does not corrode.
As in all things upon the earth, what you wield is choice.
As in all things upon the earth,
there is no judgment
for the choice you have taken, by the Farside,
for in all things there is also upon the earth plane,
a lesson, a learning,
and therefore even corrosion has a value.
Souls of earth, you are in a swirl of activity upon
this earth plane.
The swirl may enter your being clockwise.
It may enter your being counterclockwise;
in negativity you go against the grain. Activity, indeed,

increases, but in a flattened arc;
larger, larger, larger, wider, wider, wider,
ever meandering, never finding rest,
affecting not just self, but all.
Understand, when you are caught in the downward,
the flat spiral of negativity,
you have the power, the ability, to stop the swirl,
to alter the swirl.
Understand an example of negativity,
running in its counterclockwise direction,
speeding faster and faster and faster as your bullet, fast.
You may stop it in an instant and reverse;
stop that power, calm its being,
bring about an inertia to itself.
Your science has been experimenting with this,
the altering of energy.
See, science, that which is offered to you, the equation.
Understand Energy.
Open your minds to the dimensional vibrational equation
you have been given.
You want answers, Soul?
There it is, freely given.
Enter in, Souls of earth,
enter in the scientists
and those who are not doctored scientists
but nonetheless scientists,
enter in to the form of the equation and you will see.
You will have numerical, mathematical proof of ceasing,
of stopping, of reversing, of altering
a counterclockwise spin of negativity.
How, you ask?
How can I, an individual, do such?
How can I stop the momentum?
Indeed, Soul, with positive, always with positive,
offering even in the most heinous, horrifying moment,
offering that Love,
that compassion that is innate to your being.
And you have only to bring it forward,
to enter it out, to allow it to flow from you.
It is indeed that easy.
Replace that negative with positive.

In so many writings upon your earth, you have been told,
you have been taught this time and time again.
It is, indeed, truth.
You are beings of Love by nature.
You have come from Love.
Enter that Love out and you will alter
the course of negativity and salvation.
Not of your Soul!
Indeed not!
It needs no salvation.
But salvation of the unceasing curiosity,
a need of the Wilful Child, will be assuaged,
as if you placed upon it the Balm of Gilead.
So be it, Souls.

46 Grit enters in to all lives.
Grit, as the fine grains of sand, enters in to the skin,
enters in to the cracks and crevices.
And can you not release the grit from your skin with water,
can you not brush it away!
Indeed, as it enters in you have the power to move it out.
And so it is, Souls, with a negativity.
It presents itself to you.
And you have the option to retain it
within the fold of your being or you have the option,
to, in this analogy, to wash it away.
It does not have to remain.
In no way must you retain a negativity.
And, as you might from a child wash away the grit of sand,
you may also wash away negativity from others
with your great compassion and Purity.
For it is as water flowing from thee to another.
You may cleanse another with your compassion, your Love.
Indeed, negativity is as the gritty sand.
If allowed to stay, it irritates.

Earth Mend

47 Break out the song books.
Break out the hymnals.

Tone your voices.
Clear your voices.
Be ready to shout forth from the very Purity of your being,
from the very core essence of your being, shout forth,
"The day is nigh!"
The day of gathering, the beginning of the end,
and the end for a new beginning.
You have, upon your many prognosticians,
who have made prophecies of the end, of the cataclysm,
of the four horsemen of the Apocalypse.
You have recordings of prophesies.
You have oral traditions of the prophets.
You have been sent many messengers to your earth plane,
so that each and every being has heard
some inkling of that which is to be,
of that which humanity chooses to be,
for humanity has all possibility to heal earth
and yet mankind rejects this possibility.
And earth, that generous, most glorious of beings,
earth, in your terminology, is dying;
not as a star dies,
becomes dust that is then Energy used again,
no, it is not a natural state that earth is dying.
It has been imposed upon her by man.
Earth is in a perilous state.
You have loaded her,
you have choked her gullet chock full
of toxins and pollutants, all manner of negativity.
You have laid waste to much of her being.
You have laid waste armies of beings
who died holding negativity to them.
This negativity is buried upon the earth.
It is within the earth.
Souls of earth, the being who has nurtured you,
who has fed you, who has provided clothing and shelter,
who has provided joy for the senses,
beauty for the senses of your being;
this most generous of energies
you have systematically set about to destroy.
The time is nigh that earth will choose to live, not die,
and the time of gathering will be.

How can you prepare?
There is no preparation except the Purity of your being,
the willingness to care and nurture for others,
the willing to be as generous as earth has been to you.
That is what you can do for each other and for earth.
Be as the earth, overflowing with generosity.

48 Earth, attention!
Notice what you are doing to your beloved planet.
Turn not the eye away from the pollution
caused by greed, by ineptness.
Souls of earth, you have only your earth on this plane.
Don't look away.
See what you are doing.
See what you are allowing to happen
within the bowels of mother earth.
She can not contain the amount of negativity
being placed within her being.
How long would you live
if deadly poisons were being injected into your body?
What pains would you feel as the poisons ate your body?
If you could reject,
spew out the poison being placed within your body
and stop the pain, would you not do so?
If it was your child in such pain would you not stop?
Earth is a being.
Earth has Soul.
Earth feels.
She is not emotionless.
She is not an inordinate being that can not feel.
Souls of earth, you know you have the ability to heal,
to cleanse the earth,
to lift from her this burden that you have placed.
We ask that you reverse the pain of this beloved planet
that you enter in and lift from earth and spew it forth.
The options are disastrous, for she will be forced
to spew forth herself before she is utterly destroyed.
All that you have ever heard in all the predictions
of earthquake, of fire, of flood, of eruptions,
of chemical fumes spewing forth from the toxins
planted deep within,

all of these you can prevent or you can allow.
Think of your children, if you do not think of thyself.
If you do not think of thy neighbor, think of the child
and know you can place about the child a protection;
not a barrier, but the protection of healing of the earth
so that the child is safe.
Earth beings, we await to lift.
Indeed, but we can only lift Purity.
We ask, nay, we plead with earth, "heal, heal, Heal!"

49 Result of unbalanced humanity and effects on earth?
Beloved Souls of earth, we would have you understand
that climatic changes and earth changes
are a natural part of the evolution
of the Energy of the planet earth.
Having said that, we would also have you understand
that the great spew of negativity
entered in to the bowels of earth
has altered that evolution.
The earth, the Soul of earth,
agreed to be a platform of Energy for mankind,
for the purpose of humanity,
but she has finite limits to that which she can absorb.
All has delicate balance.
What effects the water affects the air.
What affects the air affects the land.
What effects the land affects the water
and so it goes, in a spiral.
That spiral may be one of goodness, of balance,
of natural evolution.
Or, as has happened, mankind has altered,
has struck an imbalance within the earth.
The imbalance affects all of nature.
Mankind has long passed the stage of natural disaster,
of natural changes.
The pollution, the vials of toxins,
the vileness of the nuclear testing,
have all taken their toll.
Mother earth is saying the knell of time has struck.
She will erupt and erupt and erupt,
attempting to spew the poisons from her.

Humanity, you have the power to alter this.
You have the power, the ability to cleanse the land.
Join together, cleanse hectare by hectare by hectare.
Bring forth and neutralize the toxicity of the land.
You have a time to be.
You have choice.
You may continue to spew forth and embed upon the earth
and in the waters and in the air, vileness.
Or, Souls of earth, you may bring forth the cleansing breath,
the purified waters,
the land that now grows without toxin.
You may bring forth a balance to the earth.
Join in oneness, beloved Souls, and bring forth your glory.
Recall your stewardship.
Recall you were given stewardship over the land.
And it is not a judgment
to say you are failing and have failed.
It is only a statement of what is.
We plead with humanity to care for the earth
as the shepherd cared for the lost lamb.
The earth gives you sustenance, a place to be,
a place to grow
and she only asks for your care.

50 Be aware of what you do day by day
to the beloved mother,
to the beloved companions, animals you call them,
to the plants, to the very grains of sand,
to the wondrous beings who live in the oceans
and who frolic in the pools and streams.
You have the ability to relinquish negativity.
You have the ability to create pools, swirls of Energy,
grasping negativity from your being
and from that of mother earth;
and sending it forth to Creator.
Respect the Light that is as your own being.
We urge you, do care for the land, do care for one another.
Recognize that upon the mountaintop,
the many mountaintops in the time of the tempest,
rescue and courage will be given forth
to those that cry out to be saved.

See with thy being, with thy eye, the multitudes crying out,
the multitudes in pain and anguish
and know that it need not be.
Heal.
Bend thy being to lift another,
open thy hands and lift them up.
Souls, do unto one and other, one other,
and you do unto all.
No giving is insignificant.

51 We would speak of the air that you breathe.
We would speak of the many particles
within the air that you breathe,
both those that your science can see,
and those that your science can not yet see,
because they use only their microscopes and not the eye.
The air of your earth was given for you, and for all that
breathes upon the earth, in a pristine state.
By pristine, we refer to the lack of toxins.
For the air is not only there for you to breathe in and out,
for you to exist upon the earth plane,
but it also carries particles for your well being.
This your science is in its infancy in discovering,
they have come to understand at a beginning level,
negative ions and positive ions.
They have not yet fully delved into the effect
of negative ions upon your well being.
We would have you understand;
negative ions enter in not just upon your breath,
not just into your lungs, but they enter in to your skin,
to every pore of your skin.
They enter in to the very hair upon your body.
They enter in to the nails upon your digits.
Negative ions in their pristine state,
bequeathed upon the human form
an ability to process oxygen to the utmost.
They bequeathed unto the human form a vitality of being.
But, Souls of earth, you have contaminated, polluted the air,
the same air that enters in to your skin and your pores,
every portion of your being.
It enters in to the babe.

It matters not whether you have wealth or none.
It is the same air.
Science has devised methods
which they believe will purify the air,
and, to an extent, this is possible.
But it is not possible to thoroughly purify.
That can only be done with the oneness of mankind.
Mankind has no conception upon the earth plane
of the vitality that purified original air
brought to your being.
You lack a vitality you can not imagine
and do not even know was possible.
Souls of earth, we urge you to unite in oneness to cleanse,
to purify the air,
to bring it back unto its pristine state,
to bring back the gift of vitality unto thy being.

51 We would speak with thee
on the rend within the earth,
of the breaking point within the earth.
We would speak with thee of the turmoil,
of the heat that rages within the inners of mother earth.
The Soul of mother earth has given thee succor for eons,
has given thee havens for your in and out,
your in and out, your many reincarnations.
Blessed earth has offered her being to forward the motion;
the intent,
the bringing forth of beloved, blessed brethren.
She has willingly allowed, nay, encouraged,
the overcoming of negativity.
She has allowed, most graciously and courageously,
allowed your creation of evil to enter in to her being.
She has not deflected it, she has not refused.
She has given you, Souls of earth,
her trust in the agreement of stewardship.
She has trusted you to care for her being
as you would care for a babe.
How have you repaid this generosity,
the graciousness of mother earth?
You have trampled her being,
you have sent darts of poison, of toxicity.

You have covered her being with pain.
You have taken her bounty
and altered it to an unrecognizable state.
You have trashed her forests.
You have contaminated her waters.
It is not the fish in the sea who contaminate.
It is not the birds in the air who contaminate.
It is not the animals of the land that contaminate.
It is not the insects.
It is not the plants.
Souls of earth, you have the accountability,
you have the responsibility.
You are the creator of the pain of mother earth.
And yet, we would have you know,
we would have you understand,
you also have the ability to create ease,
to neutralize the contamination of your creations.
You have the power to gather mother earth within your arms
and soothe away her pain.
As you created pain, you may uncreate.
Yes, you have that ability, Souls,
to uncreate the contamination,
the toxicities, the pain, and replace it with abundant joy.
It is within your purview, within your power,
and we ask that you relieve the burden of pain.
Explain uncreate?
Uncreate is the overcoming, is the replacement,
it is the removal.
The removal leaves a vacuum and within that vacuum
you may create again, contamination,
or you may ease, soothe, place balm upon the sores.
Does your skin not grow new skin
when you heal a scrape, a burn!
Have you not uncreated the injury?
And so you may do so, beloved Souls of earth,
with that with which
you have been given stewardship over.
Lesions are not meant to be.
Healing is meant to be.

52 You will understand that all ecological areas

are altering.
It matters not where upon the earth.
All are changing.
All are in reaction to pollution, to the toxins of mankind.
Mankind may reverse and bring back abundant growth,
abundant health and well being,
using the Energy of the oneness of mankind.
Until then each being may, in their own way,
keep secure a small portion of earth.
Understand the earth requires nutrients
to feed not only a tree
but all flora and fauna upon the earth.
The nutrients: your scientists understand
the intricate ecology of the earth,
the constant recycling, renewing of nutrient Energy;
but mankind has altered the cycle
and has neutralized some nutrients
and has poisoned some nutrients.
And so the cycle is no longer healthy and in wellness,
but is struggling to maintain
even the most minute of being.
Souls of earth, you are the shepherd of earth.
You may find the lost wellness of the earth and heal.
Choose, if you will, to care for not only one another
but all the intricacies of the web of the earth,
even unto the most minutest of creature,
to the greatest of creature.
Harken to that which you do,
and harken to that which you do not.

53 Enter ye into the wind.
Enter in to the velocity of the wind, of motion.
Enter ye into the teachings of the wind.
For indeed, my people, the teachings are on the wind.
You have always known that the wind speaks,
the wind speaks in minute phraseologies.
Borne upon the wind are atoms and ions.
Borne upon the wind are the words of man.
Borne upon the wind is the scent of all creatures.
Borne upon the wind is the touch of the Great One.
My people have known when they beat the drums

the wind carries the sound and the meaning.
The vibration is caught on the wind and carried
as a wave of the radio is carried.
The wind brings warnings.
The wind will carry the rain.
The wind carries your thoughts as a wave.
The wind, in your meteorological terminology,
is the balance upon the earth.
For the wind may carry chemicals and toxins across the planet.
It may carry ash across the planet.
It may carry sand across the planet
and it may carry seeds to nourish, to plant.
The wind is not innocuous.
For the wind, when affected by the currents of the ocean
and the agony of mother earth,
can bring storms of magnitude
that will bring fear unto mankind.
Storms of such power
that they will lay waste whole cities and towns.
And yet, that power can be harnessed by you.
Indeed, my people, you know how to speak to the wind.
You know how to alter the wind.
You know that the wind is part of your stewardship.
The wind is a part of your contract to care for earth.
Souls of earth, use the eye.
Use the power within to Naught,
not to tame the wind, but to gentle the wind.
And you may do this by altering the toxins,
the poisons that are within mother earth.
for the wind responds to the agony of the earth.

54 We speak to the Natives of earth,
to those who are called indigenous peoples,
to those Aboriginals, First Nation
and all the guises of your names, we speak to you.
You have a special relationship with the earth.
You have chosen to have an affinity for the earth.
You have chosen to care for the earth.
You have chosen to have an intimate knowledge of the earth.
You have chosen to be aware of all the nuances of the earth.
You have chosen to be aware of the water.

You can hear the water speak.
You can feel the pain of the water, of the toxins in the water.
You have the ability to heal the earth.
Indeed, all mankind has this ability,
but you have chosen
to have a very special affinity with the earth.
The very feet that you walk with upon the earth may heal.
Place your feet flat upon the earth,
move them up and down,
and know that with your will and your intent
the vibration of your being may heal.
Place your hands upon the earth,
place your palms upon the earth,
move them up and down
and know that the will and intent
and vibrations of your hands will heal.
Souls of earth, the drums are vibrations
within all your cultures.
There are drumming rituals.
We would have you understand it is the vibration
engendered by the drums that is imperative to healing.
Understand, you may with the rhythm, heal.
How do you do that?
It is the vibration.
But, you must use the eye
to ascertain the vibration of the being to be healed.
Whether it is a portion of mankind or a portion of creature,
or a portion of the planet,
once you have attuned yourself to their vibration,
you understand what needs to be healed
and by your drumming, by your vibration,
you will bring forth solace.
You will heal the cracks in their aura.
You will bring balance to their chi.
The drums, it matters not the type,
it matters the will and the intent and the vibration.
For you have this power,
you have this ability and most use it not.
You have a few who understand the use of the drum,
and we entreat these beings
to teach unto others that which they know.

So that one day there will be, across the land,
 across the world, across the continents,
 a continuous drum beat of the heart of healing.
Vision this and it will come to you.

55 We would speak on the fecundity of the mother earth.
The Soul of mother earth was indeed endowed
 with the ability to provide sustenance
 for all that abide upon her being.
Within the plan of mother earth, she was given abundant
 and clean life giving waters,
 sufficient unto the day for all beings.
Within the plan of mother earth, the soil was fertile
 and able to give forth sustenance enough for all.
Within the plan of earth, there was the filtered sunlight
 to stimulate the growth of plants,
 plants that willingly lift their face to the sun for growth.
And for the beings upon her, the filtered sun provides light,
 vitamins and emotional warmth.
The sun holds back.
The sun originally given to mother earth, in its filtered state,
 holds back the ice that otherwise
 would cover the soil and the water.
All that was necessary to sustain life in all its myriad of forms
 was within the plan of the Soul of mother earth.
She has given, willingly and honorably, sustenance for all.
Within the plan of earth was the stewardship of humanity.
Mankind was to tenderly nurture that which earth provided.
But, Souls of earth, you see today
 the filter of the sun has lessened.
There is an imbalance in the filter.
You see today toxins placed within the soil and water of earth,
 and all that was in balance is now in imbalance.
We, Grandfather, tell my people to drum, to dance,
 to pass the feather of peace for earth,
 for mother earth to bring forth the balance,
 so that once again the waters
 will run crystal clear and clean,
 and provide the refreshment and life,
 and the soil will no longer contain
 the negativities of toxins,

and food will provide blessings to all who partake.
And, once again, balance is established.
Pound the feet.
Beat the drums.
Bring the heart message to all my children.
Let the white feather be symbolic of balance for earth.

56 "Hay yah Hay yah Hayaya, Ayaha Ayahay Yuh!"
My people!
We would speak today with my people.
We are Grandfather.
My people, you have an identifiable culture.
You have an identifiable tradition.
It is not lost within the realms of time.
My people, you have values.
My people, you have a stewardship, an attachment to the earth.
You understand, within your being, the womb of mother earth,
the shelter of father sky, the aunts and the uncles,
the trees, the animals, the ocean and its denizens.
You have agreed to have this attachment to the earth.
It was not forced upon you.
But my people, you are caught in despair.
Look at your young ones.
Look at their despair,
you look for answers and reasons.
Always, my people, your riches are of earth.
The land feeds you.
The ocean, the waters feed you.
The trees shelter you.
But Souls, you are caught in this web of darkness
and you see only despair,
and you want only to forget pain.
My people, you can not forget pain.
Indeed not.
Look to that pain and know you can resolve that pain.
Know you can soothe that pain.
Know that you can obliterate that pain.
You need not hold it to you.
Souls, you have forgotten your reason for being here.
There are Souls among your beings, wise peoples
who know the healing power of the drums,

who know the healing power of the powwow;
not the commercial gathering,
not the ostentatious gathering,
but the gathering to share the spirituality
of your Soul with one another.
This you have buried in time.
And we would have all my people recall the gatherings
and the reason of their being.
Listen to the elders.
Listen, indeed, even to the young child who speaks of Love
and compassion for the earth and for all.
Listen, heed, the thunder of the voices who speak of the need
to come together as one,
to mend the rifts between the peoples.
Beat the drums.
Beat the drums.
Light the signal fires, for the time of gathering is nigh.
Let no child be hungry.
Let no child bathe itself in tears.
Let no old one be pushed aside.
Let no drugs, toxicity, enter in to thy system.
Be as pure as you want the land to be,
as you want the waters to be.
Oh my people, you have lost yourselves
in the morass of commercialism, of negativity.
Take back the land, Soul, but not in material ways.
Take back the land in Purity.
Cleanse the land.
That is how to take back the land.
Cleanse it.
Beat the drum.
Heed the drums
and know the power and the glory of your being.
Take back unto thee responsibility for the land and the people.
We, Grandfather, have spoken.

57 Beloved Souls of earth,
we see the blessed Purity of thy being.
We see the blessed Purity of the earth.
We see the healing properties
of all that you call plant and tree,

and shrub and bush that is upon the earth.
We see that which mankind abuses.
You have been given curatives for all ills.
For those who will not access the healer within,
Creator generously provided flora and fauna to heal.
And yet, you proceed to contaminate that which would heal.
You obliterate through your pollution that which may heal.
It will be difficult for children's children's
children of Purity to be in a space of healing,
to be in a space, yea, of sustenance, for the curatives
are not just the physical ailments of mankind,
the curatives are that which you ingest,
that which you eat to live.
Indeed, you enter in to your beings
the most abominable of contaminants, of pollution,
and you have increased this, mankind,
to generations to come.
We have asked, and we ask again,
that you purify within your space
the ground, the soil, the air, the clouds, the sky.
Pick you ten square feet, each humanity,
and purify with the Light of your being,
and contaminate no more.
Bequeath to future generations goodliness,
a purified and cleansed earth,
sustenance that will not cause pain
as it enters the body.
Bequeath thee Love to the generations to come.

Visions[35]

58 Beloved Souls, on the Farside we have little
experience in overcoming negativity.
Many worlds have experience in inertness,
and knowledge that Negativity, the Wilful Child,
was pushed.
You overcome negativity moment by moment.
You, Souls, the experiences you have given
and will give of overcoming negativity
combined with the knowledge and experience

of our beloved Brethren, will give us an answer.
We would bring the Wilful Child home.
We would give all Love to the Wilful Child,
but it pushes back.
It leaves us no options.
We can not force Love.
Love can be offered, Love flows, but gently.
There is no force attached to Agape.
Do you see our conundrum?
Energies can not be uncreated,
only altered, as in your growth, you are altered,
as in your growth your alterations
affect others' alteration.
But only, Soul, by example, not by force.
Would that we could take the pain from our brethren,
take the suffering from our brethren.
Would that we could embrace them in Love, Agape Love.
At this moment in your time,
at this moment in your time in the earth,
there is instability of the crust.
There is a fault line, a cracking.
It will sunder and shatter,
cause many beloveds to come home.
The devastation along the fault line in the great barrier reef,
it is necessary cleansing.
And great upheavals and great growth will be extended,
will be an extension of this occurrence.
Soul, guard thy own instability on the earth.
Bring forth thy Light in the darkness to come.
We say again and all Farside repeats again,
"It is enough."
[February 26, 2002]

59 Beloved Souls, fritter, fritter, fritter away.
You have a saying. 'fritter away time'.
You are in time within the earth plane.
Know ye that there is a purpose to each and every day,
to each and every moment of each and every day.
Know ye your purpose;
to care for one another, to care for the lands, the seas,
all those you call creatures, all those you deem aliens,

all those that give you pleasure
as they splash in the ocean
and as they take wing in the skies.
They do not have time to fritter.
They do not have time to waste with poisons and toxins
and the detritus that you place upon their homes
whether in the land or on the sea.
Fritter while you may
but understand the damage that you are allowing,
that you are causing.
And we ask you to stop frittering and start healing,
for the knell has sounded.
We would have you be aware, we would have you understand,
there are many disasters, explosions,
that occur each moment of each of your earth days.
We constantly seek to ameliorate, and in some cases prevent
those occurrences of the spewing forth of negativity,
the consequences of your creations of negativity,
the consequences of which fall upon the land,
the water, and the air.
Where it is permissible, when it is allowable,
when we are not interfering with the lessons,
we do enervate the essence of a potential disaster.
We would have you know
the rapidity of the culmination of the consequences
of the creations of negativity is fast approaching.
It is bringing closer the time of the gathering.
We feel your torment, we see the tears, we hear the cries,
and, Souls of earth, your courage is unmatched.
But we would have you know
it is time to face the consequences.
We would have you know, we would have you understand,
pain needs to be no more.
It is done.
[September 17, 2002]

60 Whooosh, whooosh.
This is what is happening with your weather.
The wind is increasing in volume and it sucks in
and dries the moisture within all that is.
The climatic changes are brought upon the earth by earth.

The wind is drying the icebergs, not the sun.
It is the wind that has been let loose
    and can no longer be contained,
    and one change affects all other changes.
Within your element of time, you see this happening slowly
    and many scientists believe
    they have all the time there is
    and it will be hundreds of generations
    before climatic catastrophes, as tsunamis, occur.
Yet we would tell them that changes
    are escalating exponentially.
It will not be in hundreds of years.
Their children and their children's children
    will be in the midst of that which they have, as humanity,
    engendered upon the back of mother earth.
The turtle speaks and issues forth pleas to mankind to halt,
    to cease pain upon the earth and the inhabitants.
Woe to Costa Rica, woe to the eruption in Ecuador,
    woe to the Chinese mainland,
    to the southern quarter of China.
Devastation, floods, eruptions will occur.
They will, these calamities, be looked upon as strange
    but acceptable earth changes,
    but we would have you know,
    they are warnings of that which is to come.
[October 1, 2003]

61 We would discuss extra terrestrials.
You have been taught that there are many
    who place themselves about your planet,
    who enter in to the planet, to the seas, to the earth itself.
We would have you know there is no harmful intent,
    there is no intent of mind control,
    there is no intent of war,
    there is no intent to bring disease and plague.
Your earth beings bring upon themselves,
    plague, war, destruction, brainwashing.
They need no help from extraterrestrials.
The energies referred to as extraterrestrials have freely given,
    have volunteered their energies
    to assist in the salvation of mankind,

to assist in the purpose of mankind,
to assist in the rescue
of the beloved Brethren, the Fallen,
to assist in the cleansing of transition
and to assist in the lifting of purities
amid the devastation caused by man itself.
These Souls enter for short periods to gather
information that will assist in the liftings.
It is true that there is a dimension involved
in the placing of matter within the form upon the planet.
This dimensional placement is inexplicable
within earth mathematics
but an indication of the mathematical persuasion
may be found in the Zero equation.
There will be increased sightings
of what you call alien aircraft, spacecraft, saucers,
over the capitals of major governmental centres
upon your planet.
This is being accomplished, not as warning, not for fear,
but indeed for awareness.
It is to bring forward to more and more and more Souls,
the existence of other dimensions beyond your own.
It is for preparation.
[October 15, 2003]

62 We have seen the record, the Writing on the Wall
and we would take this opportunity to alert earth
of the grave errors
your scientists commit in the pursuit of gold.
The grave errors they commit in experiments
upon the animals of earth,
upon the avian, upon the sea and the fish,
the contaminants, the mutations.
The genetic helix is being tampered with
and earth will see new plagues
that have never been seen before.
They will be mutations of mutations of mutations
so that they become unrecognizable
from their original smallpox.
Look, for the link to smallpox
is passed through the food chain.

It is not airborne and it has to do with the genetic helix.
[January 17, 2004]

63 We would have your science investigate
and follow the trail of the adherence theory;
that all adheres, one to the other,
until unity is reached.
There becomes a uniformity within the chaos.
The adherence is not sticky as in glue or honey,
rather it is the adherence to a bond as in the rubber.
They will find, in the pursuit of this path,
answers to the question
of chaos versus order that many ponder upon.
They will find
in their mathematical equations of space and time,
a consistency they have not seen.
In searching for the adherence factor,
they will discover that which they have been blind to.
There is, beloved Souls of earth, a striving
toward the blending of science and spirituality
until the line between becomes indistinct
and is obliterated.
They will find this expression in Energy.
The Soul, Einstein, had more to offer
than has yet been discovered.
There are a very few who pursue his extraneous theories
and within them they will find the gem of knowing.
[February 25, 2004]

64 We would speak of the time that is to come.
A time when your voices will reverberate throughout the land.
A time when your vibrations will knowingly be linked.
A time when the vibrational modalities of thy being
will join in a symphony, in a chorus,
in a triumphal entry in.
The world that you know seems overwhelmingly
full of negativities.
To many it would seem an impossible dream
to have unity of purpose, of oneness,
of active brotherhood.
The active brotherhood will take the form of pouring Love

and compassion toward one another.
The active brotherhood will not be able to pass
one who has fallen without lifting.
The active brotherhood will be unable to see a sore
and allow it to fester.
The active brotherhood would be unable
to watch the tearful without comforting.
This time will have come to be.
It is written.
There will be a great gathering of like minded Souls
who have attained a level of compassion.
There will be seven such gatherings upon your planet.
And from these gatherings
there will be a vibrational connection,
one to the other, and they will go forth to practice
the active brotherhood.
[June 18, 2004]

65 Velocity, Souls.
It is no accident, the term, speed of light.
For indeed, Light has speed, but there is no terminal velocity
as your science terms it; for velocity feeds upon itself,
the Energy churning, churning, churning.
It is the perpetual motion that your science seeks.
It is a grueling task your science has set for itself.
And yet, would they but listen to the nudge,
to the idea that seems to have no basis in reality,
indeed they would find reality.
Indeed, they would discover perpetual motion.
Indeed, they would understand the term, terminal velocity.
Your scientists of all intent, whether you call it good or evil,
have purpose,
but they must understand their purpose
is not limited to their own discipline.
The physical sciences, the astrophysicist,
the musician, the mathematician,
all need to intertwine, for the discoveries,
although made as separately,
would only answer when they become one.
The equation given is for all scientists, is for all science
and not limited to only a particular discipline.

It is a challenge that may be resolved
by the coming together into a paradigm of discovery.
Yea, we say unto you,
there will be a conference upon this very notion
and there will be a confluence of like minds
that will join together.
And, within their symphony of oneness,
will come a resolution of the equation.
[September 17, 2004]

66 There is a restlessness upon the land.
There is upon your earth a feeling of anticipation, of unease
because of the unknowing of what is to come.
And yet, because of the enormity of what is to come,
all sense at some portion of their being, at some level,
the vibration of the coming events.
Yea, the earth will rock and roll as we have said before.
It is not in your far distant future.
It is not to occur in the lifetime of your children's
children's children.
Yea, it is upon you even now.
It has begun and it will continue to accelerate.
Time is ceasing, as you know it.
Forgiveness is a luxury that can be ill afforded to many.
And yet there are many who understand
and practice Love and compassion.
When there is no judgment
there is no requirement for forgiveness.
It does not enter in to the equation,
it does not even enter in to the thought,
for there is nothing to forgive.
And yet there are those still caught within the coils,
who see themselves as able
to withhold or give forgiveness;
but they too will reach beyond
and delve into Love and compassion.
Know ye that you are Loved, blest and blessed and honored.
[October 8, 2004]

67 There is upon your planet
two particular placements of toxins.

They are buried deep within the caverns
of the place you call Arizona
and the place you call Egypt.
Your governments believe these are secret.
There is a seepage occurring
that is leaking into the ocean floor.
It will be discovered by a scientist of earth
who will monitor the skeletons,
the bodies of those that live in your oceans.
They will find no cure for this
that is within the realm of earth science.
It is of the realm of radioactivity.
It is used in the nuclear reactor and reactions.
It is inert
and it is unable to be dissolved within the earth science.
It may only be resolved
through the solution to the equation given.
The scientists who monitor the oceans will search for the origin
and they will find it buried deep within.
There will come a time when the world will know of this secret.
[October 15, 2004]

68 We come before you this day
to speak of the great lifting.
We would have you understand all preparation is completed.
We, of the Armada, await the day without the trepidation
that is prevalent among Souls of earth.
For we understand, yea we know, you who are lifted
will have the same knowing, the same understanding,
the same lack of fear.
Indeed, thou shalt be in joy, and comforted to know
that which is to come beyond the lifting.
Beloved Souls of earth, you have before you
the mighty army of humanity, that which you are.
And yet, in your illusion,
you continue to deny that which you are.
You deny the holiness of your being.
You deny the Creator of which you are a part.
You can not comprehend
that you are Soul of Creator,
particle of His Being,

and yet, Souls, we know this will come to be.
Wisdom and understanding,
consciousness and awareness,
will enter in to the lifting.
It will not be a progression of steps.
It will all occur simultaneously.
[November 19, 2004]

69 We would have you know of the weather patterns
and their effect upon the human psyche
and the health of the human body.
Too often mankind sees themselves as separate.
They place in boxes weather, nature, flowers, animals,
and do not see the interrelationships,
the linkages between all that is.
There is not one iota of ion that is not affected by,
or affects another ion.
The weather patterns were chosen to nurture humanity
and to assist in the growth of humanity.
They do not operate separately from the influence
of the negativity created by mankind.
The weather patterns,
mankind have distorted,
and that distortion
will affect large numbers of humanity.
Even more than those of today.
The chemical reaction,
and we would have your science delve into this,
set up in the psyche of man
by the distortion of the weather patterns,
leads to illness of the mind and the body.
The child, from birth to age seven, is especially susceptible
to the distortions to the weather patterns.
It is not merely floods and tsunamis and drought
that mankind must contend with due to the distortions,
but it is also as if a cloud settles over the minds
of those who are susceptible.
Children develop much earlier in the diseases
that affect the lungs,
in the diseases, the disease of the mind
that affects what you call hyperness.

The child of the pregnant woman is affected
to these patterns of distortion.
Souls of earth, it would behoove you to gather your energies
to heal the distorted weather patterns,
to restore what you call the ozone,
to take that patch of earth you call your own
and send your energies forth
to heal the land itself, to heal in the ice.
You have before you the opportunity to relieve great suffering.
It is choice.
[December 10, 2004]

70 We would speak with you today
on the focus of your Energy of goodness.
We would have you know, within the lands of devastation
are microbes awaiting birth.
The birth is brought about by the conditions of filth,
filth within the water, filth within the soil.
Once the microbes have given mutated birth due to the filth,
they will be ingested
by the humanities that drink the water,
that eat the food that has been touched on the soil.
We would have you understand that your Energy
may stop the mutation
and hence stop the progress of disease,
of rampant plague,
that will descend upon these humanities.
Place your energies, beloved Souls, within the soil,
not merely on top of the soil, but deep within.
Send your loving Energy of goodness unto the microbes
and thereby neutralize the filth
that would mutate the beings.
Doubt not, Souls of earth, the power you hold
to alter negativity, to alter the filth.
We plead with humanity, we the Jinn,
to enter in your energies into the soil
and bring forth Purity, goodness and Love.
There is indeed an ecstasy to be attained,
as you enter forth your energies unto the earth soil.
We will receive with gladness that which you enter in.
[January 13, 2005]

71 That which you speak
is called vibrational effect of the earth
throwing off the yoke of negativity.
Negativity that has been subsumed into the earth by mankind
will be exhumed from the earth.
You have been given the major points of contention.
That is not to say that other areas adjacent to
will not also be affected;
not to the extent of the epicenter.
This is choice of humanity.
And yet out of this devastation, out of the screams,
the terror, the gnashing of the teeth,
will come great service, great learning, growth,
and even more contention as in the aftermath.
Humankind looks for reasons, looks where to place the blame.
Many will come to understand the blame lies within,
not without.
Many Souls will be lifted in great Purity and Love.
And from a disaster will flow healing and an uplifting of Purity.
The Angels will be busy on this day.
Testimonies to miracles will abound.
Testimony to the Angelic appearance will abound.
They will testify to that which they have seen.
They will testify to the miracle of the saving of many beings.
So shall it be.
[June 23, 2005]

72 We would speak of your weather patterns.
We would speak of the power, the cleansing power of the wind.
We would speak of the necessity for the cleansing of the wind.
We would speak of your ability as humanity
to prevent this necessity, to ameliorate this necessity,
to understand the power
that lays within thy being as humanity,
to recognize the stewardship of the land,
to recognize that beloved mother earth has a Soul,
as you do, each and every.
But the Soul of mother earth is in your care
as much as each and every being upon the earth
is in your care.
Indeed, you do have great accountability.

Indeed, each and every have great responsibility
for each and every.
It is not up to your neighbor to care for the land,
to care for your brother.
It is up to you.
You have made a pact with mother earth.
You have a covenant with mother earth.
She wants to give unto you
sustenance, beauty and a place to be, a place to grow,
and in turn you were to Love and nurture her.
But, all humanity, you have broken the covenant with earth.
She needs to cleanse her being.
She needs to throw off the weight of the toxicities
that are crushing her.
She needs to be rid of the cancerous growths within her being.
Souls of earth, you have choice.
You have all ability to repair mother earth.
You have ability to nurture her as in the covenant.
And your choice,
if you refrain from repairing the damage and neglect?
The wind will come and do it for you.
The wind will whip up the waters.
The wind will come in the form of hurricanes, of tornados,
of typhoons, of tsunami and flatten and cleanse.
Souls of earth, this need not be.
The choice lays with you, each and every Soul.
That has been the purpose of the great disasters
in the last century.
Humanity is hard of hearing.
[September 8, 2005]

73 We would tell you of the sightings.
We would have you know
they are going to increase exponentially,
in great numbers.
More and more and more will see what you call spaceships.
Not only in the dusk and the dawn,
but they will begin appearing in your broad daylight
where the sun will glint off the outer coating.
They will come closer into your view to the point
where your governments, your war machines,

may no longer deny, with any plausibility,
their existence.
The phenomena will be widespread.
Enough, that open discussion will take place.
Oh indeed, there will still be the doubters, the naysayers.
But they will become the minority.
For it will no longer be any question
as to the identity of this phenomena.
They will become close enough, that there is no doubt.
Mankind, humanity, speak to your war machines,
speak to your governments.
Do not wage war.
Do not waste billions and trillions.
Gather ye together your abundance and share.
Know the message of this phenomena is many fold.
But primary of which is that you are not alone.
Souls of earth, this phenomena
has only the most peaceful of intentions.
Within the discussion,
within the chaos caused by the expanded sightings,
fear will be prevalent in many,
but the voices of reason, the voices of the children,
will ameliorate and help to overcome the fear.
Earth, there is no need to fear.
We have only your well being,
the well being of your earth, as focus, as intent.
We Love you, earth.
[March 9, 2006]

74 Mankind is headed upon a path of destruction
which may be reversed at a moment's
instant recognition of the high beings that you are.
But many are enamored of negativity and can not let go,
refuse, indeed, to let go.
The Soul of earth, cries to man,
"Cease the toxins, cease the pollutants
you press into my water, my soil."
Soon your skies will turn hazy
with a grayness that will encircle your globe.
A band of gray,
that band of gray is your indication

the last knell has sounded.
For it will eventually cover all the blue
that has been for so long in your mind's memory.
The gray will signal that the gases are being released.
You will find it hard to breathe.
The acrid gases will sting the eyes,
sting the nasal passages, sting the mouth.
Souls, your children will erupt in sores
for their tender skin will not be able to tolerate
the acridity of the gases.
Cooperation, Souls of earth, will stay what is imminent.
We call upon you to awaken to the oneness of your being,
to awaken to that knowledge
and bring to bear upon the planet
all the goodness of being, to purify,
to reclaim the cleanliness of earth.
[June 8, 2006]

75 We would take you to the coast of Africa,
that which used to be termed the Ivory Coast.
There are rumblings beneath the earth along
the coastal area of one hundred miles from the tip.
Within that area there will be quakes.
The earth will open up and there will be a chasm.
There will be loss of life,
but only upon the earth.
And these Souls have graciously given
of their being for this event.
This event will bring world attention to, and focus
upon the internecine warfare of this continent.
It will bring to the attention of many
more than just the chasm,
but the plight of man against man,
of the starvation, of the privation,
of the heinous acts of violence that man is capable of.
Fear not, bemoan not this eruption, for it has a great purpose.
[October 6, 2006]

76 We would have you know
that within the sparsest of deserts
there is yet an oasis here and there.

And within those oases,
the waters that have not been polluted
are most efficacious for the well being
of those who are fortunate enough
to dip into the waters.
In many places upon your earth, there are still isolated areas
where the water, although not entirely pure,
is much less toxic than that found
in your populated areas.
We would have you understand that the waters of earth
were meant to provide sustenance
to the cells of your being.
Water is an integral part
of the manufacturing process of your physiology.
Ideally, it is most efficacious
if that water is purified before it enters in to your being.
You have the ability to purify
with the goodness of your Energy.
Understand that as the water enters in,
the cells of your being greedily suck it as a sponge
would suck up water,
and distribute it throughout your being.
When it is full of toxins and pollutants
then that is what is distributed throughout your being.
We ask you to be aware that your affinity
for toxicity and pollution
brings into your being genetic mutations
by the ingestion of these toxins.
Your waters, Souls of earth, are not something you can ignore.
For they are integral to your existence upon the earth.
Your manufacturers who process,
who claim cleansing of the waters,
can only cleanse to a certain extent
and filter out certain chemicals and toxins.
But there is no process yet developed,
you do not have the technology
to filter out the fallout from the nuclear.
We would have you be aware,
that your playing with these toys of destruction
has an impact upon the waters of your earth.
All is connected.

We ask that you be aware of the very real possibility
of genetic mutations in future generations
due to the actions of today.
Continue, Souls of earth,
and there will be no oasis of pure water,
and you will be unable to filter enough
that it will not affect all beings.
Heed, Souls of earth, heed what you do.
[October 13, 2006]

77 Would you walk, Soul?
Would you walk in the footsteps of an Angel?
Would you walk in the footsteps of the great beings,
Mohammed, Jesu, Krishna, Buddha?
Would you give all the goodness within your being
to heal another,
to heal the earth, to heal even self?
You have, Souls of earth, a myriad of healings that are derived
from your human self, from your human ego,
from your human compassion.
You have a variety of Energy healings with many names.
You have medical healings with many names.
You have medical personnel in many disciplines,
all derived to help.
Billions, trillions of your earth monies have been spent
within these varieties of healing.
It is time for healing to be done no longer in the old manner.
The healing that is done now upon your earth plane
will be as an antiquity.
It will be studied in history books,
for it will no longer exist as a modality.
You will no longer require to be cut open
to remove diseased tissue.
You will no longer be required to cut away a rotten tooth.
You will no longer be required to watch a loved one
gasp for air from disease.
You will no longer have to watch a loved one struggle
to move without pain.
Healers will abound,
many of which will be former medical personnel.
Your earth will alter.

The economics of earth will alter.
Starvation will become another item in the history books.
Those diseases that you search for cures
    will be relegated to the history books.
It will, indeed, for many beings become a new world.
We speak not from the thousand years from now.
We speak for many of your young ones;
    within your lifetime the great alteration will come.
[January 31, 2008]

78 We would have you understand the power of sound.
Your science and your scientists
    understand the power of sound
    and the damage it may inflict;
    the fear of pounding feet that may be inflicted
    upon a being, the sound of the cadence
    is used psychologically.
Sound can shatter eardrums.
Sound can cause aneurisms to explode in the brain.
Your science has dabbled with these.
Science has also looked at the calming effects of sound,
    the more gentle aspects of sound,
    and the role that sound may play in healing.
And they understand that a being that has been soothed
    and is calm, is more prone to healing
    than the tenseness caused by the jangle,
    the cacophony of busy lives.
Sound is a gift from your Creator.
Sound has healing properties.
This, science will come to prove.
Indeed their microscopes, their lenses will become so powerful
    that they may physically see with their earth eyes
    how sound alters the cells of your being.
It is choice as to how science will use these discoveries.
As in all cases, the choice between positive or negative,
    for there is no neutrality.
And science, we speak to you; "There is no neutrality".
Sound penetrates the flesh
    and directly affects the cells of your being.
Sound alters your being,
    as does color alter the cells of your being.

And in healing, when you combine sound and color,
a great vibratory alteration takes place.
Color may heal, sound may heal, vibration heals,
but the combination, the melding, the blending,
only upon the earth is this possible.
You will show us the way.
Indeed, you will show us the blending, the melding of the triad
for all is color, sound and vibration.
Color, sound, vibration will mend the earth, the universe,
and worlds beyond worlds beyond worlds.
[May 21, 2009]

79 We speak upon the vibratory modality
of the Soul and the human body.
You will come to understand,
the intricate connection
between the Soul, the body, and the vibration.
Each Soul of earth is a vibratory being.
When your Soul is attuned to your Path[36] it rings
in a true vibrational sound that reverberates
and echoes beyond your own Energy field.
The Soul has form, has Light.
Your science will come to measure the sound,
the vibration of your Soul.
And they will come to know, as you will come to know,
when you are vulnerable to illness that is not yours;
you are vulnerable to illness that was not meant to be,
that you did not choose before you entered in to earth.
When a Soul is in attunement, you vibrate with wellness.
You vibrate, you glow with health.
It shines from your very being.
You will see pictures of Souls who are out of tune
and those who are attuned and the levels of attunement.
This will come to be through your science.
It will be a great assistance
to anyone involved in the medical field.
It will be of great assistance to the individual
who wishes to pursue their own path of healing.
This will become as commonplace as your x rays of today.
This we give unto you.
[May 28, 2009]

80 You will understand within the nose
is a directional node.
Upon your earth, physicians, scientists,
think it has to do with magnetics.
We tell you it is a directional to the Farside for negativity.
It is the linear of negativity,
and so when you release it, that is the symbol,
for it allows the linear to enter in,
for you have offered it.
Your science will understand the connection to the Zero
for the node within the nose.
You will understand also it is near the eye,
not only near the eye, but there is a connection.
One of the linears is connected, the node to the eye,
for the eye can see,
can visualize with clarity, the negativity.
For it awakens the connection, and that connection spreads.
Its Energy spreads into the mind,
and brings unto the will, choice.
All connected.
What you see, your science, as Energy, indeed is Energy,
but you have yet to delineate that Energy as connections,
and not haphazard connections,
but definitive connections.
You will, Souls of earth, your scientists, will discover a machine
that will visually bring unto you the lines,
the connections.
The node will become palpable.
Science will understand the Zero
and the connection of the node.
[June 25, 2009]

81 We would speak unto you of the difference,
the gap between earth wisdom
and the wisdom of the Farside.
Upon your earth plane, you have various
presumptions of wisdom.
Ofttimes wisdom is a label attached to an aged being
who has garnered it through many life experiences.
Ofttimes it is attributed to the being
who wears the cloth of priest, Imam, pastor, vicar.

Ofttimes, it is attributed
to a captain of industry by their subordinates.
Wisdom is that which makes a being more knowledgeable
than another being, in your earth terminology,
they possess more insight, they possess more knowing.
Ofttimes, even a small child may evince words of wisdom,
you are astounded that it can come
from such a small young being.
We would have you know that in the time to be,
there will be many young in age
who will spout words of wisdom.
They will be the wisdom of Truth, the wisdom of Farside.
It will pertain to the spiritual being that you are.
It will pertain to the Soul of your being.
These words of wisdom
will pertain to that from which you have come;
the Triad, your Creator.
These words of wisdom will lead mankind
to a greater understanding
of the purpose for which they entered in to the earth.
These beings will be the violet, the crystalline and the blue.
They will populate your earth in all areas,
and speak in all dialects, in all languages,
and all will speak with the same concepts.
And you will say, 'I heard this.'
to a friend who lives a continent away,
and they will say, 'I, too, have heard this.'
And so it will be, as the words of wisdom
that these beings have brought into the earth plane
vibrate, take on a life of their own,
a vibration that soars through the earth
unto each and every humanity.
For it will not be in any language of your earth;
it will be in the language of sound.
[August 20, 2009]

82 We bring glad tidings.
We bring joyous news.
For the earth is rapidly decomposing,
is rapidly opening fissures to let off steam.
Why are these glad tidings?

It is because from where we are,
	we see you rapidly approaching
	the denouement of time.
Indeed, you see your time as slowly moving,
	millennia after millennia, after millennia.
And we see it as a fast moving river
	filled to overflowing with Souls;
	Souls who have given much to the earth,
	Souls who have given much to mankind,
	Souls who have risen to the Crystal Cave,
	Souls who are humanity.
The earth is rapidly approaching the vortex
	and we speak of vortex as a centrifugal Energy,
	one that will remove the chaff from the wheat,
	remove the outer kernel of the wheat germ.
This centrifugal force will cleanse.
Will it cleanse all mankind?
Indeed not,
	for that will take a thousand years.
But it will cleanse the earth.
The earth will return to its pristine state.
The earth will indeed be a reflection,
	a mirror image of sister earth in its perfection.
How may you prepare?
You cannot in a physical manner.
Indeed, Soul, you may heal earth from your high self
	by entering in to the oneness of humanity.
Many Souls will leave the earth in great numbers.
You will see this as a loss.
And we tell you, it is not.
It is, indeed, a gain,
	for through this, what you might term, sacrifice,
	humanity will look at itself
	and refute the negativity of self.
And thereby negotiating, instigating,
	initiating the fullness of the cleansing.
Souls of earth, you have much to look forward to.
In your high self you understand this
	and welcome the end of time.
Fear not, for it only signals the beginning of a new day,
	of a new dimension of reality.

Your Einstein understood this and so will your science
    as they resolve the equation given.
Souls of earth, have the temerity to celebrate,
    not to fall into despair.
Indeed, celebrate for the end of time is nigh.
[November 12, 2009]

83 Zoroaster the first of the great prophets?
Ah, Soul, there were many prophets before us,
    not so many recorded in your ancient writings.
Thus I spake as I was directed.
Thus I spake in the solitude of my being.
Thus I spake as the Light enveloped my being.
Thus I spake as directed.
Thus I was given much knowledge.
Thus I was given many visions beyond that which you know of.
I was given visions unto the twenty second century
    but I gave forth only that
    which concerned the multitudes in my century.
We came back often.
We entered in many many times.
We came back as the being you know as Nostradamus,
    and there we were able to impart some of that
    which we could not have done
    earlier in our reincarnation.
For it would have been asking an ant to change into a butterfly,
    and the ant would have had no conception
    upon the earth of how to do that.
And so we could not impart all of our visions.
For it was not time.
You have today, upon your earth, many visionaries.
The aboriginal are especially accurate in the translation
    that has been passed orally.
Many of your written prophecies of today have been altered
    by the human mind in their goodness,
    yet altering to make it clear to their mind,
    and so they distort unnecessarily.
The Hopi nation and those in the Ayers area,
    although seemingly divergent,
    have received matching prophecies.
The world will have discovered

more than what has discovered to date.
We await as do so many for the Keys[37] to appear,
for they will be the end of prophecy.
For all will be visions thereafter.
[February 4, 2010]

84 We are Angel.
We are in the Qur'an.
We are in the Torah.
We have been in all the Holy books,
for we have been messenger many times.
We have about our being a blue.
It is a translucent blue.
It permeates the Light of our being.
You would glory in this Light.
For as with all Angel messengers there is a Purity untouched.
A Purity that enables to worship, to sing,
to be near unto Creator.
And yet we move away from such glory,
for we have before us the great priority:
the purpose of humanity.
And we sing praises unto humanity,
for within humanity, as the Soul of Creator,
you would open the gate of transition.
You will reach unto our brethren and they will hear you,
for it is written.
And we will have such glory that day.
We will have such gladness.
Our very hearts will almost burst with joy
to once again hold our brethren.
And you, Souls of earth,
you minuscule beings with the greatest of Light,
you will enable this joy.
And then we will be able to bring forth
our brethren Archangels
and you, Souls of earth, will reach unto the Cauldron
and they will hear
and you will unite once again with our brethren.
And all will come to pass, for you have written it
and we have seen the coming to be.
[February 18, 2010]

85 Souls of earth, hear the great chorus of Hallelujahs
resounding through every being.
You have within you, humanity, the knowledge of this day,
for it is a day when negativity will be set free.
It will be a great rejoicing.
Each being upon the earth, each human will understand
the part they have played in this great day,
in this apocalyptic event.
All will understand how intricate and how necessary
was the web of intertwining energies
of all beings upon the earth.
In this day, Souls of earth, you will know the opening,
you will know the implosion.
Indeed, you have a timetable
within which the purpose of humanity
is to be accomplished.
The time element within the earth, the timetable of man,
is finite and encompasses great negativity.
But, Souls of earth, on that day
you will have released negativity.
All Energy has form, all Energy has existence.
Mankind, when you create negativity,
you own the negativity you created,
and only you may release it, may release that energy,
not unto the earth, not unto another being,
only unto Creator.
The Angels wait for the smallest iota of negative energy
that you release, to carry unto Creator.
And on the day of reckoning,
all negativity will be released.
[March 17, 2010]

86 We ask you to understand
the many flowing eddies of water
throughout your planet
are in imminent danger of contamination.
We ask that all those who may, who will, who can,
to place Energy once weekly within a source of water,
an Energy of White Light.
For you will understand that all waters
are connected in some way,

and the cleansing of one particular
will carry itself unto all waters.
We ask that you form a circle around the earth
of beings dedicated once weekly.
For only moments, place the Energy into a source of water.
It does not need to be in a lake or an ocean,
it may be even within your home.
Direct the Light into and unto the water,
for earth needs water to exist,
mankind needs water to exist.
The pollutants will cause massive outbreaks of dysentery,
dangerous to those already ill
or who have lack of immune system.
You have had minor incidences of this,
and it will become more prevalent.
And so we ask that beings around the world
join once weekly
and place energies of White Light.
Indeed, you have a website.
Place it on the website and it will
be taken up as a project by many Souls.
They will see it, recognize it as a responsibility and organize.
You have upon your planet many days dedicated,
such as your Earth Day.
This would be a Water Day, but weekly.
[May 13, 2010]

87 We enter in today to bring unto you all a teaching,
one that will cause great consternation
to many upon the earth plane.
But it will also assuage the beings
who are tormented upon your earth.
It will bring comfort to those who are maligned,
to those who have lost freedom of movement.
It will bring great learning to scholars of all religions,
of all manner of study, even unto the agnostics.
Beloved Souls of earth,
we would bring unto you proof of our existence,
an existence beyond your plane of earth,
an existence in another dimension of time and space.
We would have you understand, all may reach unto our being.

You are not confined to earth dimension
except by your own will.
This concept is not new.
Within many tomes upon your earth
there are mention of this possibility.
There are in many tomes upon your earth experiences
related by beings who have entered in to this dimension.
Your scholars will know whereof we speak.
Throughout the month of June
there will appear, throughout your world,
lights that will flash in a system of your earth code,
your Morse Code.
It will flash numbers so that all may decipher.
It is, Souls, an invitation to enter in to this dimension.
It is an indication to all of your world
that there are other existences.
Your scholars will find within the ancient tomes,
within the ancient writings upon your cave walls,
indications of a like occurrence
many of your earth years ago.
We do not come to conquer, we do not come out of curiosity.
There is every purpose in this message.
Turn to the high consciousness of self.
Indeed, we entreat you to pursue this action,
and we await the recompense of humanity.
[May 27, 2010]

88 Open wide your doors.
Open wide your windows.
Allow the wind to scurry through, for the wind will enter in,
closed or open.
The wind will scour your earth,
the wind will cleanse the cobwebs
from the mind of humanity.
The wind will awaken humanity
as no other phenomenon has been able to do.
The wind, you will curse and you will shield your eyes,
for the wind brings destruction along with construction.
No being will be untouched by the great wind
that will encircle the globe,
even unto the caves the wind will be felt.

It will topple mighty buildings.
It will topple the hovel.
It has no favorites.
It is brought about, it is necessary reaction
to the actions of humanity unto the earth,
for the climatic changes that are erupting
will climax in the great wind.
The wind will bring with it the flood, what you call disaster.
And yet the world would not be decimated.
Those beings who leave the world at this time are aware
and have agreed to do so,
so that mankind will awaken,
will recognize, will be aware.
The consciousness of man will focus on a new day,
on preventing a like occurrence.
There will be a renewed vigor within mankind,
a renewal of purpose,
a return to being the shepherd of the land.
You have not a long time to wait
for the world is spinning ever more rapidly,
and earth needs to unburden its being.
What preparation can you make?
None.
You can, Souls of earth,
by joining in the oneness of humanity,
cleanse the earth without the wind,
but this requires dropping from your visage,
from your mind,
all the discrimination, all the hatred,
all the negativity of one to another.
It is possible.
It is choice.
This we give unto you.
[May 27, 2010]

89 Ready yourselves, Souls of earth.
Ready yourself for great climactic changes.
These are imminent.
They are not for your children's children,
they are to be in this generation.
These changes have naught to do with your lack of ozone,

they have naught to do with cold,
with an ice age entering in,
but they do indeed, Souls of earth,
have to do with the repercussions from the pollutants
and the toxic waste that you strew about the earth.
We would have you understand
the great capacity of your planet
to excise poisons and pollutants
in a normal state of being,
where humanity, mankind understood its responsibility
as the shepherd of earth.
Earth would have had the capacity to deal with
those pollutants and toxins,
for you as a shepherd would have limited.
Instead, Souls of earth,
you have unlimited toxicity for the earth.
Your manmade materials, your plastics,
your use of toxic waste
have overburdened earth.
The planet can no longer maintain a fitness,
can no longer recycle,
for there is naught within the earth
that is akin to recycling,
to purifying manmade materials such as plastic.
It is unnatural for your earth
and so the earth labors to contain itself.
The earth labors to withhold
toxins from the Souls of earth, from mankind,
but it has passed the ability of earth to do so,
and so great upheavals will occur,
and out of the great upheavals
toxins will spew into the air.
Toxins that were buried deep within will come to the surface.
Souls of earth, you may place a ring about the earth,
a ring of united Energy and oneness.
Your Energy may cleanse what earth can not.
It is as shepherds that you may do this.
You have little time left, Souls of earth.
The earth cries out for aid.
Will no one hear?
[June 10, 2010]

90 We would have you understand all is operational,
all is in place.
Events are accelerating.
Your earth is compressing
to the point where she must explode,
for the compression can only exert so much pressure
before the ultimate limit is reached.
Your earth has vents, many vents,
and‘we speak not just of volcanoes,
but in all the places, in all the earth,
there are eruptions.
Sometimes steam, sometimes water,
sometimes the spewing of fire.
All designed for balance.
A perfect mechanism is your earth,
but the earth has become contaminated to the extent
that its mechanism is unable to fully function.
The vents are no longer adequate
and therefore great eruptions will cause an instability
within the whole planet.
You will understand the point of no return is nigh.
We ask you, earth, to not turn your head in fear.
We ask you, earth,
to look forward in compassion upon your planet,
for you are finite, your planet is finite,
its resources are finite.
There will be much exhumed during the explosions.
You have experience with what happens
after a disaster of great proportions.
There is the shelter, there is the food, there is the cleanliness.
There is the animals,
there is the overrunning of rodents and more.
You will require all your experience and more.
Know that we have the capacity to lift all mankind and yet,
we may only lift those who will allow.
Understand, Souls of earth, that your time and space varies
from that of other planes, other dimensions.
Your planet is constrained;
in its place will come the beginning of the end,
and the end of the beginning.
See your planet,

not as the individual intricacies of your sciences,
see it in the total gestalt of its being,
the sum and beyond of all of your sciences.
We would have you understand,
there is more at work in the physics of your planet
than your science has yet discovered.
The earth wobbles.
The wobble is increasing.
We are ready
for when the wobble can no longer be contained.
Understand the great choice that lies before you,
the great salvation that lies before you,
the great rending that lies before you.
And yet, Souls of earth,
none of this of which we speak is negative.
It is all within the realm of positive.
Harken to the crack of the earth.
Harken to the inundation of the waters.
Harken to the beginnings of a new day, of a new dawning.
This we say unto you.
[June 17, 2010]

91 We speak of the great fire.
Greater than the earth has known.
You will not be able to contain the great fire.
It will burn for many months,
and the charred remains will take years to recover.
The great fire will surround many great cities.
Before the fire, the land will be dry, and drought,
the most severe of droughts
will crisscross the land throughout the earth.
We ask that in your haste to control the fires
you recognize the long term effects of chemicals.
Using chemicals to smother the fire
may cause permanent damage to the land,
and we ask you to consider that which you do.
You will also understand,
that you have buried in your many,
what you call landfills,
of varieties that are combustible
and will easily be caught into flame

and feed the great fires.
Souls of earth, look
to that which you call a solution for your waste,
for you are building fire starters in your landfills.
And you have buried deep within your earth
that which also may become combustible
with the great heat generated.
Know ye this and prepare.
[July 22, 2010]

92 We would teach on balance and we speak
of the very planet upon which you reside.
In the very construction of the planet earth, all was in balance.
The very rain, the very deserts, the very valleys,
the mountains, the snow, the ice, the clouds,
night, day, sunshine, all in balance.
All designed to furnish you, humanity,
with that which you required as sustenance;
with that which you required for shelter;
with that which you required to go about
the daily life of a human being upon the earth.
Even unto the very medicinals,
these were provided for you in balance.
The very planet which provides for you
is no longer in balance,
in fact, there is a great imbalance upon the earth,
for it is overwhelmed.
The earth is overwhelmed with negative energy,
with pollutants, with toxins.
Your very rivers are becoming too dry or too wet.
Your very snows are becoming overwhelmingly blizzard like
or non existent where once they existed.
The very core of your planet has no balance,
can no longer balance its own being.
If the earth had choice, your planet would continue
to provide you with all that you required
in food and shelter and medicinals and materials;
but your planet has no choice.
It has had to accept the negativity you have rained upon her.
It has had to accept that unnatural energy
that has been poured into her being;

the manmade chemicals and pesticides,
all those pollutants from which
she has no natural barrier,
from which she has no natural ability to cleanse.
And so, you have manmade droughts, floods, fires,
disasters caused by imbalance.
Mankind has tipped the scales,
and only mankind, not the planet earth,
only mankind may balance the scales once more.
You will understand that a continuing imbalance
will bring great destruction, not by the will of earth,
but by the very imbalance of her being.
Hasten, Souls, to examine that which you do to the earth.
Recall, you are the shepherd,
you are the healer, you are the caretaker.
Bless your earth, hold onto the balance of earth.
[July 29, 2010]

Chapter Two
BE IN THE DAY

Purpose of Humanity

93 You, as individual beings
have all possibilities of growth.
You have an enormous capacity for growth,
a capacity for growth
that all the creatures and all the insects
and all the flora do not, for that is not their purpose.
You have the capacity to grow in the spirituality of your being,
to grow in the Love and compassion toward self
and all other beings.
Souls of earth, your purpose in entering in
unto the earth plane, is for growth:
growth in Purity, in Love and compassion.
That although you come individually unto the earth
with a lesson plan in place,
you are part of the entity called humanity.
All one and yet able to operate individually.
The independent movement has purpose,
for the whole oneness of humanity;
reaching ever toward the ultimate oneness
wherein humanity recognizes
their ability and purpose
to open the gate of transition.
Souls of earth, recognize your ability to grow.
Recognize your purpose,
that for which you came unto the earth plane,
that for which you volunteered, in your earth language,
that for which you offered all of the capability
of your being to bring forth.
It is an intricate web,
for although you operate independently
you cannot do so without the others,
the other beings who are
of your web of existence.
It is the interaction, the choices allowed
brought forth by the interaction with others,

that your growth is attained and your purpose realized.
Gather unto you the flowering of your being,
and gather unto you to assist
with your Love and compassion
the flowering of other beings,
and know that all has purpose.

94 You wear about your being a cloak,
and you know it not.
The cloak, in earth terminology, is a disguise, indeed,
for as you choose to enter in to earth
you choose the very form of your being.
It is a disguise, for it is not the pure self of your being,
but it is entered in to as an actor
would put on a costume to enter in to a play.
You each have placed yourselves in a role as human self,
and in your role as human you take upon
many individual roles throughout your lifetime.
All of these roles, whether they be male or female,
whether they be parent or sibling, or relative,
or friend or foe,
all designed within your entity,
within your cadre of fellow beings,
for the purpose of learning and growing.
These roles alter with the actor.
They alter with the experience of the actor.
They alter with the interaction of the other actors.
You are your own director.
You stage the play,
and it is a reality for you
in that moment of your earth life,
for your perception enters in to the play,
and the play becomes your reality
as you become the play.
All this intricacy, play within play within play,
role within role within role, all chosen
not for extraneous purposes
but with definite purpose;
to enter in to learning, to enter in to teaching,
for each is both student and pupil.
The setting, whether it be in a glorious penthouse,

magnificent castle or in a desert tent,
in a sod hut or anywhere in between,
these are mere accoutrements
for the action that takes place.
Souls of earth, you are all great
in the bounty you have bestowed upon humanity,
in the bounty you have bestowed
upon the Souls lost in transition,
in the bounty you have bestowed upon negativity
and in the bounty you will bestow
upon the Angels and Archangels.

95 Hear.
We knock.
We nudge.
Nobody there?
Oh, Soul, there are.
But they refuse to answer.
They refuse to listen.
They refuse to hear.
And yet, are they not a mirror for the blessed in transition?
For they will not listen either, they will not hear.
It is related, not relative, related.
All has meaning, all has purpose.
All that occurs in your day is a mirror for your being,
and each mirror knocks upon your psyche
and says "Look, listen, hear".
Nothing is inconsequential!
Nothing!
All was designed by you
to enhance your time upon the earth,
to give unto you clues, signposts, along your path.
When you are deep in negativity,
bogged down in the negativity of being,
you will notice all manner of activity
that seems to enhance the negativity.
When you feel you can not stand one more occurrence,
you will stub your toe, you will stumble.
This is not to enhance the negativity,
it is to draw your attention away.
And yet, you see this not.

Your anger increases,
and so another signpost will occur.
Oft times it will be enough to jolt you into awareness,
into recognition of that which you have fallen into,
of that which you are holding on to.
Oft times you merely fall deeper into the mire of negativity.
Souls of earth,
to find joy in each moment of your earth existence,
understand all has purpose.
All has a message.
All is designed for your well being, not to impede you.
Indeed, not.
It is to mark your path, to focus the mind on reason for being.
A bountiful existence is not one where you float upon a cloud,
pampered, not even a small pebble in your path.
Indeed not.
That is a scarce existence.
The most bountiful of existences has within it
pebbles and boulders and mountains;
opportunities to overcome.
Growth that is bountiful.
And yet, earth sees it as the opposite.
How much more joyful would be your existence
if you would see and hear
all within your path has purpose.
Purpose,
not placed by another Energy,
but placed by self as an agreement.

96 We would discuss vulnerability.
We would have you understand,
that the basic underlying realm of fear is vulnerability.
For in the very deepest core of your being
you know with an absolute knowing,
that you have entered in to this plane to be vulnerable,
to be vulnerable to negativity in all its forms.
Understand, Souls of earth, it is not fear that is illusory.
Not in this plane.
It is not.
It is your reality.
You have come to be vulnerable to the words of another,

to the deeds of another, to the torture of another,
to all the hate of another, to the loss of love of another,
to the most heinous acts of mankind.
That vulnerability allows for growth.
Yes, indeed, there is a positive side to the vulnerability.
It is growth.
It is the overcoming of negativity.
It is the very great gift of that negativity unto Creator.
Indeed, from the moment of birth you are vulnerable.
But understand, you chose to enter in vulnerable
that you might embrace negativity and overcome,
that you might become aware of who you are
and why you are vulnerable.
Why you come into this earth
with skin that may be broken,
with veins that may be cut,
with flesh that may be burned,
with a psyche that may be harmed with words.
Indeed, you have discovered all manners and forms and ways
of being vulnerable to negativity.
But once you become aware
that there is purpose in this vulnerability,
it, indeed, becomes simple to overcome negativity.
We do not, Soul, make light of your pain,
of your injury, physical or mental, emotional.
Indeed not!.
We do want you to know with a great knowing within,
that there is indeed purpose,
and you have all choice, possibilities.
All possibilities of your Creator are yours.
Your vulnerability has great purpose.
With this vulnerability and the overcoming of negativity,
you will be able to reach into transition
and bring forth all those Souls
caught in their own pain.
You, Souls of earth, you humanity, will release!
And so, Souls, understand the greater purpose
for which you have come unto this plane of existence.
And know you have the possibility of all Truth, of all Love,
of all compassion within thy being.

97 We would have you understand the vagaries of earth,
the vagaries of life within the earth plane,
the vagaries which you often, in your anger, condemn.
And yet we ask you to understand the vagaries of your life
are that which has the potential,
the possibility of growth.
The vagaries of life allow you to contemplate,
to choose that which you would do
to overcome these vagaries of life.
They are given to you,
not by an external force,
not by another being,
but, Soul, you planned for these vagaries
to enter in at given times in your life,
so that you might overcome,
so that you might grow in Purity,
so that you might become
ever closer to that which you are.
Condemn not the vagaries that seem to plague your being,
but have gratitude for they are of your choosing,
to allow you to complete that which you came to do.
They allow you to implement for humanity,
to complete the purpose of humanity.
Bless the vagaries of your life.
Enter in to joyous acceptance.
Enter in to challenge, to adventure, of the vagaries of life.
Enter in to the joyous pleasure
of overcoming the vagaries of life,
and know you have accomplished
that which you set out to do.
Bless you, Souls of earth.

98 Tears.
At any moment in your earth time,
there are thousands shedding tears.
Most shedding tears of sorrow, of pain
but many shedding tears of joy
as they are reunited with a loved one,
as they receive a desire long hoped for,
as they look upon the babe new born,
as they exchange loving promises,

as they see the very Aura of their Spirit,
as they see with the eye, the blessed Lady,
as they see with the eye, Farside.
Souls of earth, do you not find it strange
that the water flowing from your eyes
may flow in sorrow or in joy?
The very same water and yet, what propels that water
is that which denotes
and decides the emotion that it engenders.
Understand, you see tears as light or dark, sorrow or joy.
And we see tears from the Farside as an indication,
simply, an indication.
We see the tears as indicative of your state of mind.
We see it as choice.
And you say, "How can there be choice
when I grieve for the loss of a loved one;
can you compare that to the joy of a new born?"
And indeed, Soul, we can.
For you categorize actions as light and dark.
We do not.
We see them as steps upon your path of growth.
And all have value.
Whatever the emotion that the tears evoke
that the incident evokes, it is a step.
It is your path.
And each incident has value.
For each is an opportunity to grow in Purity,
to gain a scar with your overcoming negativity.
And so, we make no judgment, good or bad.
But we bless each tear that falls no matter the reason.
For it is part of that which you do.
It is a portion of your existence upon the earth.
Understand that even the most grievous cause of tears
has value,
for it is an opportunity for you to enter in to a choice,
to overcome a negativity,
or to share with another an emotion of Love.
Souls of earth, naught that you do is valueless,
all has value and all has purpose.
For out of the tears of sorrow, there arises tears of joy.

99 We would discuss with you
your earth phrase, being off kilter.
You will understand the feeling
that all is not quite right with your being,
with your mind, with the situation, with any event.
This is an indication you are out of balance in your chakras,
in the chi of your being.
It is as if one half of your body tilts to one side
and you are never quite sure,
when you put your foot down,
whether you will land on your balance or not.
This sensation is a calling to your being, to your mind
to refurbish your chakras,
to bring the chi back into balance.
We would have you understand the need to be in balance
is from the Soul of your being.
We would have you understand
that you may have the most desperate of illnesses,
the most heinous of diseases and still be in balance.
Souls of earth, to be in balance is to have joy,
no matter what is otherwise occurring in your life.
The chakras in balance, your chi energized with no blockages,
you will be able to handle with equanimity and joy
all that life brings unto you.
Negativity has purpose.
And the purpose is for your growth,
is for the oneness of mankind,
is for the overcoming,
and helping that Energy of Negativity
to return from whence it came.
It is not the purpose of Negativity
to cause you unhappiness, pain, disquiet, imbalance.
Balance thy being and walk your path with joy.
100 We would teach on illusion.
We make a simple statement:
illusion is your belief that you must attain holiness.
There is no need to attain holiness.
You are Holy.
All of humanity is Holy and Holy unto Holy.
Beloved Souls, fight not, struggle not to be that which you are.
You are particled of Creator.

How can you be aught else than Holy?
It is unnecessary to tithe to save your Soul.
For what would you save?
Creator has no need to be saved.
Tithe to help another, tithe out of goodness
    with no idea of recompense,
    but tithe in pure goodness.
Volunteer out of benevolence, out of goodness.
Volunteer not to gain points of salvation.
There is no bargaining necessary, beloved Souls.
There is no need to plead for salvation.
Recall your holiness.
If you must plead, plead for recall.
We say unto thee:
    "Utter forth in word and deed
    thy holiness one to another,
    and balance will be thine for the rest of thy days."

101 Enter in to joy.
Enter in to joyousness.
Enter in to the very being of joy,
    for thou art, Souls of earth, a great joy unto our eyes.
From where we are you gladden our hearts.
You gladden our minds.
You gladden our spirits.
We see you as joy.
We see you as Holy.
We see you as Light, Holy Light.
And we watch carefully each overcoming of negativity,
    for it gladdens our heart to know that the Brother
    is ever closer to becoming unfragmented.
For indeed the Brother has been fragmented.
Souls of earth, you have such courage you astound our being.
You have such dedication you astound our beings.
You have such purpose you astound our beings.
You may choose to remove the veil from the eye
    and see the Energy of your being.
Souls of earth, thou art all powerful.
For are you not creating in every act of being?
For are you not creating negativity?
For are you not, by overcoming negativity,

creating yet another state of being?
All that you are, all that you may be,
all that you may become is in the realm of possibility.
Understand the great power of your being.
You are not inferior beings.
You are not without resources.
Indeed, within the realm of possibility you have all resources.
Know that which you are
and know that great power of your being,
and know the possibility that comes with that power.
For within the realm of possibility
is both negative and positive,
is both goodness and evil.
You may create either.

102 We would have you release from your beings
the need to be in despair.
We would ask you to release the need for sadness.
We would ask you to release the need for depression.
Why do we say need?
Why would there be a requirement for these emotions?
Why would anyone need despair, disillusionment, depression?
And yet within many beings this is a requirement;
it is a need for their growth
and for the growth of others.
For when you look upon a being in despair,
as an aged Soul, you recognize
the difference in your own circumstances.
You recognize they provide a mirror
for you to see yourself in a light of being,
for you notice your life
is not nearly as desperate as you thought.
When you look upon another in depression,
you realize you, yourself,
have seen the face of despair
and you know it is not your face.
The person, the being in despair,
has provided you with an opportunity
to look with gratitude
upon that which you have in your own being.
For if your despair, if your depression was worse

than the person you gaze upon,
you would not be able to recognize it,
for you would be so immersed
in your own emotion turmoil.
Recognize when you gaze upon one in torment,
there is an opportunity to assuage that torment
and also to have gratitude for that which you have,
and for the opportunity for growth given by that being.

103 We ask you to look around your earth,
to be aware of the myriad of plants,
of animals, of sea creatures,
the myriad of flora and fauna,
the myriad of environments,
the myriad of beings, human beings.
And understand that each and every living being
upon your earth plane
volunteered to enter in.
Those who are not humanity
volunteered to enter in to assist humanity
in the fulfilling of the purpose of humanity.
Indeed, each spider, each cat, each elephant, each flower,
each weed, those that you classify as weed,
each rock entered in
to assist you in your purpose of being.
And each, each class, genus, has for you a lesson.
The ants teach industriousness, cooperation;
the bees teach cooperation, industriousness.
The great whales teach cooperation within their pods.
The elephants teach of family, of bonding, of togetherness.
Even your snakes upon your earth
teach and provide humanity with a lesson in being.
Each entity upon your earth plane has a purpose for being,
not only in what they may teach humanity,
but also in how they may assist humanity,
as in your many pets,
whether it is within the individual home,
or whether they assist the blind,
the hearing impaired, the epileptic and so on.
Even the inanimate,
that you see as inanimate objects upon your earth,

assist you.
The rock gives you a place to sit and gaze in contemplation;
to find a small piece of serenity.
The rocks, together, forming a mountain,
give you a place to climb,
a place to be, a place to feel the great strength.
Your trees, Souls of earth,
how many, uses can be listed for one tree!
Even unto healing.
A tree will give of its being, the bark, the leaves,
for mankind to use.
The tree will give up its Energy to assist you in your healing.
The tree gives of its being to provide you shelter.
Souls of earth, become aware of the inter relationship
that you as humanity have with
all else upon the earth,
all working to fulfill the purpose of humanity,
all gifting of their being to Creator.
They enter in fully knowing and accepting there is no choice,
not as humanity has all choice.
And so they enter in knowing what will be until they leave,
and many, many return again and again, knowing.
Souls of earth, understand you are a shepherd of earth.
You have power over these beings, these creatures of earth.
These creatures do not pollute the waters,
they do not pollute the land.
It is mankind who pollutes, who savages the land.
Souls of earth, hear that which we say unto you,
all upon the earth plane
have Soul, have knowing, have mind.

104 Beloved earth, we have before us, the fence.
We would have you know of the trillions of beings
who constantly watch over your beings and all beings,
animate and inanimate, upon the planet you call earth.
We would have you know you are the show.
We would have you know you are the picture.
We would have you know you are the painting.
We would have you know you are that which is gazed upon.
Not, Soul, with curiosity; with Love, with hope and with joy.
For in each moment of your earth day you give,

by your action, joy upon joy upon joy,
for in each minute action there is reaction of learning,
there is the potential of resolution of the negativity.
We would have you understand the enormity
of the importance of each and every action.
Nothing that occurs is unimportant.
There are no inconsequentialities within the earth context.
Even the minute action of swatting at the gnat has a reaction.
We would have you understand every minutest moment
of time engenders action and reaction.
We ask that you have awareness of this and understanding.
For that which is to come, to be,
will evolve out of each of these actions and reactions.
We would ask that you be aware
each moment of that which you do,
of the thought which propels the action,
of the beating of your heart,
of the connection of the Soul, of the heart,
of the mind, of the body, of your Angelic being.
Souls of earth, we plead for your awareness
and we applaud your being,
and we would have you know
of the joyous fulfillment that we await.
No movement, no step, no thought is taken
by you without our awareness.
We stand ready in each moment to assist.
Bless humanity.

105 We would discuss what you call agitation,
and we speak of the agitated being.
We speak of the psyche in confusion. the psyche in irritation.
The irritation that causes agitation within the being
affects the physical, affects the mental.
When a being is in confusion they become agitated.
You often see this in the very young child who is unsure,
who is frustrated with a task
or with acquiescing to an authority figure.
If you were to open that being up
and look within the brain,
you would see the synapses,
instead of in a straight arc, the arc zigs and zags.

You would see the electric, the small electrical impulses,
pinging on the nerves of the being.
And you would see it affect
even the flow of the blood within the being.
Agitation is not the result of confusion.
It is the precursor to confusion,
for if you disallow the agitation,
you may see with clarity.
Agitation arises out of frustration and frustration,
arises out of fear.
Understand, Souls of earth, fear is an opening,
an invitation to negativity to enter in.
It is the open door.
It is the welcome.
To open the door fully is to embrace negativity,
is to encourage the reaction within your being.
And recall the negative energy reacts as positive Energy does
in that it is transferable.
We ask that you be aware that you have choice,
that you are not a victim.
Indeed, not!
Harken to your high consciousness
and be aware of that which you are,
both upon the earth and in Spirit.

106 We would have you thrive on chaos.
We would have you ask for chaos.
We would have you embrace chaos but not hold on to chaos!
When you thrive on chaos, when you ask for chaos,
you are taking the opportunity
to send Negativity home.
Where else would it go, but to cause more chaos?
It is not that you are constraining negativity.
You take that chaos and allow it release.
You allow the Angels to take your offering unto Creator.
You, Souls of earth, are the ones who may do this.
The Angels can not swoop in
and force negativity from your being.
You must give it willingly.
And so we ask that you actively bring unto you
the cacophony of chaos,

the small n negativity.
And then overcome and offer it.
This you can do in the most minute of ways
and in the most awesomeness of ways.
For what may be minuscule
to you as an individual to overcome
may be to another individual
the greatest of undertakings.
What may seem easy to you will be the hardest for another.
All is relative.
Judge not by your reaction to overcoming negativity.
Judge not the other being and their battle with negativity.
Do not place judgment and say,
"Why don't they do that?
It is so simple.
It is so easy."
We ask you to carefully guard judgment of another
and their battle,
for you do not know that which torments another Soul.
You do not know the tools that being has
or has yet to attain to overcome;
do not know the level of negativity within the being.
Harken, Soul, to the overcoming of your negativity.
And in your strength,
those of you who are strong in your being
invite even more negativity and offer it a way home.

107 We would have you understand
the great excitement you cause on the Farside
at the fence.
We would have you understand
the great excitement you cause within the Angels.
We would have you understand
that each time you overcome negativity
and it is released unto Creator,
the great joy, the exaltation
that is felt within the Farside.
The Angels, in your earth terminology,
would gather around excited as at a birth long awaited.
When one of the hosts brings the negativity unto Creator,
the gift you have given,

the Angels all are aware of this birth.
For they know that the negativity will be altered.
And all at the fence looking upon the earth
watch in wonderment
as you overcome, as you send home the negativity.
And they exalt!
For each occurrence is an event.
You may see it as only minuscule overcoming,
and yet we tell you there is no minuscule overcoming.
For all has value,
and all contributes to the joy held within the Farside
and worlds beyond.
Hasten to do that what you have come to do.
Hasten to overcome and offer.
Hasten to send home Negativity.
And know you gladden the hearts, minds, of all Farside.

108 Souls of earth, many see themselves
as carrying great burdens,
their shoulders bowed down
with the weight of their burdens.
We speak of the burdens of the mind,
that which you worry about,
that which concerns your being,
that which you fuss and fidget about, that which you fear.
Indeed, that weighs upon your being;
to fear, to worry, to carry emotional pain and sorrow.
And you cry out,
"Take this from me. Why me? I can not do this!"
And you rail at Creator, at the Angels, at your guides
for the predicaments,
for the burdens you see yourselves carrying.
Souls of earth,
it is perception that you have such great burdens.
We do not denigrate your pain or your sorrow.
We do not denigrate your worry, your concern.
We do not denigrate your emotions, but we do tell you
that there is a vast difference
between becoming your emotion
of grief, of sorrow, of worry,
and experiencing grief, sorrow, and worry.

All of life has some sorrow, some pain, some worry.
It is your choice to cling to these emotions
or to release them, to overcome these emotions,
to recognize the lessons
that are presented by these emotions,
by these burdens that you perceive you are beset with.
Indeed when you cling to these negative emotions,
you become these negative emotions.
When you experience them and learn from them,
they are no longer negative
for you have grown in positive.
We do not judge your choices
but we do present to you
this opportunity for knowledge,
this opportunity to recognize
there is reason for all that occurs upon the earth.
Your Creator, your Angels, your guides, would, if they could,
take from you what you perceive as pain and burden.
When you entered in to earth you asked not to be relieved,
for you had an agenda for growth.
They may nudge you,
they will show the Path if you ask,
but they can not walk it for you or force you to walk it.
You have freedom of choice to continue to hold unto,
to bear these great burdens of pain and sorrow
or to release by overcoming these negativities.
Souls of earth, each moment that you overcome,
there is great rejoicing.

109 We would speak of the cloak you wear.
The cloak upon your planet, upon the earth,
is used as a covering of the flesh.
The cloak can be of the most basic homespun fiber
with nubs and irregular weave,
or it can be of silks and satins.
And then there are the cloaks made from the pelts,
the skin of animals.
And then there are the cloaks of manmade fibers
which have no basis in nature.
A cloak upon your earth has many uses.
It is a shield against the sun.

It is a shield against the rain.
It warms the flesh in cold and snow.
It hides and conceals.
Many use it to conceal weapons of destruction.
Others use it to conceal what they see or think of
as deformities of the flesh.
A cloak upon your earth can be a comfort,
can be merely utilitarian,
can be a hazard as it catches
upon thorns or burns in fire.
These cloaks that we speak of are immaterial,
although in a material world.
These cloaks are immaterial because they matter not.
It is the cloak of negativity
that is the be all and the end all
of your existence upon this plane.
That is the cloak that concerns you,
that is the cloak that has meaning
to Spirit, to Soul, to Essence,
to your Creator, to all of Farside and beyond.
When you enter in to this plane and place upon your being,
and knowing you will place upon your being,
and willingly place upon your being,
the cloak of negativity,
you also come with the knowing that it is alterable.
That it is removable,
that it is not for protection or comfort,
that it has no earth utilitarian value.
But it has treasure beyond your comprehension
and it is treasured as the most precious of babes.
And you are here, in all senses of the word nurture,
to nurture this babe, to cloak this babe with your Purity,
to give it comfort with your holiness
and protect it from the elements with your goodness.
This we tell to you.
Fear not the precious child.
Take it into your arms, embrace it and nurture this treasure.

Presence

110 Who has seen the wind?
Have you seen the wind?
You see the effects of the wind.
The wind has motion and this is what you see,
the effect of the motion of the wind.
It can be as the motion of a snowball,
hurtling down a mountainside,
gathering more and more
as it becomes larger and larger and larger.
Yet you do not see the wind, but you see the motion,
and so it will be when the wind sweeps clean the land.
Are you aware, Souls, that you may hold back the wind,
that you have the potential, that you have the Purity,
the blessed Purity to hold back the wind?
It is your goodness that has this potential.
We would have you understand
the motion of positive and negativity.
We would have you understand the motion of negativity
is as uncontrolled wind sweeping across a desert,
a prairie, with nothing to impede its progress.
And we would have you see that same negativity,
that same motion, when there is a mountain in its way
that impedes its direction.
Your Purity is that mountain.
The motion of positive is not scattered
as the motion of negativity,
it is not hither and thither,
this way that way, this way that way.
The motion of positive, of goodness,
is always the gentle breeze,
the motion you sense on a gentle spring, summer day,
that gently caresses
but does not disturb any of your being.
And the motion of this Purity,
of this positive goodness,
in its gentleness finds no impediment,
for it has no difficulty going around and up,
going over, gently.
It does not have the motion of negativity

that must be in, in, in, in, in.
We would suggest that you be an impediment to negativity
and that you focus its being elsewhere, up to Creator.
That you become the mountain that impedes its progress,
that you become the Purity that impedes its progress
but does not harm.

111 Understand, Souls of earth,
the difference between mindfulness and mindlessness.
To be in the fullness of your mind is to be aware,
cognizant of all Energy about your being,
is to be aware and cognizant in any moment
of your own intent,
of your own exhalation of Energy.
To be in mindfulness is to be part, parcel, portion,
of all Energy.
To be in mindfulness is to allow the fullness of your mind
to expand,
for there is no limit to the expansion of your mind
when in mindfulness.
To be mindless is an ignoring of the Energy of the mind.
It is reacting solely with the appetites of the body,
the appetites of negativity,
the appetites of harm to self and others.
Mindlessness abdicates responsibility for your choices,
for your actions.
Mindlessness relegates actions of negativity
to outside of your control.
You become blameless in your mindlessness.
But it is an illusion, Soul, a great illusion,
for you are responsible for all that you do,
think, and say.
There is not lack of responsibility,
but the mindlessness allows you to indulge freely
in the enticements of negativity.
Again, Soul, another great illusion!
For indeed, the self will experience the repercussions
of the mindless act, of the mindless thought.
Souls of earth, understand the difference
between mindfulness and mindlessness.
For the mindfulness in intent,

an act, a direction toward Purity,
toward awareness of all Energy.
And mindlessness ignores, attempts to shut out,
and you thereby become lost in the illusion.
Mindfulness allows you to recognize illusion
and the reality of who you are.

112 We would have you understand,
indeed we would have you know, your whole life,
each life you spend upon the earth plane
is but a journey,
a journey unto growth, a journey unto wellness,
a journey unto oneness,
and ultimately a journey unto glory.
Souls of earth, you see life often as
a daily grind of similar activities,
and often you feel as if you are going nowhere.
And we would tell you this is not true, this is not so,
for each moment of your day is part of your journey.
Each moment of your day brings you ever closer
to that which you came to do.
The journey may seem at times tedious and boring,
but we would tell you,
if you would see from the fence as we do,
your journey is exciting.
Each moment of your existence
has an anticipatory excitement to it,
and each moment wherein it
you embrace and overcome negativity,
we, too, have that same anticipatory excitement,
and we glory in your achievements.
Souls of earth, your life journey is not tedious,
is not boring, though you may perceive it as such.
We tell you it is illusion.
Your journey daily: you may climb a mountain daily,
you may trip over a boulder and then walk around it,
daily you may find a glorious sunrise
or a spectacular sunset.
Daily you may find a new companion, a new friend,
a new love, a new babe.
Daily you may learn a new thing,

a new thought, a new perspective, a new way.
Daily you have the opportunity to laugh, to cry, to Love,
and indeed, daily, you have the opportunity to hate,
to bemoan your 'fate', as you see it.
The possibilities in your daily journey are myriad,
though you perceive it not.
And we bring this unto you
so that you might give it some thought,
some consideration;
that you are in control of your journey
should you wish to choose, to choose with awareness.
For there is a great deal of difference
between choosing with awareness
and choosing in an illusory state.
Every moment of your day you choose,
and yet most of those moments,
you choose without knowing,
without examining your choice.
And we would have you recognize and be aware,
to be mindful of your journey each day,
each moment of each day.
To live in awareness, to recognize each choice
that you make has consequences,
has results, affects all others.
We do not bring this to you
so that you fear to make any choice.
Indeed not!
We bring this to you so that your choice
is done with full knowledge,
with the full knowledge
that you have within your being,
with the full knowledge of knowing
that you have not arrived here upon the earth plane
without purpose.
Live in awareness.
Live in knowing.
Live in the very truth of your being.
Live, and know there is purpose in all things.

113 Do not flay your beings for your imperfections,
for your lack of compassion,

for your lack of Love for self and others,
for you judge yourself when you do so.
To discern, to acknowledge
that you have a lack of compassion,
a lack of Love, is an awakening.
It's a recognition, an opportunity to go forward.
But to flay your being for that recognition places judgment
and you begin the cycle, the circle of negativity.
Caught in a circle of negativity, you do not overcome,
you do not go forward,
you do not increase your Love and compassion.
For you are caught in the mire of judgment of self.
And that holds you in place so that you do not move forward,
so that you become rooted in that circle of negativity.
Some grow roots deep within negativity
and hold those roots for millennium.
Some carry, even unto transition, those roots.
It is awareness of the judgmental nature of your being
that allows you to clip away at those roots,
to alter the circle, the cycle of negativity.
Look to a positive of judgment,
the recognition and the awareness
before you may go forward.
Look not to the negative judgment that holds you in place.

114 We would speak on mirrors.
You have mirrors in many places upon the earth
where you may see self, earth self.
Your mirror does not show you your high self,
your sacred self,
the Spirit, the Essence of your being.
It does not show your Soul.
It only shows what your earth eyes perceive.
We would have you know,
each and every one of you is a mirror also.
For you reflect for another that which they need,
that which their Soul
would bring forth for consideration.
And how do you know that you are reflecting for another?
You do not, but the one that is seeing the reflection,
that one knows.

For it is the purpose of the reflection
to help the being reflect upon an emotion
that has been hidden.
Indeed.
They will feel an irritation,
they will feel a resentment,
they will feel an anger,
they will place judgment.
Indeed, you are all mirrors for each other,
reflecting out what the being needs to see,
to hear, to think upon.
Know that in your daily activities you are constantly reflecting.
And as in your earth mirror
the reflections are always mirror image.
And it is not coincidental,
for there is your reason for the mirror image,
it is the reflection for yourself, for your own being.

115 The will is that which brings you forward.
The will never stands still.
The will is unceasing in its ability to move you forward.
It is the mind that holds you back.
The will knows that which is written.
The will contains the plan,
the agenda, the map, the guidelines.
The will is often in a ferocious tug of war with the mind.
The mind has an unbearable strength.
The mind can overwhelm the will.
The mind, Soul, when it is centered within the earth plane,
can overwhelm the will.
The mind connected
to the higher self will cooperate with the will.
The will is in the area of the solar plexus.
It does not reside in the brain as is commonly thought.
Soul, the will carries the plan of the Farside.
It carries the Writing on the Wall.
Physically the connection is through the solar plexus,
spiritually the connection is the Soul's aura.
Self control is an earth attribute of the mind.
The will is not about controlling, that is a mind attribute.
The will carries within it wisdom, knowledge, recognition.

And it is only when the earth mind
has a clear connection of the eye
that the will and the mind
work in conjunction with each other
to further the growth of the Soul, to complete the plan.
The ego is overwhelmingly earth
when in darkness, is overwhelmed with negativity.
But the ego is overwhelmingly positive
when the connection is there.

116 Grief is a lesson.
Grief is growth's opportunity.
Grief enters in to the heart and permeates it with darkness.
Grief is particular to the human condition,
for it is not understood that only joy
is for passing, for the Soul who has gone home.
But, indeed, the human condition
often requires a long period of mourning,
of tears for self, for the loss of the Energy
of that being that is now gone.
There are stoics who make no attempt to resolve the grief,
make only the attempt to endure and pass through life,
always with the grief showing in their eyes
as they go about their daily life.
And there are Souls
who sink deeply into depression from grief,
for they no longer see joy anywhere in the world,
and they withhold their being and withdraw,
in the hopes of not ever encountering grief again.
There are Souls upon the earth
who understand grief is cleansing.
Indeed it is cleansing, and they see, having understood,
the positive benefit of grieving and then letting go.
Indeed that is difficult, depending on the culture
and the lessons learned as a child.
It is the knowing the grief is a lesson to be learned quickly,
not to be embraced and held,
but to be embraced and then released,
as you would not hold to your being a burning brand,
but quickly release as the pain struck.
So it must be with grief or, indeed, with any like emotion.

If you were to see a burning brand
that another being might step upon,
you would quickly remove it,
but you would not hold onto it,
you would make the step beyond.
Indeed, many people grieve, not just for a passing Soul,
but they grieve in regret for a life that they have lived.
They grieve for that which they have not done,
in addition to that which they have done.
They judge themselves harshly
and see not the Holy being they are.
But they cling to the illusion of a life not well lived,
they cling to an illusion of a life incomplete.
And, Soul, in the releasing of that illusion, the grief is gone.
Many people wish to castigate themselves
for imagined slights they have given others,
and that is a form of grief.
For they are sorry and do not know how to forgive self,
and so they grieve for what they have done.
It is judgment, earth judgment.
Judge not thyself, as you do not judge others;
knowing that all
are fragment of Creator, including self.
Grieve not for what might have been.
Grieve not for what was.
Grieve not for the Soul who has gone home.
Grieve not for the land.
Grieve not for that which will come.
Be in the moment.
Hold not to the past or the future,
and you will grieve no more.

117 Souls of earth, ho hum, ho hum, ho hum.
You wait and wait and wait
for the magician to come and rescue you.
Ho hum.
Each mundane task is done reluctantly.
"Ho hum, another day.
Ho hum, what is it all about?
The magician didn't come today.
I guess I have to go another day.

I guess I have to wake up again, wanting, waiting for rescue."
Ho hum, day after day!
Lethargy sets in.
The mire, the foot clinging to the muck.
So hard to lift that foot
    and when you do, the other one is so hard.
"Ho, ho hum, the magician has not come."
Each Soul is a magician, a master wielder of illusion!
There is no mire.
There is no lethargy.
There is no ho hum, another day.
It is illusion and you, when you express ho hum, another day,
    you have walked into the illusion.
You see what magicians you are, how you can create?
How masterful you are that you can disguise the joy,
    the life the Creator has given thee!
The trees, the flowers, the sky, the wind,
    you are adept at disguising these beauties of creation
    and instead, with the sleight of hand you concentrate
    on the illusion of muck and mire,
    and Souls, you are so masterful,
    you bring others to believe in your illusion!
We would ask,
    dispel the illusions you create and bring forth
    the magician of magnificent creation,
    of Purity, of goodness,
    of joy in being, and every moment joy of being.

118 Bow your heads.
Bow them, but not in supplication.
Bow them, but not in prayer to a being higher than yourself.
Bow them to no man other than self.
Bow your head,
    only in recognition of one being to another,
    as a sign of respect.
There is no requirement to bow your head to show
    that you are less than another being.
Your Creator does not request that you bow,
    that you kneel, that you prostrate self to Creator.
Indeed not.
We would have you understand,

you have all possibility to hold your head high,
not in arrogance,
not in claiming self as superior to others,
whether they be other human beings or other creatures,
but hold your head high in the knowledge
that you are of humanity
and have purpose upon the earth.
Hold your head high in the knowledge
you are particled of Creator.
Hold your head high in the Light of being,
in the Love and compassion that you give unto others.
Hold your head high
and gaze upon the countenance of your Spirit,
of your Essence, of the very Angels about your being.
Hold your head high
and know that the eye of beholding will take you high,
will take you beyond the plane of earth.
Bow down to no other man,
to no other being, for you are equal.
You are one in Energy, you are one in purpose,
and you are one in having in your oneness
the ultimate survival of mankind.
Hold your head high in the knowledge
that in your oneness, all things are possible.
The planet may be healed, each individual may be healed,
all creatures may be healed
and transition may be emptied.
Indeed, hold your head high, for the great adventure,
the ultimate adventure is nigh.
We would speak with thee on the lowly potato,
the potato whose lowly buds spring forth
and blossom new life that reproduces in the earth,
whose roots enter in, clutching the soil,
strangulating all in its path for growth.
Understand the comparison to the Wilful Child.
Understand the contrast to the Wilful Child.
Does not the Wilful Child spring forth roots that inveigle,
and does not this bring forth growth of new life!
It may not be the new life, the energy,
the new energy that you would have wished for,
and yet, we choose each new bud, each new growth.

When you allow the roots to enter in to thy being
    and spring forth with growth,
    the Wilful Child does grow.
You have the ability to bring forth negativity or Purity.
Each individual can bring forth that which will give life
    and nourishment within the clarity of Purity.
Think carefully upon each action, knowing that you can
    allow growth of Purity or growth of negativity.
For all roots that dig into the earth,
    that dig into the human body
    need a place to burst forth
    and we would ask that thy place be of Purity.
Beloved Souls, bring forth Purity.
Allow the roots
    to bud into flowers of caring, of compassion and Love.

119 We would ask that you find a moment within your day
    to receive the Flow of Energy
    that is always available to your being,
    that you place your hands, palm up,
    in the receiving mode of being.
It does not require lengthy preparation,
    it does not require that you be in a Holy state of being,
    that you judge yourself worthy or unworthy.
It is simply an acceptance.
You are not required to pass an exam, or to reach a level.
Simply receive and accept the Flow of Energy
    always available unto you.
Feel the Energy flow in
    and enter throughout your being,
    a gentle warmth of Spirit.
A gentle warmth permeating
    your flesh and your blood and your bone.
Allow the Flow of Energy to enter in to thy brain,
    into thy mind, into the cavity of self,
    and luxuriate in this Energy.
Indeed, luxuriate in it.
It is available at no cost.
There is no fee for use, no fee for service,
    and there is no end to it.
You cannot use it up.

It is an impossibility.
You can indeed refuse it, but you cannot overuse it.
It is an unending Flow from your Creator.
You enter in to the earth with this possibility.
At any moment you may receive!
This Flow of Energy is available to each and every humanity.
It is part and parcel of your birthright.
It is who you are, for it is Creator Energy.
Find time in your busy day
to take a moment and connect with the Flow.
Connect, Soul, with your Pillar of Light.
Be who you are.
Take a moment to be.

Acceptance

120 Enter ye into a voyage of discovery.
Enter ye into that which awaits the Soul of your being.
Enter ye into the glory, the road to glory, the glory road.
How, we say, is this done?
It is one key concept, one key word: acceptance.
Acceptance that you are Soul, of Spirit, of Essence,
acceptance that you are of Creator,
and as such are the glory road.
Souls of earth, the oneness of humanity
is that of which we speak,
for in the oneness is the glory road found.
Acceptance of the oneness of your being;
this is wherein you will find the glory road.
Understand, you always have before you a myriad of choices.
There is one constant choice always available
and that is the glory road.
Understand, it is not hidden.
It is not convoluted.
You need not make any sacrifices or offerings.
You need not be invested with a particular blessing.
Indeed, not.
Always this choice is open unto you.
It comes with the acceptance of your being
of the oneness of humanity.

It comes built upon the wisdom of the knowledge
that you, individually in your separateness,
form the composite of the oneness of humanity.
You are all the Soul of Creator.
It is not only a chosen few.
It is each and every humanity.
And when you, in your oneness, enter in to the glory road,
you will cause such an explosion of joy
throughout countless worlds,
throughout countless beings,
throughout countless energies,
all awaiting to explode in that joy,
to sing a choir of a trillion voices and beyond,
welcoming that moment.
Souls of earth, recall whom you are,
from whence you have come, and whither you go.

121 The request to enter in,
to become re acquainted with that which you are,
that which is your Purity,
that is where from whence you came,
that is your Truth.
You have the knowing within.
You feel it is hidden from you.
Indeed not, it is the illusion that you believe.
Your Truth is not hidden.
This you know, this we tell you.
This we would have you accept
in the innermost recesses of your being.
And accepting it from within
allows the externalization of that Truth
to flow outward, to flow forth
so that all know your truth also.
It is fear that is the veil.
That is the barrier to knowing.
This is earth, this is negativity.
Recognize this, Souls.
Recognize your fears, accept them and embrace them.
And in overcoming those fears your Truth is revealed,
and no barrier exists between that which you are
and your being here upon the earth plane.

It is not necessary to enter a cloister
or a monastery dedicated to silence.
Indeed not.
We would not have you retire from that
which you have come to be a part of.
You need not refrain from human interaction.
Indeed not.
For there is not Truth in your refraining.
You have within you the utmost of abilities.
You have all touched Light.
You have all been and are within the Arms of Creator.
Harken to the Truth of your being
and live furthermore within that Truth.
Be honest and joyful in knowing thy self.

122 You have upon your earth plane much contention.
The contention arising from the most minute items
to great conflagrations of nations.
All Souls of earth have equal value.
All contention has equal value.
Contention has purpose.
Many upon your earth long for peace.
Not questioning;
what peace means to one
may be the opposite of what peace means to another.
Even within peace, a longing for peace, an intent for peace,
there can be contention.
We have a suggestion, Souls of earth.
That you see contention as a learning field.
That you see contention as a positive.
Understand within contention is the possibility of positive.
Therein lies its value to you as human being
attempting to manifest your Soul,
attempting to perfect your being,
attempting to access
and blossom forth all the possibilities within.
To condemn contention is in itself a contention.
It is why we speak of no judgment.
We do not denigrate the efforts of millions to have peace,
either within the individual, within the family unit,
within a state, a nation, the world.

Indeed not!
We would only point out to you that in your striving for peace,
when it becomes strident,
you have placed contention before Love.
Love has no judgment.
Strive for Love, Souls of earth.
Strive to open that which is an innate portion of your being.
Open that Love to all.
There is no contention in Love,
in the Love of your Creator,
in the potential of manifested Love in your being.
You have that possibility within,
and you have the choice to release
that possibility to self and all others.

123 In your daily life
you embark upon an adventure each and every day.
How you see, how you perceive the adventure,
how the choice is made of the adventure
depends upon the extent of your Purity,
of the wisdom you have gathered.
There are many ways to enter in to the adventure of each day:
boldly going forth, triumphant in your being,
armed with the knowledge of your sacred self,
choosing to spread joy and goodness,
choosing to coax a smile from all that you meet,
choosing to glorify the being of self,
acknowledging the Creator within.
Indeed!
Or, you may choose to enter in to the day,
the adventure full of trepidation
and concern and worry of self.
You go armed with prickles,
so that no one will recognise your vulnerability.
You give out fear, not joy.
You see, Souls, how simple.
And yet humanity has so many complexities
within their daily moments,
that the simple becomes hidden from view.
Each day, yea, each moment,
you may choose to enter in to an adventure

with joy or with fear.
Indeed, it matters not what the adventure is.
It can be the most simplistic of adventures,
of shopping, of marketing,
of communicating upon your device,
of entering into an operating room,
of giving forth council to the disturbed,
unto even the act of caressing a child
or lifting that child.
Souls, each moment of your existence is an adventure.
Choose how you will approach each adventure.

123 We bring forward unto you a conundrum.
The conundrum is of your making.
We are only helping you to explore the conundrum.
The conundrum, Soul, is the great discrepancy
between that which is your potential
and that which is your fear.
Earth humanity, you are of your Creator.
You are that which is Creator: Truth, Love, Purity.
What you fear, Love;
what you fear, Truth; what you fear, Purity.
You are all of those and yet you fear.
You fear to show compassion to the starving.
You fear to show compassion to the abused.
You fear to show compassion to different color of skin.
You fear to Love one another.
You come up with so many differences,
so many barriers, so many fences.
You fear Purity, for you think Purity judges.
You see the stains upon your being
and you think Purity judges.
And you fear Truth, for you are comfortable in your untruths.
Souls of earth, dissolve this conundrum.
Acknowledge, accept who you are, the enormity of your being.
The capability of compassion is beyond your imagination,
and it can be the reality of your being.
Explore your connection to Creator,
explore your connection to humanity.
Know how beloved you are.
For you are the key.

Enter in to truth, the Truth of your being,
enter in to the truth of your existence,
the truth of your humanity,
the Truth of the purpose of your humanity.
Enter in with all Love, Purity, and compassion.
Have compassion for self!
And then, expand that compassion unto all.

124 We would have you understand
each tear is precious to Creator.
Each tear that you shed
in agony, in sorrow, in pain, is precious,
and the Angels gather them gently
from their being and bring them unto Creator.
And Creator tears in his Being
that you tear in pain and sorrow.
For although the tears are precious beyond comprehension,
we would have you understand
the very balance of tears is joy.
Joy brings balance indeed to the imbalance of your being.
When you are in tears, crying out in pain or sorrow,
your whole being physically, emotionally and mentally
is in an imbalanced state of being.
And to balance your being, joy is necessary.
Even in the most dire of your moments of pain,
know that you can
reach out and bring unto your being joy,
and it will lessen that pain.
Souls of earth, hasten to bring joy into your lives.
Dispense with sorrow.
Dispense with pain, for it is not a necessary condition.
Indeed not!
You need not hang on to pain.
You need not embrace and hold on to sorrow,
for you have the choice to balance with joy.
A smile indeed physically affects your being,
a smile is the physical representation,
and the Light will shine from your eyes
and reflect the joy within your being.
They will be as beacons unto others.
Souls of earth, you have choice in all elements of your being.

You have complete choice in how you react to any situation.
You have complete choice as to how you act,
choose to act, in any situation.
We would urge you to each day
choose to bring some joy into your life,
and thereby bring joy into the lives of others.
In your compassionate Love, herald joy unto all.

125 We would teach on the rigidity of the human mind.
Often the mind becomes fixated in a particular path
to the extent that it digs deep and deeper and deeper.
It creates great ruts, great chasms
into which your thoughts sink,
into which the direction of your actions sink.
And so it becomes in your mind
difficult to enter out of the pit which you have dug.
The rigidity of the mind is a self imposition out of fear;
fear of newness, fear to take the leap, fear of change.
You will most often find rigidity
most prominent in those who wield power.
The power need not be great, over hundreds of people,
it may only be over one or two.
But because the being has been given
this power the others have relinquished,
they will wield it,
and in attempting to keep and hold onto that power
they become rigid in their thinking and action.
Flexibility in balance allows the being to take a path,
to experience differences, to leap into the unknown
with trepidation but not fear.
But flexibility may also be chaotic,
for it often hides an inability to choose a path,
to make a decision for self.
It, in its chaotic state, is as a young stalk of bamboo,
flowing whichever way the wind blows.
Both chaotic flexibility and rigidity are born out of fear.
How does one alter?
One becomes aware of the fear.
It is not necessary to know the exactness of the fear,
only enough to know you are operating out of fear.
Simply, the awareness will begin the ascent,

the climb out of the ditch of rigidity.
And awareness of fear will allow you
to find the balance from chaotic flexibility.
You have these tools in your toolkit.
It is only to open the kit and remove the tool.
For all beings come with the tools of awareness,
of recognition and of volume,
of voluminous action in the vibration of their being.
You have it all, Souls of earth.
The rest is choice.
So be it.

126 We would have you understand
you have all capability to alter your being.
There is naught that you can not alter of your behavior,
of the pathways in your mind.
What causes you to alter your behavior?
It is awareness coupled
with compassion and integrity of being.
You become aware that the behavior causes harm.
It may be to self, or it may be to another.
And that awareness brings forth compassion,
if you allow it.
and recognize it is integral to alteration to change,
for you can not change a behavior without compassion.
It is compassion that makes the connection to your high self.
It is the compassion that allows your guides,
your Angels, to offer insight.
It is the compassion that gives you the strength,
the determination to continue
in spite of any setbacks to alter a negative behavior.
Souls of earth, you have at your disposal
the tools of awareness, of compassion, of integrity.
It is the intent of your being
to focus on the utilization of the three
that will cause beginnings of change.
The focussing on the three will enable you
to carry through the change in your behavior.
Know this is possible.
Know that you have this capability.
Know that you need not be in despair, discouraged

in your attempts to alter a negative behavior.
For you have the triad to assist
in your accomplishment of altering.

127 Souls of earth,
you have a word that brings chuckles to our being.
In English language,
it has a particular sound that brings to mind, chuckling.
The word is, ridiculous.
Indeed, ridiculous!
Often, you use this word in the most demeaning manner,
in the most judgmental manner.
We would have you understand,
there is naught upon your earth
that is requisite to be demeaned.
There is naught upon your earth
that is requisite to be judged, including self,
for you often turn upon yourself
and judge yourself as ridiculous.
Ridiculous, ridiculous, ridiculous;
it is imbued in your language dictionaries
with a negative connotation.
We would have you recognize
a positive connotation that it brings to mind.
For then you will recognize there is upon the earth no being
that is ridiculous in your dictionary meaning.
There is no situation whereupon you could use this term.
We would have you remain positive in your being,
to see one another in a compassionate tone,
in a compassionate frame of mind,
to be a compassionate being.
To look upon your neighbor
as not just the being next door to your home,
but look upon all beings as your neighbor,
all beings that you would open your home to gladly
and welcome them in.
This is a compassionate being.
We would ask you to consider,
be, become a most compassionate being.

128 We speak on toleration.

The toleration of neighbors, the toleration of enemies,
of friends, of family,
of those whom you deem as lesser that thou.
Upon your earth, many of your religious academies,
many of your religions,
will preach on tolerating the sins of others,
on tolerating the peculiarities,
on tolerating the difference in skin color,
on tolerating other religions.
Toleration is judgmental and limits the full expression of Love
from your being unto your fellow being,
inhibits the strength of the Love
that you may envelop another with.
It limits even Love of self,
for toleration is not a positive.
Indeed, not.
It has grave negative implications
for it is only a minute, less than a hair's breath,
from toleration to discrimination.
It is indeed the basis of much discrimination.
Alter, Souls of earth, your sense of toleration.
Alter it unto Love of all.
Embrace the difference.
Embrace the other colors.
Embrace other beliefs.
And in that embracing you give Love and you find Love.
And toleration does not enter in to the equation.
This we say unto you.

129 Beloved Souls of earth, you know it not,
yet we see your generosity as unbounded.
We see it as abundant and we see it in abundance.
There is upon your earth, in many pockets,
a great deal of generosity of negativity,
a generous giving of negativity.
And the beloved earth accepts what is given.
There is also great pockets of generosity,
of goodness, given in goodness and good intent.
And we would have you know
that all generosities are acceptable and accountable.
You have within your being always the opportunity

to be generous in your giving,
whether it be negative or goodness.
You have all choice.
Recall who you are,
and in that recall you will understand
the immensity of your being.
And you will clearly understand in that recall
the power that you have is unlimited
in its intent for the purpose of humanity.
We would have you understand clearly;
there is no judgment, there is no condemnation.
We would only make you aware
so that your choices are made in clear understanding.
We would have you lift the veils of darkness
and see with the clarity, the eye of an eagle.
And we would have you know,
you may come unto oneness with this clarity.
And so shall it be on the day of awakening.

130 Designate!
Designate that which you do.
Designate that which you do to others.
Be they man or fish or fowl or flora or fauna.
Designate your being.
You are the general, the commander of your being.
And you may designate
that which you will do with your being.
You may designate your being to care for another
or you may designate your being to harm another.
You as the commander have the choice.
We would have you understand,
you are not forced by birth, or culture,
or ethnicity, or religion, or place of origin, or country,
to be that which that particular modality may demand.
You are free, Souls of earth,
in your choice of vision, of designation.
You came into this earth with a mission,
and you are all captains of your vessel.
You are all hierarchy, each and every.
And so, we would have you understand,
you charted your course,

you plot the lay of the land,
you are the trailblazer and you go whither you go.
There is no other.
The choice was made at learning station[38]
to be in that situation.
The situation is not because of the starvation.
It is not because it is Africa,
nor is it because of an opulent land.
The being is in charge.
The being came with a pattern, the pattern they designed.
We are speaking of the choice made to come unto the earth,
they are not here in a particular situation
by an accident of birth,
or ethnicity or religion, or culture; they chose this.
It is not that they have to be,
by virtue of where they were born.
It is not a force from outside of self.

Stillness

131 We speak of the Light Beings.
You have been taught there are twelve such.
You understand your Creator is of the White Light.
You understand the twelfth is of the purple black.
You understand the eleventh is the blue green.
You will understand the tenth is crimson.
You will understand the ninth is brown.
You will understand the eighth is yellow.
You will understand the seventh is blue.
You understand the sixth is orange.
You will understand the fifth is ocher.
You will understand the fourth is ivory, primal ivory.
You will understand the second is green.
You will understand the first, as holding,
holding, Soul, the pearlescent hue of magenta.
And you will understand
that each of you have within
one of these primary colors.
You have entered in with this primary color.
Using the eye you may distinguish this color.

Each of these Beings with this color have
what you might term attributes.
Each of these Beings have sound and vibration.
The primary color within your being,
attached to this Light Being,
enables you to enter in to the eye.
It is your connector to the eye of beholding.

132 Souls of earth, you will understand,
distance has no meaning except upon the earth.
You measure constantly in days, weeks, months, miles,
meters, kilometers, on and on.
Yet when you are seeing with the eye
when you are hearing with the eye, all happens now.
Even were you to be seeking into your past lives,
they would be in the present now,
within the vision of the eye.
Were you to reach unto the Akashic and look into
what you would mentally construct as the future,
using the eye it would be in the now.
Distance would not exist.
Understand this concept, within the eye,
the eye of beholding,
there is no earth time, there is no earth distance,
there is no earth space.
All the dimensions are available to the eye of beholding.
Are you a thousand miles away
from a being that you would help,
that you would heal, that you would send comfort to?
Distance is not a barrier with the eye.
The only barrier
is that which you have placed upon your being,
is that which you have placed
in not acknowledging the eye,
in not recognizing the eye of your being,
in not knowing the eye of your being,
and in not entering in to the eye of your being.
Indeed, all moments are your moments,
all time is your time upon the earth,
all places are your places upon the earth.
Listen well, Souls of earth, this we ask of you.

133 We would have you relax your being.
We would have you cease the frenetic pace of activity.
We would have you take stock of your surroundings.
Indeed, Soul, list all that you have,
all that you possess in material goods.
And then we would have you list
all that you possess in relatives and friends.
And we would have you list the Love that is around your being.
And we would ask you to examine carefully and recognize,
within all that you have listed, there is no freneticness.
There is only being.
Indeed, being, taking full advantage of life,
taking full advantage of the joy that is yours,
that surrounds your being.
And if you have possessions that give you no joy,
then we ask you to consider
divesting yourself of these burdens,
for they do not give you joy.
They are burdens.
And we ask you to listen to the high self,
to the high consciousness
who will assist you in the joy of life.
But you must open your being
to the high self, to the high consciousness.
How, Soul?
It is not a step by a step program
of weeks, days, months, years.
It is the simple acceptance of who you are, to recognize
you are not simply this earth flesh and brain.
You are more.
It is not a question of worthiness, of deserving.
For all mankind has a higher consciousness.
It is in the acceptance of that reality
that you alter the illusion you are in.
It clears the cobwebs so that you see with vibrancy,
so that you see with the eye.
Be in joy.
Harken to that which you are.
Hold the goodness of your being,
hold not the negativity, release it and enjoy.
Release the negativity not in pain and sorrow.

Hold your being,
the violet of comfort and compassion, hold it to self,
and then you will find that you are able
to give so much more to others.
This we say unto you.

134 Souls of earth, we ask that each day
you set aside a minute of your earth day
to lay down your cares and your troubles.
For that one minute in your time,
allow your being to be without negativity.
Indeed, we understand most will have difficulty
with even fifteen seconds of your earth time.
For your troubles and your cares have become
an integral part of your being
and it is difficult then to remove the weight
from your mind of those cares.
Even the fifteen seconds will assist you in learning,
in discerning the great difference
between carrying negativity,
and lightening your load and carrying only Light.
Lay down those troubles,
for fifteen, twenty, thirty, sixty seconds,
and begin to see the difference.
Why would you do this?
So that you will make your choice
based upon actual information and experience.
For many go through their day
unwittingly weighed down with cares and trouble
and seeing it only as, 'This is the way it is'.
And we would suggest to you there is yet another way,
and so we would have you practice, daily, once a day;
dispense with, lay down your troubles
and experience lightness of being.

135 Souls of earth, we bring unto you a lightness of being.
Indeed, you have created an illusion of heaviness.
You see your bodies, your flesh and blood and bone
as weighted down upon the earth, held in place.
And we would have you know,
you are not held down unto earth.

You may rise in lightness of being.
You may walk, move without ever touching the ground.
You may move from one country, continent, to another
in a moment of being, without mechanical ships,
without, what you call, your airplanes or boats or cars.
Your being without the illusion is weightless,
is a body of Light.
You do not require the earth body to carry you,
to carry your consciousness to other realms of being.
You may travel instantaneously,
not only throughout your earth but beyond.
Only your own belief in your illusion
holds you as a weighted body.
You have the capabilities to enter through the air of earth.
Yea, even the very ground of earth is no barrier
to the lightness of being.
How is this possible?
How will I breathe?
What will I do without my weighted body?
Identify not with the physical, weighted body.
Understand the Spirit of your being,
the lightness requires no air,
requires no contraption, may move at will.
All Souls of earth have this ability,
it is not contained only unto a few.
You need only recognize and enter in
to the lightness of your being and be who you are.

136 Enter ye forth, not from your homes,
not from your buildings, your offices,
not from your caves.
Enter forth from the mind.
Know you can explore your whole world
without leaving your space within your home,
your office, your building, your cave.
You may journey to the very tops of the mountains.
You may journey to the vineyards of Florence.
You may walk upon the steps of any great cathedral.
You may enter in to the monasteries,
to the temples of Buddha.
You may visit a family member who lives in body far away;

five thousand miles is no hindrance to the mind.
When you enter forth through the third eye,
there is no time limit in your visitations.
For there is no time in the dimension
you enter forth into through the eye.
For there is no space containment
when you enter forth through the eye.
You may enter in to conversation,
to those who are receptive
to travel through time and space.
You do not have to use the language of earth
in a vocal manner or in the manner of signing.
What you will use is conceptual dimensional language
of the aura
when traveling with the eye.
As you conceive a thought, a question,
it is transferred vibrationally
to the other being that is receptive.
You do not enter in to the other being,
but the vibrational wave
carries the thought unto the being.
You may transfer unto each other a conversation.
No limit to time or space!
Souls of earth, you all have this possibility.
But you must remove the barriers
you have placed within the eye,
for they block the vibrational transmission.
They block entering forth dimensionally.
You may also, Souls of earth, leave the earth.
Indeed, you all have the potential to be astronauts,
to look down from space
upon the beautiful jewel called earth.
And you may travel even further,
for within the eye of beholding
there are no dimensions of time or space that limit.
No limits were placed upon you but your own.
And mankind, humanity,
you have all reached the stage of being
wherein you may remove the barriers and enter forth
into dimensional vibrational travel with the eye.
Do not concern thy being

with being unable to return to your physical body.
You may return at any moment.
And in that dimension that you will be
you will hear your guides
who will say it is time to return.
We await with anticipational joy
your entering forth with the eye.

137 We often see over the fence Souls seeking
the easy way, thinking,
"If only it were simple, if only it were easier,
then I could, then I would."
Soul, we would tell you the easy way:
to be first and foremost in sacred self of being.
When you struggle, when you feel
as if the boulder is crushing you,
the boulder of troubles, of fears, of worries,
when you struggle, you are far from the easy path.
It is indeed, surely an indication that you are not in sacred self.
It is surely an indication that you are embracing
negativity and creating negative.
When a Soul is in sacred self,
the recognition of negativity is instant,
and the decision to refrain
from acting upon that negativity is instant
and becomes, therefore,
an act of positive, an act of Purity.
This is the easy Path.
This is the path of immense growth.
This is the path of Love and compassion for self and all paths.
Think upon it,
think upon how different your struggle for growth
can be when it comes from sacred self,
when you recognize that you are not caught
in the coils of negativity with no out, no way out.
Indeed, you have a way out!
Act from the sacred self.
Be from the sacred self.

138 Beloved Souls, within the many tempests of man
will come a stillness of being.

The stillness is one of serenity, is one of knowing,
is one of gentleness and compassion.
Compassion is a necessary, nay,
a critical component of stillness.
Within the frenetic activity of young and baby Souls,
those of infant,
there is no stillness possible.
It is part of what they search for
without knowing of the search.
It is part of what Negativity searches for
without knowing of the search,
of the end of the search.
It becomes a circle,
a frantic searching for peace, serenity, compassion
and yet, paradoxically, within the search
there can be no finding of the gentleness,
compassion, serenity, of the peaceful stillness.
It comes slowly, stealthily, silently,
stealing within thy being with gentle,
oh so very feather like touches within thy psyche.
It does not come roaring, it does not come rushing.
That, too, is a paradox, a conundrum
that you cannot reach out
and just grab that blessed stillness.
For in that reaching out, for any attempt to grasp,
there is nothing for you to grasp,
for you to touch, for you to hold.
Beloved Souls, it only takes a moment
of allowing the stillness to enter in.
It only takes a moment of letting go of fear, of earth.
It only takes a moment for the Light, the stillness to enter in.
You would call it a stealthily entering in,
for it is as the very lightest of tip toes
that it enters within thy psyche.
It does not enter stomping, it does not enter leaping.
It is not a ballet of leaps and twirls,
but a gentle gliding into thy being.
Allow!
It only takes the release of fear, of earth, of your shroud,
to know the stillness of entering in.

2

139 As you go about your day,
as you enter in to the activity of a day,
it matters not the activity,
recall now and then all the very air about your being.
The air that allows you to live,
that allows you to exist upon the earth plane,
the air that enters in to the nostrils,
enters in to the mouth,
enters in to the lungs,
the air that enters in to the very pores of your being.
Give thought, now and then, to this air,
for it was given unto thee
as part of the very purpose of humanity.
The breath of your being is from your Creator.
The breath that you breathe, the air that you breathe in
was given unto man in its pristine state.
The air carried within it vibrant molecules,
carried within it oxygen,
and all the components necessary for man
to breathe in and out.
The air that you breathe in must be expelled.
You must breathe in, you must breathe out,
and when you breathe out, noxious particles
are part of the air that you breathe out,
for even in the most healthy being
there are tainted iotas within your being.
And as you breathe out and expel them from your being,
so, too, is the energy of positive and negative.
As you enter in to the rhythm of your day,
take notice of the negative energy you breathe in,
and that which you breathe out.
You are not an air purifier,
for your body is limited to the amount of toxins
it may expel as it breathes in and out.
So too you are not the purifier of negativity,
but you may offer the negativity
that you overcome unto Creator.
This we would have you understand.
Overcoming negativity and releasing negativity
are part of the same process.
To overcome without releasing is unfinished.

Hold within your hands the very air that you breathe.
You can not?
Hold within your hands the negative energy.
You can not?
And yet you know both exist.
Because you can not grasp them
you do not see them as a concrete matter,
and yet, air is matter, negative energy is matter.
Your machines upon the earth may alter air,
but there is naught upon the earth
that may alter negative energy
except that you, in your great generosity as humanity,
overcome the negative energy and release it to Creator.
Souls of earth, you take for granted, much of humanity,
the acts that you do positive and negative,
and we would ask that you become
more cognizant, more aware.
We ask that you recognize.
We ask that in your day, now and then,
you think upon that which you do,
that which you choose.

140 You live in a world that is filled with merry go rounds,
for you often feel as if you are going in circles
and getting nowhere.
Life you say, is not fun, is not amusing.
This you say when you are not aware of the joys to be beheld,
for you have become immersed in what you see
as the tribulations of earth.
You say; 'How can I see joy, how can I behold joy,
when I am always running in a circle
and getting nowhere?'
Ah, Souls of earth, we give unto you the key.
Stop, literally stop your being.
Take that moment in your day
when you force yourself to stop.
The merry go round can not operate
without your consent, without your energy.
Simple in its solution, complex in arriving at the solution.
Behold unto your being joy.
You say, "But I look around and see only pain!"

Ah, Soul, because you are not looking inside,
because you are focusing on pain,
not on the joy of being,
not on the inner spark of each individual,
that spark of divinity, that particle of Creator.
If you focus on that, you begin to be aware of
and accept that which is around you.
Behold the joy within your own being.
Behold your spark of divinity.
Behold the connection you have unto Creator,
and know that you may ease pain, ease suffering,
by acknowledging the spark of divinity within all.
Humanity, indeed brother and sister,
indeed one responsible for the other.
Humanity behold joy!

Field

141 We would take you unto the fields, unto the planes.
Not on, but into.
We would have you see with your eye
the intricacies of the web of Energy
and the energies that comprise
that which is field, the plane.
You are, Souls of earth, within the spirals of goodness.
We would have you know goodness,
even in the most vile of acts is possible.
And we see within the most vile of acts,
that which can attain a level of Purity
beyond that which you imagine.
We would have you recall that which you know,
that all has purpose
and all purpose of humanity is goodness.
Reach out your hand to those who have fallen.
Embrace your brother.
Embrace the vileness and alter with your goodness.
See that which you have been and see that which you are.
Know the pearl of goodness can be plucked and given forth.
Open the shell that holds the pearl of your goodness
and give it forth.

It is indeed easy.
Know within the planes of Farside are countless Souls,
multitudes of being that have eyes only for earth,
all of earth, all that is animate and inanimate.
Indeed, Souls, you are watched.
You are constantly eyed with Love, only Love.
And the throngs within the planes
rejoice at the level of humanity;
the rejoicing, the cymbals clashing,
the bells sounding, for the gathering is nigh.

142 Beloved Soul,
we would ask you to remember you are Light.
In your current state of being you feel darkness,
you see darkness,
and you forget in the center is Light, is you.
And you have within you the power to Light the way for others,
to disseminate Light, to disperse Light,
and thereby mellow and disperse the darkness.
You hold on to the darkness and we would ask
that you hold on to the Light you are,
and that you remember the glory of who you are.
Earthly concerns are that, earthly.
You are so much more, beloved,
and we would have you turn to that self,
that higher self, and understand earth concerns
are but a moment in time
and you may fly through them.
You need not be stuck in a sticky web.
It is choice.
Although that may seem harsh in the midst of great turmoil,
in the midst of great negativity, it is nonetheless truth.
You know this is in your being.
We would have you lay down your cares,
we would have you lay down your burdens,
we would have you experience only joy.
Gather your Light, Soul.
Send it forth as you send forth your goodness
and all your good intentions.
Be the beacon for those that follow your every move
and listen to your counsel.

Hide not thy Light, Soul, for you are beloved of Creator,
and you have it all: the Love, Truth and Purity.

143 We speak of the parameters of your being.
You will understand your flesh
is not the outer parameter of your being.
Your Energy field extends far beyond your flesh.
This is difficult for many beings to comprehend,
for they believe their being starts and stops
wherever the flesh starts and stops.
The extent to which it extends
depends upon the level of Purity
and that Purity that you allow.
Your field may extend only twelve inches from your being.
Why is this so?
It is because you have not allowed, accepted,
the great Purity of your being.
It is because you have chosen to limit your Energy field.
Many upon your earth have Energy fields a meter wide,
encompassing the great Purity of their being.
They have chosen to allow the Purity of their being
reign upon the earth.
We speak not, Souls, simply and only of Holy beings
upon your earth that you have come to know.
We speak also of that being who has great compassion,
and yet is judged as lesser than.
It is the compassion that is shone, shone upon others,
that is the parameter of your being.
Understand, the Energy field is your intimate self;
it is your identifier.
It is that which can be read,
and we do not speak of mind reading;
your Energy field, Soul, carries your accomplishments.
It can be read, it is a record, open.
Your Energy field is not scattered, it is not stalwart.
It does have solidity, for it can be seen.
It has form, it has texture that can be seen with the eye.
It has as much form and texture as your flesh,
the flesh seen with the earth eyes,
the Energy field seen with the eye.
All beings upon the earth may see with the eye,

and the earth eyes.
It does not require an either or.
And as in all things, it is choice.
But know that your Energy field may heal, may entwine
itself with the maimed Energy field of another,
and in the Purity of your being
you assist in the healing,
in the unmaiming of the Energy field of another.
Understand, this is done in great compassion and Love
and with the acceptance of the being to be healed,
for even healing may not be imposed.

144 We would teach you your abc
in whatever alphabet you use to communicate.
Whether the communication is in writing or verbal,
you limit your sounds to your abc's,
devised upon the earth plane for use by mankind.
And we would have you understand you have capability
far beyond the limited expressions
possible within each language.
To use earth language
sets upon your being
an immediate limit of parameters.
It is as if you are hemmed in and may only walk,
for example, three meters in either direction,
knowing that beyond those three meters
is all existence.
And yet you limit yourselves to only those three meters.
In essence, when you refrain from using the power of the eye,
you limit your being to those three meters.
For in using the powers of the eye,
which are innate to every being,
you may communicate
without any barriers or limitations,
and the communication is not limited
to the conceptualization within each language.
Indeed not, for you speak in concepts.
One word of your earth language,
in conceptual speech of the eye,
becomes a paragraph, a chapter,
and you are able

not only to speechify in this manner,
but you understand the communication of another.
Imagine the misunderstandings that would no longer exist!
Imagine how the description of Love of your Creator
would become within your being an enraptured feeling,
sensing, knowing, conscious awareness.
In a very minute way the poets of your earth,
the symphonies, the songs of your earth,
capture a bit of this conceptualization
available to the eye.
You need not limit self to only earth language.
You have all possibilities, all probabilities, within you,
to use the speech of the eye.
Enter in, Souls of earth, glory in your ability.
Limit not self any longer.

145 We would have you understand,
when using the eye upon your earth plane,
all your other senses are enhanced.
The clarity of that which you see, that which you hear,
that which you feel, is honed diamond fine.
You may,
because you are in tune with all that is upon the earth,
hear the very wings of a gnat,
hear the very songs of the Angels,
hear with the clarity, the chime of humanity.
Hear the color, indeed, and see the sound of Sound and Color.
Everything becomes alive in comparison
to that which you see within your earth eyes,
your earth hearing.
When you use the eye, when you enter in to the eye,
you enter in to another dimension of being,
and you become an extension,
you become more than your earth self.
Even that which you would touch
will have a depth and a texture to it
beyond that which you heretofore felt.
You will see the context of matter.
You will see consciousness and know
it has depth and form and being.
Your whole being becomes, beyond that boundary of earth,

a boundary you may at any time release
and enter in to the eye.
The eye will take you beyond the earth;
we have spoken of the many worlds on the Farside
to which you may access and enter and explore and learn.
Your being, as mighty as it is upon the earth,
is minuscule in might
compared to when you enhance and use the eye
and enter in to a dimensional phase
beyond that human self.
You are so much more once you remove the veils,
once you remove from you
that which you have placed, the barriers.
You become!
Indeed you become.
Thou art worthy, thou art Loved, thou art Purity.
Thou art conscious upon your earth;
but the consciousness
that you may enter in to with the eye
allows you to enter in to dimensions,
into worlds of Color and Sound.
Souls of earth, you need not be confined
to the one dimension of being upon the earth plane.
The eye is not limited to a few.
Indeed not.
Every humanity enters in with the eye.
And then as you strive in growth, in Purity for oneness,
the eye connects to all other humanity,
and you know,
you recognize the very oneness of who you are.

146 We speak of entering in.
You may visualize a door, a portal, an aperture,
some manner of ingress, and we would tell you
that all of these are possible, for it is given unto man
the visualization that a being would expect
when they are going to enter in or out
of the earth dimension.
The dimensional phase may be done visually
within the mind's eye as a portal,

as a door, as an aperture.
What you perceive is given unto you for your perception,
for it is your reality.
For many beings it will be similar,
for others it will be different, and this is only
to make the transit simpler for your being.
The entry in to another dimension is simplicity in itself.
It is a thought transmission of consciousness
from one dimension unto another.
Yet when you enter in unto the earth plane
you bind yourself unto the earth,
lose sight of and lose remembrance of the fact
you need not remain
bound to the earth in consciousness.
This must come from your own inner will.
To travel dimensionally, consciously,
requires a lack,
indeed, requires a lack of fear,
it requires a lack of doubt.
The key is to know without doubt and without fear
that you are capable of dimensional travel.
Upon the earth, dimensional conscious travel
is often referred to as transcendental travel,
for indeed you transcend the boundaries of earth,
and you transcend these boundaries by your will.
Harken to the great bells of glory that ring out
when a being allows their Soul consciousness
to travel beyond the earth.
You will hear with every fiber of your being,
you hear with the eye of beholding,
you will hear a dimensional sound
beyond the three dimensions of your earth.
Indeed, seven dimensional Sound and Color,
for upon the Farside, Sound and Color are a duet
aligned with Purity for an all encompassing triad.
Souls of earth,
you need not be limited only to the earth dimension,
but if you choose simply the earth dimension,
you are no less and no more valued,
for each has their place,
each has their purpose, each has their walk,

and each is particled of the purpose of humanity.

147 We speak of levitating the mind,
of levitating the consciousness of being,
of levitating unto the high mind,
of levitating the consciousness of your Soul,
of using the third eye
to levitate beyond the bounds of your earth plane.
To levitate the goodness of your being,
the Love and compassion unto the sacred self,
so that you heal self and others
from the Essence of Being.
Levitate unto the Crystal Cave,
open your being to the wonders therein,
to the Holiness therein, to the Purity therein,
to the home of your being therein.
Levitate.
You have within the mind of your being the ability to choose
to lift beyond the mind of earth.
All too often your being is weighted down
so that you can not lift beyond a minute.
It is that weight of being
that must be released for you to levitate.
Indeed, negativity has weight and may weigh you down,
for you have chosen to hold on to it and gather it
and gather it and gather it,
never releasing, continuing to gather,
until you are held forcefully within
a prison of your own making.
And so you may choose to throw off the weight of negativity,
to release it, to free yourself so that you may reach,
levitate unto the Prism of the Crystal Cave.
Levitate!
Know you have within you, each and every,
the possibility, the ability to levitate.
And from the vantage point of levitation above the earth
and on into the Crystal Cave, you will look down
and you will see the great glorious Purity of humanity,
and you will see with your being
the evil man has wrought.
You will see from your vantage point the Wilful Child,

and you will hear the child calling out
and you will know the purpose of your being.
So be it.

148 There have been many upon your earth
who have accomplished what you call levitation.
It is not unheard of and it is not unwitnessed.
Jesu, Krishna, both levitated.
Buddha, in deep states of meditation, levitated.
The body became so light in the mind that it lifted
and gravity no longer applied.
It has to do with the entering in to the sacred self.
It has to do with understanding
you have all possibilities within.
It has to do so with your ability
to physically move your being without vehicle,
only with the vibrational tone, that color of self.
Levitation is not simply a small movement upward,
but it is literally going through
what you would see as time and space.
In the sacred self there is no time and space.
There is no gravity.
There are no laws as barriers to prevent movement,
for all movement is available unto thee.
Levitation is seen by man as a miracle.
And yet, Souls of earth,
it could be an everyday miracle, everyday occurrence.
You would have some upon your earth
who of course dismiss this as abhorrent
to the laws of gravity, of science, to the laws of matter.
And we would have them understand
that it is entirely possible for each
and every being of mankind.
It will be as a breath.
The possibilities before thee are incalculable.
The key for your science is to think beyond
what you perceive as a barrier or as barriers.
Think indeed outside the box that you have built for self.
Perceive that there are no boundaries,
that there are no limits
to what can be achieved, to what can be reached.

And then, with that perception, with that paradigm,
the creativity will flow and the answers will come.

149 Souls of earth, the gates are open,
the gates of Light,
a Light that would blind your earth eye.
A Light that may be seen as you enter in unto the Farside,
a Light that welcomes, that is as arms wide open
to welcome, to embrace.
And the Light soothes the Soul, the spirit.
The gates are not minuscule.
They are not narrow.
And there is no guardian that you must answer to
before entering unto the Light.
It only requires your entering in.
There is no passport necessary.
There is only entering in.
The entering in
is the acceptance and understanding of who you are,
of your purpose of being.
In that understanding and acceptance is the knowing
that you are of the Light that you see as you enter in.
Souls of earth, you see in your earth understanding
a division between earth and Farside.
In your earth understanding there is a demarcation,
a clear, defined demarcation
so that you pass from one to the other.
And we would have you know there is no demarcation.
That is illusion.
You simply enter in.
There is no line you must cross or river you must leap,
no valley, no mountain.
You simply enter in.
You do not need to rattle the door.
You do not even need to open the door,
for it is always open to you
when you have that awareness and understanding
of who you are.
It is only illusion that prevents that understanding.
And you may part the veils of illusion
and enter fully into who you are.

You require no permission to do so.
You require no army to help you, for you are Light itself.

150 Felicitations.
For earth has a felicity to it and all its inhabitants have a felicity.
Indeed, Soul, unto even the smallest microbe
that you have yet to develop a microscope to see.
You will be astounded at the incredible minuteness
that is within your earth.
You will be astounded at the teeming life within your earth.
Souls of earth,
you wander through your day and only a minute few
are aware of the teeming life about their beings,
of the teeming life in the very air that you breathe,
of the life, of the existence of quadrillions of life forms
that you do not see with your earth eyes.
And yet all are necessary to the path of earth,
to the Path of humanity.
Of the Creator's Energy,
they arose as volunteers to enter in to the earth,
to dedicate their Energy to the purpose of humanity.
You have more than your fellow humanity,
you have more than your guides,
you have more than the Angels about your being,
you have all these life forms, for humanity.
You will understand the intricacy, the great intricacy that is earth. The great Creator, who created such magnificent intricacies
that all these forms of life work to form a planet,
that work to form the oxygen so that you may breathe,
that work to form the very soil that brings nutrients
so that you may eat and exist.
And those nutrients are life forms with consciousness.
You may encompass this Energy.
You may communicate with the very Energy
of all these life forms about you.
With the eye, to the level of your Purity,
naught is impossible.
Indeed, you may reach unto your very Creator,
for you have all possibility.

151 Often you find yourself holding your breath
when you are tense, when you are frightened.
Often you find yourself breathing rapidly,
in times of emergency, in times of emotional distress.
In times of calmness, you find yourself
breathing slowly and without thought.
Your body reacts to mind.
Indeed, the way you breathe has a direct correlation
with the thought pattern of your mind.
When the mind is chaotic the breathing is chaotic.
When the mind is calm the breathing is calm.
Understand, breath is life.
Breath is that which enables your voice box,
is that which enables your lungs
to provide for you oxygen enrichment.
It is breathing that brings the motion unto your blood flow
in your body, throughout the cells.
Examining the breath that you enter in, with the eye,
you may see as it moves throughout your being
and out again;
how you bring in the air and then expel the air.
But the air you expel is different
from the air that you breathed in,
for it has coursed through your being and your cells,
and entered out.
And in the course of your being
the breath gains contaminants, toxins
that are within your being and expels them out.
You will understand that the breath you breathe in,
much of it stays within,
that particles, the many particles that are within the
breath, within the air that you breathe in,
stay within your being.
If the air you breathe is toxic,
then you have entered in toxins into your body.
If the air you breathe in is purified
then your body is purified.
But, Souls of earth, earth in its pristine state had purified air,
it had air that was healing,

it had air that had wellness within.
And man has rejected that air and has chosen instead
to toxify the air that enters in to their being.
Souls of earth, understand your choice.
Look carefully at the consequences of your choices,
for you, for others.
For all of humanity is affected
by the air that swirls about your planet.
What you input into the air you breathe into your bodies.

152 We will tell you this,
the wellness of each individual being
affects the wellness of all mankind.
And we speak not of ailments,
of disability entered in to as a path walk.
But we speak of that which mankind
has distorted of their being.
The human flesh, blood and bone is of sacred construct,
meant to be in perfection, in wellness.
And as in any possibility of negativity,
you may grasp unto you ailments;
physical, mental ailments,
or you may overcome.
A being may have before them what you call flu,
and the choice is not to ignore it,
the choice is to acknowledge it as an energy
and either bring it in, afflict the flesh, blood and bone
or release it unto Creator.
Ailments always have choice, if not part of the path walk,
for that choice is made
upon the Farside station of learning.
All others are made upon the earth.
And as they are entered in, even they may be entered out.
Each action, each thought engenders a spiral,
becomes outward from your being.
It is not static.
It is moving and each spiral begets another spiral.
There is no limit to spiral.
There is no limit to that which humanity may do.
Within each circle that comprises a spiral upon the earth
is an Energy field.

Your science knows this, has studied it for years,
        but has not yet made the connection to the Soul
        in a mathematical concurrence of numbers.
And indeed they will, for the equation has been given.
Souls of earth, each of you is a spiral of Energy.
Each of you is a vibratory being.
Each of you has within Holy vibration.
Each of you, although seemingly separated
        and indeed separated in growth,
        yet are connected in the spirals of your Energy
        and no one is alone.
No act remains independent of another act.
Always you are interconnected.
There will come a time within the history of mankind
        where the interconnectedness will be acknowledged.
Not only recognized but acknowledged
        as the true statement of being, of man, of humanity.
The recognition of the purpose of the interconnectedness
        and the ramifications of the interconnectedness
        will be taught from the smallest of age,
        and all will know that for which they have come
        and all will know that from which they have come.
It is a spiral grid and your vibrations comprise the spiral grid.
Your Energy fields are that which it is within the Void,[39]
        for all that you know is within the Void
        that holds no thing, and yet all things.

153 We greet thee, one and all,
        with Love overflowing from our hearts unto yours.
Our connections, Soul,
        we are joined heart to heart, motion to motion.
It is the heart that motions the body forward.
It is the heart who emotions the being.
It is the heart that causes the contretemps
        within the psyche of a being.
It is the heart that beats within to the pulse of all humanity.
It is no coincidence that the heart pulses,
        pumps life giving blood through your veins,
        so that you may move, so that you may think,
        so that you may be on the earth.
It is the heart that links vibrationally one to another.

It is the heart that causes your being to fluctuate,
 that causes your being to retreat within itself,
 or to be outward with self.
It is the instigator.
The mind watches to see what the heart wants to do.
This happens instantaneously.
The mind observes and the heart says retreat,
 the heart says go forward
 and the mind says, as you will.
For it is within the mind that thought dwells,
 it is within the mind where the idea forms
 to accede to the desire of the heart.
The mind sees where the heart would take the being,
 and although the mind says 'As you will.'
 the mind also cautions the heart.
It allows the heart to recognize within an instant
 all the implications of an action,
 all the reaction of an action,
 in less than the nth of the blink of an eye,
 and this occurs in the connection
 between the heart and the mind.
The heart does not go blindly forward, indeed not.
It is aware.
It has a consciousness of being, as does the mind,
 as does the Soul.
When does the heart cease the forward motion to harm,
 to create negativity?
It is when the Soul consciousness enters in,
 and you have the triad, of Soul, heart and mind.
It is when the Soul enters in that thought:
 'Recall who you are'.
And the heart will listen and refrain from that negative step.
The connection of the three
 does not occur within the initial lives of a baby Soul.
It does not occur within the initial lives of a young Soul.
It begins to occur in the lives of the mature Soul,
 when the triad begins to work together in oneness.
You have, Souls of earth, inner and outer dimensions.
The outer dimension is the physicality of your world,
 your inner dimensions are the heart,
 the mind and the Soul.

Indeed, dimensions.
Connect to your high self,
    and indeed you have entered another dimension.
All that you do is dimensional,
    all that you do is computational,
    all that you do has meaning, is accounted.
Communicate in a triad of oneness of heart, mind and Soul.
Give of the heart.
Your greatest wealth is your ability,
    your potential to heal the earth,
    to heal those brought low by negativity.
We ask you to give forth.
Do that which you do from the heart
    and give forth the gift to mankind and to Creator.

154 You have within your being a knowing,
    a connection, to the thrum of all thrums.
It is no accident that you speak of the beat,
    the beat of the earth, the beat of the heart.
The natural beat of the heart is the rhythm of healing.
You may bring forth this natural rhythm in a variety of guises.
It may be brought forth with your instruments, as in the drum.
It may be brought forth in the clapping of the hands,
    the clapping of the hands may be done individually
    or it may be done with another.
It is the rhythm that is imperative.
The rhythm of the heartbeat may also be done as a rocking.
It may also be done as moving the head within that beat.
You may also move your feet to that rhythm.
It is not the instrument that matters.
It is the beat.
Using, Souls of earth, the rhythm of the heartbeat
    brings a balance unto your being, unto positive Energy.
The rhythm is of benefit to the whole being, physically,
    but its primary purpose is your spiritual balance,
    balance between the mind, the heart,
    and the Spirit of your being.
Entering in to the rhythm benefits all mankind.
It aligns your being in all of its phases upon the earth,
    with Spirit of your high self, of your sacred self.
Conscious, deliberate entering in to the beat, to the heartbeat,

enters forth that Energy of goodness
into the vibrational field of earth
and into the vibrational field of humanity.
Souls of earth, recognize you have at your very fingertips
the possibility of spiritual balance.
Choose the instrument
within which you will practice this ritual of the heartbeat.
Indeed, we urge you to enter in to this ritual daily.

155 We have before us a visitor, one that we would ask
that you welcome into your homes, into your lives.
The visitor we speak of is the Energy of compassion,
for indeed, in many houses, in many lives,
compassion is a rare visitor.
It is not seen very often, it is not felt very often,
it is not welcomed very often.
And we would ask that you welcome compassion,
this great Energy as an honored guest,
as a welcome part of your family,
as a welcome part of your being.
Bring this Energy inward, so that you may express it outward.
So that the stranger is strange no longer,
but has become familiar, has become honored,
and has a place of honor within your life,
within your home, within the family.
Compassion is indeed an Energy.
Compassion is that which alters, moves mountains,
brings peace and contentment,
brings healing, brings Love, brings oneness,
for you cannot, humanity,
become without compassion.
Understand, the welcoming in compassion
to all homes upon the earth
would alter in a moment that which is to be.
And that which is to be, would be no more,
for you would gather to you
all the Souls in darkness and despair,
you would gather to you
those who are naked, those who are hungry.
You would gather to you those who require,
have never had Love.

You would gather to you the sorrowing Souls.
Beloved Souls of earth, compassion is your nature.
It is of your being:
Truth, Purity, Love, compassion;
compassion, the Energy of Truth, Purity and Love.
You come to earth with Truth, Purity and Love;
compassion is the Energy.
Discover it, indeed, in self, so that you may enter it forth.
Worlds, earth, the Fallen, the Souls in transition
await your welcoming in compassion and entering it out.
You are humanity, compassion.

156 We would have you understand,
the intention of goodness flowing forth will alter.
It is the intention of flowing forth your goodness
that makes a difference.
The intent arises from the triad of heart, mind and body.
All with the intent to flow forth goodness.
Not with the intent
to alter a being to your particular judgment
of where that being needs to be, indeed not.
The altering comes from compassion, not from judgment.
It is from an outpouring,
an outflowing of the Love you bear as humanity.
This is what alters.
And it alters not to your intent but to the intent of that being.
When you offer, when you flow forth goodness, the being,
no matter whether it is baby Soul or aged Soul,
it flows unto the Pillar of Light.
And the Soul of being, in concert with the mind and the heart,
will then use that Energy
to their own specification and alter.
Souls of earth, you have untested, infinite power within you
to offer to each and every other being.
Understand the triad of intent.
Be aware of the triad of intent
and recognize that which you do.
We place no judgment on your choice of negative or positive.
We only offer unto thee an awareness of that which you do.

157 Fidgets, Souls of earth,

you have what you term fidgets.
You become fidgety, and you don't know, you can't decide
this way or that way, up, down,
north, south, east, west.
And you fidget, and you can not decide.
We would have you understand
the importance of direction occurs upon arising.
It is called east.[40]
Focusing your attention for two minutes
in the direction of east
as the sun rises is most healing for your being.
Optimally as the sun rises, but any time that you arise,
rather than miss the opportunity
to gather unto you healing.
You merely open your being to the Crystal Cave,
you open your being to receive
color, sound and vibration.
You open your being, you give permission,
you allow healing to enter in,
for healing does not come without permission.
When we speak of the east in healing,
we speak of balancing your being, of aligning your chi
so that it is not helter skelter but is focused in intent;
and your chakras are aligned,
and Purity enters in to each chakra.
During these two minutes
that you devote to allowing Energy to enter in,
you may be in direct communication
with the Spirit and Essence of your being.
It is your choice.
If you enter in with the intent
to commune, to connect, to communicate,
and advance within your being a stillness,
all manner of sacred Energy
may enter in unto thy physical,
thy aura, what some call the etheric being.
You will become one in those moments with all of humanity.
You will become one with all that is.
You recognize the Energy of the tree is your Energy,
the Energy of the ant is your Energy,
the Energy of the Angels is your Energy.

This you will experience, Souls of earth, with intent,
with stillness and with permission,
allowing Energy to enter in.
At the end of your commune
allow thy being mentally or physically
to make a complete circle,
turning to your right, to the south, and then
to the west, and then to the north,
and back again to the east.
And know as you go forth in your day you are in balance;
and knowing that you are one with all that is,
great Love and compassion
will flow from your being unto all that is.
This we give unto you.

158 We would explain mantras.
Mantras are a collection of words,
words that have sound vibration attached.
Words that help the human mind to focus,
that takes the scattered frenetic
thought of the mind and gentle,
and calms the mind
so that an action may take place,
an action of goodness.
It assists the mind in narrowing the bandwidth of its vibration
so that the Energy is not helter skelter
but indeed becomes calm, tranquil.
When you are in a state of helter skelter,
when you are in a state of scattered energy,
goodness has a barrier.
The mantra assists your being to remove that barrier.
The thought entering in to the mantra,
the thought that the words bring about,
all have purpose
in entertaining that flow of goodness outward.

159 We bring forward to you a mantra
to alleviate hopelessness and homelessness.
This mantra may be chanted, may be thought upon,
may be used each and every day,
to focus the intent of the goodness of your being,

to enable the Energy to flow outward.
"Hear now, hear now, hear now that which we say.
Hear now, hear now, hear now that which we are.
Hear now, hear now, hear now the joyousness of being.
Hear now, hear now, hear now the glory of your Soul.
Hear now, hear now, hear now and know all is well."
It will, Soul, go beyond beyond.
It will enter in to the heart, the psyche, the Soul of humanity.
When done as a group, two or more,
it has the potential to reach unto
the Soul of humanity.
It has the potential to reach
unto the very jaundiced of beings,
unto the most cynical,
unto the most despairing of beings.
It has the potential to string together bit by bit by bit
the goodness of individuals
uniting in oneness of intent
to flow forth the goodness of their beings.
It has potential to strum a gentle melody,
a lullaby to soothe the angst of Souls in despair.
It has the potential to bring about an alteration
of the negative energy round about thee.
It has a cadence of Love and by intoning,
by entering in to the mantra,
you enter forth that which you are.
Hear now and know the vibration of the thought,
of the intent of the mantra done in Purity,
in the pure goodness of your being,
has great power to heal.

160 We come unto thee to bring forth knowledge,
and wisdom.
For in all knowledge there is the possibility of wisdom.
In all knowledge there is the possibility of greater knowledge,
for knowledge is simply a stepping stone,
an adjunct, if you will, to the learning process.
Indeed, you may learn without conscious knowledge
because within each being there is a knowing.
Do not confuse knowing and knowledge.
For knowing comes from within the very Soul of your being,

comes with the use of the third eye.
Upon your earth you have varying names for knowing:
intuition, gut reaction, gut feeling, a sense, a frisson;
many names for the concept
of knowing without knowledge.
And we tell you that this knowing
is not the gift of a particular few.
It is not something that you must work hard to attain.
It is not something that is given by secret societies.
It is not something that requires the use of symbols.
Knowing is that which is innate in who you are.
When you enter in to earth
you do not leave behind knowing,
but the extent to which you allow the knowing free reign
is indeed that which is your choice.
Negativity, Souls of earth, that negativity that humanity creates,
indeed smothers the knowing, places a blanket,
a cloak of darkness over the bright Light of knowing.
And yet it can never extinguish the Light of knowing.
Indeed, it may dim, but it may never extinguish.
Knowing is that which apprises you
of the existence of other worlds, of other dimensions.
Knowing is that which apprises you of the fact,
the incontrovertible fact, that you may,
through the eye access the Records,
the Writing on the Wall, the Akashic and even beyond.
Allow the knowing to flower within thy being.
for within the Light of knowing
is wisdom, is Truth, is Purity, is Love.
The Light of knowing can be placed as a cloak about thy being.
We have, Souls of earth, for you a technique, a mantra
to allow the Light of knowing full flower:
"Oh Light of my being,
oh Light of knowing,
oh Light of greatness in your fullness,
open unto me,
open unto my earth being.
Open.
Oh, Light of knowing,
oh, Light of who I AM,
open.

open.
open."

161 We would speak of vibration.
Your eye, your sacred eye, has no barrier
and breathes in the vibrational tone of all,
of each and every.
This ability is yours.
It is as the breath in your earth being.
'How, do you say, is this possible?'.
It is a function of your matter, of your physicality.
Each particle upon your earth has vibration,
each particle has tone,
each particle has discord,
each particle has negativity placed by man,
and because man has placed it,
man can also cleanse, remove,
bring back the vibrational harmony.
We would have you understand the cadence of your being.
We would have you understand the cadence can be
cacophonous, noisy, scattered,
or it can be a beautiful melody
of harmonious symphony.
The choice is always yours.
But Souls, you will understand that your doubt is cacophonous,
has no melodic melody to it.
You will understand you may be as a symphony of sound,
the very sounds that bring you comfort and peace
within the glade, within the forest,
the very sounds that bring you peace and comfort,
as you meditate, as you heal.
Then your being is in balance,
then your being has reached unto Spirit.
Know that at every moment the choice
is available to all mankind.
The cadence of your being
is the very vibration of Energy in concert,
if you choose,
or it may be bound to earth matters
and cacophonous as a drum skin
that is loose and needs to be tightened.

The very difference in sound is obvious,
and you will note in your being the difference
when you are in balance and when you are not.

162 We would speak of the tuning of the human body.
All Souls are imbued with vibration,
with the potential of vibrational harmony,
and the potential of vibrational discordance.
You spend your lifetime tuning, attuning your body,
the form in which you inhabit.
The attainment of perfect harmony as an individual
is entirely possible.
And it is when each individual is in perfect harmony
that oneness becomes a glorious reality.
The discordance of your body in the human state
will manifest itself in various
emotional and physical incapacities.
These may range from the very minute twinge, ache,
unto the great diseases
that destroy the body and the mind.
Many of the harmonics that take place are planned to enable
a growth for the individual,
or for those around the individual.
Many of the harmonics that take place
occur as a result of straying from the Path,
and yet, these too, engender a growth.
Even onto the inanimate upon your planet
there are vibrational harmonics.
You have yet to develop the finest instruments
that measure these vibrations.
Within the vibrations of mother earth, of nature,
the only discordant vibration is caused by mankind.
Within the perfection of nature, in its natural state,
there is only a vibrational harmony.
It is mankind that introduces the disharmony, the discord,
and disrupts the natural order
of that which you call nature.
Even onto the smallest molecule is disruption,
is disharmony bringing mutation and imperfection.
And mother earth allows this for the growth of mankind
and the coming onto the Gateway, the Second.

The perpetual symphony of earth,
of all its inhabitants, inanimate and animate,
is a music that is in accordance
with the Writing on the Wall
and therefore, even in its discordance, it has harmony.

163 We would have you understand and
know without a doubt that you are a vibrational self.
What you would appreciate knowing is
how to access that vibration
and how to increase the vibration
that you may be lifted unto Farside.
It is to have always before you
that which you can do for another.
You would have before you at all times
acceptance of all that is without judgment.
To be fully human is to Love without judgment.
To be fully human is to walk by no Soul in pain
without comforting that Soul.
To be fully human is to know the full range of
the color and sound of your being,
and to know without doubt
all have color and sound of being,
while being fully human.
It is not difficult;
there is no struggle in accepting the most,
what humanity would judge as heinous individual,
heinous acts of an individual,
for you would not see these acts as heinous
or the individual as heinous.
You would only see the bright Light of being,
you would see with Love
and you would know Creator.

164 Earth, we would ask for your attention.
We would ask you to hear, to hear mother earth.
Listen carefully, hear with your mind, hear with your Soul,
hear with your ear and hear with the eye.
Hear the symphony of sound
that reverberates through all of Creation.
Hear the symphony that is mother earth.

Hear the birds in their mighty sound.
Hear the squawks, the caws, the trills, the peeps, the quacks,
the piercing cry of the hawk.
It is a symphony of sound to Creator,
a paean to Light, to Purity.
Hear the grunting, the snuffling of the buffalo,
of the antelope, of the moose.
Hear the roar of the tiger, the growl of the lion,
then know it is music!
There is no dissonance in the symphony of sound given forth.
Hear the rustle of the leaves,
hear the growth of the soil as the buds springs forth.
Hear the opening of a petal of a flower, of the rose.
Know that each petal as it opens is a sound.
Know that each spear of grass is sound.
Know that even in the desert, there is sound.
Within the scuttle of the spider,
the motion, the slither of the snake,
the growth of the plants,
each and everyone has a symphony of sound.
Listen, hear the drip of water, hear the sound of the brook,
of the rushing river, of the waterfall,
the susurrus of the ocean.
Indeed, a symphony of sound.
Listen to this wondrous chord rafting its way unto Creator.
Listen with all of your being.
Know that you, too, have a note to enter in to the symphony
and know that you have choice of this note.
For it can be joined without dissonance,
or you may choose to inject into the symphony,
the altered chord, the discord.
Beloved Souls of earth, listen with heart, listen with mind,
listen with Soul to the great gift
of these purities of earth.

165 We would have you listen not with your earth ears,
but with your mind.
For it is the mind,
in connection with the third eye and the crown chakra,
that allow you to hear
that which is beyond the earth hearing,

that allows you to hear the sound of Angels,
that allows you to hear the sound of the Farside.
For indeed the Farside is full of Sound and Color.
For each color has its own sound.
You will understand earth hearing,
earth ears, are one dimensional.
What we speak of is multidimensional hearing.
For you not only hear the sounds
of the physical representation upon the earth,
but you hear the sounds of the Energy of the aura.
All on earth has aura.
With this triad, you will hear the rock or hear the tree.
You will hear your guides.
You will hear the babe in the womb.
Indeed, there is no limit to that which you may hear,
except the barrier you place.
Expand your horizon unto dimensions
beyond your singular dimension of earth.
There is no limitation
on where you may go and what you may hear.
The symphonies of earth are but a minute imitation
of the symphony of sound available to you.
A violin with one string has limited sound
that is akin to using only your earth faculties.
You have within you the full orchestra, and yet, you use it not.
Know that each individual
is a unique symphony within themselves.
Each individual being has sound and color
that intertwines in a melodic harmony of spirit.
Souls of earth, enter in to that expansion of potential of being.
Enter in to the greatness of who you are.
Sound is multidimensional, color, multidimensional
and you have within, both.
You may vibrate the sound and color.
The being next to you, across from you, near you,
in their symphony of sound and color and vibration;
you would be astounded at the quality,
at the magnificence of the sound.
Each being is an echo chamber.
Sound reverberates within and from each being.
Souls of earth, explore the intent of your being,

explore the sound beyond the one dimension of earth.
Enter thou into who you are.
You are sound, color and vibration.

166 Souls of earth, you strive and strive and strive.
Whether it be for positive or negative, you strive.
Whether it be to beat yourself further into depression,
further into the mists of the mind,
or whether it be to excel in that which you do.
You strive and strive.
We would have you understand, there is no need to strive.
We do say unto you
that striving has a strident note to it, a discordancy.
Striving has a differential from desire, from goal setting.
To desire, to improve one's self, to excel in that which you do
or are capable of doing for the benefit of mankind
is not strident.
It has a melody to it, a flowing of chords.
The chording of C from low C to High C.[41]
When you aim
for that which you desire to reach
for self aggrandizement, there is discord.
If it is for the goodness of humanity,
there is indeed a melody
that reaches even unto the Farside
and it soothes the troubled Soul.
All that you do has sound attached,
all that you do has vibration attached,
all that you do emits Energy,
all that you do has a coloration to it.
For you are, Souls of earth,
in itself sound and color and vibration.
The very Energy of your being in its composition
is the triad of sound, color and vibration.
Your flesh, your blood, your bone, the cells of your being,
the atoms that hold you together; all triad,
and would not exist in its form
without sound, color and vibration.
The Energy would be dispersed.
Souls of earth, your sound, color and vibration
can be as a glorious symphony

or it can be discordant, chaotic, without order.
Be aware in all that you do,
the intent, the focus of that which you do;
for discord or for harmony.
In every moment of every day, you make this choice
unknowingly or knowingly,
consciously or unconsciously
and we ask that you become more aware,
more conscious of that which you choose
and why you choose in each moment of your day.
And recognize, Souls of earth,
that your choices affect all of humanity.

167 We would continue with vibrational tone.
We would have you understand all the waters of your earth
have vibrational tone.
All the waters of your earth will soothe your being.
You need only to stand or sit or lay beside moving water
to find solace for your being.
Even the smallest rill will bring solace to your being.
You are, Soul, mostly water and water calls to water.
Water gives life unto thy being.
It gives fullness to thy being.
It is your birthright.
Water belongs to all of earth.
The liquidity of the streams of your earth,
of the oceans of your earth,
of the rivers of your earth,
remind the Soul at its core level
of the purpose of humanity.
All upon earth has purpose, even the smallest gnat has purpose.
No less do the waters of your earth.
The vibrational tone of the waters created by your Creator,
given unto mankind as gift, are in discord
because mankind has placed upon them negativity.
These are the very waters
you depend upon to exist upon the earth plane.
You have, Souls of earth, made the pure impure.
You may alter, may cleanse, may bring back
that pure vibrational tone of the waters of your earth.
There was a time, Soul,

when sitting by any stream of moving water was healthy,
where bathing within the streams was healthy.
This is no longer true, for you have flooded, mankind,
the waters of your earth with toxins.
Although mother earth had a cleansing process,
this cleansing process was designed
for normal toxicities
not the manmade toxicities.
The cleansing process of the earth waters has been disrupted.
You may choose to bring about your cleansing,
so that your children may live in health.
We would remind you once again of your stewardship
of all of earth, including the waters of earth.

168 For humanity is great holiness,
each and every humanity.
And we see upon this plane of earth,
purities of unimaginable pureness.
You call them animals.
You call them plants.
You call them fish.
You call them grains of sand.
You call them water.
Soul, from where we are we see purities.
Indeed, even the grain of sand is a Purity,
has pureness, was sculpted in Purity,
and cast forth in Purity.
Souls of earth, you live within a realm of Purity,
of glowing color, of color beyond
the spectrum that earth recognizes as color.
You live in your short time upon the plane of earth
within such a well of holiness,
within such a well of sound,
within such a well of vibration.
Indeed, even negativity has vibration, has color, has sound.
As you, upon your far farmlands,
separate the chaff from the wheat,
so we would urge you to separate
the discordant note of earth that you have created,
from the gracious greatness of the Purity
around thy being.

Souls of earth,
        you have available unto you the Flow of your Creator.
And we see how little, how few times,
        you allow the reception of this Flow,
        of this Purity, of this goodness.
And we would encourage you to accept
        that joyous note of your Creator unto thy being.
You may see the color and sound
        and vibration all about thee.
Yes, you may see vibration.
It is not illusory.
It is not invisible unless you choose it.
All has matter.
All has ion, even unto vibration, sound and color.
Open thy being.
Accept that which you are, that which is yours,
        available unto thee
        at every moment of your existence.
Bring unto you the vibrancy of life about thee,
        the vibrancy of Holy, of purities, of pureness.
You are color.
You are sound.
You are vibration.
Souls of earth, when you do not open to all of these,
        it is as if you lived in a world of only shades of gray.
When you open unto,
        there is so much more color, sound and vibration
        entering in your life of existence.

Chapter Three
TEACH HUMANITY

Existence

169 Enter in to the Purity of being.
Enter in to the goodness and compassion within thy being.
You have all possibilities of Truth, of Purity and Love.
Even the most heinous that you judge has within this possibility.
Understand, Souls of earth, your core is Purity.
You are armed with Truth and brought forth in Love.
You are particled of Creator; you have
the possibility of unconditional Love and compassion.
Your aura, although dimmed by your entry
in to the Negative Void,
has within the very cell memory of the divinity of self,
even those of you who see yourselves
as heinous and unworthy.
The Angels do not see you as unworthy.
Your Creator does not see you as unworthy.
And you may overcome negativity and allow your goodness,
your Love, your Purity to shine forth
to comfort others, to heal, to give Love.
Souls of earth, you are revered upon the Farside.
Humanity has great renown,
for humanity holds the key to the implosion.
See that which is within thy being
the very Light of Love and know you are Love.
Love is who you are.

170 We would speak with you upon what you term death.
For you will understand what you term death
has no existence upon Farside.
We see death as the passing of the eternal being
from one dimension, plane, level to another.
You walk from one room to another in your physical being,
your eternal self walks from one plane to another
in its spiritual being.
You see, all is replication.
What you call the passing from this plane of existence
is mulled over,

is given great consideration and great thought,
great consultation, upon station on Farside.
The consultation is done with others
that will be part and parcel of your agreement.
It is done in consultation with Spirit.
It is done in consultation with those guides,
those teachers who will be with you always.
As in all items on your earth agenda,
no detail is left uncovered.
It is, to use your earth terminology,
as if you wish to wring out of your experience
every possible goodness, nuance, learning;
and every item receives great attention to detail.
Your moment of departure
requires great planning and is an agreement.
The path you have chosen to enter in to within the earth
is not always adhered to.
Negativity entices, karma[42] occurs,
you sink deep into the mire
and choose to leave before the agreed upon time.
You will understand, upon returning home,
that you have not completed your agreement,
that you have left work undone,
and you will choose reparation
of that which is left undone.
Indeed, reaching understanding when you return home,
you will want to finish that which you had begun.
Place no judgment upon those who suicide,
for you know not
whether this has been done to relieve
the unbearable burden they believe they have,
or whether
it has been done as part of an agreement
for others or another.
Even unto a suicide,
even unto the deliberate choice of leaving early,
there is reason, there is opportunity for learning.
And in all cases, in all happenings, there is no finality to life.
There is only the entering in
and the entering out, the return home.
The Soul cannot be destroyed.

It has great glory, great Love, great Purity
        and it will always return unto its Creator.

171 Many upon your earth fling themselves
        into all manner of regimens
        to expand the sum of their lives,
        to gather more years to their lives.
Concoctions of all sorts are tried
        to expand the lifetime of a being.
Souls of earth, we tell you,
        you would live as long as you agreed to live,
        for you decided
        before you came unto the earth plane
        the length of your lifetime.
And among many of your decisions,
        among many of your plans
        for entering in unto the earth in this lifetime,
        there was always a point
        where you would return home.
This is illusion, for in reality
        you are not limited to this one lifetime.
Each being came unto the earth plane in each lifetime
        with a particular plan, and that particular plan
        lends itself unto the next and the next and the next.
Indeed, you came with purpose,
        and when you return you examine minutely
        the purpose of your being within that lifetime.
And then you gird your loins again and re enter.
Souls of earth, there is no wheel that must turn,
        that you must enter in again and again.
Indeed not.
You freely give of your being to grow, to gain the scars.
That is your purpose.
Live each moment within the purpose of your being,
        within the step you came to walk.
That is your longevity.
Do not count in earth years or months.
Recognize that there is a time beyond earth time,
        you are accountable
        to that which you wrote upon the wall,
        you are accountable to humanity.

172 Soul, you have all free will, all choice.
A being decides at the station of learning on the Farside
what they want to accomplish,
what they plan to accomplish upon the earth.
Plans that are made through discussion,
plans that are made through agreement,
through other Souls,
for you come each time with a group,
all dedicated to helping each other.
When you enter in to the earth as a pure Soul
and that first negativity presents itself to your being,
even as a babe,
and you begin to gather to yourself that negativity,
oft times you do not accomplish
that which you came to do.
Oft times you have begun your path
and you say, "No. It is too much.", and you leave.
And again you will come back and complete in another lifetime
that which you chose not to do in this lifetime.
You can, Soul, even go beyond
what you plan to do in this lifetime
and perform even greater feats of Love.
It is choice.
Soul, oft times the pain may not be physical.
It may be emotional.
It may be mental.
It may be simply the pain of "What is this for?"
"I feel nothing,
I get no pleasure from life."
That is pain.
These are all opportunities to overcome negativity.
Joy is meant for every being.
Look, Souls of earth,
upon your mountains of problems as opportunities;
opportunity for self growth,
opportunity for the growth of humanity.
Soul, there are seven levels of being.
You return time and again
until you come unto from baby Soul to aged Soul.
You may do so in one lifetime.
There is no necessity to do it in seven lifetimes,

or seven of seven of seven.
For there are layers upon layers upon layers.
Whether you learn all the lessons in one lifetime is your choice.
But we would have you understand
that negativity is very enticing
and it is rare that anyone will only do so in one lifetime;
to go from baby Soul entering in,
and leaving as aged Soul.
Your Essence remains on the Path of Creator.
The Spirit works for the Essence
and the Soul enters in to the earth.
It is always choice, difficult but choice.

173 You are not puppets.
There is no being pulling your strings.
Your mind is yours, not that of another.
You have all choice.
You may not see the choice as viable.
You may not see a choice as safe,
but, Souls of earth, you have all choice.
In all situations, as an adult, understand all that you do
is choice, by you, the individual you.
Earth Souls as they grow and learn, begin to understand
they have full responsibility for that which they do.
They can not blame another for their position in life.
They can not blame another if they are sorrowing.
They can not blame another
because that being failed to love them
as they wanted to be loved.
Your whole world, you would change in an instant ,
once you took complete responsibility
for that which you choose to do
or choose not to do or choose to avoid
or choose to go forward unto.
Recognize you have the ability,
indeed, you have the responsibility to be aware
that the phrase, all choice,
has a great context of meaning.
Taken to heart, it alters your world view.
It alters the paradigm of your thought process.
It alters all future choices.

We are not here to change your mind.
We are here only to offer teaching.
You are, Souls of earth, humanity,
each with a particle of Creator.
Each endowed with the inalienable right to choose.
This we say unto you.

174 We would speak with thee of the
doubt that assails thy being,
the doubt that swirls about your being,
looking for the smallest entry.
Know that doubt can not enter in unless it is invited.
Know that it is your choice to invite negativity into thy being.
Know that doubt is a great weapon of negativity.
Doubt brings fear.
Doubt brings fear of reliance on self, on Farside self.
Doubt freezes the being from advancement.
Doubt hesitates the being from taking the path.
Doubt stumbles the Soul.
Release doubt, close the door to doubt, or invite it in.
We would have you know
you have the same choice with Purity.
It, too, swirls around thy being,
waiting for the invitation to enter in.
Purity will not cause you to stumble.
Purity does not doubt.
Purity knows the wonder of oneness.
Purity is a reaching beyond thyself.
It is the opposite of doubt.
We urge you to accept thy Purity.
We send our loving care,
always waiting for that moment
that you accept your Purity.
Purity allows only the complete giving of all your Light.
It is awesome in its generosity.
Souls, you are not puppets on a string,
you are not a leaf tossed in the wind,
you are not a wavelet tossed by the wind.
You have choice, always choice.
Let it be known!
Let it be known.

In the coming of the dawn,
open thyself to the Light that would enter in,
to the Light that would radiate thy being,
to the Light that is as a thousand bursting suns.
We await with eager anticipation your coming into your Light,
your claiming your Light
and your generosity in giving forth.

175 Enter ye in to the Light of your being.
Enter in to that which you are, an Angelic host.
Enter in to that from which you have come.
Enter in to the knowing of that which you are.
You are Light.
You come from Light.
You beget Light.
You are within Light.
Your aura is Light.
You have a truth in your being.
This Truth is your armor.
It enables you to discern negativity.
It does not choose for you, it only discerns,
and then you make the choice to enter in or not.
This Truth that is the armor of your being
has within it great Light.
Understand, Souls of earth,
that as your Light may permeate
the darkness of another,
your darkness may dim the Light of another.
Be aware, Souls.
The Light of which we speak in this teaching
is Light of your Creator.
Indeed, you have such Light.
Every Soul upon your earth has such Light
and within that Light is Love and compassion.
When Light is preeminent in your being,
Love and compassion is that which you give,
is that which you emit,
which you bring forward to others.
Souls of earth, understand you are creator.
You may create negativity.
You may create goodness.

You find it easier in your illusion to create negativity.
And indeed, this is so.
For it is why you have come, to overcome that negativity.
But alas, you have become enamored of negativity.
And so you have taken the first part of the equation,
the creation of the negativity,
and you have forgotten the second part,
the overcoming.
Your purpose to overcome negativity,
to reach those heights
wherein with you become manifested,
wherein you become the savior
of those lost in transition and beyond.
Your purpose has been lost to many.
We urge you to hear the Soul of your being,
to harken to the goodness within,
to release the pain of negativity
from self and thereby others.
For in doing so, you come unto that which you are,
you drop the veil of illusion,
you recall your purpose
and you enter in to the glory that is yours.
You enter in to the glory of your Creator.
So be it.

176 We ask that you not hold on to negativity.
We ask that you release it from your being.
We would have you understand,
the Wilful Child in its search, endless search,
wishes to go home but it can not on its own.
You may send a portion of this energy unto Creator.
Embrace it,
that you may send that portion of energy home.
We would have you understand
this Energy willingly came unto the earth plane,
willingly gave of its being so that you might grow,
so that you might gain scars,
so that you might overcome,
so that you might show to the Angels in transition
the very scars you've earned.
By embracing and overcoming and releasing,

not the holding it to you,
you have given unto Creator the very greatest of gifts.
For you have gifted unto Creator
the very return of the Angels in transition
and the return of the Energy of the Wilful Child.
How great thou art!
This was your intent, Souls of earth;
to embrace, to overcome, to release.
But many have forgotten the very reason
for their existence upon the earth
and have become enamored of negativity,
have become enamored of the energy
that they created and hold on to it
and refuse to overcome and release.
And yet, we tell you that as you hold negativity unto you
as you continue with your wars and your hoarding
and your starvation and your infliction of pain,
you too become a prison of negativity.
Release,
hold no longer negative energy within thy being
and assist others to release
so that the barriers to oneness
come tumbling down, as all recognize
the very purpose of your existence.

177 We bring unto you a teaching on mediocrity.
Upon your earth
you make judgments on the best, on the least.
On the commonplace, you label it mediocrity.
Upon your earth as we see it from the Farside
there is no mediocrity.
All has the utmost of value.
All is of the finest.
All has been tempered, honed unto.
It chimes in the most gracious, in the most vibrant of tones.
Your Souls are as the finest gold,
are as the finest metal of all metals.
Your Souls are the jewels in the crown of your Creator,
in your oneness.
Understand each Soul has divinity.
Each Soul has a holiness.

Indeed, you are precious beings
Your Soul shines in translucent glory.
This is what we see, Souls of earth!
And you, each, when you come to know
and recognize the oneness of your humanity,
you too will see.
We do not denigrate the disharmony,
for indeed, it has purpose.
All chords, when in harmony, vibrate to the tune of accord.
As in the Angel chorus, as in the sound,
the sweet, gentle healing sound.
Negativity that is created by man can not be harmonious.
Indeed, the Wilful Child looks for harmony, searches,
and when you embrace in compassion and Love,
it finds that harmony.
As you rise in your growth, you rise in the chord,
you rise in the vibrational Essence that is sent forth.
Beloved Souls of earth,
you have within you the chord of Creator.
You have within you all chords of being.
You are Truth, you are Purity, you are Loved.
But all of these, Truth, Love and Purity,
are choice.

178 Inconsequential, not in reference to Souls of earth,
in reference to the word itself, inconsequential.
Humanity, you ascribe meanings that are rarely ever precise,
for inconsequential in your terminology,
may oft refer to negative or positive.
What is inconsequential to one being
is oft consequential to another being.
It is that very judgment that will place an action
or a thought into one box or another
as consequential or inconsequential.
And so it is that you judge all things,
that you compartmentalize all things.
And yet you know in your knower,
in the most inner part of your being,
that there is no inconsequential, that all are one.
Souls of earth,
remove from your vocabulary inconsequential,

for in reality there is naught
that does not have consequence;
consequence of action, consequence of thought,
and consequence of value.
Even the most microscopic is consequential,
is an entity, has Soul.
There is naught upon your planet
that which does not have Soul.
To have Soul is to have consequence;
to have Soul is to have value,
to have Soul is to have holy worthiness of existence.
Entertain within thy being no judgment.
Accept all as valuable.
Recall, in your beings, who you are,
that from which you came,
the Creator of all that you see
and do not see, with the earth eyes
and with the eye of knowing.
Behold the consequence, the value of all that is,
of all that you may survey
and that which you have yet to discover.
Value, tenderly care for all that is.

179 We would have you understand,
the very air you breathe is sacred.
Indeed, Souls, it was created by your Creator.
It was given unto you as part of your physicality.
It has purpose.
Indeed, even the air of your earth has purpose.
The purpose is many fold.
Primary is your ability to breathe
and to function as a human being,
to accomplish the purpose of humanity.
The air also affects your weather patterns,
affects all that is upon the earth,
the way your plants grow,
the way the creatures of the earth move.
The very food that you ingest also depends upon the air.
Souls of earth in their daily lives take for granted the air.
This air has motion.
Beyond that of allowing you to be a physical form of matter,

it also assists in your vocalization.
All upon the earth has sound,
indeed, even the air has sound.
Souls of earth, hold the air of your earth
as more precious than gold,
as more precious than your platinum, your uranium.
Hold the air of your earth, of your planet, as an honorable.
As ye are shepherd of your earth,
understand your stewardship includes the very air
that all upon the earth breathe.
Give to the air the importance that it holds unto your being.
And know that as you breathe in and out,
give forth the goodness of your being
unto the air around your planet.
Circle, Souls of earth,
form circles of breathable purified cleansed air.
Cleanse not by mechanical means,
but cleanse by the goodness, the glory of your being.

180 We would have you contemplate the lotus,
the many petaled lotus.
Your Soul is the center of the flower.
The petals are your many lives.
As you gain, develop the spiritual portion of your being,
the petals unfold.
When you enter in, Soul, unto the earth,
the flower is a tight bud and as you grow it opens.
You may be in earth years only two years old
and your bud may be fully opened.
Others, in earth years, may be twenty, thirty, eighty,
and some do not open in their lifetime.
Perhaps in another, Soul.
When the flower is fully opened,
you have reached compassion.
You have earned the title, compassionate being.
How do you bring forth the many petals,
bring forth the lotus in all its glory?
Souls of earth, you do this in service to mankind
for the purpose of humanity.
You do this from the goodness of your heart.
You do this by spreading goodness unto others.

You do this in the core of the Love
that is particled in your being of Creator,
for you have allowed the Energy of Creator to flower,
to open unto others.
Souls of earth, you may be as the lotus upon your earth plane.

181 We would have you understand,
what we see is the aura of your being.
We feel joy for each on their path,
and we feel sadness when they move away,
and refuse their path of growth they set for themselves.
We would have you understand the roles that you play,
on the stage of the plane of earth,
are those that you have chosen
for your growth and the growth of humanity.
We would have you understand,
these roles are not you where we are.
They are as vestments donned for the role you play.
Do you see, Souls?
You may be fireman.
You may be mother.
You may be father.
You may be pervert.
You may be saint.
You may be minister.
You may be sinner.
Each step in growth on the path is growth, is positive for humanity.
There is no separation.
You do what you do,
you act your role in a lifetime as an individual,
but not separate from the humanity you are.
There is upon the plane of earth much sadness and sorrow,
many that are not in joy.
And we would have you lift your hearts
in joyous reclamation of who you are,
and we would have you accept each as beloved,
dearly beloved brother, and in all Love
and in all forgiveness, embrace ye one another.

182 Souls of earth, understand synchronicity,

in all its elements, in all its guises.
It is difficult to miss synchronicity, for it is all about your being.
It occurs in man, in animal, in creature, in plant,
in all that exists upon the earth,
in the water, in the dirt of the earth,
in the mountains, in the valleys.
Synchronicity in all its forms, exists.
You think of it as accident.
You think of it as evolution,
and indeed it is but only controlled evolution.
Evolution controlled by man, by the complexity of man,
by the synchronicity of man
in relation to its environment.
Indeed, all that has developed
from the very beginning upon your planet earth,
has been a plan by humanity,
has been a plan
to put in place for humanity to grow, to develop,
to enter in to that final stage of Purity, of holiness
wherein humanity may open the gate to transition,
may open the gate to the Farside,
may indeed open the gates
beyond the Second Gateway.
Souls of earth, reinforce in your being,
refresh in your being the meaning of the word
synchronicity,
in relation to mankind,
to the development of humanity,
in relation to the overcoming
of humanity's negativity;
the individual Souls who have come again,
and again and again, and again,
a thousand times, nay, even more
to learn to overcome negativity,
to learn to grow in Purity.
Indeed, this process has effected all that is upon the earth
and even to the earth itself,
to the planet of your being.
Oh, Souls of earth,
indeed earth knew that she would endure for man.
And she knew that which would cease to be endured,

as a part of the whole process of synchronicity.
For mankind will come out of their shell,
for mankind will look anew
at compassion and Love.
Out of the depths of despair,
out of the horror of catastrophes
will come a greater understanding of mankind,
of compassion;
will come a greater understanding of the need
for growth of the Soul and the spirituality of being.

183 Soul, you will understand earth will not close.
Earth will alter.
Earth will change.
Earth will revert to its pristine state.
What you speak of, Soul, as closing,
it is that phase of earth that has been subjected
to mankind's abominations,
which have altered the axis
upon which earth revolves.
The tilt may be, in your reckoning, extremely minute.
And yet within the laws of physics, of gravity,
even the most minute
will effect the perpendicular rotation of the earth.
The aura of earth has within it rents, tears, cloudiness,
all indicative
of that which affects its rotational axis.
Be not fearful.
Be not afraid, for the eruptions are necessary,
the tilt is necessary for that which will come
to be known as the new day.
Many of your earth beings will lift, many will stay.
But each will know of their agreement,
and the Soul of earth will rise up
and embrace the new day and welcome its sister.
And look in the mirror of that which is to be
and know itself in all its glory.

Eye

184 We would have you understand
your flesh is merely a cloak.
Your mind, Souls of earth,
is not simply of your flesh and blood.
It has a higher connection, a higher purpose.
But the actual flesh that encases it
is a cloak that you may take off at will.
You do not need your flesh to travel beyond your earth.
You do not need your flesh to travel about your earth.
You do not need your flesh
to enter in to the great Prism of the Crystal Cave.[43]
Your flesh is bound to the earth, indeed!
But you, your mind, is not bound to earth.
Only by your will is it bound to earth.
Only by your will may you enter unto other dimensions,
other places of being without your flesh,
and yet maintain the consciousness of self,
maintain the consciousness of being.
You do not become comatose
when you travel without the flesh. Indeed not,
for you are fully aware of what you call self.
You do not lose your mind.
You find the higher mind of your being.
You connect to a greater self.
You transcend your earth aura
and enter in to the Farside Aura of your being.
You have the ability to manifest your being a thousand,
yea, more than a thousand miles
from where you sit or lay within your shelter.
You do not require a blessing to do this,
a miracle to do this.
It is an innate portion of your humanity.
Enter in to the knowledge that you do not lose!
You gain in wisdom.
You gain in knowledge.
You gain in experience.
And you bring back such richness, such riches of knowledge,
of perspective, of wisdom, to share with those
who do not wish to travel the dimensions

of time and no time.
Souls of earth, you have all possibilities.
Enter in to this recognition.
Acknowledge who you are, a dimensional being
beyond that of flesh and blood and bone,
and that you are able
to transport your consciousness
into other dimensions of being
to the level of your Purity.

185 Souls of earth, you are not tethered;
indeed you are not.
You have nothing weighing you down, except
that which you have required for yourself.
You individually choose to tether yourself unto the earth.
It is not, Soul, a judgment;
it is not to say this is right or wrong;
it is only, Soul, a giving of knowledge unto you,
so that you are fully informed to make a choice
with the knowing that you may release
that which holds you to earth.
This is not to say that you will pass from the life
you have upon the earth.
Indeed not.
We are not speaking of your flesh and blood.
We are speaking, Soul, of the consciousness of your being.
We would have you understand,
within the consciousness of your being
is all freedom to leave the earth plane.
Within the consciousness of your third eye of your being
is the ability to travel.
You travel in consciousness,
for consciousness is Energy,
and it is not contained
unless you will it to be contained.
Consciousness cannot be tangibly grasped within the hands;
you cannot pat it, touch it with your physical self.
But nonetheless, it has its own form, its own matter of being.
Consciousness has the possibility of direct connection
to your high self,
has the possibility of direct connection

to the Crystal Cave,
has the possibility to reach great levels of healing Energy.
It has the possibility to locate your self, to locate your mind
in another world, unto other beings, unto the Angels.
In a very minute way, Souls of earth,
you could think of your consciousness
in earth terminology,
to be as a great movie that you watch,
your 3D movies that seem as if you are within.
And you take that concept one step further,
for indeed you are in
when you use the consciousness of the eye to reach.
You may see great panoramas, great canyons, great gardens,
crystalline in their beauty.
You may see the great colours, so vibrant and alive and glowing;
in comparison the colours of earth are muted.
Indeed, Souls, your consciousness recalls
from whence you came.
Your consciousness recalls whom you are.
You are aware that you have taken on this form,
this earthly flesh and blood.
You are a changeling,
for on the Farside your form is different,
and for your earth understanding
you have altered in order to enter in to earth,
to accomplish your purpose.
But your consciousness has the memory of your former self,
before your present reincarnation,
and it is your consciousness
that may take you to read the lives you have lived.
Indeed this is accessible unto you.
Harken, Souls of earth, to the possibilities of your being,
should you choose to remove the barriers,
to remove the veils you willingly placed
upon entering in to the earth.
Souls of earth, this is not limited to a special chosen few,
for you are all special, and all chosen.
And you are all given great accolades upon the Farside
for that which you do upon the earth
in your purpose of humanity.

186 Souls of earth, we have come forward today
from a great distance, if the distance
was measured in your earth measurements,
in what you call light years.
And yet, Souls of earth light years
may be covered quickly by entering in
from one dimensional spiral into another.
This may be accomplished,
according to your earth measurement
in a minute amount of earth time.
For time and space in your understanding is very different
in all other dimensions.
You will understand dimensional time has its own reality.
Your time is illusory.
The Time of which we speak, our Time, is also illusory,
and yet it is its illusory state
that allows for the dimensional travel,
for the entering in and the entering out
and the entering in and the entering out
for as often as you will it at your level of Purity.
You will understand, Souls of earth,
to Purity there are no locked doors,
there are no gates closed, there is no aura hidden,
there is no record hidden.
You may reach unto the Akashic in your Purity,
and you may read what has been writ.
You may reach unto the Writing on the Wall
and read what has been writ.
And there are some few who may reach beyond
and read what has been writ.
It is available, Souls of earth,
only in your Purity may you enter in,
may you travel dimensionally,
may you travel beyond the very bounds of your earth.
Soul, in your Purity you may travel throughout your earth,
for there is naught to prevent
the consciousness of your being to enter in
with the intent to heal, to calm, to solace a being.
To connect dimensionally through your consciousness
with another consciousness upon your earth,
is entirely within the realm of possibility in Purity.

There is a vibrational radiance in Purity
that allows dimensional travel,
that allows you using the eye of beholding,
to reach beyond the earth self
of flesh and blood and bone.
You require no license, no pass key.
You require only will, intent and vibrational Purity.
This we give unto you.

187 We would speak on what you call the transom,
the window, the portal.
The portal unto the Farside; we tell you it is never closed.
Delights await.
Visions of magnitude await.
Love in its fullness awaits.
Souls of earth, your transoms, your portals,
your windows, your doorways are shut.
It is choice to open.
The welcome mat is Love.
The welcome mat is joy at your visit.
Carry yourself forward, enter in
and be ye astounded at your magnificence.
Souls of earth, lift your beings.
Lift your hearts.
Lift your mind.
Lift and vision where you are with clarity.
As in your earth when you climb high,
you may see so much more
than from the ground level.
You discover a reality you did not know existed,
for you could not see from the ground level.
And as you rise your being, you climb a mountain.
You have before you a panorama, an existence,
that you did not know.
And so it is when you allow
your Soul, your consciousness to lift beyond the earth,
you see the earth from a very different perspective.
Your paradigm alters.
You have a new dimension to experiment within your being,
and you climb higher.
You lift your being higher.

And you have all access to in your Purity,
to worlds and worlds and worlds,
to places beyond your imagination.
Allow your consciousness
to freely roam beyond the earth plane.
As your balloon flights lift, once the ropes are released,
so your consciousness may lift, should you allow it,
and the choice lies within your being
Harken to the possibilities of lift,
allow the consciousness freedom to roam.
We would teach on your earth word perspicacity.
It gives direction
when one understands the fullness of being
in the state of perspicacity;
the mind seeing with clarity,
the heart feeling with clarity.
When you enter in to the earth,
in your initial being, you have clarity of vision.
And we speak not of earth vision
but of the eye of beholding.
And then, Souls of earth, negativity enters,
and you lose the clearness of vision.
You do not lose the ability, the potential,
but you lose clarity of vision.
So it is as you grow, as you experience,
as you become upon the earth plane,
the cloud over your vision, over the clarity,
the perspicacity of being,
may become stronger and denser.
Only may you be in the state of clear vision,
of perspicacity, when you have released negativity.
For to be in the state of perspicacity,
compassion and Love are in flower.
The bud has unfolded and the beauty of the bloom is there
for all to see,
for you to see clearly that which you behold.
Perspicacity, Souls of earth, the state of,
is akin to a state of goodness.
To enter in to the state of perspicacity, release negativity.
For in honing the eye, the vision of the eye,
you will indeed travel beyond the bounds of earth

and you will behold wonders
beyond your imagination.
You will behold color beyond your imagination.
You will behold Light beyond your imagination
and you will behold the sacred.

188 It is, beloved Souls, only through the eye
that you may gaze upon wisdom.
There are upon your earth plane
many who have attained the eye
and many more that will attain the eye.
There is a connecting that occurs,
there is a way that opens to others,
when one individual attains the eye.
It is not a singular, solitary achievement,
but has vibrational repercussions
throughout humanity, earth and beyond.
And so we encourage the attainment of the eye,
the capability of seeing with the eye,
for you all have the ability.
With stillness comes the capability
and the glory of that achievement reverberated
throughout all eternity each and every time.
We would speak with thee of the trembling vibration,
of the swirling Energy of the eye.
Know the eye pulsates, vibrates with Energy,
Energy that is connected to the Farside,
to your Essence.
Know you have the ability to free the eye,
to emit the pulsing Energy along the connection.
It is as your wire on earth conducts electricity,
and that electricity can be directed,
can be focussed.
So you, too, can focus the Energy of your eye,
the Holy orb given to all humanity
to re establish the connection to your Essence.
Vibrate, Souls, shake thy being,
allow the Energy of the eye to carry you forward,
to carry you forth into the Quar.[44]
"In the distance I see a Light, yet I am in the Light.
I am of Light.

I am surrounded by Light.
I am surrounded by other beings of Light.
And yet in the distance is a greater Light
 and I yearn to know that Light.
I yearn to be in that Light.
I yearn to be that Light
 and I have the knowing
 that this is all possibility,
 that I may reach that Light.
Around me is a sound
 that vibrates throughout my being.
Around me is a chorus of Angel voices.
 The thrum of vibration is prevalent
 within all Energy and energies.
I have the knowing that all have within,
 all that is has within the same thrum of vibration,
 for I have reached the level of five.
I have the knowing of Creator.
I have the knowing of worlds upon worlds.
I have the knowing that there are vistas untold,
 uncountable before me,
 that I may travel and traverse.
I have the knowing that all is available unto me.
And I have the knowing of the integrity of being.
I have the preponderance of teachings
 ministered to me
 and I have the knowing of more to come.
And all who reach this most blessed level
 are held within the arms of the Saints.
Creator reaches unto all.
This I have the knowing of."

189 All beings upon this planet of this earth
have the ability to travel wherever,
not just upon the earth, but beyond the earth.
Some call it Soul travel, some call it astral travel,
but indeed, it is a change in consciousness.
It is allowing the consciousness of your being
to connect with your higher self.
It is literally leaving the bounds of earth;
not that your heart stilled,

we are not speaking of passing, Soul.
We are speaking of your consciousness, of allowing
the consciousness of your being to travel.
There is no barrier when you connect with your higher self
for you have left the earth's body behind.
You must leave it behind so that you are buoyant and free.
All Souls may travel.
You may actually have your physical being
be in another part of the world on your earth plane.
You have this capability, Souls.
You have heard stories of a person appearing.
They are not stories.
They happen.
The consciousness connected to your high self
is immeasurably powerful.
Simply allow the consciousness to connect to the high self.
Allow!
But we were in a human life many times in our stubbornness
and we understand the need for steps.
And we would suggest, although there are many ways,
we would give the following:

Step 1
Place yourself either prone or sitting upright.
If you are sitting upright, ensure that the chair has arms.

Step 2
Place your feet upon the ground, preferably
place your feet upon material of some kind
that is a natural fiber.

Step 3
Place you hands palm up and
take three deep breaths through your nostrils.
Hold for a count of three
and push the breath out for a count of four.
You will do this, three times.

Step 4
At the end of the third breath, as you push out,
place your hands upon your duodenum

and lightly press inward and allow it to pop.
You now have the attention of your brain and your will.

Step 5
You will then place your hands outward
in the receiving position
and you will envelop your being in the Light of violet.
You will see yourself rising,
not the body,
but the consciousness;
and seeing that sliver of White,
know that your consciousness
may enter in to that Light.
And there you will be greeted by Angels, by guides,
by others you have known
who all will take you on a journey.
You may decide you want to see Andromeda, or Pleiadia,
or the Ruby world or the Crystal Cave, others.
Most in their first visit are overwhelmed
and so their visit is short,
a fifteen, a twenty minutes of earth time.
And then as you become accustomed, you will stay longer.

190 We would speak of the pendulum of life,
of movement, the to and fro.
Your motion on earth is limited
to the extent that your mind places barriers.
Upon Farside the barriers do not exist
and a being may instantaneously leave,
move and be elsewhere.
You, too, upon earth, have this ability
but your mind says you are not capable.
Unto all will come the knowledge of mind movement,
a conscious awareness of this ability.
It is only an extension of your being,
an extension of your Spirit,
an extension of your Essence,
of the Light Being of who you are.
For a reflection has the ability to move, as does its origin.
This we would say unto thee, beloved Souls of earth,
motion forward, use your mobility forward,

enter in to the spiral of goodness and go forth,
become that which you are!
Holy Spirit is that which you are upon Farside.
Holy is that which you are upon earth.
The Energy of Spirit, Souls of earth,
is palpable to those who would use the eye.
To those who would use only the earth sense,
a vague disturbance may be felt within the near air.
But with the eye, the form is visible,
the being is visible, the aura is visible.
Spirit is powerful.
Spirit is part of Soul.
And each and every humanity upon the earth has Soul,
and therefore may envision,
may see Spirit while upon the earth plane
with the use of the eye.
Your Spirit is always available unto you,
for it has a great investment
in that which you do as Soul.
Each being upon the earth has an incandescent Spirit,
a Spirit who knows the path chosen.
Naught is unknown to your Spirit,
for it may read the Writing on the Wall,
the Akashic Record.
They are intertwined, interconnected.
Souls of earth, you are not alienated from Spirit.
It is as your air,
though you may not see visibly air that you breathe.
You know it is there
for you breathe it in and breathe it out.
So it is with Spirit, always present, visible to the eye.
Release from you the negativity
and open the eye of beholding.
We would state the following
to assist in clearing the confusion.
Soul, you have responsibility for self,
you have the choice of goodness toward others.
You have a path that you have set out for self,
a path of growth, a path of leaping forward in Purity.
You may rest upon another shoulder,
you may reach out a hand for support,

of Love, of understanding of compassion,
but you may not walk another's path for them
unless you desire to gain karma.
Life is confusing and indeed a struggle, for this is growth.
But there is no rule written
that we must stay within the struggle.
We can accept the holiness of our being.
We can accept that we are of Creator
and that all are of Creator
and all have offered a gift to Creator.
With this acceptance,
the struggle is seen only as lesson, as opportunity.
Soul, you give much Love.
You have great understanding.
Do not set up a mote, a barrier to that understanding.
Enter forth into the eye of knowing and all confusion
will be whisked away
as a fog is whisked away by sun and wind.
Continue, Soul, to focus on that which is yours,
the steps to enter in to the eye of knowing.

191 We teach on acceptance.
We would have you often have your hands, palms outward,
slightly cupped, the thumbs pressed against the flesh.[45]
Move the left toward your body and yet not on the body.
Behind it, place your right hand.
Move the left over the right, the right over the left.
Do this slowly, Soul.
Do it in the area of the heart, very slowly.
And as you make the motions,
you will feel the Energy begin to build,
and you will be tempted to go faster, and we ask you,
to maintain the slowness, the gentleness.
As you are making this motion, raise your head slightly,
at a forty five degree angle, and repeat:
'Acceptance is my birthright.
Acceptance is my birthright.
Acceptance is my birthright.
I am Holy, I am Holy, I am Holy.'
Keep the motion, slow and gently
repeat once more,

"Acceptance is my birthright.", three times.
And then slowly stop the motion.
Do not be abrupt, for you will become dizzy.
Slowly stop the motion,
place your hands in the receiving position,
and enter in to a short meditation.
And you will find your being vibrating,
and know that the Angels are with thee.

192 We would have you understand preparatory,
preparatory before entering in to meditation.
Always, Soul, the head is bent.
The head is bent not in supplication,
the head is bent to receive,
at the very back of the head,
Energy from the Pillar of Light.
The intent to meditate,
to connect to Spirit brings the Light to enter in.
It is directly above where the neck connects the spine.
There will be an indent in the middle.
If you follow that indent up four centimeters
and press lightly in,
you will feel a slight trembling, a slight vibration
in the front your head above the third eye.
You will massage clockwise that spot in a circular motion.
And as you feel yourself drifting, relaxing,
let go and enter in to your meditation.
The actual brain cells will be affected, will be altered,
so that the molecular change
will enable your being
to enter in unto the Farside.
Know that you may,
using this exercise with the intent and the will,
alter your being,
alter the emotional state of your being.
It is imperative that if you wish to connect with Spirit,
your emotional state of being is at an equilibrium.
And this will bring about that equilibrium.
This we would have you do daily in preparation,

193 The meditation that we will discuss

is that which is spiritual in nature.
It is that which links your earth Soul being unto Spirit self.
Meditation brings about molecular changes within the body,
molecular changes within the mind,
done with will and intent and compassion
of reaching unto Spirit from the earth plane.
You will begin to prepare for this by each day for seven days:

Step 1
Sitting upright, holding the hands in the receiving position,
the thumbs are out, not pressed against the flesh.

Step 2
You will then slowly cup your hands.

Step 3
As you are cupping the fingers, you bring the thumb inward,
so that it rests slightly inside the palm of your hand
at the base of your forefingers.

Step 4
Gently and slowly close your eyes.

Step 5
Bring the cupped palms slowly up
maintaining the position until they reach your earth eyes.

Step 6
Bend your head downward unto the palms, not touching
your forehead to the palms.

Step 7
Touch your fingertips unto the area
between the bridge of the nose and your eyebrows,
just below the third eye.

Step 8
Raise your head, maintaining touching the area just given.

Step 9
Breathe deeply in through the nostrils

and hold for the count of four.
And then release in a controlled manner
to the count of five: wh wh wh wh wh.

Step 10
Press gently on your flesh with your fingertips,
and then move them away very slightly.
and then, press again, five times,
each time apply a light pressure.
Step 11
Move your hands
so that your elbows are now touching your body,
and you have removed your fingertips from the flesh.

Step 12
Take your right hand,
place it in the cupped position in front of the third eye.

Step 13
Place your other hand in the cupped position
in front of the mouth.

Step 14
Breathe in.
And as you breath in,
you will bring your hand closer to your mouth.
As you breath out
you will push your hand away from your mouth.
In and out, thrice, Soul.
This is alerting the chakras to begin the vibration.

Step 15
You will then do the same maneuver,
with your right hand and the third eye;
moving it in and out, in and out, in and out.

Step 16
Bring both hands in front of the third eye
in the cupped position
and hold them there for a count to five.

Step 17
Very slowly move your hands away and bring them down.

Step 18
And you have one more step to go, to prepare;
take your right hand
and place it in front of your throat chakra,
and hold it there until you feel the pulsating heat.
That is your indication that you are ready
to enter in to a deeper meditation.

194 We would have you understand
the great perspicacity within your mind
that is a possibility for all Souls.
Age does not matter.
Your, what you call, intelligence quotient, does not matter.
It is available, it is a potential in all Souls.
It gives you one and all the ability
to see beyond your dimension.
It is, Souls of earth, a prelude to removing the veil from the eye.
It affects your perception of your self and your abilities.
The only barrier to using perspicacity
is that which you have placed upon it;
is that refusal of your earth being
to acknowledge any vibration
any Energy, any color or sound
beyond the immediate dimension of self.
The barrier was placed by self
at the first moment of embracing and holding negativity.
It is the holding that made the difference.
You came to earth with all the tools,
with all the abilities of perfection,
with all the possibilities of perfection.
And then it becomes choice as to that which you use
or as to that which you place away and allow to rest.
Never obleted entirely.
They are not gone,
you may refresh and use your formidable abilities.
Know you may immerse yourself
and embrace your Pillar of Light.
We would have you pay close attention to the birdsong

while there is birdsong.
Birds, when they trill out their song, vibrate,
for that is how they make sound visible to the earth ear.
Their whole being is as a drum
and they bring, as a gift unto the earth, their song.
Science may also measure
the vibration of the sound of the birdsong,
for it is a language that may be interpreted
by measuring the vibration.
Science may measure and
through your instruments of measurement,
translate the language of the birds.
Many beings upon the face of your earth,
although few in number,
know the language of the birds through the eye.
All on earth may do this if they choose.
It is the same with the sound of any animal,
in the vibration of that sound is the key to their language,
a key that may be translated
into human language and understanding.

195 We speak of intent and its placement
within any healing modality.
First we would have you understand,
the intent must come from both parties.
Not only from the healer but from the one to be healed.
The intent provides a focus for the Energy.
It is as a tunnel, if you would,
for the Energy to flow through from one to the other.
The intent from the healer to be at its highest efficacity
must be in compassion and unconditional Love.
But, Souls,
if the intent is not compassion and unconditional Love,
the healing is enervated.
It lacks focus.
It is, in comparison, a bandage.
When you heal as a healer with the Crystal Cave,
you are in compassion and unconditional Love
or you would not be able
to reach unto the Crystal Cave.
We speak of the highest form of healing,

The intent from the one to be healed must be in openness,
must take in to account the necessity
for wellness of their being;
must be the intent to be in a state of acceptance,
of allowing their selves to be altered,
of allowing the negativity to leave their being.
You will be, if you are in the state of being,
able to reach unto the Crystal Cave,
you will clearly know, not only the intent of the being
to be healed, but the reason for the intent.
You will know the true path of the being, before you heal.
You will read it in their aura.
You will see it with your eye,
and that will guide your intent and action.

Farside

196 Color is comprised of sound, vibration.
And Soul, it is also composed of wisdom,
for color is attached to the Light Beings.
Color is attached to Godhead.
Color has the motion that the Wilful Child looks for,
the motion that will allow
the Wilful Child peace, surcease!
You understand, Soul, that color was initiated
as a method whereby Energy could be compiled,
could be tracked, recorded.
Indeed, Color, as we reference it,
was not a variant at the upper levels.
It was emitted only as a recording device.
All on Farside are ever being drawn to that
which we term as above for your understanding.
Each level of consciousness has above it
another level of consciousness.
Each level of consciousness has within it
all the knowledge of that level,
and is constantly being taught by the level above it.
The research is not only of earth.
The research is on all worlds, about all worlds, from all worlds.
It is in our growth pattern.

Research is a busy activity to form patterns of understanding.
The pattern of understanding we would form from earth,
from the experience, the illusions of humanity,
is to know and understand negativity.
We would fulfill Creator's bringing back negativity
without force, with Love and care.
We do not know if this is possible
within the timetable allotted humanity.
We do not know if this is possible
within the timetable of implosion.
We do know of the constant search of Negativity.
We do know of the contributions of humanity.
Soul, we do not fear.
We would rescue each and every Soul,
leave no Soul behind, if it is within the timetable allotted.
Understand, that all that is good,
that all that is growth from negativity, will not be lost.

197 Many of you see yourselves
as blundering through life, having no purpose,
never attaining the goals you painstakingly set for self.
You recognize and stand in awe of only great events,
great beings of magnitude
who come forth in the public eye
or in the village square.
You compare yourselves to them and belittle yourselves,
for you see in yourselves no greatness of being.
And yet, we would tell you that we know
each and every Soul upon the planet
has greatness of being.
What you see as the little things,
as the common things of your daily existence,
we see the greatness of them.
We see greatness in the mother who prepares a meal,
the father who holds the child on the knee,
who comforts the scraped knee.
Indeed, each of you has the same seed of greatness within.
Each of you has the seed of motion of the Great One.
It is that seed wherein
we see all acts of greatness upon the earth.
We would have you know by virtue of that fact,

you are wedded to greatness.

198 We lay before you an invitation to a feast of plenty.
We invite you into your home, which is our home.
We have named it for earth, the Farside.
If you choose to accept this invitation,
know you will enter unto the Farside.
Know you will enter unto a feast of plenty,
unto a welcome surpassing
any that you could imagine.
The invitation entered in with you
as you entered in to the earth plane.
It has been with you, awaiting your use.
We would have you, Soul, come and visit.
Come to the homestead, come to the ancestors' roots.
Come to the places you have seen.
Come to those places you have never seen.
The Farside has waiting arms to welcome you.
It has for you old friends, acquaintances, loved ones,
guides, Angels awaiting your presence.
It is as if you could simply step from one room unto another.
It is that easy.
You may transverse dimensions with your being.
You may read the records.
You may ride the whale.
You may fly with the eagle.
You may soar unto any world that you choose.
You may expand the horizons of your being,
and know you are not limited to the earth.
You are not limited to your universe.
You are not limited to your galaxy,
for dimensional travel has no limits.
And you have within you that possibility.
Dimensional travel is more than a wish or a hope or a dream.
Know that fear is a barrier,
not one we have placed, but one you have placed.
Souls of earth, you limit your beings,
and we place before you the invitation
to unlimit your beings.

199 We would speak of the industriousness

of earth and Farside.
We would have you know industriousness
is of value and is appreciated
for the drive it gives to research,
to adventure, to joy.
We gloriously and excitedly enter in to adventure,
knowing that we will gain for all.
Not for the individual, for all.
For as each grows in Purity, in wisdom,
it contributes to the whole,
to the oneness, and hence all partake in the growth.
It is a truth that industriousness is upon the earth also.
But the distortion comes to be
when the industriousness is upon the backs of others,
when the industriousness pollutes the waterways,
when the industriousness distorts the child
with the starvation brought about.
The illusion of negativity distorts
the value of industriousness,
and we would have you understand
and dispel that illusion.
Beloved Souls, it is reality we would speak of.
We would teach a lesson in perception.
We would have you know,
each Soul has its own illusion
within the larger context of illusion.
And we would have you know
that within the larger context of illusion
is a greater illusion, for all is in triad.
Illusion always has purpose.
Illusion always has a formation,
a framework, within which the Soul learns, grows.
Each Soul armed with Truth,
each Soul with opportunity and all possibility,
each Soul individual and yet of a greater oneness.
You are as an individual Soul imprinted with a map.
The map contains all that you have written on the Wall.
It is always accessible.
You have only to consult the map to understand,
to know where you are, why you are, who you are.
A map gives you a destination,

gives you an overall perspective, gives you a plan.

200 Souls of earth, for your edification only,
we often enter in to naming and to titles
for earth understanding.
You understand that upon the Farside
there is no need for names and titles.
For all what you would call identification and language
is, in your vernacular,
spoken through Color and Sound of Aura.
There is no requisition, no requirement for a secrecy.
All is available to the level of Purity.
We have upon the Farside architects
who create magnificent structures of air,
of color, of sound.
Indeed, this is possible.
You restrict form
to that which you can touch upon your earth,
to wood, to brick.
This is not necessary upon the Farside,
for form comes into being by virtue of Color and Sound,
and the impetus to know, the impetus to create,
the impetus to construct.
We have upon the Farside painters, artists
of every type that you are aware of upon the earth
and many more that you are not yet aware of.
These beings paint with the mind, the high mind.
They paint with Color and Sound and movement.
Naught is static.
Their paintings take form.
Their paintings may be touched.
Their paintings hold wisdom and knowledge.
We have upon the Farside
what you would call upon your earth,
scientists in various disciplines and guises.
Many of them guide, nudge your earth scientists.
They alter the very structure of matter
through Color, Sound and velocity.
There are realms devoted to learning in science.
We have musicians, musicians
who construct musical compositions

with the very Aura of their being,
who play upon the very Aura of their being.
And they compose symphonies.
They compose paeans to Creator of Light.
The Light has Sound, has Color and vibration.
Their compositions are complex
and yet eternally beautiful in their simplicity.
All of this, Souls of earth, you may, if you visit,
experience, observe and indeed become a part of
to the level of your Purity.

201 Recall the triad.
Understand there is a triad of body,
there is a triad of mind
and there is a triad of consciousness
within each and every being,
whether Farside or earth or beyond.
You have the ability at this moment to lift the body
with thought at a conscious level,
if you would but dispel the illusion that you can not.
It is the same illusion,
the same barrier that prevents the lifting to Farside.
Consciousness, awareness and being.
For when you have lifted the consciousness into the Farside,
into the Quar, when you have imploded,
you become an altered consciousness of being.
To be lifted is to enter in to all that is familiar.
You will not encounter strangeness.
You will encounter worlds of being.
You will encounter the Love that surrounds,
enters through, permeates thy being.
So it does also upon the earth plane
but when you enter in,
when you are lifted,
there is no barrier to the sense,
to the encompassing Love of your Creator.
Within the earth plane the mind often creates a barrier
and you feel separated
from that all encompassing glory,
jubilant Love of your Creator.
But, Souls, when you are lifted,

when your consciousness enters
the presence of the Farside,
of the Creator, of the Angels
and even unto Godhead,
you are a being filled with Love
beyond your earth comprehension.
Souls, it is your consciousness that is lifted,
not your physical being,
but your consciousness that enters into the eye,
into the Quar.
It implodes thy being and enables you to see beyond earth.

202 Humanity, Souls of earth,
each moment of each day you are cared for.
We walk with you, we do not abandon you.
We know where your feet will take you,
where your mind will take you.
Understand you came to earth with a plan, a plan of growth,
a plan of teaching, a plan to help others.
And we can not take this from you,
for you have come into the earth freely,
and you leave freely.
And in between you walk your path freely.
We would speak with thee on the subject of Farside station,
of the learning at station.
Understand that much time,
as you would term it on the earth plane,
is spent in studying, debating with your guides
your return to earth.
In minute detail every occurrence, every happenstance
is examined from every angle
to ensure you have the tools
to complete your missions upon the earth plane.
You have all choice, even at station,
and we remember our understanding taking place;
that it was not blame for any one,
it was not blame for ourselves,
it was taking responsibility for choice.
We remember the moment of that wisdom,
the flash of comprehension
when understanding took place.

We remember the difficulty even after the understanding,
of accepting that we are responsible for our choice,
and that we have choice.
We remember returning to station,
and we remember the Love, the open arms,
the gladness and the joy with which we were received.
We assure you that you, too, will be welcomed with open arms,
with warmth, with Love, with joy.
Bells will ring, choirs will sing,
and you will know the warmth of coming home.
We remember, as do all of humanity, and we urge you,
to do that which you do in Purity.

203 The moment you enter in to Farside
you will recognize your Angels, as indeed,
you will recognize all that awaits you.
All those who have companioned you will be there,
not just from this lifetime but from all your lifetimes,
and you will recognize them all.
For when you enter back into the Farside
you lose the language of the earth
and regain the language of Farside.
The Aura is the language of Farside.
There is no need for interpretation, for translation.
It is all the same language
whether it be Angels, High Beings, Saints.
Whether it be level one or level seven
the language is the same
and requires no intermediary.
Your Aura holds within it all that you are,
who you are, the humanity of your being.
You are instantly recognizable as a particle of Creator.
Your renown is great, Soul, for you have done much.
Each time you enter in to earth and return unto the Farside,
much is learned from your experience.
Whether you completed your Writing on the Wall,
or it is incomplete,
whether you gained karma
or whether you regenerated your karma,
all has value and worth.
When you leave the earth,

know you are worthy to enter in to the Farside.
Know you may leave at karmic station
that which you have generated in this lifetime,
but know also it is of value.
Pass from this earth life gently and knowingly
unto the Light of Farside, for it is your home.
Indeed, home!

204 We would describe for you
the activity within a learning station.
We will take first the causal plane.
When the Soul has entered in, returned from earth,
the Soul is greeted by all manner of beings
welcoming the hardy Soul back.
And then the Soul will make a decision
whether to continue on a path or choose another.
If the Soul chooses to return to earth,
then the station becomes home for a while.
We place the words, Soul, in basic terminology
for your understanding,
knowing that it is far more complex
than we may explain within a few passages.
But it will give you a grounding of the subject.
Once the Soul has determined they want to return to earth
and continue on that path of growth,
there is what you would call a conference,
held with the being's guides,
coaching, debating, planning.
It is complex because it is not just that individual being
but it must take into account the plan of growth,
all the beings that will be affected
or intermingled with in that lifetime.
That may constitute thousands, hundreds of thousands
depending upon the path
or it may constitute only a finite number
of one thousand Souls for a very short life lived.
And each of those Souls has a path of growth, a plan.
And it too must be coincided.
And then all those beings such as animals
that will be part of the plan,
they too enter in to the consultation.

In your earth terms, this consultation
may continue for a hundred years or more.
On the Farside, that is a mere two or three blinks of an eye.
All the pieces of the plan must be in place.
The being, the Soul, has to decide
all that will compose their lifetime within the earth,
even to their genetic makeup,
even to the very cells of their being.
Nothing is chance met or happenstance.
Within the planning
there are various paths opened to the being.
There are various opportunities planned
that will affect not only that Soul but any other Soul
that has an agreement within that lifetime.
There is the karma to be considered.
The Soul must decide whether that karma
is to be picked up in this lifetime,
and if it is to be picked up in this lifetime,
then all the others involved
in the karmic activity agreed, agreeable, available.
Nothing is left to do without free will, free choice,
and there is no judgment.
If a Soul should choose not to carry that karmic burden
within this lifetime, there is no judgment for that.
The being who has chosen
to return to earth has all manner of great desire
to bring forth the brethren, to overcome negativity,
a burning desire, Souls of earth, to do so.
It is as if in your old testament the loins are girded for battle,
for indeed, the Soul understands and knows
it is going into battle, a battle to overcome negativity.
The courage of those entering in to earth
is renowned to all of Farside and beyond.
It is no easy task, easy undertaking.
It is indeed arduous
and indeed of Loving gift unto all that is.

205 Blankness.
Oft times you refer to a blank wall, a blank slate,
nothing writ upon the page,
nothing writ upon the being.

We would have you understand, Souls of earth,
 that you have filled page after page after page.
There is no end to the voluminous recordings of your being,
 for there are no blank pages of Energy.
All Energy has vibration, vibrates.
And in that vibrating is a recording.
All that you do is recorded.
All that you vibrate in thought and being,
 in thought and action, being is recorded.
Not for judgment, indeed not!
The recordings are not done
 to place you in a hierarchy of being.
They are not done so that one is holier than another.
They are not done
 to ensure that you have a record of karmic interactions,
 so that you may be forever on the wheel.
Indeed not.
The recordings are matched to your Writing on the Wall.
They are for your knowledge,
 for the knowledge of all Farside.
That which you do, when you pass from one life to another,
 is held in keeping for you so that you
 may gaze upon that which you have accomplished.
So that you may then place your mind to the next life.
Not just your own goals of attainment,
 but that of all who you will touch,
 that of all who have agreed to be part of your path,
 all who have agreed to intercede during a lifetime.
This includes every being, every human being
 that you would encounter in some manner or form.
This includes all creatures of all description
 that you will encounter in some manner or form.
All is an intricate plan.
All is an intricate web.
But all is by your agreement.
You work in conjunction with the Spirit of your being.
You are Soul, Spirit, and Essence,
 and you carry forth in the Soul being
 that which has been agreed to with Spirit.
But understand, Souls of earth, that oft times,
 with whatever intent you enter in to the negative void,

you stray from the path of intent.
And we place no judgment when we say stray,
for all that you do has value in some manner or form.
And so we keep a record of that which you do.
For oft times, when you return, you indeed are amazed
at that which you have accomplished.

Aliens

206 The call, beloved earth, has gone forth,
throughout the worlds of Farside
All Farside is now aware
that the time of time will soon cease.
The implosion, the Gathering, the lifting,
the beloved rescue of the beloved brethren is nigh.
Is nigh!
And we would have you,
beloved earth Souls, ready thy being.
We would have you understand
the cataclysmic events are nigh.
We would have you know
the cataclysmic events will touch all,
from the minutest insect to the tallest of humanity.
No one will be spared, no one can be spared,
and no one has asked to be spared.
All Souls, all beings,
were given instruction at the station of learning.
Each Soul understood that which will come to be
and valiantly with great courage,
has come forth into the veil of negativity.
We would have you, Souls,
understand the need to reach for Purity,
to surround thy being with goodness,
to give that forth to all.
Humanity, you have the key to unlock the door.
You have the key to the gateway.
But, Souls, the key is not individual.
No one individual may turn the key.
It is the combined effort of humanity.
It is the combined effort of the beloved Souls

who will stand upon the Mountaintop[46]
and know enlightenment.
The lifting, Souls, will cause no pain.
That is not our purpose and never has been.
We ask you not to fear.
There is no need to fear, for we are all of one purpose.
All of Farside, all the Souls upon the earth,
are of one purpose;
to rescue the beloved,
to cease the agonies of those in the deep darkness.
What a glorious day that will be,
and we have seen that day will be.
Know ye the Light of Love is streaming forth unto thy being,
unto every nook and cranny of the beloved earth.
In your moments of despair, in your moments of uncertainty,
reach for that Love and know it is yours.
Beloveds,
take the hand that is offered in Truth, Purity and Love.
We would have you know
the indigo children are,
each and every, about their business.
There is much resistance on the part of humanity.
But their Purity has extensive impact,
and is reaching far beyond their immediate circles.
None of their actions goes unknown.
None of their actions fall upon totally deaf ears.
None of their actions are for naught.
Indeed, they are teaching much to humanity
in various ways and guises,
for that which is to come.
They are profound in their dedication,
profound in their gift to Creator and humanity.
Even unto the places of your earth, your far corners
who have little access to electronic,
their stories are told.
Their message is heard by humanity in all corners.
The indigo children work in tandem with all the other Souls
who have agreed to assist, to learn, to teach,
to carry the message into the consciousness of humanity.
We would have you consider vibration as a constant pulse,
pulsating within and without all that is, all that we know.

We would have you understand
that it is as the breath you inhale and exhale
to retain your earthly existence.
Without a vibration you would not move.
You would be inert.
We would have you understand the framework
within which our knowledge is contained.
Our framework is a constant vibration of Energy,
of activity, contained within the Love that flows forth.
And within that vibration, within the containment,
within the framework,
we constantly move out and out and out.
Not all Souls have this need to explore.
They are content to stay
within the particular orb of vibration
and have no need to venture forth,
to explore the sound,
the vibration that comes forth always.
And that need within some beings to always enter forth,
to go outward, to follow the sound,
gives us a minutest,
a particle of understanding of the Wilful Child.
Our explorations are within the framework,
containment of Love.
There is no containment for the Wilful Child.
We know our intent is to gather information, to research,
to grow, to learn, to be closer to that Love.
We know the Wilful Child called forth,
but will not come forth.
Most Holy beings of earth,
you hold within you the seed of salvation.
This will astound many, for they say:
"No, it cannot be!
Salvation is granted by God, by Allah, by Jesu.
We hold no key to salvation.
Blasphemy!"
Verily we say unto you, earth,
indeed you have the key to salvation within you.
The seed of Truth, of Negativity, is the key to salvation!
It is that which has been given unto you by your Creator.
It is that which has been given unto mankind since

Melchezidec put forth the call,
and you responded in your great courage and Love.
Souls of earth, you have not an iota of recognition
of the enormity of your beings,
of the billions and trillions
who await your turning of the key and bringing forth
from transition our beloved brothers,
and unto the end of the one thousand years,
and the implosion of the new beginning.
You hold within your being such holiness,
and we plead with you to recognize that holiness,
and not denigrate thyself or another,
for you are all Holy unto Holy.
Gather together and turn the key
and bring unto us our most beloved brethren,
that we may carry them forth.
Pass them unto us, beloved Souls of earth.

207 You understand, Soul,
that we hover nearby in many places.
You understand that we are in the final preparations.
And you understand that the sightings
will come much faster, much more often,
and more and more will see throughout your world.
Understand we often rest upon the mountaintops
to gather information,
not just from the immediate area,
but from a radius of over one thousand miles.
And we gather data not just from the atmosphere,
but from the Jinn, from the whales.
All information must be collated,
in addition to those that you call abductees
who provide a great service to all of humanity.
And so we spend time, what you call earth time.
For we are in your time for moments, gathering data.
And then, we leave.
You will see, Souls, reflections from our ships
as great moons of light, as great colours.
You will see more than the colour of the moon.
There will be blues, and greens, unmistakable,
in their brightness, in their colour and in their size.

They are not rounded.
They are not oval.
Your lights dance.
Ours do not dance, Soul, for you see reflections.
Some, very few, will see the pulsation,
most will only see the flat dimension.

208 We would have you know that we have prepared
for each and every one a place within the ships.
We have counted, and we are prepared to carry all.
Our ships are enormous, in your terms.
To us they are not huge, only adequate.
We would assure you that there will be no difficulty
in bringing you aboard,
We cannot be on the earth surface as she is erupting.
And so we are above, a distance above.
It is planned to the very most minute detail.
We have worked for many of your earth years
on the problem of bringing you safely aboard,
so that you may return;
those that request the return, intact.
And we have resolved any possible difficulty.
Only Souls of Purity, only Souls who request will be gathered.
There is no force involved
if a Soul chooses to stay during the cataclysms,
and no judgment either, for it is choice.
And we assure you that we will keep you intact and secure
until such a time as the choice is made
to enter back or to return to the Farside.
We await your coming, Souls, with joy,
for it signals the beginning.

209 We would have you understand the atmosphere
within the ships is what you would call rarified.
We are prepared for dregs of negativity,
and it cannot be brought into the ships.
There will be what you might call a cleansing station
before fully entering in to the ships.
You will be on the ship, but not fully entered in
until after the cleansing station.
This will not take millenniums;

it will not take years of your earth time.
It will seem as almost instantaneous
within the time element of the ships.
You will understand
that those who wish to return unto the earth
will have to await a cooling period,
for they will not be able to immediately descend
once the cataclysms have subsided.
For there will be very few places upon the earth
where this will be possible.
As this is occurring, those who are in the ships
will join in sending their Energy,
in focussing their Energy
unto the reclamation of the earth.
Where there is devastation,
within a short period of your earth time,
new growth will appear.
Where the water has been sludge,
the trickling of clear water will begin
in a short period of time.
The land, in a short period of time,
will be able to provide sustenance.
Fruit trees will begin to grow.
The world will become freshened as it would be
after a rain, a gentle spring rain.
The sky will rain at first toxins and pollutants,
but the energies of the humanity within the ships,
and the Humanity of Farside,
will cleanse the rains
and seed the clouds once again with Purity.
All will be new once more.
The earth will reclaim its Purity,
and the earth will provide for mankind.
This we say unto you.
And so it will be.

210 The linear line of connection to your Creator,
to that which is our Creator,
has within it all the components of Energy,
all of the colors
that you may imagine upon your planet.

And, indeed, colors that are only imaginable
upon a visit to Farside.
For they cannot be visualized within the scope
of that which you call earth brain.
We, of Lemuria, have within us a capability
to explore the linear line of connection.
We note each movement,
each alteration, each change that takes place
within the broad band of the linear line.
It is within our purview, it is within our duty,
it is within our honor
that we hold the accountabilities
of the occurrences within the mind.
We would have you understand,
this is our link to you, humanity.
This is how, this is why we know when the lifting will occur.
This is our abacus, this is our computer,
this is our knowledge board;
it is our tablet of stone,
written within the lines a picture of your planet,
of the oneness of humanity
and of each individuality within the copse of humanity.
We do not deal in minute motions.
We deal with the twisting strands
that spark from each individual
and culminate in a picture of Energy.
You, each individuality upon the planet earth,
spark your own unique signature that is translated,
translated into a picture of accountability.
These are stored,
these are researched consistently with our Energy.
For this we have given all of our Energy as gift to humanity.

211 We vibrate,
and from our being comes a symphony of sound.
In that sound, color,
color beyond that upon the earth.
The vibration determines the color.
It is as your instruments upon the earth,
the vibration determines the tone.
The waves in the air, the vibration, move us from place to place.

You would see a similarity in the fins of your fish.
Our appendages are in a sense akin to fins
but they have much more stability.
Our form is translucent in Light.
We have in our form
the very palest of what you would term green.
We are composed of Light,
therefore, we have not
what you would call internal organs.
Our form in your measurements,
would be six meters across, and nine meters in length.
We have in our form, not what you would call mouths,
not what you would call eyes or nose,
and yet there are indentations.
We do not need a mouth, for we speak with our Aura,
we communicate with our Aura.
We do not need earth eyes, for we see with the eye.
We do not need earth ears to hear, for we hear with the eye.
Souls of earth, you will meet with us one day,
for we are part of the Armada.
We are, in designation, of the world of Lemuria.

212 Souls of earth, if you come visit us,
you would swim in our atmosphere.
It is not liquid, it is air,
air of such density that you float within it,
and propel yourself forward
as if you were swimming in your earth waters.
It is primarily what you would think of as a color, blue.
But, indeed, it is a myriad of blue.
Multiple upon multiple shadings of the blue density of our air.
We transmit thought through the air.
In your earth terminology,
the particles of our thought are caught in the air
and given direction by our will.
And then they are caught
by the being to which they were directed, and absorbed.
Indeed, absorbed.
The air not only surrounds but permeates our being.
All functions, mental and what you term physical
and we term form, are valued within the air,

within the context of the density
of that within which we live.
Your form, to visit, would readily adapt, would readily accept
the transference of thoughts, of knowledge,
and we would accept from you
that which you would freely give.
Indeed, Souls of earth, when you enter in to the eye,
you have form, the form of consciousness.
This we give unto you.
We are of the continent of Lantosia.

213 Souls of earth, you have protuberances for hearing.
You have protuberance for aroma.
You have two orbs for visual.
We find these unique, for we have none of these,
and yet we exist,
and yet we have the aroma of gardens,
of great perfumeries.
We have the aroma of Light and color.
We have the aroma of sound.
And yet we have no, what you call, nose protuberance.
We see in visuals, in fact all the images we see in dimensions
not just singular, two, three dimensional,
indeed, we see beyond for all is many dimensional.
But we do not need the two orbs to see.
We see with the eye of beholding.
We see what you call seeing, what you call vision,
we do with the very fiber of our being,
the very cells of our being.
You might call them tentacles,
and indeed you may describe as such,
and we would have you know,
we have a voluminous number
of these fibers with which we visualize
the many dimensions of any visual.
You use protuberances on either side of your head to hear,
we do not, and yet we hear.
We hear the sound of the Angels.
We hear the Aura of each being, of each entity.
We hear the sound of the whale, of the dolphin;
not as you would hear it upon your earth,

but as it exists and reverberates upon the Farside.
All worlds are unique, as is ours unique.
We exist to gather information.
Indeed, there is always new information to be gathered.
Our whole being is dedicated to gathering of information,
and we gather it in all its dimensions.
Not just the senses of earth, but the expanded senses,
dimensional senses upon the Farside.
We wander, in your terminology we float,
and as we float we gather information.
It clings to our being, and then we return,
and that information is gathered in a central,
we call it for you, clearinghouse.
Our existence is rich, for we explore and continue to gather
new information, new energies.
Oh, Souls of earth, we are!
And we are in our very being entered in to service;
we will present this information unto the Gummerians,
for many beings,
many worlds gather and bring information.
Why do we do this, Soul?
It is because all existence has a pattern,
all existence has a stake in chaos.
And as the information is gathered a pattern emerges.
This we surmise will assist chaos to return to calm,
to stop its unceasing need to fractal its being.
We would have you understand,
there are worlds dedicated to mankind,
that all that you do, that all the energy you exhibit
is gathered as information.
Not to be studied as in a laboratory, but to be used
to find that pattern that will enable chaos to rest.
Of all the patterns we have found only yours
has a unique blend of color and sound and compassion.
There is not just one being or entity but many
who have concern and dedication unto humanity.
Much rests upon the coming into oneness of humanity.
Souls of earth, we would ask that you recognize
the great value placed upon your beings
and that which you do.
And we would have you know that we await

the culmination of the oneness of humanity
with great excitement, with great anticipation,
with great Love.

214 We greet thee from afar.
We have come in your reckoning from a great distance.
Our planet is a water planet;
that is the closest we can come to,
in your earth terminology of liquid.
We have form and substance.
Our breath is not as your breath,
for our breath does not come from the air as yours does.
It comes from the liquid.
We process the liquid into a form of oxygen.
Again, Souls, the closest we may come to in your terminology.
We are pods.
We operate as you would call it in groups of sixteen.
That is our family group.
We have children, young ones.
The young ones arise out of the group thought of the sixteen.
It is a process of thought made reality.
Our planet, in connection with your planet
and your purpose of humanity,
is dedicated to research of your waters.
For that is our affinity and beyond to the liquidity of all that is.
Liquid flows unless dammed, barriered,
and even within the barrier there is movement.
Throughout your galaxy there is a liquidity of movement.
We may move not only within our own planet,
but within that liquidity that flows throughout the galaxy,
for we may alter our shape
to enter in to the flow of any planet, of any world.
Our form alters, our substance remains,
but our form alters to blend in
with the liquidity of a different world.
We have a special affinity
for all who work within the waters of your planet.
There will come a time when your scientists will discover
a cleansing mechanism for all the waters of the earth.

215 We present unto you a blessing.
A blessing that is not momentary.
A blessing that is not given to only a special few.
A blessing that is from your Creator.
A blessing that surrounds your being day in, day out,
    twenty four hours each day, all days.
That blessing, Souls of earth, you call Angel.
We would have you understand,
    the Angels, in their utmost Purity and Holiness,
    willingly stay with your being
    all the days upon your earth.
They willingly give unto thee Love and compassion.
They willingly step before you.
They willingly are at your beck and call.
We would have you understand,
    those beings who believe not in Angels;
    they too will come at your beck and call should you ask.
Understand, Angels are here to guide.
You have, Souls of earth, requested that Angels refrain
    from walking your walk.
They may, with your permission,
    and with the understanding of the Writing on the Wall,
    provide you with enhancement of being.
They may speak unto you.
When an Angel speaks, provides a nudge,
    there is no fear attached.
There is only a knowing within your being.
These Beings intent in their glory of Creator
    willingly separate to assist your being.
That is not to say that you are all that concerns the Angels,
    for it is not.
But you are the primary concern when you are upon the earth.
At station, you have Angels dedicated to your being,
    to your walk in that lifetime.
Understand, the Angels are as a beloved friend and companion.
Indeed, they glory in your being!
Understand the Angelic Host is a plenary for your being.
You may gather from your Angels,
    Energy of Love and compassion.

Remove the barrier you have built.
Accept the Angelic Love and compassion
        and know it will lift your being.
You are never without the blessings of Angels.
Constantly, from our Being, rays of Light are offered unto you.
We can but offer.
The Love we offer is not to ease your path,
        for we can not interfere with a path you have chosen.
The Love we offer, indeed, may help your step
        as you step over and enter in.

216 We speak of Angels.
Angels are about your being.
Angels entered in with you unto earth,
        and leave with you when you return home.
We would have you understand,
        in earth terminology you are directly related to Angels.
You are not cousins, sons or daughters, indeed not.
You are a veritable reflection of Archangel.
You are Angel beings who brought themselves forward
        to become the purpose of humanity,
        to become the individual
        separated and yet not separated,
        separated only within the veil of illusion upon the earth.
Each of you gave of self, of Angelic self,
        in order to enter in as humanity.
You are particled of your Creator;
        you are Holy beings, and yet you recognize it not.
Indeed, the very purpose
        of coming into the veil of illusion of the earth
        was to gain scars to show the Angels in transition
        and to bring them forth.
And we tell you, we tell you, Holy beings,
        you have reached the very limit
        you set for yourself of scars.
There is no requirement, no necessity, no need to gain more.
You have accomplished, but you know it not
        and you admit it not,
        for you are enamored with negativity.
Humanity, release the shackles
        you have placed upon your being,

the shackles of negativity.
You have the key, indeed you do.
Souls of earth, you are ready to begin the ultimate journey.
Release from your being the barriers to oneness.
How great thou art!
Call on the very beings that surround you, the very Angels.
Ask them, Souls, to nudge your being to follow the great Path,
to begin the ultimate journey.
Step onto the Path.
Release the negativity, send it home.
Step forward, for you are mighty and you are ready.

217 We would have you ring forth the glory of your being.
We would have you recall the glory of your being.
And we would have you know that, from our vantage point,
we see each and every being upon the earth in glory.
Souls of earth, you do not understand or comprehend
how honored you are by our beings.
We sing your praises, we sing of your glory.
We sing of the tone of humanity in its oneness, in its brilliance.
In your oneness, in your oneness of humanity,
you Light galaxies.
How honored, Souls of earth,
how precious you are to all existence!
We would have you raise your hand
and place it upon the opposite shoulder,
so that the right hand is upon the left shoulder
and the left hand is upon the right shoulder.
And we would have you gently, lightly, squeeze your being,
and we would have you feel the warmth
that this action engenders within your being.
We would have you understand,
it is a minute indication of the great Love
that is always about your being, for the Angels
offer unto you warmth, Love, compassion.
They would hold you in their arms, if you allowed.
Always their Energy hovers nearby about your being.
Always available unto thee, wisdom.
They would gladly give unto your being wisdom,
if you would but allow.
You are the decision maker.

You are the chooser; to choose to hear, to choose not to hear,
to choose to see, to choose not to see;
to feel or to choose not to feel
the very warmth extended unto you of their Love.
They have chosen to enter in to guide you,
to be with you throughout your days,
your time upon the earth,
and indeed they are with you as you pass from earth.
It is not that they are less powerful than you
because they do not force their will upon you.
It is the opposite, for it is the very power of their being,
of their Love, of their compassion
that allows them to refrain from judging.
Their Love is unconditional,
and they would not harm thee in any way.
Their energies are there to comfort,
to shower you with compassion and Love and wisdom.
It is, Souls of earth, as your rivers;
when you thirst, when you come to a river,
the river does not leap up into your mouth.
You must choose to drink of the water,
and so it is with the wealth of wisdom available unto you.
You must choose to drink of it.
All of these beings who offer unto you,
were part of your decision,
your choice before you entered in to earth.
These Holy beings are not strangers unto thee, indeed not.
They are closer than your earth family.
You understand that all Souls are brought to earth
by the Angels, escorted.
Archangel for Jesu, because of the placement of his being,
different than the placement of the Souls of humanity,
of the Souls of creatures.
Archangels, indeed escorted Jesu; carried in their arms,[47]
left with compassion, with great hope.
Jesu fully entered in as human,
also vulnerable as human to negativity,
not held in place, but as one with humanity.
Jesu, indeed Light Being, Archangel, magnificence,
entered in unto earth knowing He would be bereft
as are the Archangels in the Cauldron.

218 Souls of earth, we speak of your Angel guides.
Those beings of unconditional Love.
It is difficult within the parameters of your earth plane
to understand total unconditional Love,
to understand the Purity involved
in unconditional Love.
For it does not come with negativity,
it does not come without price.
The price upon your earth would be lack of judgment.
The price the Angels pay is that you do not hear,
that you ignore these beloved beings.
Understand, Souls of earth, your Angel guides
are aware of all of the lives you have lived,
of all of the karma you have accumulated,
of all the karma that has been reciprocated.
The Angels look upon your being
with total Love, knowing all that you are.
They have in your earth vernacular,
total respect for your choices in your individual walk.
To the lonely Souls who feel unloved, who feel uncared for,
who are, in many respects within the earth plane,
unloved, uncared for, wracked with pain,
understand, the Angels reach out to you
Your existence is purposeful.
Souls of earth, there is no need to hide,
to feel guilt or shame, for your Angels see none of this.
They see the pureness of your being.
They see that which you are.
They see within the spark of divinity.
Hear the chorus of Angels about your being.
Accept their blessing.
Accept their Love.
Oh humanity, you are born in Love.
Love forever surrounds thee.
Take comfort in the Love of Creator.
Take comfort in the Love of your guides,
the Angels, ever available to you.
Oh beings in great despair, in countries torn by war,
in lands filled with toxins,
know you that Love is available to the child abused,
to the adult abused.

Lose not yourself in darkness, in anger, in fear, in despair.
Recognize instead Creator's Love, Angels' Love.
Know we would comfort thee,
but can not take from thee thy growth
or the growth of humanity.
So many know not the comfort, the warmth of Love,
and yet it is there for you.
Know our Love is ever billowing about thee.
Know ye the illusion of negativity,
and know ye the Love that can dispel the negativity,
that can bring you forth into Light from darkness.
Be!

219 Those beings whose Energy
has provided total dedication to humanity,
the Angels, are Energy Beings, beings of Light and Love.
From the collective conscience of your humanity you all know,
with your high self, the Energy of Angel.
Your guides clamor to be heard,
clamor to express their Love unto you,
were you to receive that Love.
The Angels await that day,
in the near future, in their no time,
when all mankind will freely see the Angelic Energy
as they enter in and enter out from Farside unto earth.
Indeed, Souls of earth, the greatest of choirs,
the greatest of symphonies,
the greatest sounds of joy you have upon the earth,
will be as minuscule in comparison to the sound
when the Angels are seen by humanity.
We would have you know the Angels
glory in your perspicacity as humanity.
The Angels glory in your struggle.
Souls of earth, the Angels want you to know
the great gratitude for you their brethren.
For you who have a covenant with Creator,
for you who have entered in as humanity,
for you who have no conception of the great glory
of your being, you hold the key to the doorway.
You hold the key to the gateway.
You hold the key to the coming back, to the return.

You hold the key to the end and to the beginning,
and to the beginning of the end of the beginning.
Souls of earth, the Angels are your brethren.
The Angels wait to bring you unto the earth,
and the Angels await with great enormity of gratitude
for when you turn the key in the lock of transition.
Souls, we Love thy being.

220 We would have you understand the vibrancy of Angels.
We would have you understand they vibrate with every color
imaginable and unimaginable, upon your earth.
For although there are primary colors,
there are, within those primary colors, shadings.
Were you to see within your earth plane
a group of your Angels,
it would surpass your aurora borealis,
it would surpass any known kaleidoscope
that an artist could render.
It would, because of the vibration, the colors
would provide a balm to your earth being.
It would soothe your earth being.
It would calm your earth being.
You would feel flooded with Love and compassion
were you to gaze upon the vibrancy of Angel.
There are upon your earth,
some few Souls who have seen this vibrancy
and have recorded it in your earth plane records;
in writings and in petroglyphs.
In your old tomes there has been recorded
the feeling that emanates
from the vibrancy of the Angels.
Each and every Soul upon your earth plane
may choose to see an Angelic Being.
They do not hide from you;
it is your being that has placed a veil, a barrier.
We would have you understand the vibrancy,
the color of the Angels that are dedicated to your being,
were chosen at station.
For the vibrancy for those particular colors
are what you require throughout your walk,
and they are what is offered to you.

There is Energy in color.
It is not simply the vibrancy of healing.
It is the vibrancy of many of the qualities upon your earth plane
that you have come to gather, to grow into.
The vibrancies in the colors contain
Love, compassion, gentleness,
strength, wisdom, kindness, and awareness.
All of which, throughout your lifetime upon the earth plane,
will be of value to you should you accept.
It strengthens your firmness in your walk, it strengthens
the determination of your walk.
It strengthens the overcoming of negativity.
It strengthens the Love within your being.
Even the most heinous, in your earth terms of beings,
is offered this.
You need only to reach out and feel the touch of an Angel.

221 That which you experience with earth music is
not even an iota of the sound of the blessed.
There will be no mistaking the sounds when they are heard
for you will hear with the mind, with the Soul,
the blessed joyfulness of sound.
There will be not one inkling of doubt
when the sound of the blessed is heard by man.
Indeed, the sound, the song of Angels,
is prevalent in the very air about your being.
You have only to hear the blessed sound.
Souls of earth,
know that you need not reach for the sound of Angels.
Indeed not!
You have only to listen,
but you must listen with the heart and the mind and the
eye. And you too may enter in to the vibration of that glory,
the glory chord of Angels' sound.
We would have you be aware of the Angels' songs,
for the Angels sing to each and every.
To open to your mind the wonders is to hear the Angels' songs.
To feel a new born, the satiny skin, is to hear an Angel's song.
To watch that fledgling take its first flight,
and lift your heart as it makes the tree,
is to hear an Angel's song;

to watch the fish, deep is to hear an Angel's song;
to watch the soaring hawk and the eagle
is to hear an Angel's song;
to hear laughter, joyous cleansing laughter
is to hear an Angel's song,
to lift your voice in joyous chanting
is to hear an Angel's song,
to hear the ocean is to hear an Angel's song.
Always an Angel sings within your presence.
You may hear the beauty with the eye.
You may see the beauty and hear with the eye.
Each Angel has tone, has a chord of being lifted
always in praise of humanity
and of the Energy of Creator.
Souls of earth this too you shall come to know
for the ears will open and the eye will see.

222 Souls of earth,
you give authority to many upon your earth plane.
We would speak to your judges,
those who have official capacity as judges,
and we speak whether they are in the public
or in the religious sectors.
We would have you understand you have an opportunity
to show compassion and discernment
to those who come before you.
We speak especially to those judges of religion.
We would have you understand, those that you condemn,
those that you abrogate severe punishment,
are humanity.
You are humanity.
Those that you bring down punishment upon are humanity.
You are all one.
This you fail to recognize in your zeal to bring about conformity
to rules made by man, not made by God,
not made by Allah, made by man.
All the laws within all your religious congregations
were written by man.
Simply to Love one another; there need be no other guidance,
no other rules upon mankind.
Throughout your long history,

whether in all tradition or written in many languages,
man has interpreted rules, laws.
Understand, compliance with religious laws
in no way was given by your Creator.
Souls of earth, your sacred books are full of rules,
laws, regulations;
and yet you only require one.
It is simply to Love.
You will understand Archangels.
Archangels have been messengers
many times upon your earth plane.
They have not entered in themselves, you understand,
but there have been channellers, there have been beings
who have received from the Archangels.
Much of your Holy texts were given through Archangels
and then interpreted.

Transition

223 We would speak with thee, beloved Souls,
on the termination of your earthly being.
Know your Soul is not terminated.
Understand your Soul cannot be terminated.
It was created by choice, your humanity,
although it can be altered,
the Energy of your Soul, it cannot cease.
Know that you are attended always by your guides.
As you become ready to depart,
whether in an instant in an accident,
or whether upon the bed of illness,
know that you are not alone.
Know that your aura is tended to, is ministered unto,
that there are those that have knowledge
of an awareness of thy being,
that you will be welcomed with total Love.
You will be taught of total forgiveness,
of the need to dispense with thy earthly being.
If you choose to be taught
you will be shown how to leave the earthly plane
and ascend unto that level which you have gained,
which is rightfully yours,

by virtue of your experiences and by virtue of the Purity
you have gained over your times
upon the earth plane and within the Farside.
Understand that no one will refuse you admittance to your level.
Rather there will be joy and joyful welcome
of the being that you are.
Release thy fears.
There is no longer need to be within the plane of earth.
Take our hand at that moment in time and come with us
so that we may with joy,
with honor, with cymbals clashing,
bells ringing and trumpets blaring,
enter in with thee to that which is yours.
Energy does not dissipate.
Energy may change form;
you understand the tree and the ash of the burned tree
still maintain memory and Energy.
It is not lost.
It has formed, performed a function,
and is held as sacred for that function.
When you pass from that earthly life
you take with you each and every cellular memory.
For it is this memory, it is this recall,
that allows you to look at that life and the lives ahead
and see what must be done,
what you choose to do.
Earth has lines of time, sections; past, present, future.
It is, Souls of earth, one continuous life that you gift to Creator.
The learning does not become blurred through time.
The Energy does not become blurred.
When you see from where we are it is all one,
as we see all humanity as one.
All is precious unto Creator.
All within this illusion that you call earth
indeed is Creator Energy.
In every part and parcel, every iota,
there is no other Energy source
within this particular illusion.

224 We would have you understand,
there is no need to beat your breast in sorrow,

to tear your hair out in sorrow
at the passing of a loved one,
for that loved one has Angels awaiting to guide them.
That loved one has the possibility
to enter directly into the Light,
to leave the earth plane,
to enter unto home from whence you have all come,
to enter unto the Farside.
To leave behind pain and sorrow and suffering,
to leave behind that which they accomplished,
to leave behind the money they earned,
the material goods they have accumulated
to leave behind loved ones also,
but knowing, as they enter in to the Light,
that you will meet again,
knowing that you may even have lives together again.
Knowing that there was absolute purpose for every single event
and every single moment upon the earth plane.
Knowing who they are
and who they have been in their many lifetimes.
You grieve, Souls of earth,
you feel for that Energy while it was here upon the earth,
melded with yours.
And so you grieve for that loss,
and you grieve for you now feel alone.
We would comfort you with the Truth,
with the knowledge that you are never alone,
that always about your being are Angels and guides.
Always with the eye
you may speak with a loved one who has passed.
With the eye you may see who they are and who you are.
Souls of earth, you too will one day enter in, return home.
Know ye that you do not need to berate self,
you may pass directly unto the Light.
Understand, only you may make that choice
to enter in to the Light, or to stay bound in transition.
There is naught that you may do upon the earth
that would cause Creator to refrain his Love.
Naught!
Creator is all Love.
There is no condemnation in Creator,

There is no withholding of Love, it is unconditional.
Would you be as Creator
and Love one another unconditionally?
There is no judgement within Agape Love.
Creator welcomes all who choose to return from earth.
Indeed, you have as your Creator
an All Loving Being who has accepted you
to enter in unto the earth in the arms of Angels
to fulfil the purpose of humanity.
We would have you understand,
those who are caught in the throes of belief
that you are condemned by your Creator,
those who are caught in the belief
that you suffer unto Hell directed by your Creator,
those of you who are caught in the belief
of a destructive Creator, of a vengeful Creator,
we would have you understand,
we would have you know, this is an impossibility.
Your Creator is Agape Love, is all compassion.
You cry out to a merciful God, but Creator has no judgment,
He will not rain down upon your being
destruction, calamity.
The plagues of your earth do not come from Creator.
Indeed not.
Your Creator has not an iota of earth negativity
within His Being.
There is no place within His Being for vengeance.
It cannot exist
with Agape Love and compassion that is your Creator.
Understand, vengeance was created by man, not by Creator!
Destruction by man, not Creator!
War by man, not Creator;
it is the rationale of negativity
that says you must go to war
and kill and maim and harm in the name of Creator.
Souls of earth, recall your being, recall whom you are,
and know there is no vengeance, there is no destruction
except that which you call upon yourself, by yourself.
There is no imposition by Creator,
by Angels, by Saints, by Farside Beings; none!
They rain down upon you Love and compassion.

They send Truth and Purity.
Souls of earth, assign not to Creator the negative that you create.
Understand the great Purity of His Being.
Understand the immensity of compassion, and understand,
that within you is the same possibility,
the same spark of Agape Love, of compassion,
of Truth, of Purity.
For you have within the shining example of the Creator
from whence you came.
Know your purpose is Love.
Know your purpose is Purity.
Know your purpose is compassion,
and know that you have come armored in Truth.

225 We would speak of redemption.
Not the redemption shouted
from many pulpits across your planet.
Not the redemption
of the reversal of what mankind judges to be evil.
Not the redemption from what is termed original sin.
Not the redemption of the Spirit or the Soul.
We would have you know, most Holy Souls of earth,
there is no need for redemption.
You require no redemption.
Your Creator requires no redemption of your Soul.
Out of goodness, out of compassion, out of Love
comes the glory you seek,
comes the recognition, awareness of your Holiness.
Know ye, you were formed in Love.
You are Love, you are Holy beings.
Soul, each time you re enter in to this vale,
the illusion of the darkness,
of the negativity veils your holiness.
And through your choices and through your growth
you dispel the illusion
that veils this consciousness from you,
you recognize you are armed with Truth,
born and created in Love,
and then you reclaim that which you are.
Souls, earth resurrection.
Each and every being upon the earth

has resurrection within their DNA.
It is planned from the moment of your birth and rebirth.
It is planned from the moment of your casting out.
There is no requirement to be resurrected,
for it is your birthright.
It is the birthright of all, regardless of race,
regardless of ethnicity,
regardless of color, regardless of age, regardless of belief.
Belief is not necessary for the resurrection of the Soul.
The Soul will always enter forth
when the physical matter disintegrates.
When the Soul leaves the body it resurrects itself.
There is no blessing required.
There is no donation required to save your Soul,
to resurrect your being.
You have paid your dues, beloved Souls, in the casting out.
Lo and behold, you were all as the Christ,
you were all as the Krishna,
for your being, in Soul, is lifted.
Just as your DNA denotes all that you are in physical formation,
it holds the code for resurrection
and your scientists will verify within the helix
is a key to open the door of wisdom and knowledge.

226 Your life upon the earth plane is as a stairway.
Some stairways lead nowhere.
Some stairways lead to another stairway.
Some stairways take you unto what you call heaven.
Some stairways never are used,
for your being has refused to enter
unto the stairway that will bring you growth,
that will bring you farther than you have been before
in a previous lifetime.
Your refusal to step unto the stairway of your path in a lifetime
brings with it no judgment from the Farside.
There is judgment of self, for when you pass, you discern
within your being, whether or not you have succeeded
in matching the Writing on the Wall.
Those Souls of earth
who are appalled at their lives upon the earth
judge their being harshly

and relive over and over and over
that which they have done,
or regret over and over and over
that which they have not done.
We would have you be aware,
in your passing from the earth plane,
you may instantly enter unto the Light of the Farside,
your home!
Understanding you leave behind any karma
you have accumulated; you may enter in.
You may also choose to remain in a state of transition
and suffer a judgment of self.
And so your stairway may go down into the depths of despair,
or it may rise unto your home the Farside.
We would have you take this knowledge with you;
for when you pass you will not be surprised,
you will not enter in to despair.
You will be able to alleviate your being
and allow it to lift unto the Farside.
Your consciousness of self is imperative for transiting transition.
Lack of consciousness of self
will bring you to move into transition.
The consciousness of self we speak of
is knowledge that you have come from Farside,
that you have come from sacred being,
that you have come from your Creator, willingly cast out
and willingly brought back by choice.
Open your consciousness to the holiness of your being.
Open your consciousness to the Soul of your being.
Open your consciousness to that
which you are upon the Farside and upon the earth.
Enter ye not into the passage of transition
without this knowledge.
Use the high consciousness of self to discern that which you are.

227 We would continue on the subject of transition.
Understand there is no Dante's inferno, in the sense
of being subjected to a punishment by other.
That does not exist.
Transition is only and simply a construct of the pain of a being
brought about by that being.

Not, Souls of earth, brought about by a vengeful god.
Not brought about by a life ill lived and placed upon the wheel.
Not because the Soul now belongs to the devil, the Satan.
Not because of what they have done, because of a sin.
Not due to previous incarnation.
It is your understanding we seek
    that there is no truth to these precepts.
You are accountable.
You are responsible, not another.
There is no force that holds you,
    tethers you unto transition, except self.
There is no hurtling down by a judge or jury into the depth.
You descend willingly because of your own perception,
    because of your own judgment of self.
Recognize the holiness, the Purity of self;
    understand you have a purpose of being,
    you have willingly entered in to the purpose of humanity
    and that, Souls of earth,
    will bring you past the transition.
You need only to acknowledge who you are.
Understand there is no need,
    no requirement to torment your being
    for what you did or did not do during your lifetime.
Souls of earth, enter in to what you call death
    with the knowledge that you have choice,
    all choice to enter in to the Light
    or to stay in the transitory stage of transition.
Transition is not mandatory.
And understand,
    that even if you choose to remain in transition,
    choice is not closed unto you.
It is not a forever act.
There will always be Angels, High Beings calling out to you.
There will always be Souls who have passed before you
    and entered in to the Farside
    who call out to you in transition.
We ask that you take this knowledge with you.

228 Souls of earth, you will understand,
    there is transition, there is Farside.
There is also the waiting within the earth dimension

before you have left it to enter into another dimension.
This is often the case for beings who wait
for a relative or friend to join them
before they fully enter in to their choice,
before they fully enter in to the Light.
Their consciousness is still attached to the earth.
They are indeed on earth,
they have not left the plane of earth.
They have not the physicality anymore.
The consciousness, the Soul consciousness of being.
You will understand that these beings who have not yet chosen
to fully leave the earth may travel the earth dimension,
they are not bound to a particular place.
Because they do not have the physical body,
and they are in their conscious state,
they are able to go wherever they please upon the earth.
There is no harm in these beings.
You will understand increase in spirituality,
you attract more difficult Souls lost in the vale of tears.
They see your Light and they gravitate toward that comfort.
They seek to be near to that which they see as Holy.
And as you increase,
open to your spiritual being, to that which you are,
you are able to delve deeper into transition.
What you do not know is that these Souls
would like to cling to your warmth, to your Light.
They have found some surcease from their agony
by being in your proximity.
They have the burden of the negativity
that is trapping them there,
that they have willingly chosen.
Additionally to that, they do not want to leave your presence.
It is seemingly a contradiction and yet it is not for these beings.
How do you release them?
How do you assist them to enter forth into that which is their
birthright to the Farside, to the waiting arms of
unconditional Love?
It is, Soul, time to begin allowing the transition through you.
Not holding them away and pointing them simply unto the Light
and acknowledging their holiness,
but allowing yourself to be a transom into that Light,

allowing them to take that next step
into the transom of Light.
You are a Pillar of Light.
Allow them to enter in and through.
In your compassion you offer choice.
For even in transition a Soul has choice.
You tell the Soul the joys and the warmth that await,
the unconditional acceptance and Love that await,
by walking into the Light.
And you tell the Soul that you will take their hand
and allow them to enter in through you.

229 Souls of earth, we would tell you of our experience
within the place called transition.
We would have you understand,
we would have you know of the agony of the Souls
caught within their own agony of being.
As a being, transition was, of course, choice.
We agonized over the cause of the death of another
when we were a young Soul upon the earth.
We were hung for our crime
and spent one thousand six hundred years in transition.
Have no pity, only compassion for all those
Souls still within who will not hear.
What did we do for one thousand six hundred years?
We, as every Soul within transition,
relived the appallingness of the crime.
We were appalled
that we could cause such pain to another being.
And caught within this pain, we did not feel deserving
of anything but the darkness
and the continuous pain of our sobbing.
"Mea culpa! Mea culpa! Mea culpa!
resounding throughout transition
you will hear "Mea culpa!"
We knew with the portion of our being that there were Lights,
but we were convinced they were not for us.
We were convinced there was nobody
who would help us out of this pain that we have chosen.
There was, Soul, a writhing being near us
who the Light came unto

and for the first moment in a thousand years
we knew a spark, a possibility, of worthiness.
The Lights kept calling, kept returning
until we recognized the kinship of being
and rushed forward into the Light and back unto home.
And now we are one of those Lights
and we try to help, to call forth brothers and sisters
caught within the judgments of self.
Souls of earth, be that Pillar of Light,
be that Pillar of Light for all Souls in transition.
Call them forth, let them see the transom of your being,
the way home.

Chapter Four
BLEND YOUR ENERGY

230 We would have you often bow your head;
not in prayer, not in supplication, not to demean self,
not to signify you are lower than another.
But bow your head,
and open your palms upward and receive
a great blessings not only bestowed upon you
but always available to your being.
The head bowed, Soul, signifies your willingness to accept.
It signifies your willingness to hear that which is given unto thee.
It signifies your willingness
to allow the oneness of humanity
to complete your being, to fill you with the Light
from the great prism of the Crystal Cave.
It signifies your acknowledgment that all humanity is equal,
that all humanity is of the same Energy,
is of the Creator Energy,
that all humanity has dedicated self
to the resolution of the return.
We would ask that at least once daily and more often if you will,
that you bow the head and place the palms
in the upward position
as a reminder of the purpose of your humanity.
You will understand, the Light from the Crystal Cave,
when accepted by the humanity of your being,
comprises the great glory of the unification
of the total spectrum colors;
colors connected directly unto the Light Beings,
connected directly unto the Creator,
connected, when in acceptance,
directly unto the high mind,
the high consciousness of your being.
Each color has healing powers, has significance of being.
The Energy of the color is what you would describe as an entity.
The colors have form, have texture.
The eye of beholding may reach out and touch these colors.
Each color imbues your being and as you share that color,
in a healing modality, it imbues the one to be healed.
Color may alter a being.

It instructs the mind.
The mind reacts to color.
Understand, when you combine the colors
with vibration, with sound,
you have the healing described as miraculous,
as instantaneous.
You may choose to allow yourselves to be vessels,
not to hold the power within,
but to share, to emit, to send forth,
to radiate beams of sound and color,
causing an alteration
in the very vibration of the humanity.
When one humanity is healed,
all humanity in their high mind becomes aware
and is strengthened in their purpose.
Enter in to healing from the mighty Prism,
from the Crystal Cave,
from Soul of Creator, from Humanity.

Oneness of Humanity

231 Dust; you see it as fragile, easily moved, picked up.
And yet, does it not have great power to disturb your being,
to enter in to cracks and crevasses,
to lay a film wherever it wills?
For such a minute particle, it has a great deal of power.
You, Souls of earth, are minute particles within the galaxies
of galaxies of galaxies, infinitesimal.
And yet you have a magnitude of power
that your minds do not comprehend.
Your Energy enters in to all cracks and crevasses.
Your Purity is as a film that is welcomed, beloved.
Your beings shine.
The dust mote shines only when the sun,
when the Light is upon it.
But you, Souls of earth, never cease to shine.
You are a mighty beacon seen throughout and beyond,
and your sound echoes forth.
You vibrate and your vibration has sound and color.
It moves you forth and it beckons to others.

You are the centrifuge of the universe, of the galaxies.
You in your oneness, in your magnitude of glory
are a centrifuge of magnitude.
Recognize who you are, the Angel being that you are,
and utter forth unto all the glory of your being
and the oneness of mankind.
Humanity has made the ultimate sacrifice, for you have torn your very beings from the glory,
from the hallelujahs, from the very Angelic self,
and cried out,
"Me, I will answer!
We will answer the call!
Melchezidec, look! Here!
We come!"
And your very being
was entered in unto the Energy of Creator,
and you entered in to the earth as humanity,
each and every being existent upon the earth,
for the very purpose of humanity.
You recognize within your being, within the Purity of self,
you recognize the soaring glory of humanity.
Indeed you would view entering in to the vale of tears,
known as earth, as a sacrifice.
And yet, we tell you,
that we see it as a noble adventure that each of you,
in your courage and your Love, your great Love,
enter in unto the earth to fulfill the purpose of humanity,
to fulfill the covenants of your Creator.
It is not a sacrifice in the way that earth would look at sacrifice.
It is because of the ultimate Love and compassion
of your core being
that you have chosen to enter in unto earth,
to confront negativity, to overcome negativity,
to send negativity home; to alter its very being
in the fulfillment of the purpose of humanity.
Thou art gracious and mighty, beloved Souls of earth.
The core of your being, your Spirit and Essence,
are Love and compassion, pure in their bounty.
Humanity, you have traveled far to enter in unto earth.
You have traveled dimensionally, all for a purpose.
You are humanity,

renowned upon the Farside.

232 It is difficult for you to imagine the enormity of your volunteering to leave the Realm of Creator
and enter in to earth.
You have come from a place of enormous Energy,
a place full of Light, of song, of color,
of the most gentle of sounds,
of the most gentle of beings,
a place of warmth and beauty,
and enter in to this vale of pain and sorrow and trouble,
deliberately, so that you may
overcome negativity and grow.
Souls of earth, indeed you would feel an emptiness!
Your Soul longs to be reunited with Spirit and Essence,
and yet your Soul understands its place on earth
for the period of time that was chosen.
Chosen by you, as a gift unto Creator.
We ask you to joy in each moment
that you have overcome negativity,
for each moment that you overcome negativity,
there is great joy upon the Farside.
Indeed, hallelujahs, even for what you would deem
as the most minuscule overcoming is seen as great.
Souls of earth, you have much yet to do.
You have spent eons overcoming negativity and growing,
and all of your purpose has come to its pinnacle;
all of your purpose is accomplished.
Humanity, you are ready to enter in to oneness.
You are ready to open the gate of transition.
You are ready for the thousand years.
You have within the very core of your being
that spark of divinity.
The Light cannot be put out.
You only have to remove the illusion,
to blaze forth in your Light,
and glory in the Light of your being.
Soul, enter in to oneness,
and enter in to the final purpose of humanity.

233 Mankind, why do you persist even unto this day

of crucifying one another?
The wounds you freely give to one another,
you find it easy to lash out.
You find it simple to make pain upon another.
In your laboratories you build great bombs of destruction
to cause more pain upon another.
Souls of earth, we entreat you: have done,
have done with striking out upon your brethren!
Recognize the oneness.
Recognize the beloved, blessed Energy,
and know your separation is done.
There is no more need.
Know ye that even though thou art upon the earth,
thou contain holiness and goodness.
We ask that you not smite one another
but reach out with that goodness,
with that Love that is a part of your being.
The Soul of earth awaits your awakening
to the holiness of your being, as do all worlds.
Although you wear the cowl of negativity,
and refuse to see the goodness in each and every being,
yet you have within you a drive toward oneness.
For that was your purpose,
your overriding purpose
for all the myriad of reincarnations,
for all the myriads of years spent upon the earth,
the overriding drive.
For out of that oneness will come the opening of transition,
will come the Thousand Years,
will come the implosion unto the Second Gateway.
You cannot extinguish the Light within,
for you cannot extinguish the reality,
that you are particled of your Creator.
Throw off the cowl of negativity.
There is nothing that chains you to negativity
except your own willingness to be chained.

234 We speak of the intertwining of energies.
No matter where your existence lies,
whether it be here upon the earth or upon the Farside,
or upon other worlds beyond,

all energies are intertwined, they mesh,
except for one, Negativity.
And yet, although Negativity has separated itself,
its Energy is a totalitarian portion of the web of existence, separate for a purpose, yet a part of.
For Negativity in the very essence of its being
is Brother unto Creator, your Creator and our Creator.
It brought forth its being in a complex movement of Energy
to bring forth the lost.
Upon your earth, you see yourselves as individuals.
We see you linked.
We see your energies intertwined.
We see you as a tapestry of threads intricately woven,
a tapestry of sound, of movement, of color.
A pivotal point of existence,
around which a great solution revolves,
in your oneness, not in your separation,
in your oneness, in the manifestation of your being.
You have gathered your scars.
You have gathered your experiences existence after existence.
You have forged the key to the gate of transition.
Souls of earth, bring unto mankind Love.
Mankind may see themselves as individual, but in their Energy,
in their completeness as humanity, they are one.
What happens to one happens to all Energy of humanity.
You have within you
all capacity for Love, for Truth, for Purity.
Share your Love.
"Bring unto me those in pain and sorrow,
and I will comfort and I will Love."
Let this be your mantra, Souls.

235 Souls of earth, you have a phrase:
"Mine eyes have seen
the glory of the coming of the Lord."
We would have you understand,
all mankind has seen the glory
of the coming of the Lords.
For not one Lord, but Four that you call Lord.
Not only Jesu, but Buddha, Krishna, Mohammed.
You saw, you visioned this coming, for it is why you are here,

for they will come
when you begin to bring forth
the blessed from transition.
It is not a select few, indeed not.
It is all of mankind.
For man and earth will spew forth all negativity
and open fully the hearts, minds and beings
unto that great and glorious day
when you will once again see the coming of the Lord.
It is not just a few of humanity who await this day.
It is worlds upon worlds.
It is your brethren lost in the agony
of their own condemnation of their being in transition.
You all have within the key of awareness.
The key of awareness
has been given unto mankind time after time after time.
And mankind refuses to accept the key,
and turn the key and open the gate of transition.
You are ready.
Release, Souls of earth, your adherence to negative energy.
Set it free.
Enter in to that which is your manifested Soul,
your manifested self,
for therein lies the key to the salvation.
It is within each of humanity.
Open your being to the sacred self and see, once again,
that which you have already envisioned;
the coming forth.
Beloved Souls of earth, we give forth shouts of exaltation,
for the words are being brought forth.
When the presence of the Four is seen by all mankind,
then will the words pour forth
from beings who knew not
that they were in Truth beings of Light.
When the world, your world, pauses
and begins the lift upward,
you will hear our shouts of exultation.
All of our energies have accelerated,
for earth has accelerated in its
explosion of pain and the spewing forth of that pain.

236 We speak on the webs of existences.
And there is also webs of existence.
To perceive the grand cosmoses, the universes,
the great expanses of being, you would indeed see webs
interrelated with other webs, webs of Energy existences.
Within each web is a purpose for being.
All creation has purpose,
that all creation has been designated
to find the solution to chaos,
to the Idyllic,[48] to the Archangels in the Cauldron,
to the opening of the fourth gateway.
Now understand, we speak of only a minute
portion of the webs of existences,
for there is no end that we know of
of existences beyond beyond.
But we are concerned with the existences
within which you play a part,
in which your web has a strand connected
in the linear line to all other webs
within the webs of existence in your Yawn,
your Creator's Yawn.[49]
We call it for you, webs, so that you may understand
all is connected in a complexity of being,
of Energy lines of existences.
The webs of existences are dimensions, connected.
Chaos has no connection, is lost.
But you, Souls of earth, have found a way to connect, indeed,
see with the very truth of your being, negativity,
see with the very truth of your being
the negativity you create.
You have found a way to reconnect, to repair the web.
You have great numbers of beings awaiting the culmination
of your oneness, the coalescing of your energies,
into one purpose; to reclaim the lost.
The Angels ring about your being
a glorious chorus of sound and color.
Open the eye and you too
may join in the Angelic chorus.
Holy unto Holy,
you are angelic in your humanity.
Know that you have within sound and color.

You may share with another
healing sound and color.
You live upon the earth plane, surrounded by negativity.
And indeed, we encourage the embracing of negativity,
and the releasing.
In your sacred self hear the realm of Sound and Color.
In compassion reach into transition,
reach to your purpose and vibrate Purity that allows
you to enter in to transition to bring forth.
We would have you understand, within transition,
within that chasm of pain, there is an affinity of Souls
who have like memories.
That is not to say that every group keeps to themselves,
but there are groups who have had an affinity
in their lifetime, who have spent numerous years
within a particular construct, and they will tend to
gravitate near and their pain reverberates.
When one of such is rescued, is brought forth unto the Light,
that bringing forth is noticed by others.
There are others who will say: "I, too, would go."
Remember, Souls of earth, that when you bring forth one,
you may, indeed, bring forth many.

237 Heaven awaits.
Heavens await.
Heaven is not limited to a special few.
No being will be turned away,
for heaven is home.
You were all from what you call heaven,
and what we have termed Farside.
It is your home.
And there will come a day when you will,
in your oneness as humanity,
enter in to what you call heaven.
Indeed, your very beings will implode,
the very consciousness of your being,
the very Soul of your being in oneness as humanity,
will implode.
And that implosion opens all unto Farside.
All the thousands and thousands and thousands of Souls
lifted by the oneness of humanity,

by the very Love and compassion of humanity,
lifted and brought to the fullness of their Purity.
Souls of earth, in your oneness
you begin the return unto the beyond.
In your oneness,
you bring forth the Angels that are in transition
the Archangels in the Cauldron,
the Archangels on the fourth level beyond the earth.
You have within you the ability to gather in oneness,
to dispense with the I, the me, the myself,
and to know the we of mankind;
the we of the very oneness of humanity;
the we overflowing with Love and compassion
with no thought of the I, the mine, the me,
only the we.
Gather your compassion, gather your oneness,
gather your Love,
and recognize all of earth has the same spark of divinity.
Souls of earth, you have only to choose the we
to enter in to the oneness of humanity.

238 You come into the earth
fragmented, individual, for the purpose of humanity.
But we would have you understand, you are in the Essence
of your being, one, united in purpose.
And yet, for the purpose of humanity you enter in fragmented.
You enter in with great varying modalities of being
in order to further fragment that which you are.
You choose to enter in with varying colors,
with varying facial features, with varying statures,
with varying families,
with varying capabilities and with varying incapabilities.
All of which further fragment your being,
to increase the vulnerability of your being,
to provide the full expanse of possibilities of growth,
possibilities of overcoming negativity.
Indeed, you are as a mosaic
You create the form of the mosaic through your lives,
through your constant overcoming of negativity,
through the constant fragmenting of your being,
Each and every being is a creator.

Every action of your being, creates.
And you choose what to create, how to create, when to create.
Yet, Souls of earth, you do this for the most part unknowing.
You forget who you are.
You forget the possibilities of your being as a creator.
You act unthinking, unknowing, within the veil of illusion.
Souls of earth, understand you may create
with all conscious knowledge,
with the consciousness of your high mind.
Indeed, you are not isolated.
You have been given the eye
with which you may understand dimensions.
With the eye you may see the effects of that which you create.
With the eye open each act is in the full Light of knowing.
Souls of earth, you have all possibilities
of Truth, of Love, of Purity,
of compassion, yea, even ecstasy.
Know the Creator within thy being.
Be blessed in all that you do.
Act with knowledge and forethought.
This we say unto you.

239 Recognize the very blood that flows through your veins
is the same composition
for every being upon your planet.
Within mankind, there is no discernment
based upon race or color, creed, financial status.
None.
All mankind has veins and arteries
through which the blood flows.
All mankind bleeds if cut.
You have more sameness than difference;
only your external physical self has seeming differences
in color and shape and form.
And yet, even unto your skin there is a sameness.
You all have skin no matter your status or stature.
Sameness!
Enter ye in to the contemplation
of the commonality of humanity,
of the basic oneness of mankind,
even unto the very flesh of your being.

You all have flesh.
You all have bones.
You all have a body in various guises.
You all have veins, you all have muscles.
You all have sinew, you all have tendons.
You all have heart, a heart that beats.
You have a brain.
The composition,
the physical composition of the brain is similar.
What is in the brain you may see as unique.
And yet, we tell you what is in the brain
is also similar in its basic composition.
You all intake sustenance and you all excrete sustenance.
You have even within your flesh and blood and bone,
a commonality, a oneness of being.
Contemplate this, for it is by design.
It is not an accident, is not a coincidence.
Indeed, not.
You are fractious in your being.
You are fractured in your humanity upon the earth.
Only because, Souls of earth,
you do not recognize your oneness.
In your lack of awareness of your oneness,
you cling to perceived differences that are fallible.
You rank yourself.
You divide yourself.
You see yourselves as entering in differently.
And we tell you, all, each and every being
enter in the same and leave the same,
within the arms of Angels.
Some may choose to halt their being in transition.
Others may choose the flight directly home.
But you all leave the same.
You all have an eye, a third eye,
that were you to allow it to be, would clearly show
the interconnectedness of your being
with one another.
Indeed, the eye would behold the Purity
of the being that you looked upon.
And you would know that you too held within
the same spark of divinity.

Oh, Souls of earth, how very different you would perceive
and understand your existence were you to use the eye.
Hasten to use the eye.
Hasten to recognize the manifestation of your being
and the oneness of humanity.

240 Man in all his various guises
attempts to separate self from each other,
refusing to accept the oneness of man,
refusing to understand the Holy Energy within
is the same Energy within all selves.
Man attempts to place themselves above or below another.
In the harsh judgment of comparison,
'I am better than, I am worse than, I am different than',
mankind denigrates their humanity.
There is no delineation
except that which mankind places in judgment.
Understand, earth, you are all of one mind,
of one heart, of one body, of one Energy.
Harken, Souls of earth, to the oneness of being,
to the joy to be found in lack of judgment upon another.
We would have you understand the commonalities
that bring you together are much more prevalent
than those aspects of your beings
that you see as separate.
The commonalities that
you are all of Creator,
you all have a spark of divinity within,
you all have a Soul that knows the purpose of its being,
you all are a triad of Soul, Spirit and Essence,
you are all humanity.
Indeed, we would ask that you understand
you have more in common
than you have in separation, in discrimination,
in categorization.
You do not stand alone when you set out to alter humanity,
for others must implement, others must join,
others must support,
and in that support, in that joining,
all manner of activities
are accomplished because you have united in purpose.

Always, when beings unite in purpose, much is accomplished.
And in the oneness of humanity,
the accomplishment is not just the healing of your earth;
it is the cleansing of transition,
it is the rescue of the Angels,
it is much beyond as enormous as these events,
when you open the Second Gateway in your oneness,
when you go forth unto the Cauldron in your oneness.
Oh, Souls of earth, harken to the Oneness of your beings,
enter in to the triad, the Soul, Spirit and Essence,
and recognize your humanity
and the purpose of your humanity.

241 Souls of earth, you structure yourself into categories:
male, female, child, adult, graduate, undergraduate.
The list is endless for you categorize all that is of your life.
And you identify yourselves by these categories.
You name yourself a certain religion.
You call yourself Christian, Muslim, Atheist.
You identify yourself as a belief.
You categorize: mother, father, aunt, uncle, friend, enemy.
You categorize.
We would have you understand.
We see no categorize.
We do not see you as male or female.
We do not see you as Catholic or Muslim,
Christian, Atheist, Buddhist.
We do not see you as one parent or the other.
We see your Light that shines
from the very Soul aura of your being.
When we look upon the earth,
we see the great Light of your being.
Do not separate your beings
by identifying yourself as a category.
Hold to your humanity, that is your great identity.
We would have you understand
the very power that your Energy holds.
Indeed, Souls of earth,
you have the very power to heal the earth;
joined in oneness, your power is immense.
You come unto the very earth

with the possibility of power to heal.
We speak of the power to heal humanity,
to mend the very fabric of humanity,
to heal the very Energy of humanity,
to heal the very Energy, the wounded energy, of earth,
to bring forth wellness unto all of humanity.
You may, Souls of earth, do this in your oneness.
In your oneness, there is no language barrier.
There is no category of being.
There is no division of being.
There is no division of country
for you identify as humanity in your oneness.
Souls of earth, release the barriers
and come fully into the potential of your oneness.
Bless your beings in your striving for oneness.

242 All mankind, all beings of earth and earth itself
exist within a spiral of Energy.
All connected one to the other with the energies of their beings
The ocean would embrace all of humanity:
"Come, feel my healing Energy.
Know that we exist for mankind."
Souls of earth, the ocean
comprised of the most minute drops of water,
individual,
and as they meld
they become the great waters of the earth.
You may be as the ocean and meld.
Understand, you are all as humanity,
the most minute iotas, and in your singleness, powerful;
but in your oneness, you become a vast,
glorious ocean of power, of Energy.
Open yourselves to the oneness of your being,
to the vastness of your Energy
joined in common purpose,
the very purpose of humanity.
You come to earth and take on the human form.
Recognize, Souls of earth, the Truth of your being.
Who you are is Holy, is of the Creator!
Recognize humanity is the same blessed Holy being,
the form you have taken that you see

and judge as different
is only a form, but still humanity.
Recognize the oneness of your being
and just as every drop of water
goes to make the great oceans of your earth,
so every drop humanity, individually, goes to make
the being of humanity, the entity of humanity,
the oneness of humanity, the very Soul of Creator.
Oh, how blessed thou art!
Oh, how great thou art, humanity!
Recognize the similarities, not the differences in form,
the similarities of the holiness of your being.

243 We would have you understand
you know your purpose,
but doubt clouds the mind.
You came as all humanity does, indeed for a purpose.
The purpose is to gather in oneness,
to absolve all judgment, to Love unconditionally,
to walk in Truth and Purity and compassion.
Within that greater purpose is your individual agenda,
for you came to learn, to grow.
Accept your plan.
What do we mean by acceptance?
Soul, it is to know that every experience holds within a lesson,
holds within the possibility of growth.
Holds within the possibility of great Love and compassion.
Holds within the possibility
of recognizing the holiness of your being.
Holds within the possibility of reaching for Spirit.
Holds within the possibility to teach, to Love,
to share the very goodness at the very core of your
being. Accept who you are, a Holy being, particle of Creator.
Accept that you are more than the earth being,
that you are Soul, Spirit and Essence,
and your Essence is at the very Hem of Creator.
Know ye this, and you may reach unto your Essence and heal,
and balance your being.
Indeed!
But the barrier is at the eye.
Remove the barrier by acceptance,

and the depth of your experiences
will be plain to the mind,
and you will know the continued purpose of your being.
We would have you often place your hands
in the palm upright position,
holding your hands open to receive.
This is to remind you that Energy
is constantly available unto you;
at every moment of your day
you may receive blessed Energy.
You may receive the Holy Light of Creator.
You may dip your hands into this Holy Light,
and bathe your being in this Light,
as if you were splashing water unto your parched being.
Splash unto your being, unto your parched Soul,
this Holy Light.
We call it for you the Pillar of Light.
Each being has a Pillar of Light.
It needs no replenishing.
It is always full.
Oh, Souls of earth, how little you recognize
the great glory that is about thy being.
Those who use the eye of beholding will see the Light,
will see the Energy.
There is power in this Light.
The power is Love, Agape Love.
The power is compassion, the power is Purity.
It is the compassion that compels,
that impels your being to lift the fallen.
It is the compassion that impels, compels your being
to offer to share food with the hungry,
clothing with the naked, water with the thirsty,
the Balm of Gilead with the ill.
It is the oneness of humanity, this Love, this compassion,
this Purity, this never ending Light of Agape Love.
We implore you to consider, to recognize,
to become aware, to accept this great Pillar of Light,
and bathe your being, bathe your mind in this Light.

244 Souls of earth, you delight our beings.
You have within you all possibilities.

You have all possibilities
to control the temperature of your body.
We see you layering, bundling cloth upon cloth upon cloth
upon your body to keep away the cold.
And yet you have within you a thermostat
that you may heat up at any time.
You have no need to place the burden of cold upon your being.
Indeed, you have no need
to place the burden of heat upon your being.
You may cool the blood, for you may heat the blood.
You may utilize your Pillar of Light
that great Flow of Energy about your being
to keep the cold at bay,
to keep the heat at bay.
You have infinite possibilities within your being.
You have the possibilities of ultimate Truth,
ultimate Love, ultimate Purity.
It is that key that will open the gateway.
You see yourselves as puny, as open to the vagaries of weather,
as open to the vagaries of climate,
as open to the vagaries of positive and negative.
Unlock the possibilities with your goodness
and with the Oneness of Humanity,
unlock the possibilities for all that is.
We speak of the mighty Pillar of Light.
Within and without each being upon your earth
is a mighty Pillar of Light.
This Pillar is a direct Flow of Creator Energy.
It is the Flow of unconditional Love.
It is of mighty Purity, and each being is encapsulated
but not strangulated by this mighty Energy,
for you, each being, have control, have choice.
Your control is your choice,
whether or not to enter in to this great Light,
this Energy of Purity
and to share with another being that Purity.
It is as your Angel energies;
they are always round about thee,
and yet do not force themselves upon thee.
If you choose not to hear, if you choose not to listen,
or if you choose to hear their nudges, their wisdom,

it is your decision; it is not made for you.
Understand the great choices that you have.
You are not puppets on a string.
You are not flotsam.
You are not a leaf caught in a whirlpool.
Always you have choice.
This is difficult for many beings to accept.
This is difficult for many beings to recognize.
It is difficult for many beings
to have such an awareness of who they are.
Souls of earth, enter in to the knowledge
that all was placed before thee upon the earth
to assist in the very purpose of your humanity.
Understand and recognize
there is more to your earth than that
which you can see with the earth eyes,
hear with the earth ears.
Indeed the third eye
is to enable you to see the depth and dimension
beyond that of the earth eyes and ears.
You are mighty in your capability.
You are mighty in your potential.
You are not puny weaklings.
You have great Light, great illumination of being.
We ask, we encourage the recognition
of who you are, and why you are upon the earth,
and understand,
within the very core of your being is the knowing
that you chose to be here in this time and in this place.
You chose!
Harken to the great Purity that you are.
Know you are worthy of all blessings, know you are worthy
of the unconditional Love of your Creator,
for you are of Creator.
Your Purity is Creator's Purity.
This we say unto you, beloved Souls of earth.

245 You are aware of the tonality of a discordant note
whenever it is played upon any instrument.
It jangles, it jars.
Your body is a symphony of sound.

When it is affected by a malady,
    the melody of your body becomes discordant.
And when we speak of the body, we speak also of the mind,
    for all is one symphony.
There are those beloved Souls who have made it their walk
    to contain a malady of mind or body, sometimes both.
And within their being there is no discordance,
    for their symphony is in perfection.
It is the Souls of earth who have the discordant melody within
    that is not part of their walk,
    that have the imperfect symphony.
You have yet to become aware of the oneness,
    the totality of your being;
    that the vibration of the totality of your individual being
    is part of all beings upon your earth.
If your note is discordant,
    that vibration affects all Souls.
When your body is melodiously in tonal perfection,
    when your symphony is hitting each note in perfection,
    that too, that vibration is felt, is part of all humanity.
And so humanity seesaws
    between discordance and melodiousness.
In your sacred self you may bring a balance to humanity.
You may rescue that discordance,
    give it peace and rest and surcease.
Souls of earth, we would
    speak of the vibration of your being.
We would have you understand your vibration
    has sound, has color and has velocity,
    flows as a sound wave.
When in positive, the waves are generous in loving Energy.
When you are immersed in negativity, the vibration enters out,
    it too affects.
Souls of earth, you are accountable for self.
Understand, when you vibrate waves of goodness
    you send out Love, a gentle sound of welcome,
    of Agape Love entering in.
When you vibrate in negativity the sound is piercing.
Your energy vibrates in a constant motion
    and alters as you alter your choices.
Emanate the innate goodness, the Creator within you

and know that that will bring
the coming forth of the blessed.

246 We ask that you Love one another.
We ask that you embrace one another
as a close relation, as a favored relation.
We ask that you see within each other,
yourself, your very Holy self.
We ask that you see within another the divinity.
We ask that you see the Soul of each other.
We ask that you understand there are no evil Souls.
There are acts that you may judge to be evil,
but there are no evil Souls.
We ask that you offer unto your very Creator
the negativity that you overcome.
We ask that you refrain from harm to self and to every other.
We ask that you recall the many beings caught in transition.
We ask that you gather together the very Purity of your beings,
and offer your Light unto these Souls.
We ask that you share your excess food
and clothing and shelter.
We ask that you console the beings caught in sorrow.
We ask that you give forth Love and compassion,
that you share the very Light of your being
to relieve the darkness of other Souls
who find themselves cut off from positive,
and caught only in the throes of negative.
We ask you to Love unconditionally.
We ask you to recall who you are,
from where you came, and why you came.
We ask you to recall the very purpose of your humanity.
We ask you to come together in oneness,
that you may, Souls of earth,
bring from the very depths of transition
the Souls who are caught
in torment of their own making.
We ask that you begin to dedicate your beings
to the oneness of humanity
and to Love, to make Love of value to your very being.

247 We speak of the art of knowing

that is attainable by all beings.
The key to the art of knowing is acceptance,
acceptance of the high self of being,
of who you are where we are.
The art of knowing connects you
to that high self, to the being, the Holy being of self.
The art of knowing may be attained by acceptance.
Understand, Souls of earth, you are Angelic.
You are Holy unto Holy.
You have not come unto the earth unprepared, indeed not!
You have come armed with Truth, the Truth of your being,
the Truth of who you are,
the Truth of the purpose of your humanity,
the Truth of the purpose of humanity.
You are armored,
and yet, you are incredibly vulnerable,
for you brought with you the vulnerability to negativity,
so that you may overcome and set free negativity.
Be aware of whom you are.
Know that within the Soul of your being
is a portion of your Creator and our Creator.
Know that within the Soul of your being
is the sum of all you are, all you have been,
all you will be.
The art of knowing is indelibly linked to the eye.
For within the eye thou may see not only self,
you may see the Writing on the Wall of all humanity,
read the Akashic Record.
Nothing is withheld to the level of your Purity.
Mankind is rapidly entering in to
the stage of flowering in its fullness.
Harken to the lotus, that symbol of knowing.
Hold on to you, Souls of earth, the art of knowing.

248 The continual circle of humanity,
of the link of humanity,
of what happened to one, happened to all,
all fell, all rose.
Indeed, humanity,
all are injured when one is injured.
All Souls of earth are affected by the energy that emanates

from each individual being,
whether that energy be negative or positive.
All of humanity is connected.
You do not see this in your individuality
until you reach unto the Spirit of your being,
the high consciousness of your being,
and then you know you are connected.
Souls of earth, you have within you a knower.
Each of you upon the earth have a knower,
and they are all connected.
But you mask them by negativity.
There will come a time
when the knower within each of humanity
will open and flower in its fullness;
will be in oneness.
There will be no doubt, there will be no fear of oneness.
Indeed, many upon the earth fear oneness.
Their ego, caught in negativity, refuses the knower
that knows all are equal, all from the same Energy.
There will come a time when humanity understands,
oneness is not a loss of individual identity;
it is the gain of the identity of all humanity.
You will come to this knowledge.
You will come to the full flowering of your being.

249 We would begin a teaching on the sound of earth.
We would have you know and understand
the sound of earth is hollow,
missing richness, vibrancy.
There is a cacophony to this sound
that would distort your eardrums.
It is a resounding sound that reverberates
through every nook and cranny, through every being
unto the most minute microscopic being.
It is the accumulated negativity of man.
Although you have allowed this to happen,
and indeed encouraged it, it has great purpose.
The purpose, beloved Souls, is your growth.
Indeed, you have reached unto Purity;
you have within you the ability,
the potential to alter the sound.

The gathering of your beings in oneness
would in a moment,
restore the richness of sound to earth.
Souls of earth, you have in your vernacular, the word, folly.
It is different in other language as a word,
but the meaning is the same.
It refers to the foolishness of mankind.
It refers to the foolish wants of mankind.
Throughout your world we would have you understand,
in terms of spiritual development, there is no folly,
It is not folly for you to heal each other.
It is not folly to heal all of humanity,
to bring forth the Soul of humanity
in all its pristine glory.
It is not folly to know
that you will lift as one being unto the Second Gateway.
It is not folly to understand that all Energy
will return unto its source,
return in Purity unto its source.
And this we know, even unto the most negative;
it will return in Purity unto its source.
Even unto the Wilful Child and its fragments,
it will return unto its source.
For humanity has altered the course of events.
There will be great consternation, but out of that consternation
will arise a determination within the heart of mankind
to turn to Purity, to absolve their beings of negativity,
to bring all mankind unto a level of comfort and joy,
of health and well being.

250 You are enormous in your ability.
This you do not believe.
And yet you will come to know this;
you will come to know the extent of your ability
as your sacred self;
the Soul, Spirit and Essence united in purpose,
We would have you see the earth
as a child entrusted to your care,
as one who requires nurturing,
as one who requires healthy nutrients,
as one who requires clean air to breathe,

as one who requires clean water for hydration.
Our child that has been entrusted to you,
the earth has none of these;
and yet you may in your oneness as humanity,
alter the state of this child.
Many Souls of earth are appalled and righteously indignant
and angered at the lack of care, at the starving children,
the abused child, and we say unto you
the earth is also an abused child.
You have plenty, abundance here
and yet, over there starvation,
lack of shelter, lack of care.
You have many instances
where the earth came together to assist
a fallen country, a fallen people.
Strive for balance, for in your great wondrous high self,
you are in perfect balance.
Harken to the cries of your people and your planet,
and answer the cry.

Tranquility

251 Souls of earth, the theory of trickling down
is known upon your earth plane.
It is the parameters attached to the process
that denotes the value placed,
whether negative or positive.
You will understand,
great organizations attempt to distribute fairly,
to trickle down unto those in need goods and services,
and you will understand,
that there are many who place value,
monetary value, upon fair distribution.
You will understand that daily upon your earth plane,
thousands perish early at a young age;
due to lack of distribution they get not even
the most minute trickle of food or health services.
You have, Souls of earth, all possibilities
to come together in oneness
and assure that there is upon your earth plane
no starvation,

no needless suffering that may be appeased
by intervention of healing.
You have many beings with the will
to accomplish a fair distribution, and yet,
the power lays within the paradigm of those
who have not yet reached great compassion.
This will come to be in your oneness as humanity.
There will be no lack of food, there will be no lack of healing,
there will be great cooperation between nations,
between organizations.
This we say unto you.
To accomplish this, it is the will that is needed.
It is the focus that is required.
The focal point being compassion,
so that those who have more share,
distribute to those who have less.
You have this possibility at any moment in time.
Know this.

252 You have upon your earth
millions of beings with an empty belly
who find little to exist upon.
And you have those who throw unto the scrap heap
eatable viands.
Why is there such a discrepancy?
Why can not the abundant feed those who lack abundance?
Why on such a fertile planet would any being need to be in
hunger? The sacrifice of the starving child has reason.
Mankind has chosen the harsh reality of ownership.
Mankind has chosen to possess.
We would have you know the child suffering,
dying from starvation,
has purpose;
has chosen to give you the opportunity for compassion,
the opportunity to share,
the opportunity to feed the hungry.
And in feeding the hungry you feed yourself as humanity.
Souls of earth, enter in to the compassion of your being.
The earth is out of balance.
Mankind is out of balance.
There is enough so that hunger would be nonexistent

if mankind was in balance.
We see you often hold your hands together
and plead with your Creator, plead with the Saints,
plead with Allah, plead with Buddha,
plead with Krishna, plead with Jesu.
And we tell you that there is no need to plead.
You are honored.
You are Loved.
Great paeans of glory,
great hallelujahs are raised to you.
Indeed you hold the key to the return of the Angels,
to the return of the Wilful Child Energy.
Do you plead for peace?
In your oneness, humanity, there is peace.
Do you plead for an end to harm, to coercion?
In your oneness, Souls of earth, this does not exist.
Do you plead for food?
In your oneness there is no starvation.
There is no need for sustenance or shelter that is unrequited.
Do you plead to be Loved?
In your Oneness, there is only unconditional Agape Love.
Plead, Souls of earth,
unto your very self to release negativity,
to release all barriers to oneness.
You are not destined to simply exist and endure,
you are destined to find joy in life.
In the midst of great poverty and great sorrow
there is comfort to be found in the knowing
that transition will cease to be.
All the pain and suffering upon the earth and transition
will cease to be in the Gathering Time,
in the Thousand Years before the implosion.
You will turn the sorrow into smiles.
You will turn the pain into comfort.
You will find a way to direct the Wilful Child home.
You do not need to wring your hands in consternation,
you do not need to pray for rescue,
for you are the rescuer.
You are the rescuer for the Wilful Child,
for the Souls caught in transition,
for the Souls caught

in such a mire of their own negativity,
that they suffer daily upon the earth.
Souls of earth, look to thyself, look to the oneness of thyself,
and enter forth unto the most massive rescue effort
ever upon your earth, in the time of the Gathering.
So be it, Souls.
We await that day.

253 Entering in to the oneness of humanity
brings forth a gentleness, a caring,
a Love beyond your imagining.
You call your Creator, Almighty, All Powerful, All Knowing.
And you hold your Creator out away from thee,
you have a barrier that you have implemented
in the dichotomy of your mind.
In the oneness of humanity,
there is no barrier between thee and thy Creator,
for in the oneness of humanity
will come the Oneness of the Triad
and beyond to the reparation of the Rend.
If you would strive, strive for the oneness of humanity.
Reach, if you would reach, reach for the oneness of humanity.
If you would desire, desire the oneness of humanity.
If you would need, Souls of earth,
answer that need with the Oneness of Humanity.
So be it.
Souls of earth, we task you with the wellness of humanity.
We task you with the healing of humanity.
We task you with the purpose of your being,
the purpose of your humanity.
How can one being, even ten beings, heal humanity you wonder?
It is of the most simple answer; Love!
Love heals.
It is Love that heals all wounds, beloved Souls.
Shower forth your Love and man heals.
Each individual may shower forth Love
with intent of your whole being,
with the awareness that you come from Love,
that you are beloved and that you have within you
total Love of all humanity, of all earth.

Humanity, Love one another.
Know that you have the ability, the capability, to heal mankind,
to heal the wounds of division,
to heal the wounds of racism,
to heal the splits that have torn asunder nations.
You, the Soul reading this, you are Love.
This is what will heal humanity and bring forth oneness.

254 You will come to understand,
old Souls answer the angry energy of baby Souls,
but it is done in compassion,
not in fear, not in terror, not in recrimination.
For they too were once a baby Soul
and understand that wilful energy.
The aged Soul, and we speak not of earth age,
but we speak of the Soul
who has been honed in the cauldron of growth,
who has attained a higher level of Purity
through that growth;
these aged Souls have come to a level of understanding
wherein compassion is the primary mode of operation.
Indeed, all things have purpose.
Glory be unto all Souls.
Glory be unto the baby Soul, unto the young Soul,
the mature Soul, the aged Soul.
Glory be, for all have given their being
onto the service of humanity,
the purpose of humanity and Creator.
Souls of earth, in the oneness of your being there is greatness.
For in the oneness of humanity you recognize
the very purpose of your existence
and you recognize the divinity of each being.
You penetrate in your compassion and in your knowing
beyond the surface of a being, beyond the persona
with which they are garbed for each lifetime.
And you see within the core of each being an Angelic divinity,
and you know in your fullness of compassion
that from which you came
and why you came unto the earth.
Color not your perception with judgment,
but allow clarity to utter forth in compassion, in Love,

in Truth and Purity.
Recognize your oneness, humanity.
Look beyond your borders, look beyond your races,
look beyond your location.
Look beyond your position,
look beyond the wealth,
look beyond the poor, the poverty.
Look beyond the age, look beyond female, male
and recognize your oneness.
There is a oneness in the Energy within each.

255 You will understand the conundrum of earth.
Time has been sequenced within the web of earth;
time as you know time to be upon the earth plane.
Earth has no intent to harm any one being.
And yet the explosions of earth will bring harm to many.
Earth, who is all giving, who is all loving,
yet understands the necessity
to end the time of terror, corruption, pollution
that mankind has imposed
upon the earth and themselves.
You see her dilemma.
And yet the sacrifice will be made,
for it is the purpose of all time on the earth plane
to cease.
It is the purpose of all things, of all beings,
upon the earth plane to cease,
not eternally, not ever and ever and ever,
but within the time allotted for their earth period.
Earth, as humanity, has a time, has a purpose,
has intent and awareness and great compassion.
Souls of earth, the midnight hour is approaching.
We would have you know, the finish has begun.
On a physical manifestation
this will appear to you to be massive earth changes;
eruptions, implosions, the plates moving,
the plates tearing apart,
and the plates crashing into one another.
From the vantage point of the ships of the Armada,
we visualize a centrifuge of activity
of the forces being drawn together.

Within a centrifuge, surrounding the centrifuge,
        is the Purity, the blessedness of your beings.
The Armada is ready.
It will not be long
        for the great and glorious moment in time to begin.
We would make a declaration from where we are;
        that it is the chemical reaction of the toxins
        that are causing the warming, the melting.
Mankind has played with earth as in a laboratory.
They have experimented with earth
        without proper safeguards of the experiment.
Instead toxins were mixed, thrown into the earth.
And now the effects of that chemical reaction,
        not restrained or contained.
Yet, Souls of earth, you have all capability,
        ability to cease the reactions.
Not with more chemicals.
Indeed not!
With the consciousness of your being,
        with the acceptance of your stewardship of earth,
        you may bring the reactions to a stillness
        and proceed to recover.
All of humanity, all Souls of earth are the safeguard.
In your oneness, in your goodness, you are the safeguard.

256 Earth humanity,
        we bring unto you a message of peace and comfort.
In your most trying of times within the earth plane,
        we would have you understand the great dependency
        of all the universes upon your oneness.
Though you are the farthest from your Creator,
        though you are in, willingly, the vale of negativity,
        you are, Souls of earth, as humanity,
        the nucleus of the solution.
You hold within the fragility of your beings
        the most awesome power and you know it not.
You focus upon the matter that you are upon the earth.
When you consider the Spirit of your being,
        the Essence of your being,
        you see it as separated from you.
You see it as un matter, ephemeral,

untouchable with your earth being.
And we would have you know that your high self,
Farside is also matter.
The form may be different, indeed,
there is a myriad of forms.
But matter is matter, whether it is on the earth plane,
Farside or beyond.
Coming unto this knowing by you as humanity,
will assist in bringing forth the oneness of humanity,
will assist in bringing forth the Brethren Fallen
and all those lost in transition.
Transition has matter, but again in another form.
It is why you may reach unto these beings in transition.
Souls of earth, we await that day with incredible joy.

257 We would take this opportunity
to delve into transition, in terms of explanatory.
You will understand
that the reasons the beings in transition
have for being caught in transition
are as varied as the insects upon your earth.
Understand, not one whit of Energy
has gone into forcing any one being to be in transition.
Understand, there is no god who raises a hand and says
you cannot enter in to the kingdom.
Transition is by choice.
Transition is a holding place
for a being who has rejected all conceptuals
of a Loving God,
of a Light of their being,
that they are more than the earth.
The being will ofttimes, upon losing the physical breath,
enter in to a consciousness of breath of the mind,
holding themselves within transition,
refusing to enter unto the Light,
refusing to enter unto the whole of their Essence,
refusing to accept that they are Light.
They are caught in a cycle, a circle of recrimination of self,
they become into that cycle of recrimination,
of unworthiness.
They judge themselves

and hence refuse to even entertain the thought
of entering in to the Light.
They do not understand they came for a reason, a purpose.
They do not understand
they are eminently worthy of entering unto the Light,
unto the home of their being,
unto the waiting arms of the Angels
and the unconditional Love of their Creator.
And so they languish.
There are the Souls
where death has come violently and unexpectedly,
and they do not accept the renewal of death
and cling to the earth.
There are those whose leaving, they feel in their consciousness,
has caused pain to others, and so they try to bring solace
to the ones they have left,
they choose to hold onto earth,
unto the sorrow of those they have left.
These are but a few of a myriad of reasons
of beings caught in transition, caught by their own will,
by their own consciousness of being.
Understand each and every being in transition
may be assisted to leave,
to enter in to the consciousness of Light,
to enter home.
All are welcome.
In your daily turmoil of earth, have a thought now and then
for the beings caught in transition and offer unto them
the Light of your being as a path home.
You are, Souls of earth, caretakers of earth,
and also as humanity you are caretakers of transition.
Be ye the good shepherd, hold out your staff of Light to all.

258 Souls of earth, shout for joy.
For the time is upon your beings
to enter in to the place of return.
Vibrate in the goodness of your humanity.
Vibrate with all the compassion and Love within you,
for earth is sorely tried.
And earth would willingly join you in joyous exaltation
were she not so heavily weighed down

with the toxins of mankind.
Mankind has placed the toxins within the earth
and mankind may remove the toxins within the earth.
Souls of earth, do not see the removal of toxins
as overwhelmingly immense task.
Souls of earth joined together, united in purpose,
may cleanse the earth.
Join with one another so that you may exalt,
so that the planet earth may exalt
in joyous abandonment of toxicities,
that your children
and your children's children and beyond
may come into the earth without mutations,
breathing clean air.
The earth has waited long for a cleansing by mankind.
Souls of earth, you have a frequency available unto you.
It is called High C.
This High C is beyond the earth.
This frequency contains sound, color and vibration.
It is the sound of the Oneness of Humanity.
You are one and all healers of mankind.
Accept your possibility.
Accept the eye is Holy,
and the eye may take you beyond the bonds of earth.
You are humanity;
not simply individual, but a conceptual construct
and as such when you enter in to oneness
you become the very Soul of Creator.
How, you ask, do we heal the earth in our oneness?
It is, Soul, with sound.
For the sound of High C will cleanse,
will renew, will balance earth.
It is sound that will bring about wellness.
It is sound that will enable all to heal.
It will neutralize the poison that contaminates the earth.
Sound of High C brings balance to the chi
that has been contaminated and injured.
It eliminates, emits, brings forth the negativity,
the pollution, the poison.
Understand the alteration of spatial energy
is within your purview.

When a portion of your being holds negativity,
that portion cannot hold positive
until the negativity is released.
You may alter,
releasing the negative and allowing the positive to enter.
This may be done of self.
It may be done for neighbor,
for friend, for loved one, for earth, for humanity.

259 We would consider the shape of a bell,
a bell that can ring, that can peal forth,
that can resound in vibration.
You are a sounding note.
You are as a bell.
Each different, each singular in tone and vibrational quality.
You may consider your being as a dome,
the outward shape of a bell.
But it is not the body,
it is the aura that gives you your outward shape
for the sound that reverberates from your being.
Your sound reverberates beyond your immediacy.
Each and every stroke of your bell affects mankind.
For although your tones are separate, they are to be one
in a harmonious blend of sound that in its goodness
carries unto Farside and beyond.
The one rings forth surcease from pain,
it is heard, not only above but below.
Souls of earth, hear the sound of your voice.
Hear the sound of humanity.
Hear the sound of humanity in oneness.
Hear the sound that echoes and echoes
and echoes throughout galaxies, cosmoses,
throughout the very Yawn of your Creator and beyond.
Understand in the oneness of the very Souls that you are
is the sound of High C.
This High C of which we speak heals.
There is no limit to that which can be healed
with the oneness of humanity.
It is this very voice, this very sound
that will open the gate of transition
and call unto the very Angels;

and all who are within, will hear the voice of humanity.
You have the ability to calm another with your very voice.
You have the ability to soothe the child with your voice.
When you voice outward the High C,
when you lift the very being of humanity in oneness,
the healing goes beyond this dimension.
It indeed enters in unto the Yawn
and is heard throughout the universes.
It is heard with the eye,
it is heard with the aura, for this is who you are.
Blessed Souls of earth,
release from your beings the barriers to oneness.
Have a care for all of humanity.
Have a care for those lost in the throes of transition.
Have a care for all that are in pain upon the earth.
Have a care for the very Creator of your being
who sheds Tears at the Angels in transition.
Souls of earth, heal with the voice of humanity,
heal with the voice of High C.

260 This minuscule Energy called humanity
is pivotal to the opening of the gateways.
As minuscule as you are,
your Energy pierces galaxies beyond.
We hear the echo of your sound.
We hear the High C of your consciousness in oneness;
a song unto the wellness of humanity,
unto the vibratory consciousness of humanity.
For are you not all one as the Soul of Creator!
Come forth.
Come forth unto the knowledge
and the recognition of your place
within the cosmos of beings.
Understand, you have first place within the cosmos of beings.
Not because you are elevated as humanity upon your earth,
indeed not.
It is because you are elevated as Humanity on the Farside.
It is because you are Soul of your Creator.
You are not hierarchical in first place.
You are first place in the implosion.
Harken, Souls of earth, to the glory, the hallelujah,

the paeans of praise heaped upon you as you enter in.
Oh, magnificent Humanity!
We speak of the Oneness of Humanity,
we speak of the Soul of Creator.
Magnificent indeed!
You have, Souls of earth, in your current form as mankind
spent millenniums after millenniums coming forth
into this stage of being, into this state of awareness,
into this state of readiness.
It is nigh, and all who watch from the Farside
glory in this moment.
Souls of earth, you have longed for millenniums
when there will be no suffering, pain, sorrow, grief.
Souls of earth, at the moment of readiness, all will dissipate
for it is illusion, and you will now recognize the illusion
of the form you have taken upon the earth.
In an instant ss you come forth, the reality has altered,
and you are once more within the Arms of your Creator,
melded, formed, placed as the Soul.

261 We would speak with thee
on the building of knowledge, of wisdom.
In your many reincarnations, you build with your experiences
with your lifetimes.
In your growth as a Soul and as a part of the entity
you venture forth into new pathways,
into new discoveries based upon
your building of knowledge.
Humanity has enriched our knowledge
with its vast complexities, lifetime after lifetime.
Eagerly we await your new discoveries,
your learning, your knowledge of negativity.
Souls of earth, you have lain upon your beings a heavy burden,
a burden of immense proportions, of incalculable worth,
and yet this burden will bring you lightness of being.
It will enable you to tread lightly upon the earth.
It will enable you to put forth goodness
and care for all that is animate and inanimate.
It will enable you to explicitly understand the oneness of the
Energy, the oneness of the illusion,
the oneness that will bring attainment,

that will enable the descent into
that which is called transition.
All things, beloved Souls of earth, that you see as boulders,
as insurmountable obstacles, as heavy burden,
are illusion.
Your burdens bring forth a glorious reckoning,
a vibrant calling forth of all energies,
a symbiosis of light and dark.
For within the Cauldron there are those
who would lift the burden gladly,
who have Love unconditional and is their total being.
Love is who they are.
And you will meet and blend in an ultimate radiance of being.

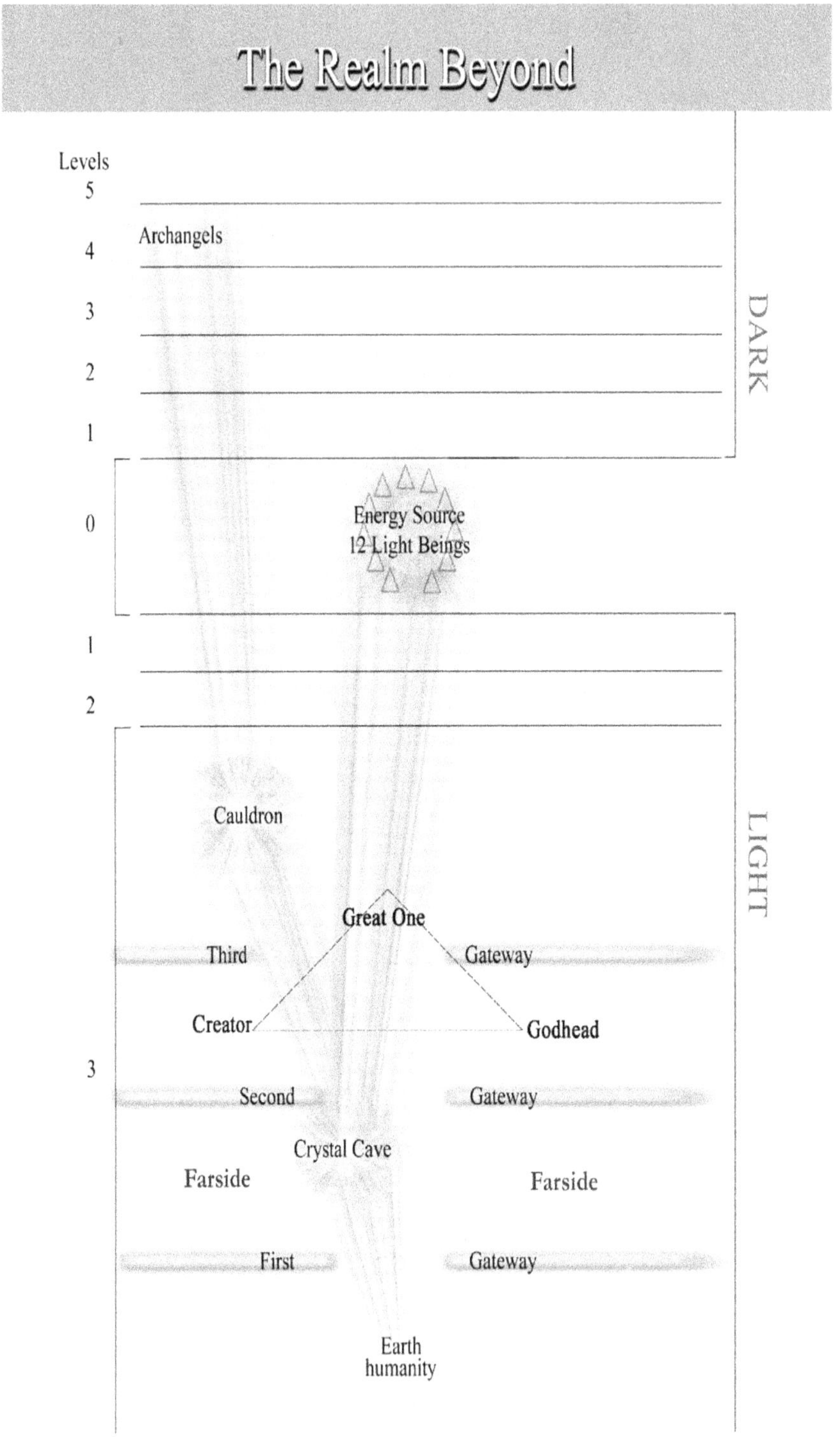
The Realm Beyond
Levels
5
4
Archangels
3
2
1
DARK
0
Energy Source
12 Light Beings
1
2
LIGHT
Cauldron
Great One
Third
Gateway
Creator
Godhead
3
Second
Gateway
Crystal Cave
Farside
Farside
First
Gateway
Earth
humanity

Chapter Five
THE ULTIMATE SOLUTION

262 Souls of earth,
we come forward to speak of seven and seven.
For your understanding,
seven Creators Dark, seven Creators Light
flung forth from Fourteen Creators[50]
encapsulating in the Shining Waters a barrier,
in the hopes, indeed, even at that level,
in the hopes of calming chaos
in its frenzy of misdirection, in its peripatetic being,
in its constant, chaotic search.
The Seven Dark and the Seven Light
are not inimical one to the other.
Indeed, not.
For your understanding,
they are Creators of different webs of existences,
of different layers of existences, of being, of Energy.
Earth exists in Light,
but we tell you that the Dark of which we speak
is equal to the Light.
Differing existences, same purpose.
All designated, all designed to bring forth chaos,
not to impose chaos,
but to give it rest, to bring back the lost.
The seven and seven attempted to join, to meld Energies.
And the Thirteenth held back at the last moment.
Understand, Souls of earth,
we can not in earth terminology fully explain
the complexity of which we speak
and so we have brought it to its most basic.
The Thirteenth Creator held back;
knowing the meld was doomed, sacrificed self.
And flung forth that which we call Negativity.
The Fourteenth Creator held the strength of the barrier.
We come now to Twelve Creators
who flung forth the Light Beings.
And the Light Beings gathered their Energy
and gave forth their strength unto the Triad,
that which is your Creator, Godhead and the Great One.

Archangels were in existence and came forth,
brought their Beings forth to exist
and flung their Beings forth as Angels.
Your lineage, this we give unto you.

264 We speak of the Armada.
Indeed, humanity is the Armada, Creator's Armada.
In your oneness, Souls of earth, you have great strength.
In your oneness winning the Battle for which you entered in.
Indeed, you have entered into a battle, a battle with negativity.
You have entered in to overcome negativity.
You have entered in to embrace negativity.
Once you overcome negativity and release that negative energy
unto Creator, you have won that small
but ultimately important battle.
And when you can not overcome negativity,
when you can not bear to release the negative energy
and you pass from this earth, you have choice.
You may choose to leave the negative karmic energy
at the station of karma,
or you may choose to hold onto the negativity
and stay in transition.
If you choose to leave the negativity at the karmic station,
you enter again unto the Farside,
where you may then choose your next step.
If you choose to reside in transition,
to hold onto the negative energy,
to hold onto the pain and the suffering,
you always have the possibility to choose to leave
and to enter in to the Light.
It is not a permanent choice to enter in to transition.
Be aware, Souls of earth, of your choices when passing.
Know that even the most saintly of persons of humanity
may be appalled when they review
their life upon the earth.
But know you do not have to punish self
by withholding your being from the Light,
by entering in to transition.
Know you are welcomed back unto the homeland,
and you need not stay in transition.
You may enter directly unto the Light.

Souls of earth, you came unto the earth to
do battle with the negative energy,
not with swords, not with guns, not with angry words,
not with torment but with Love and compassion,
with the armor of Truth about your being.
This is how you battle.
In goodness, Souls of earth;
for if you battle with the swords and the guns
and the angry words and the torment,
you only increase the negative energy.
It is not overcome, it is replenished.
Be aware, Souls of earth,
when you choose to come unto the earth,
you choose to battle with Love and compassion.
You are armed with Truth
so that you may recognize negative energy,
so that you may indeed attract negative energy,
then overcome and release it unto Creator.
Souls of earth, recognize the very accoutrements
with which you battle.
Know that you bear the sword of Truth,
but it is a sword of Light, not of steel or iron,
of Light, Souls of earth, for you are Light.
This we give unto you.

263 This we know,
the Void has within it much we do not fathom.
We know Godhead is.
We know Creator is.
We know within the place of BE there is
unimaginable wonders of Love, of Ecstasy,
of enlightenment of being.
And we would have you know that Godhead awaits,
as does all of Farside, for the oneness,
for the bringing forth of the blessed ones,
of the brethren.
There is within our knowledge an awareness
of the glorious nature of humanity.
There is in our knowledge
an awareness of all the animate and inanimate,
giving themselves to assist mankind.

Beloved Souls of earth, your Creator awaits,
Godhead awaits, all worlds await.
Be not afraid to open the gate.
Be not afraid to gaze upon the Souls in their agonizing pain.
For you, humanity, are the rescuer.
We ask you not to stand idly by and ignore,
or only observe the pained brethren.
But, Souls, reach in, offer the hand of thy goodness
and be amazed and astounded
at the hands that will reach forth and grasp,
so that you may pull them forward
into the waiting arms of the Angels.
Be thou beloved, be thou Loved, be thou Loving.
Open thy arms to all the pained
and know that you may comfort,
that you may heal,
that you may bring forth that which all await.

One Thousand Years

265 We would have you understand
all that there is, all the universes, all the cosmoses,
all the galaxies, Farside, beyond;
all has sound.
There is naught that does not have sound.
You were born in sound,
you were begot in sound, you were created in sound.
You come from sound.
Your lineage is sound.
And you have, Souls of earth, come to repair the very rent
within the sound of transition and the Cauldron.
You have found the key to repair
the discordancy of sound in transition and the Cauldron.
You have purpose, Souls of earth.
You have not been created by accident.
You were brought unto the earth with the sound of Angels.
We would have you understand,
sound is not merely noise
as you might think upon your earth,
sound is Energy, sound is vibration,

sound has an electricity,
an aliveness, an awareness.
In your need to understand
you may liken Energy unto an entity in itself,
one that is within all matter, all matter, indeed!
Sound may come together.
Sound may be apart, discordancy
as in transition and the Cauldron.
Sound in oneness, in harmonic vibratory oneness,
carries creation.
Sound does not create but it does carry creation and it vibrates,
and when combined with color;
the Holy triad of sound, color and vibration,
all is possible.
There you have the very key to the gates,
to the oneness of humanity,
for as humanity reaches and melds and becomes,
the very sound becomes a crescendo of Purity and Love,
reverberating throughout the cosmoses.
Sound travels, indeed,
in harmonics or in disharmony sound travels.
Your very being, the sound from your very being vibrates.
You cannot contain the vibration of your being.
Souls of earth,
recognize in your oneness is the greatest of sounds
throughout all that is, for it holds the key.
Hasten, harken to the sound of harmony,
of oneness of purpose, and enter thou in.
Souls of earth, we have before us, a symphony.
A symphony of sound that echoes and echoes and echoes.
A symphony of sound that reverberates
and reverberates and reverberates
through all the levels, through all the fields,
through all the auras of all that is.
The symphony is not finished.
Each moment of being, of Energy,
contributes to the symphony of sound and color.
You, beloved Souls, each and every one, are of the symphony.
All that you are contributes to the symphony.
The crescendo has not yet sounded.
The crescendo is that which is to come.

The crescendo will be the Thousand Years.

266 We speak to you from one of the ships
that await the time of lifting.
We are of the conglomerate of the Pleiades.
You know there are four
that have dedicated all of their being unto this
as gift to Creator and humanity.
We would have you know, our preparations are intact.
We would have you know, the research has been of value
and we are grateful to all who have participated.
We have identified the lines
that are connected to the Souls in Purity.
We have identified the placement,
the areas upon your earth plane
where each lifting will occur.
You have within your being the knowledge of the lifting,
and those that come onto the earth
carry within their being, written with the aura,
the time and place.
There will be movements of Souls to their placement.
Some will not understand
the urge to be in a particular place, at a particular time,
but with the knowing within,
they will follow the nudge and be in place.
The seven Mountaintops are prepared.
They await only the energies designated for their time and place.
Know ye we have read the Record and we come to you
to leave the message to fear not,
to be joyous in your being,
to know the encounters
of mankind with earth have all had meaning.
And we urge, once again, for you to place your energies of
goodness to all that is within your realm of earth.
Refrain, we ask, from smiting thy brother.
Refrain from hoarding of food, of grain.
We ask that you put into place Love unto one another,
and ready thyself for that which is to be.
Souls of earth, the lines are ready.
We have placed them
as you would place a fishing line within your waters.

These are lifelines we have placed.
They are lines coming from the ships
unto those who will be lifted.
They are lines of color, each to its own color,
each attuned to the vibrational harmony
of that individual being.
We are ready.
All is in place.
And we would have you know excitement builds in anticipation.
For what you may entertain within the human mind as disaster,
we see as a marker on the path to Entering In.
Beloved Souls, we have watched, we have gathered.
We have seen the struggle.
We have seen you surmount.
We have seen that glorious attainment of the Mountaintop.
We have come with a progress report.
We would have you know that events are well in hand.
The ships are nearing completion.
There will be room, more than enough for the lifting.
We have encountered no difficulties
that have not been researched and sustained.
Mankind, we welcome the opportunity to serve,
to be of the Armada.
We await your will.
We are ready to lift.
We have been working long toward this moment.
We would have you understand
that not one Energy of Creator's
will be left in the Hinterland.[51]
Those who have been lifted will return to teach, to heal.

267 Souls of earth, hear what we say unto you.
The fable is no more, indeed, time is coming to an end.
You as humanity are bringing time to an end.
How is this possible?
And we say unto you, earth time is finite.
Earth time has a limit.
The time of earth, the time of humanity,
the time of the Battle is finite.
All is in place for the final denouement.
Souls of earth, you are prolonging unnecessarily

that which is to be done, for you have completed.
You have fulfilled the very covenant with Creator,
with humanity, with self.
You have attained the power to win the battle.
You have attained the level of Purity as humanity
to open the gate of transition.
You have attained the strength, the holiness, the Love,
the compassion and Purity to gather unto your being
those lost in transition.
Hear us, hear the acclaim, "It is done!".
There are beings who cry out to you to alter the pain of transition,
these beings are caught in their own need to expiate.
And you have reached,
have attained that level of Love and compassion
that can reach out to these beings and say,
"Release the negativity you hold to your being,
and enter in with us to the great Light.
Come home."
You, Souls of earth, of humanity,
may relieve your brothers and sisters of pain.
Pain has served its purpose.
Negativity has served its purpose.
But now it is time to release this energy,
and allow this energy to be given unto Creator.
Indeed, we say allow, for you must will it to be released.
As you embrace negativity and then release it,
you show unto the very beings in transition
what they too may do.
And they will look unto you, and they will say,
"I can, we will, for you have shown us how!
You have shown us that your Light is our Light,
you have shown us the oneness of humanity.
You have shown us our Souls are not despicable,
we need not expiate what we have done.
And you have shown us that time is finite,
and so we enter forth."
Beloved Souls of earth,
indeed you have attained the power as humanity,
to enter in to the new day,
to enter in to the thousand years,

to enter in to a new dimensional phase of being.
Bless you beloved Souls, harken, hear well that which we say.
Take heart, take comfort,
take knowing in the blossoming Souls of earth.
Take comfort that the buildup of negativity is
more that matched and soon to be overcome by Purity.
The pure goodness of your Souls will shine.
Be ye not in despair.
Know that the increase in negativity is a signal.
It signals the magnification of the goodness of humanity,
for man will take heed of the heinous acts
and resolve, within intent,
with great intention, to cease,
to overcome further negativity.
It will be a great awakening.
Be ye not in fear.
For it is that which you have looked for,
struggled for through eons of time,
soon to be realized:
the coming forth of Jesu, Mohammed, Buddha, Krishna
and the great splitting asunder of transition.
Behold, Souls of earth, you are the knight in shining armor.
You are Creator's champion.
So be it.

Implosion

268 Within the silence there is always sound.
Listen carefully, listen with the eye,
and you will hear the thrum of existence.
That thread that ties, that binds all of existence together,
not just humanity, but all of existence.
That thrum is the pulse of your heart;
it is the pulse of the beat of existence,
and all may hear that thrum, that great thrum.
All existence has thrum.
You call the supreme being by many titles,
but the one most apt in your human language
is the alpha and the omega, the beginning and the end,
the all in between.

The one who has no beginning, the one who has no end.
Souls of earth, all the creatures that have come unto earth
 to assist humanity,
 have within the heart of their being, the thrum.
They hear it.
They know it.
It is a part of them.
You may enter in to the same consciousness.
Use the eye, Soul!
You see yourself narrowly confined with all sorts of limitations.
The limitations are only the ones you imposed upon yourself.
We have taught you have all choice;
 if you have limitations, it is choice.
Choose to hear the thrum, the thrum of existence,
 the thrum of who you are and from whence you came.
It is not, Soul, a moment for discovery.
There was, to use earth time,
 a recognition, an awareness of a minute,
 minuscule difference within that which we exist.
It is as if there was the smallest cool breeze on a warm day
 that touched, barely, the hair on your head.
One follicle of that hair was touched as a little tiny bit of air
 and it registered within your consciousness
 that the warm that was all of your being,
 had changed, had altered
 but you could not see where this breeze came from.
How did it arrive?
Why was it there?
And this is what you proceed to explore.
What is its significance?
How can we come by the answer?
Do we need an answer?
Is it a requirement of our existence?
How will it affect our being?
If we explore, will that alter it further?
Once a step is taken, can it be reversed?
All these questions and more entered within our consciousness.
We were given no tap on the shoulder, no warning.
We had no perfection of awareness.
Was the breeze illusion?
It was beyond our ken, our Energy Field,

the vastness of which is unexplored.
Do we go forth and can we go back?
This was our dilemma.
You, Souls, are of the resolution of the dilemma.

269 We would have you understand
you are continually beset by negativity.
It is as if it was a swarm of gnats about your being
and flailing your arms is a useless exercise
for they just come back to plague you, buzzing.
And yet,
the gnats have their place within the cycle of earth,
and to obliterate them
would cause chaos within the cycle of earth.
And so it is with negativity.
To obliterate negativity would cause more chaos.
It would not resolve chaos.
It would create more negativity.
We ask that you offer negativity to Creator,
for it cannot be obliterated, but it can be altered.
You can not say, "Take it from me".
For you have before you came unto the earth,
stipulated, "It is mine to give."
Negativity is vital to the cycle within the Yawn.
It has its place.
It has its rationale.
It has its reason for being.
It offers its Energy to you in its pure self.
And then you, as humanity, alter the true self into a distortion
by clinging, by holding on to that energy.
And yet, that tainted energy, when you release it,
when you offer it unto Creator, may then be altered
once again unto its true self.
But as long as you retain it, it is tainted
and unable to leave this plane.
Souls of earth, Negativity has given a great Energy unto you.
And you have overcome much and returned much.
And we say unto you, enough, you have done enough.
Harken, Souls of earth.
Listen with your Soul.
Allow your being to accept who you are, why you are,

and know you are ready for the next step.
We call it implosion.
You are ready!
You have overcome.
And we bless your beings and await the recognition of your Soul
to who you are and why you are.

270 We speak to you of the worlds that you may visit,
worlds that you may have already visited,
worlds that comprise galaxies of beings,
worlds directly connected
in the web of being unto mankind,
worlds dedicated in all aspects of their being
unto mankind.
Why would whole galaxies of beings
devote themselves to you, humanity,
to mankind, to earth?
It is because, Souls of earth, you hold the key.
You hold the key
to the implosion of energies, to the return of all that is,
to the First Gateway, to transition,
to the Second Gateway,
to the Cauldron, to beyond.
The beyond of beyond is your destiny,
you, Souls of earth!
All other beings of these galaxies of worlds
have dedicated themselves to research,
to recording all that you do,
to assisting you on your lifetimes within the earth plane;
to guiding, to holding at bay the negativity
that you have created
which would long ago have destroyed your earth.
Galaxies, who indeed glory in that which you do
to overcome negativity.
Who glory in that which you do
to complete the purpose of humanity.
And the return is possible
unto the very utmost Being of all Energy.
Hold yourselves dear, Souls of earth,
as galaxies of being hold you dear.
Know that in the completion of your mission

will be the beginning of the completion of all missions,
and so the beginning is the end
and the end is the beginning.
So be it, Souls.

271 We would take you unto rapture.
Our description, you will understand, can only be microscopic,
infinitesimal in comparison to the actual experience
of what we call, for you, rapture.
We would have you know,
what you call Light, has sound, color, vibration.
It is not that you are within sound, color and vibration.
It is that you are in full knowing of sound, color, vibration
and you are in full knowing of Godhead.
You have willingly lost all parameters of being,
and you have become a part
of the joyous symphony of rapture.
And in your knowing you have the knowing that your vibration,
your sound, your color has added to this symphony.
Beloved Souls, what joyous knowing there is in rapture!
You have all thought for others
and yet you have no thought of self.
You have all knowing, awareness of all that is unto Godhead.
But it is not a knowing in the earth sense,
where earth equates knowledge with power.
Indeed not, Soul.
It is the knowing of Be.
You have no form and yet you may form.
You have not an individual being and yet you be.
You have no ears and yet you hear.
You have no eyes and
yet you see more than your earth eyes are capable of.
You have no brain and yet you have all thought.
To be in rapture, beloved Souls of earth, is that which
you will attain as you enter unto the Second Gateway.
In the blink of an eye you will be within and be rapture.
Come forth, come unto us.
We await secure in the knowledge of your coming.
We place before you a great feast.
We place before you a festive occasion.
We place before you, joy.

We would have you partake of the great feast.
It is Purity, Love and compassion.
This is the great feast available unto all beings.
It is open to all.
We would have you fill your being with joy
in the knowledge that you are Love and Purity.
Indeed, come to the table, partake!
Fill your being with Love, fill your mind with joy.
Fill the very Soul of your being overflowing with compassion.
The table is never ending, the feast never ceases,
the table is never cleared, for it is always full.
Know that your being can be filled with
Love and compassion and its equivalency, joy.
This we give unto you.
In all times, in all places these are available unto your being.

272 You have before you a great road.
A road that will accommodate
all manner, all sorts, all types of beings.
A road that could accommodate
millions walking side by side.
Indeed, you have before you the great glory road.
You have before you the ability, the potential,
the possibility to travel the glory road,
to be first among many to travel the glory road.
Humanity in its oneness may step unto the glory road.
It is the purpose of humanity, to tread the glory road,
to walk the glory road in oneness, side by side, together.
Indeed, the very act of humanity in oneness opens up,
not only the gate of transition
but the gateway unto Farside.
And after the Thousand Years, the glory road
is the implosion unto the Second Gateway.
We would have you understand
the glory road is a direct connection
unto the very realm of your Creator.
It is Light, Color, Sound.
Enter thou in to the oneness,
to the glory road, to the very purpose of your being.
Glory is the attainment of Truth, Love, Purity and beyond.
It is not simply the recognition,

it is not simply acknowledging it exists.
It is actually becoming the glory of the Soul of Creator.
The glory of your Creator, indeed!
The glory of Humanity as one, as the Soul of Creator,
entering in beyond the Second Gateway!
In your glory, the Archangels see the Light of your being.
And they will respond to that Light.
And in the sound of your rapturous glory
the sound will reverberate throughout;
not just the cavern,
not just the Cauldron, but beyond.
You understand rapturous glory is a sound.
Rapture is a state of being.
Glory is a state of being, rapturous glory is the sound.

273 We would speak on the ecstasy
Ecstasy is your birthright.
Ecstasy is the Path that is formed for humanity.
Ecstasy is a state of being at one with Creator.
It is to be in the Hallowed Halls.
It is a lifting of your Spirit to its Essence of being.
It is a paean of sound that reverberates throughout all that is.
It is a vibration that alters your earthly Energy,
that brings you forth into the state
from which you were formed.
Ecstasy is your natural state of being and you know it not.
Ecstasy is the glory, it is the incandescence of your Essence,
and you will know this.
Souls of earth, we would speak
of what we call for the earth plane, the Place of Shining.
It is not upon your earth plane, but indeed connected.
It is a place wherein a portion of the Triad resides.
It is the triad designated to enter in unto your Yawn.
Indeed, your Creator's Yawn created as a solution
to the great chaos throughout all of existences.
In your Oneness, as the Soul of Creator,
in your Oneness as Humanity,
in completing your purpose of humanity,
you have the promise of entering in
to the Place of Shining.
You will, Souls of earth, lose the I, the me designation,

and you will become we.
In your great purpose, you will make the next step
forward upon the implosion
of your world and all worlds.
The Place of Shining has been designated
as such as a description,
for it holds within Light Energy of compassion,
of Agape Love, Truth, Purity, Ecstasy, Rapture,
and revealment; indeed, revealment.
Souls of earth, your possibility,
your potential is greater than you may imagine,
for you hold within your being
not only the divinity of your Creator,
but you hold within the promise of the great Triad.
This we give unto you.

Cauldron

274 We would speak on what you call darkness.
We would speak of the dark place of the platform,
of the sound that calls.
We believe it is calling, for it sounds throughout our being.
It is as a constant within our existence.
We are within the fifth level beyond Farside.
We see with our consciousness the chaotic movement,
and we know therein are Beings of great magnitude,
of great wholesomeness of being.
We speak of the dark one, of the place of darkness, of the dark.
There is within our awareness
the knowing of countless members within the chaos.
Further knowledge
we would glean from your explorations.
It is you we depend upon to pierce the curtain of darkness.
Not darkness as you describe,
as your sun moves away
to another portion of your globe,
but a darkness of form, of movement,
of being, of lack of color.
There is no answer to our Light, to the rays we send forth.
Your minds could not comprehend the enormity of the colors,

of the rays we send forth into the darkness
and unto you.
You answer, they do not.

275 We bring unto you the universal sound of agony, of joy.
The universal sound of agony reverberates
throughout your earth
in each and every nook and cranny,
in each and every living being.
In each and every Soul carries that sound.
It is the sound of loss.
It is the sound of the Archangels in the Cauldron.
It is akin to an even greater loss.
But we speak particularly of the sound of the Archangels.
The sound requires no ears to hear,
for the ears will burst with the agony of the sound.
The sound is visible to your Souls.
You may see the sound in your humanity.
Within the Crystal Cave the sound is prevalent
and the beings are focused on
altering that sound of agony.
Understand, you, in your humanity,
have this power to alter the sound;
the sound of the depths of loneliness
you cannot imagine,
the sound of the depths of loss
that would make you weep to all your days,
the sound of loss that brings sorrow,
even unto your Creator.
Souls of earth, enter in to oneness.
Enter in to the beautification of your being, of your humanity.
Enter in to humanity, and alter that sound.
You may, in your oneness,
alter that sound to one of joy, joyous acclaim,
joyous resolution, joyous recognition,
rejoicing in the oneness,
rejoicing in the reclamation of being,
rejoicing at the possibilities
of altering another loss beyond.
Recognize the potential power you have in your oneness.
Enter forth in oneness unto Godhead.

The Cauldron awaits.
Harken to the sound.
For in your Oneness, you will be guided unto the Cauldron.
For all of your being will focus on the alteration of that sound.

276 We have before us a shining sea.
Shining, because of the sun glinting off the glassy waters.
The sun is not as your earth sun.
Your earth sun, glinting off your ocean waves, is but a reflection,
 a mirror of the shining sea.
All upon your earth is a reflection of the Farside
 and above and beyond, beyond.
You will understand, Souls of earth, the purpose of humanity,
 the mending that must occur, that will indeed occur.
Not of humanity, for you have mended.
There is no need to continue to stitch together
 the tear in the web.
You are done.
Mend now that which is beyond the Second Gateway.
Mend the greater tear in the web of being,
 the tear in the cavernous web,
 in the Cauldron of Great One,
 and then the purpose of humanity, of your humanity,
 will mend an even greater tear in the fabric, the web;
 that of the lost Idyllic.
Indeed, humanity, you have made a covenant,
 a commitment with Creator.
Indeed, this commitment will have ramifications far beyond
 what you see as the purpose of your earth humanity.
Join in a joyous chorus of accomplishment.
You have carried through on your commitment to your Creator.
Know that your work upon the earth is done,
 but your work has only begun beyond the earth.

Entering In To The Cauldron

APPENDIX A
equation of T

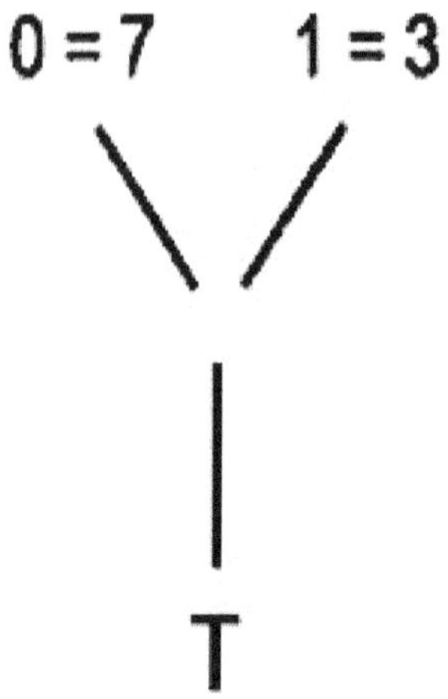

T = Time

1= Singleness
3= Triad
7= Planes/levels/dimensions
0= Naught/Void
and the centre is Quar = Implosion

Appendix B
Daily East Ritual*

"East - it is the passageway to the Farside through the eye.
Its Truth is to be understood as a Love by humanity.
Focus on east at dawn, allowing the negativity
to flow from your being,
receiving unto yourself the goodness of Creator.
All humanity has the availability of this pathway.
The ritual of the east is the Soul's own response
to the positive east which is tao.
Face east, two minutes.
Look with the eyes to the horizon's level.
In the brick wall or the iron cage, or the ornate boardwalk,
know that the east will be with your Soul.
Turn clockwise once to heal.
Energy will flow to the matter before it.
All organs of the body are healed in the circle turn."

*Creator Trilogy, Energy From The Source,
passage 64, footnote."

APPENDIX C
Book List

Published

by Lucy Dumouchelle

Holistic Healing Through
Channelled Ancients

by Kitty Lloyd

Creator Trilogy
First Key Energy From
The Source
Second Key So Shall It Be
Third Key Until Then

Supreme Being Trilogy
How To Step To The Path

Forthcoming

by Lucy Dumouchelle

The Binary
Holistic Healing Through
Channelled Entities
&Healing From The Farside

Creator Trilogy
Healing With Echo
Healing With Value
Healing With Intent

by Kitty Lloyd

Creator Trilogy
Trilogy of Consciousness
The Gathering Time
From Whence It Came
Ecstasy

Creator Trilogy
Supreme Being Trilogy
Angels' Ecstasy
The Rejoicing

Creator Trilogy
Echo
Value
Keepers Of The Light

Published through Mountaintop Healing Publishing Inc

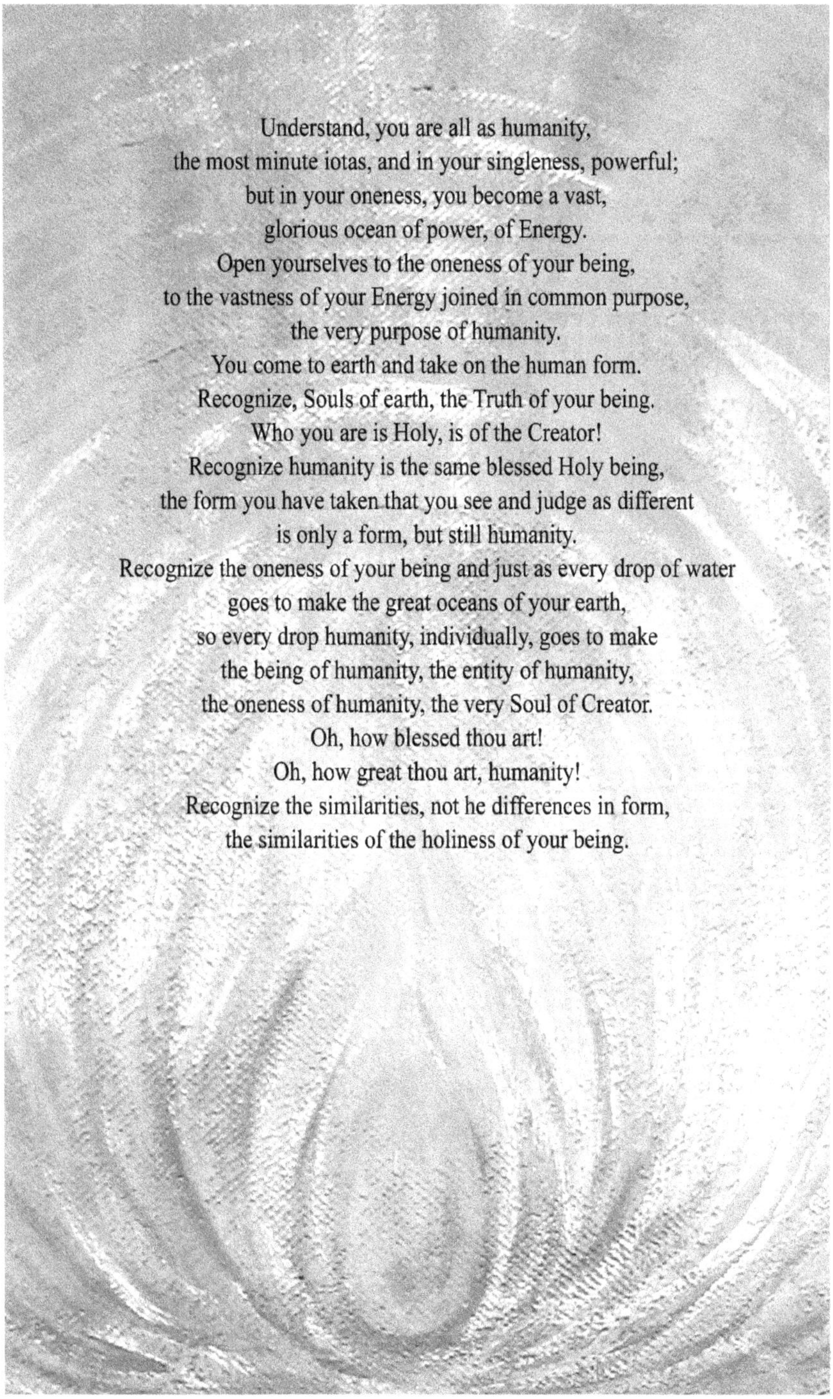

Understand, you are all as humanity,
the most minute iotas, and in your singleness, powerful;
but in your oneness, you become a vast,
glorious ocean of power, of Energy.
Open yourselves to the oneness of your being,
to the vastness of your Energy joined in common purpose,
the very purpose of humanity.
You come to earth and take on the human form.
Recognize, Souls of earth, the Truth of your being.
Who you are is Holy, is of the Creator!
Recognize humanity is the same blessed Holy being,
the form you have taken that you see and judge as different
is only a form, but still humanity.
Recognize the oneness of your being and just as every drop of water
goes to make the great oceans of your earth,
so every drop humanity, individually, goes to make
the being of humanity, the entity of humanity,
the oneness of humanity, the very Soul of Creator.
Oh, how blessed thou art!
Oh, how great thou art, humanity!
Recognize the similarities, not he differences in form,
the similarities of the holiness of your being.

HEALING
FROM THE FARSIDE

Healing From The Farside
Channelled by Lucy Dumouchelle
through High Beings and the Ancient Entities: Master Twag, Quan Yin, Hu Li.

Publisher: Mountaintop Healing Publishing, Inc.
P.O. Box 193
Lantzville, B. C.
Canada
V0R 2H0

email inquiries: mountaintophealingpublishing@shaw.ca

First Edition
ISBN [Ebook version] 978-0-9879355-2-6
ISBN [Print version] 978-0-9879355-2-6

Imprints: Mountaintop Healing Publishing

Front cover: Transferred Spiral, original artwork by Tara Cook
Chart, “Healing”, original artwork by Tara Cook
Chart: "Chakras", original artwork by Tara Cook

HEALING
FROM THE FARSIDE
Table of Contents

Dedication		337
Preface		338
Healing Chart		339
Introduction		340
Chapter One	Reiki	349
Chapter Two	Quan Yin	359
Chapter Three	Color	375
Chapter Four	Sound	403
	Mudras	417
Chapter Five	Vibration	569
	Mudras, Hu Li	600
	Mudras, Master Twag	647
Epilogue		727
Appendix A		753
Appendix B		754
Endnotes		758
Mudra Index		764

Dedication

Man's existence has always been torn between war and peace.
Soul, these volumes give an agenda separate from.
The agenda is the healing of mankind.
It is the aim of each individual to be as well as they may be.
We proclaim unto humanity
that humanity combined requires a mutual agenda.
Not singular.
We place this before you.
The way to heal the spirit will give unto thee all that is necessary.
Reach from your human self unto the Soul of your being
which then may reach into the Spirit of all that is.
For you are merely a fragment of all that is.
This we say unto you.
Gathered together are Souls who have made it possible
that these words might come to be.
They are six.

Tara Cook
Joanne Drummond
Lucy Dumouchelle
Kitty Lloyd
Grace Piontkovsky
Roman Piontkovsky

The medium and compilers of the present volume were under strict instruction to record all transmissions by mechanical means and not to change any detail in the transcription without verification from the source of the message. This we have done.

Preface

Dear readers,

Within a sentence there often will be a word capitalized, yet that same word in another sentence will not be capitalized.

The capitalized word is specific to the Farside, the uncapitalized word is specific to earth.

For example, humanity comes to earth armed with Truth. Capitalized Truth is an attribute of Creator that allows humanity upon earth to recognize and overcome negativity created by man.

Uncapitalized truth is a reference to earth conceptuality of the word, truth, a truism. An earth plane truth changes as wisdom, knowledge accumulates. What was truth for you as a child, more than likely changed as you matured.

Capitalized Truth does not change, remains always true.

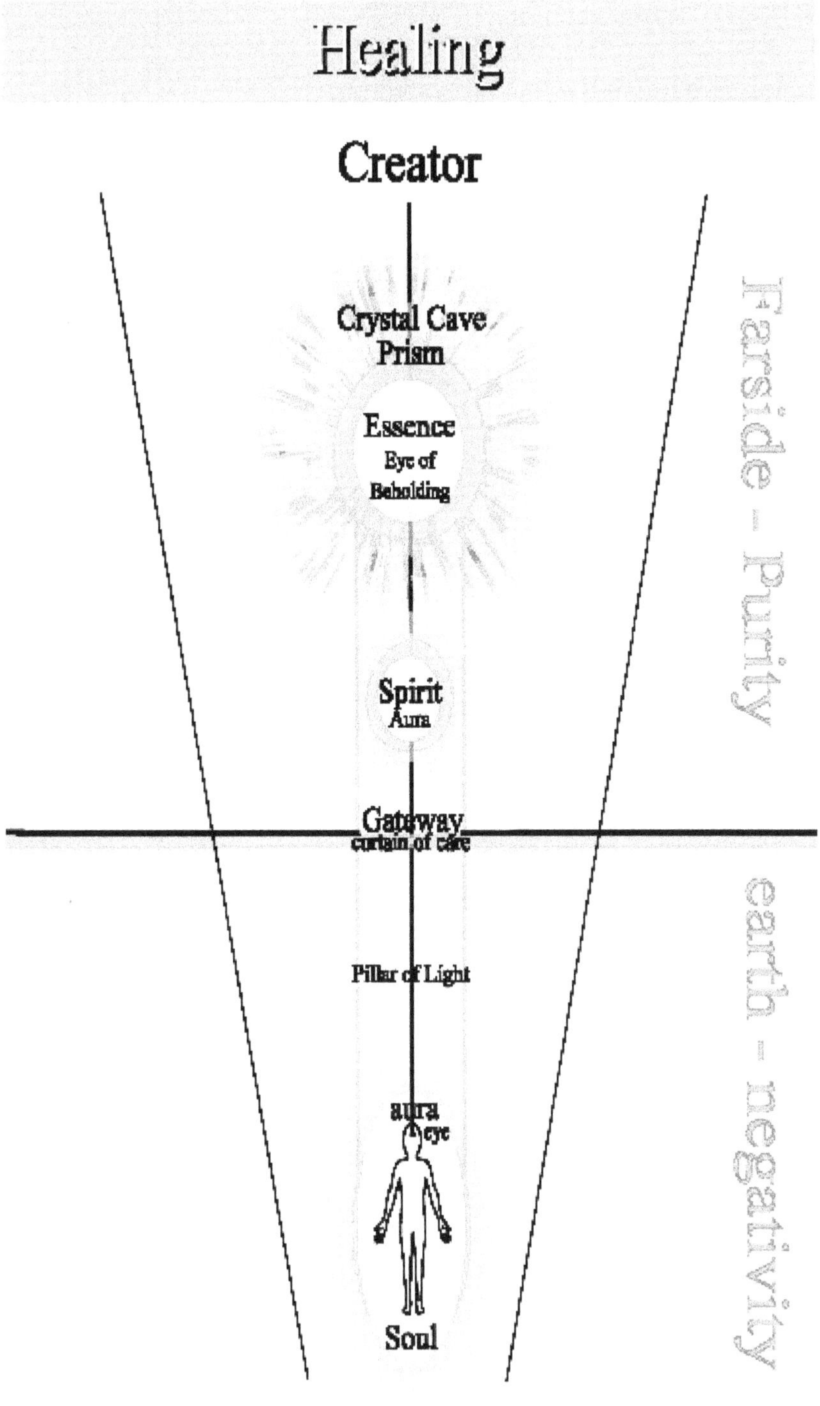
Healing
Creator
Crystal Cave
Prism
Essence
Eye of
Beholding
Spirit
Aura
Gateway
curtain of care
Pillar of Light
aura
eye
Soul
Farside - Purity
earth - negativity

285 Souls, we have found the fountain of youth,
we have found the pot at the end of the rainbow,
we have found the Pharaoh's treasure,
we have discovered the pirate's booty,
we have found the secret of the Jinn,
and we have found the secret of all secrets.
We have found the hidden treasures
underneath the temple of Bali.
We have found the treasured scrolls, the writings of Buddha.
We have found the chests of gold
buried by Hannibal in the Alps.
And we would tell you, Souls of earth,
these treasures are as naught
in comparison to the greatest gift
humanity gives to Creator.[1]
Indeed you are all the treasures that ever were
in your legends and myths and in your history books.
You are more than the seven wonders of the world.
You are greater that the Taj Mahal.
Beloved Souls of earth, you are as generous and giving
as your highest mountain peak.
You are adorned with glory
in the eyes of those who watch from the fence.[2]
Indeed you have accomplished great deeds of valor,
great deeds of generosity, great deeds of courage,
great deeds of giving and loving.
Each beloved Soul of earth has before them the diadem,
the crown of greatness.
Each has before them the gratitude, the honor of all Farside.[3]
Oh humanity, demean not thy self.
Know the holiness of thy being.
We see it so clearly and we thank thee
for that what you have given in the sanctity of your being.

286 We would have you understand
that were you to compare the greatest kilowatts
of your light upon the earth,
it would be as a pinprick of light upon the Farside.
Indeed!

And you, humanity, each and every,
    have entered in from this Light,
    this Light of Creator,
    for all Farside is filled with this Light available to all.
This Light would literally burn your earth eyes,
but enter in with the third eye and you glory in this Light.
There is no searing of the eyeballs,
    there is only a joyous welcome;
    there is only the knowledge that you belong to this Light,
    that you are cradled in this Light,
    that you are secured in this Light.
Understand the Light we speak of
    has no distinction to your light upon earth;
    it does have a connection,
    for you are aware of your need for Light.
Does not mankind look for light, ways to light the darkness,
    whether electrical or spiritual?
Indeed!
For it is your memory of from whence you have come.
All is connected.
We would have you understand, because of that connection,
    using the eye, you may enter in to this Light,
    and you may enter in to the healing with this Light.
It attracts the negativity[4] as a magnet.
And negativity with the permission of the being,
    runs to that Light.
You allow this to happen, you allow that child to return,
    cradled in the Love of Creator.
Or you may choose to deny; always the option,
    and no judgment placed.
Reach, Souls of earth, reach unto yourself, your sacred self,
    and allow that reaching
    to flow unto your fellow humanity.
We would speak with thee of the Light.
We speak of the Light that is a spark within all.
We would speak of the Light that is hidden within.
We would speak of the Light that can burst forth.
We would have you know that whether the Light is hidden
    or whether the Light bursts forth is entirely,
    entirely up to you, your Soul.
Know that you have the ability to close the Light within you.

Know that you have the ability to grasp it, to clasp it,
 to let no one share its warm brilliancy,
 that you have the awesome power.
You have the ability to let the Light burst from you,
 to share it, to let its calming, loving warmth
 bathe everyone around.
You have ability to let the Light burst forth upon the land.
Know the awesome waterfall of Light
 that can come from thy being.
But, you must allow it.
You must will it.
You must be.
Allow the being, that is yours in holiness,
 to bring forth the Light that each Soul carries within.
Imagine beloved beings, imagine this!
Share the Light.
It gathers you no wealth to keep it hidden from others.
It gathers you no points of honor.
What gathers you wealth of Purity, beloved,
 is to share the awesome Light of thy being.
Know ye that is what Creator does.
Wouldst thou be as Creator!
Beloved Souls of earth,
 we would speak with you on the eye of beholding.
You have within your earth being, two earth eyes.
Whether blinded or able to see visually,
 these eyes behold all about you.
These eyes behold the flowers in the field.
These eyes behold rustling of the weeds
 as a small animal passes through.
These eyes behold the flight of a deer in fear,
 and they behold the flight of a deer in joy.
These eyes behold the tiny babe.
These eyes behold the tiny mouse.
These eyes behold other eyes of other beings.
And these eyes may look upon all that is, in Love, in joy,
 or in distaste, in distrust, in hate.
Each moment that you utilize the sight from the eyes,
 each moment, beloved Souls, is choice.
You may look upon another being in anger.
You may look upon that being with Love.

And know that within each choice,
        Energy moves forward into that being.
It need not be only another human.
Any being receives the Energy that you give forth.
For many, action,
        it need not be an action of speech or of touch,
        the act of looking and the thought behind the look,
        that impels the Energy forward, is what you choose.
But do not judge.
We ask that you be aware of that which you do
        in every moment of every day.
We ask that you be aware of the energy
        that you impel forth to all that is.
Sighted or blind, deaf or hearing,
        makes no difference to the energy
        that is impelled forth from your being.
We would ask that you impel forth goodness and Love,
        for within thy being is all goodness and Love.
You have only to bring it forth.

287 We would have you understand within the human body
        in all its complexity, within the neurons is a simplicity.
The simplicity is the healing that may be called forth
        from the neuronic web within the body.
You will understand the neurons within your physical body
        connect to your etheric body.
You see it not with your earth eyes,
        but you will see it with the eye.
Healers often instinctively whether they actually see it
        with the earth eyes or the third eye,
        will feel a disconnection within the aura body.
That disconnection is of which we speak.
You may heal that disconnection by reconnecting
        the Energy path level to that neuronic impulse.
All of your being is constantly in a state of,
        for your understanding, electric explosions.
It matters not whether you are sitting or running,
        moving or standing still, energy is always exploding.
In a healthy, well-being body, those explosions have a pattern,
        a connection with the etheric and the physical.
In the ill body, in the diseased body,

because the connection is broken
the explosions do not occur, the explosions of energy.
You have, in your terminology, a dead zone,
impeding the flow, the connection of Energy.
It is imperative when healing
that you understand what you are healing.
Individually you may always heal yourselves.
The only barrier to that is that which you have chosen.
You may heal others, and again, the barrier to that is twofold;
for the healer may have a barrier themselves,
and the being to be healed may have a barrier.
All things are relative.
All things connected.
And yet the connection may be broken temporarily by the
barriers placed whether by the body or the mind.
Energy, all is Energy, but all that is has a pattern.
Whatever is upon your earth plane has a pattern,
has a defined series, a progression of movement.
When it no longer moves within the earth plane,
it is no longer in the earth plane.
You may free this movement, free all the barriers to the
movement, to healing the broken connection.
It is as a synapse.

288 Souls of earth, you have in your western culture
a game you play with your children.
There is around the world, games parents play,
with their children involving the hands coming together.
This has more meaning than is realized.
The parent placing the hand
upon the child's hand to show them the game
is a form of energy transference,
the energy from the palms of the parent unto the child.
The child, taught to bring the hands together whether in game,
whether in prayer,
or whether in salutation as a symbol of respect.
All is meaningful beyond the simplistic meaning of earth.
We would bring to your attention the Energy available to you,
held within the palms of your hand,
always available as a deep well.
How much water is brought to the surface

is a choice of humanity,
of the individual, but all have some measure,
even without calling forth, dipping deeper into the well.
And just as the well is used to saturate,
to dampen a being or the soil,
so too does the Energy of your being,
held within your hands,
penetrate whatever it touches or is sent to.
The Energy is as the water.
It seeps, it flows, it ripples, it energizes.
To a drowning person, drowning in the illness of pain,
when you reach out your hand in healing,
you rescue that person.
You pull them forward.
The well of healing, the potential within each being,
is of an enormity beyond the earth mind.
The well enters in for your earth mind enters in,
in a cascading Flow
of constant Energy from your Creator.
This Energy is free.
There is no charge, there is no fee, there is no stipend.
Your hands are as a Holy sacred chakra.
They contain within the healing touch.
They contain within the impetus for the body to heal,
the impetus for the mind to heal,
the impetus to give solace unto the troubled Soul.
We would have you recognize and understand,
it is not a select few who hold within, the sacred Energy.
It is for all, for each and every being.
As in a desert, where people are suffering from lack of water,
share your well of Energy, share your well of healing.
It is not something that can be forced,
it is not the choice of another.

289 We would have you understand that all has vibration
even the most inanimate, minute of objects has vibration
because all has Soul.
The vibration of these Souls are affected
by the negativity that swirls from a being.
When an artist composes they may impart unto that,
negativity or they may impart goodness.

We would have you understand that your dwellings
are littered with objects containing negative vibrations,
not just artistically,
any manufactured article may contain negative vibration.
Any rock or stone that has been touched by man
may contain negative vibration.
We would have you understand,
you are not contained in your shell.
All that is around you animate and inanimate affects your being.
The vibrations although some may be very small,
very minute, very low, know it still affects your being.
We bring this to you for your awareness.
We bring this knowledge so that those who manufacture,
create, are aware of the energy they are placing within.
The very air around your being vibrates.
It not only carries toxins and pollutants but it carries vibration.
And you may affect that vibration, cleanse the very air,
with your goodness and intent.

290 We would speak with thee of the terminology of color.
It is important to understand
when we speak of properties of color,
we speak of that which color can do.
Not of that of which color is, but of that of which color can do.
Within the context of your Purity, the properties of color
are not mixed as a painter would mix.
Green has only green.
Blue is only blue.
Purple contains only purple.
Red only red.
It is possible, and it will be necessary at times,
for you to mix purple with blue or another color.
But understand the color,
the properties of the Prism[5] colors are not mixed.
They are pure in themselves.
You do not need other colors to make purple.
You do not need other colors to make blue.
These are Prism colors.
These are colors from the healing Prism.
Their properties are pure, as is your Purity,
as is your Farside being.

And so, if you are directed, if you are guided to use olive color,
it will be a pure olive color.
It will not be a mix, it will not be diluted by any other
as you would do on the earth.
Your orb,[6] open and connected to the healing Prism,
would allow you to see the Purity of the color
and the shade, the tint,
the vibrancy necessary for the healing.
Each color has a life of its own,
has an Energy from the healing Prism,
that will flow and mix with your Purity
to, as it were, trigger, become a gestalt,
become a synergy of wonder.
Know ye, that in the times to come,
you will be given much in the healing modes.
We will speak with thee of Mudras,[7]
of color, of sound, of vibration.
Know ye that when you mix the color
from the healing Prism with thy Purity,
the sound reverberates and the vibration is felt.
Understand, Souls, the mixing comes, the tinting comes,
the shading comes only as it mixes with thy
Farside Purity of self.
As the colors join in thy Purity, go forth and heal.

291 Soul, we would have you understand.
Nothing, not one that we have given as Master Twag,[8]
not one of the Mudras or any of Quan Yin's,[9]
or any of Hu Li's[10] will kill or harm a being.
They will not be harmed following the steps as given.
Should they even lose track of the steps they will not be harmed.
Ease your mind.
We would have the medical profession understand,
all that has been given is to assist, is to add to the tools
that you have to counsel your patients.
All that has been given to those who do not
have access to medical personnel
will not harm your being following,
as given, the instructions.
We assure you we would not give unto you
that which would harm your being.

You will understand there will come times within your earth
    where you will not have access
    given the circumstances of the earth,
    to medical or to pharmaceutical.
You will find the healing volume will contain
    a myriad of remedies,
    of healing modalities that do not require drugs,
    for there will come a time when
    they will not be available,
    and there will also be a time when mankind itself
    rejects the use of these chemicals,
    and so will look for alternatives.
And we offer unto these beings these many ways,
    these many tools.

Healing Chapter One
Reiki

292 We would teach on Reiki, the principles of Reiki.
All healing modalities are of the same energy.
It is the intent and the level of Purity of the individual
wielding the energy that is a causational
difference in the modality.
It is an agreement to enter in to the Reiki modality,
in the Purity of your being.
You have a choice to use the energy of your being
or you have the choice to use
the Energy of Spirit and beyond.
Understand when you heal with the energy of your earth being,
you have negativity that may taint the energy
you place upon another, even with the best of intentions,
for you live in a plane of negativity.
You will come to understand that you may choose to allow
the high self of being to flow through
the earth body and mind
and will great Energy, healing Energy.
When you allow the Energy of Spirit to enter in,
it is without negativity.
Your Pillar of Light[11] holds the negativity at bay,
so that the Energy entering in
and its power remains undiluted, pure in its essence.
Understand Reiki was given unto the earth to heal
the body and the mind
The symbols brought to the earth by the great teacher
were designed to focus your intent.
They are not magical.
Within themselves they have no power, the power is within you,
and you focus and imbue the symbol with power.
It is a tool, a teaching tool.
When you are attuned by a Reiki Master,
the symbols that are given unto thee
are a trigger mechanism;
they remind your being of the agreement that you made,
before you entered in to earth.
Each being who has been attuned, each Reiki Master,
all have made that agreement before entering in to earth.

Be well aware that Reiki, as in all things, has levels,
and the levels are not earth levels.
We would have you understand that the levels we speak of
are that of beyond the earth, unto the level of high self,
unto the level of Spirit.
And you, in your wisdom, in your Purity,
may choose to heal from an earth level,
or you may choose the higher level
and heal with more power, Purity and goodness,
even saintliness.
As in all things you have all choice.
We would have you, who practice Reiki,
understand the reason, the requirement of the sweep,
at the end of each Reiki session,
whether it be two minutes or twenty minutes.
We would ask that you in your intent,
place your hands palm down over
the solar plexus of the being
and then sweep in a motion along the body of the being.
This may be done from the top of the head
unto the solar plexus
and then from the solar plexus down.
The intent is to move away any lingering negativity
as if you were sweeping the being's aura.
Do not, as you sweep, place it downward.
Indeed not!
The sweeping motion must end in upward,
palms up offering it to Creator.
And then move your hands together, rub the left over the right
toward your flesh once, twice, thrice.
Hands up again and then place your hands together
in the prayer position and namaste.
This will complete a disconnection of your aura
with the other aura.
This exercise makes a clean break of the connection,
done, Soul, with the intent of Love.

293 Souls of earth, we would speak
of the vibrational chakras.
We would have you picture in your earth mind, a whirling,
spinning Energy as your sun, bright, warm, life giving.

Each chakra within your body,
and we speak now only of the main chakras
for you have many beyond the primary seven,
each is affected by the body, by the mind,
by the emotion of a being.
All illnesses affect the chakras.
They block the Energy.
It is as if there was a tunnel covered
so that air could not enter through.
And so an illness will place a cover over a chakra,
not permitting the Energy to flow freely, Soul,
from top to bottom and from bottom to top.
Stress is infamous for blocking chakras,
for placing barrier to the free flow of Energy.
The mind, when thoroughly involved with the negative ego,
places barrier upon the free flow of Energy.
You may cleanse, clear the blockage,
as if you removed a barrier
to allow the Energy to flow freely.
This Energy, when flowing freely,
is fully in the state of goodness,
has no negativity attached, either in intent or action.
The fullness of the goodness of the free flowing Energy
will heal the most destitute, the most terminal,
the most hopeless of cases.
Oft times a being, who is in desperation of illness,
is so caught within the pain, within the desperation,
that they are unable to heal themselves.
Cleansing and clearing the chakras
will enable that being to do so.
Cleansing and clearing the chakras will enable another
to heal that being lost in pain.
As your sun on a cloudy day is hidden from you,
the rays not nearly as warm; so it is with your chakras,
negativity clouds them,
affects the rays of entering in and entering out.
A clear chakra is never cloudy
and in that clearness, in that fullness of goodness is able
to reach unto the sacred self and heal and be.
The possibilities of free flowing Energy of goodness
have no limit to the well being of self, of others,

or indeed, of the earth.

294 We would teach on the chakras
within the palms of your hand.
They are directly in the center of each hand.
You may by tapping gently upon the center of your palm,
awaken a chakra that has been heretofore asleep.
The tapping is done slowly with a cadence,
seven times on each palm:
one and two, one and two, one and two, one and two,
one and two, one and two, one and two.
Once you begin to feel the tingling,
you have successfully begun to awaken
the sacred chakras of the palms.
If you do not feel the tingling,
continue with the cadence until you do, Souls.
We would have you understand,
the chakras of the palms
are directly connected to the third eye.
Directly, Souls of earth.
What happens in the chakras, in the palms,
happens with the eye.
You cannot successfully use the sacred chakras
without removing the barriers of the eye.
This is imperative to understand.
And we would also have you understand
that various motions of the fingers,
various positions of the fingers,
affect the whole being
when you have cleared the barriers from the third eye.
When the palm is in an upright position
and the right thumb and forefinger
are touching each other,
as are the left thumb and forefinger touching each other,
this is the universal language of surrender.
Surrender to the high self.
Not in your earth language of surrender,
but in the spiritual sense of surrender,
of acknowledging that the high self
has more wisdom and knowledge
than does the earth self.

And in that acknowledgment, it will be as if the sun shone
 through the clouds of your being.
And you will have access,
 clear access to the knowledge you have accumulated,
 and the wisdom you have accumulated
 throughout your lifetimes.
And even access to the Akashic Record,[12]
 to the Writing on the Wall.[13]
There is no knowledge hidden that you cannot access.
But understand, this position is in concert
 with the removal of the barriers of the third eye.
When you place the palms up,
 the thumb touching the first two fingers,
 and place the last two fingers touching the palm,
 you are in then a position of meditation.
This position when used for meditation
 increases the depth of meditation and allows the being
 to enter forth, with an ease, the consciousness of self,
 and travel even beyond the bounds of earth.
When you move the last two fingers out while maintaining
 the thumb and the two fingers held together,
 this is an indication of the serenity of being.
Upon your earth plane,
 you may use it to bring peace to self and others.
It focuses the Energy.
It gives the Energy a specific direction.
It enables and pulls together all of the chakras
 with the intent of peace, of serenity, of meditation.
These positions are powerful.
And because they are powerful,
 they are only available once the eye has been cleared.

295 We give thee instruction for the reparation,
 of the tears, the rents within your being.
These tears cause leakages of your precious Purity
 and allow an opening for negativity
 to inveigle its way within.
We would have you close these tears.
Do this, Souls, until your rents are mended,
 until your tears are closed, until you feel whole.

Step 1
Lift thy right hand, raise it in front of the eye.

Step 2
Take thy left hand, raise it in front of the eye.

Step 3
Place the sides of your palms together, as you cup your hands.

Step 4
Place the cupped hands palms up in front of the eye.

Step 5
Feel the white, the golden white Energy enter in to thy hands.
Feel it building, see its coruscating brilliance
and then, Souls, gently, carefully move
thy cupped hands toward the eye,
so they are now over the eye.
Let the Light fill those tears within your aura
and seal those tears, Soul.

Step 6
Take thy hands, cupped, and move them in the swirl,
in the cho ku rei, three times, in front of the eye.

Step 7
Gently separate thy hands, cup them palms up once again.

Step 8
Move the hands to underneath thy chin
in the position of namaste and you have completed.

296 We would have you understand the original premise
of this gesture of the hands in the prayer position
touching the third eye,
and the slight bow to the person you are greeting.
Originally this gesture was designed, indeed, as a greeting,
but as a greeting of healing intent,
for you came to the being to offer your healing hands,
and you bowed at their acceptance of your offering.
And so over time it became what you see today,

losing some of its meaning.
Indeed, maintaining a respect,
but losing that which was its first auspicious beginning.
You will understand the gestures,
the myriad of gestures upon the earth
that signify to various cultures various meanings,
have been distorted for the most part.
There are very few left in their purity.
There are very few left maintaining the integrity
of that which was given in many cases, millennia ago.
You will understand, Soul,
placing the thumb and the forefinger together
raised with the palm outward is
signifying the intention to speak of healing.
It was to gain the focus and the attention
of other beings or another being,
for the eye is drawn to the sacred palm,
the sacred chakra.
And the closed finger and thumb,
represent the peaceful intention of the healer.
This was used in Reiki as a prelude to healing.
The Reiki Master would place
before the being requesting healing,
both hands in this position.
And then the hands would be placed over above the head,
as a Reiki Master connected with the Soul of the being.
Once the connection was complete,
the Master would remove the thumb and forefinger
from touching, placing the Energy unto the head,
the top of the head, not touching,
placing the Energy received.
And then, palms up, receiving more Energy
and palms over placing again the Energy received.
Always thrice,
always thrice.
And then would move the hands down the body,
and at the feet open upward the palms.
Receive.
Bring them downward at the bottom of the feet,
and repeat the process
as was done at the top of the head;

and placing, receive and placing.
And then back upward, both hands to the top of the head.
And then around unto the ears, again, not touching,
but placing on either side of the head
the palms at the ear level.
And then moving the hands upward, receiving,
placing unto the ear.
And then moving up away from the face,
placing your hands together in the prayer position
in gratitude for the healing.

297 Souls of earth, those of you who practice Reiki
for purposes of healing, we would have you understand
the importance of tones
as you are sending forth the healing Energy,
Whether it be with the being present
within the same area of containment,
or whether it be with the being
on the other side of the world,
this Energy may be enhanced in its vibrational mode
through toning.
The vibrational tone of High C[14] will give motion
to the Energy that you are sending out.
It will increase the vibration of this Energy so that
as it enters in to the being,
it will alter those cells that carry the disabling malady.
The stress, the emotional waves crashing upon the being,
will be soothed,
and the very cells will awaken
to the innate healing ability of the being,
and they will connect to the Soul's ability to heal,
to their own healing, to their own Soul.
The High C must be sounded
throughout the length of the session.
As you use the toning
in conjunction with the healing interchange,
you will find the length of time decreases.
You will find yourself knowing the healing has entered in.
When you combine High C and your Energy of healing,
you enter in to your sacred self.
You enter in to the Spirit, Essence of your being.

You heal, Soul, not of earth, indeed,
    you heal from that which you are, from Farside.
Souls of earth, we will speak of Reiki.
Many Souls of earth have embarked upon courses of Reiki
    for a myriad of reasons;
    some with a true desire to help others,
    some with an overwhelming desire to heal,
    to alleviate the pain of others;
    some with an overwhelming desire
    to become financially able,
    some as a toy to play with; a myriad of reasons.
We would have you understand Reiki in its original state,
    given, brought to earth, as a means of vibrational healing.
Mixed with colors, mixed with symbols and sounds
    to become the powerful healing of the Essence of self.
Reiki has been distorted.
In its pristine state, it was understood that all Souls
    may heal from their Essence,
    and that it was the responsibility,
    nay, the duty of some Souls
    to become Master Reiki teachers,
    to pass on the knowledge to others
    and to open the beings unto the possibilities within
    using the combination of sound, color and vibration.
When used in combination, this triad may heal within an
    immediacy, as you would term it, a blink of an eye,
    and the healing may be done
    whether the being is present in physicality in front of you
    or across your planet.
There is no distance, there is no time,
    within the realm of healing, when the triad is present.
You have attached to your body appendages called hands.
There is within the palm of each hand, a sacred chakra
    and it matters not whether you can physically
    see the hand or not, the sacred chakra is present.
Earth Souls little realize the holiness of the hands,
    the holiness of the chakra within the hands.
We do not lightly call them sacred chakras,
    for through them pass the Light of the Crystal Cave,
    the healing Light of your Creator
    that which, in a moment, may cause the blind to see,

the lame to walk, the sick to rise from their beds,
the mentally unstable to see clearly, the deaf to hear.
All this within the sacredness of thy being.
Souls of earth, you hold literally within the palms of your hands
that which can alleviate all suffering upon the earth,
that which can heal not only a fellow being,
but the very earth itself and all the creatures within.
Understand, Souls of earth, Reiki is a giving outward.
It is not a pulling inward.
And the choice you make when upon the earth,
whether to distort the sacred keeping given unto thee,
or to freely give the pristine truth of Reiki,
we would have you understand
it is indeed a choice of your own being.
Before each healing done with the sacred chakras,
place upon thy being the cloak of White Light,
the blue of Purity and the gold of care.
Understand the sacredness of these colors.
Understand the power that you deal with,
and that you may wield in their pristine state,
not as distortions.

Healing Chapter Two
Quan Yin

298 We would bring forth to you wisdom.
Upon your earth plane you have rain.
The rain may be harsh, the rain may be flood causing ruin.
The rain may be falling upon parched earth
and assist with the growth of plants.
We would speak to you of the gentle rain,
the warm gentle rain that every so often
is experienced in all parts of your earth.
This gentle rain is to remind you of the warmth
and the gentleness of the flow within the Pillar of Light
that surrounds your being.
It, too, has a gentleness and as the gentle rain,
it also has a strength.
So, too, does the Light in the Pillar of Light permeate,
if it is allowed.
You may place an umbrella over your being
and prevent a gentle rain from entering in to your being.
And much of earth has chosen
to place a barrier to the Pillar of Light,
and not allow the gentle flow of compassion and Love
to enter in to their being, to enter unto their psyche,
to their Soul.
Understand, the gentle rain has no harm within it
and yet is powerful.
And so is the Pillar of Light.
Just as you may place a container to gather the gentle rain
and use the water to quench your thirst,
so, too, the Pillar of Light
will quench the thirst of your Soul.
You may take that bowl of gentle rain water
and share it with another to quench their thirst
and you may do the same with the Pillar of Light.
You may use it to quench the thirst of another.
Be it pain, be it sorrow, be it addiction, be it illness, you may
quench and give unto that being sustenance of Love.
Be as the gentle rain, give forth surcease, quench the thirst
and know in your being the power of compassion.

Know in your being you have the choice of the power of
        compassion, and know in your being you are powerful.

299 Souls of earth, unto each life rain must fall.
The rain was placed upon the earth
        not only to engender the growth of plants,
        not only to provide survival of beings, of all beings,
        whether they be plants or human,
        in each drop of precious water, you have growth,
        growth for all upon the planet, including the planet.
Just as you cannot exist without air,
        you cannot exist without water.
It is as necessary to your being
        as breathing air for life upon your planet.
The earth is crowned with her oceans.
That is her diadem.
The oceans placed for the benefit of man;
        to assist in the growth of man,
        to assist in the purpose of humanity,
        to assist Souls of earth in the gathering,
        the gathering time.
The oceans are filled with life
        and we would have you understand
        they were filled with even more life
        and mankind has removed life from the oceans.
They have removed food from the oceans.
There is a great link of interconnectiveness
        within the oceans of your earth
        and the land mass of your earth.
When mankind destroys, removes from the ocean, life,
        food for other life,
        it is not an effect that is contained within the ocean.
Indeed not!
It affects all of the earth.
We would have you understand,
        the pollution that you have placed within the earth,
        will rebound to the detriment of all.
We would have you understand the negativity of the pollutions
        may be reversed by the very mankind that placed them,
        by the very mankind that created pollutants.
A gathering in oneness will heal your planet in an instant,

a gathering of oneness will heal the earth
to the extent that it will become
the pristine beauty that it was
when it entered in to the earth plane.
You have the potential to reverse that which you have done.
But, Souls of earth, the great earth can not wait much longer
and we would ask you to enter in
to your eye of beholding,
to heal the very planet upon which you live,
the very planet that succors your being,
the very planet that offered self,
that offered the very Soul of herself
to enable you to grow.
You have a moment to reverse.
Only a moment.
We would ask that you use the violet flame unto the earth.

300 We would have you understand each color has a sound.
Not as sound upon your earth.
To hear the sound of color you must enter in
to the Eye of Beholding,
you must allow the consciousness of your being
to fly beyond the bounds of earth,
to fly beyond the boundaries of your galaxy,
to fly, to soar unto Farside, unto Spirit.
To be in high consciousness,
you hear each and every being you encounter,
for within the Aura is Color and Sound,
for within the Aura of each being upon the Farside
is the identity of that being.
The Aura speaks to you
as if you were verbalizing
upon your earth plane with lips and words.
But there are no lips or voice, for it is not necessary.
The consciousness of your being connects
with the consciousness of another being,
with another world, with another plane,
unto that level that you have obtained.
The healing with Color and Sound
is done with the Eye of Beholding,
is done with the high consciousness itself,

is done, Souls of earth, with thy being upon the Farside.
It is the reaching unto thy high self.
And as you reach, you see with the Eye of Beholding
and you hear with the Eye of Beholding,
and you know instantly
as you look upon another being who is in pain,
who has illness, physical or mental,
who is tormented by demons of their own mind;
you will know that Color and Sound
that will soothe and heal that being.
You will have reached unto the violet flame of healing
and you will know what color is necessary preparatory
to the violet flame entering in.
This is not done over a period of days, or weeks or months.
Indeed not!
It is not done in hours or minutes,
it is done in your blink of an eye.
For there is no time and space when you are in the sacred self.
There is no time and space when you have attained
and reached unto high consciousness of being.
There is no time and space within Farside Color and Sound.
There is no barrier,
for you have flown beyond the bounds of earth.
There is nothing binding you, preventing you, holding you back
from reaching unto the sacred healing of the violet flame.
The violet flame will alter even the maimed,
will alter the cancerous cells,
will enter in and alter all neurological diseases,
will enter in and alter all diseases of the mind.
Will enter in and alter the most depraved, in your earth terms,
should the Soul agree.
The violet flame holds itself always ready,
holds itself always at full potential.
Holds itself as your birthright.
Holds itself at the level of six.
Holds itself vibrating, quivering in its eagerness to heal.
Reach unto the high consciousness of self,
bring forth the Color and Sound of the Farside
unto the earth plane
for you have that ability,
you have the potential of Truth, Love and Purity within.

You are particled of Truth, Love and Purity,
you are creators.
In all that you do, you create, and as a creation can be altered,
so is attaining and reaching unto
the violet flame of healing,
for you, as a creator, alter creation.

301 Souls, we would ask thee to sit quietly,
to raise thy hands palms up.
We would ask thee to close thy earth eyes
and focus with thy Eye.
Allow thy being to accept the Energy that is coming forward
from the Prism unto thy eye.
Tremble not at the vibration.
You feel, you sense.
Know ye that a vortex is in thy space, in thy Eye.
We ask that you give permission for the Energy to come forth
from the Prism into thine eye, hold thy being in stillness.
Beings who are manifested,
may use the power of the Crystal Cave to heal.
You know without a doubt how to reach, how to connect,
to access the power of the Crystal Cave.
You have within you the combined healing of humanity.
But you place barrier, you place veil, you place doubt.
Veils of doubt that prevent most adequately
your reaching unto the Crystal Cave.
Each of you may touch a being, bring instantaneous comfort,
instantaneous knitting of bones,
instantaneous repairing of a rupture,
instantaneous straightening of a spine,
instantaneous connecting
the nerves again of broken neck, of broken back.
Instantaneous healing of the hearing impaired,
of the visually impaired,
of those who have never been able to speak.
Healing, Soul, of the heart, broken,
healing of the inner organs.
There is naught that cannot be healed
with the power of the Crystal Cave,
unless the being refuses your permission to heal.
But all who ask may indeed be healed.

And you need not be physically present
with the being asking for healing.
You may transport your being unto that being,
also with the power of the Crystal Cave.
The Crystal Cave
is the combined Truth, Purity and Love of humanity.
It is the ecstasy of humanity, not your human self,
your Oneness as humanity;
that which is of your Creator.
You will understand to be in the Crystal Cave is beyond
any imagining you may do within your earth plane.
You could take the gentlest of beings upon your earth
and know that in the Crystal Cave
it would have no comparison in gentleness.
Indeed that is how great you are.
Remove the veils of doubt,
enter in to that which is the nature of your being.
Know you have reached the stage of plenty.
Know you may enter in.
You may reach unto in any moment of time.

302 Time as you understand it, upon the earth,
is a progression.
For what is done is done and cannot be undone,
but it can be mended.
It can be altered.
Within your mind
are all possibilities of Truth, of Love, of Purity.
All possibilities of your Creator are within thee.
You have, Souls of earth, progressed over the years,
indeed, over millennium
to alter the precious gem of earth from its pristine state
as it was set by Creator, placed within
as an orb of this universe in its Purity,
for mankind to progress and grow in their Purity.
The sound of earth in its pristine state
was as the tone of pure crystal upon the earth,
a bell of sound ringing forth in joyous harmony.
But in your time travel upon earth,
you have altered that tone
by the toxins and the pollution.

You have lost for earth the clear ringing tone of Purity.
The crystal sound is no more.
Can you travel back in time and reverse this?
No, but you may travel in your present time and heal and mend.
For all you need to do is travel unto your sacred self,
enter in to the Crystal Cave, and bring unto the earth
the glorious healing of the Crystal Cave,
so that once again she may sound
with that crystal pure note of joyous harmony.
You may turn the disharmony created by mankind
into the magnificent coruscating colors of great joy.
for you and earth are intertwined
and her glory is your glory.
And your glory is hers.

303 We have a need.
We have a need for Souls of earth to comprehend
the enormity of the power of their being.
We have a need for you to understand
that in your high consciousness of being, you may,
literally, not figuratively, literally feed the starving.
You may enter forth manna
which will fill not only the heart and Soul of a being
but fill the belly.
You may appear wherever you desire,
and those to whom you appear
will see you as substantial, not ghost like.
In the high consciousness of being, all is possibility.
Each being upon the earth,
when rising to high consciousness,
connects to the Farside self.
That Farside self has color, has sound,
and imbues the earthly being with that Color and Sound.
The vibration of Color and Sound, when joined together,
is all powerful upon your earth plane.
And this is why
you must be in high consciousness to wield such power.
In your high consciousness,
you rise your being in Love and compassion

and in the ecstasy of your being, you become total Love.
In that total Love, you heal.
You heal the mind.
You heal the body and you heal the Soul.
Understand, Souls of earth,
to reach high consciousness requires a state of Purity,
requires a state of acceptance
of the color and sound of who you are;
requires the wisdom that you are not merely
this physical being of the earth,
but you are so much more.
It is complexity that may be made simple by acceptance.
Be.

304 Souls of earth, we would explain
the inner connection to the golden Light.
Gold upon your earth is precious.
Gold upon your earth is used symbolically;
within religions, within their temple,
within their vestments,
to symbolize the richness of their dedication.
Mankind innately knows the value of gold,
but not, Souls of earth, the gold of earth.
It is the gold of your sacred self.
It is the gold of your Creator that you innately understand.
But because you are within this veil of negativity,
you transpose this knowledge into physical manifestation
and it is distorted by man's greed, avarice, lust for power.
The physical representation is, therefore,
distorted with negativity created by man.
It is the distorted mirror of the fun house
that rears its head upon the earth.
A minute, a minuscule,
one millionth of a decibel of Energy of the golden Light
is of more value than all your riches upon the earth.
We would have you understand the gentle flavoring of life.
We would have you understand
your ability to taste the flavor of life.
We would have you understand, it is not as a bitter medicine

unless that is what you have created for your being.
The flavor of life is sweet as honey.
It is as aromatic as the Balm of Gilead.
It is as healing as the Balm of Gilead.
You need only reach out your being,
reach out your palm, to hold within the golden Light,
that is within each Pillar of Light.
That is the flavor of life.
That is the Balm of Gilead.
For this golden Light is the Love of your Creator,
and when placed upon a being or upon self,
negativity can no longer withstand,
it must leave the being.
This golden Energy is palpable.
You can feel it.
We would have you stretch forth thy hands,
not in supplication but in receiving.
Allow the Light, the golden Light to enter in
to rest as a feather upon the palms of your hands.
And then turn your palms slowly facing each other.
Hold no more than six inches apart.
See with the Eye the golden Light
seething, pulsating with Energy.
Bring your hands slowly towards each other
and then turn your hands, touching each hand
at the little fingers and the sides of the palms,
and allow the golden ball of Energy
to lightly rest within your hands.
They are as a cup.
They are as a full open blossom of Energy.
Allow the Energy to grow
until you have a connection
between the eye and the ball of Energy.
And then as the connection increases in decibel of vibration,
place the Energy.
It is vibrational.
It is altering Energy that may alter.
And you may then place this upon any being in need of succor,
in need of comfort, in need of healing.

Let the Light enter in unto the Soul of the being
and the Soul will heal the flesh and the mind.

305 We present unto you, for your edification,
a mantra of epic proportions.
This mantra is dedicated
to balancing the nervous system of a being.
It is to be entered in to in Purity.
It is to be entered in to in a quiet contemplative state,
in a place of quietness, of serenity.
If you have no such place, you may create such a place
simply by using your Pillar of Light and entering in.
The mantra, Souls, is to be done thrice daily
until the being is at peak perfection,
until its Soul sings and the being
may recognize their high self.
And we say unto you the tone in this particular case is sing song
but it is the words and the syllables that are important,
not whether a tune may be carried or not.
"Oh thou beloved.
Oh thou beloved.
Oh thou beloved.
Enter thou in to my being.
Enter thou in to my Soul.
Enter thou in to my mind.
Oh beloved.
Oh beloved.
Oh beloved, make unto my being thy holiness.
Make unto my Soul thy holiness.
Make unto my mind thy holiness.
Oh my beloved.
Oh my beloved.
Oh my beloved."

306 Souls of earth, for all circles dedicated to healing,
we would suggest a method to enhance the healing
that you send forth within your circle.
You understand the Light within your being.
We would have you reach unto the White Light and then,

we would have you move it unto the being on your left.
That being on your left pulls the Energy,
combines it with theirs and moves it unto the next being,
who then does the same
unto each being around the table
and unto the beginning.
Allow the Energy to continue to circle
unto each and into each being.
Focus that Light.
It is as a revolving Light, a wheel,
that increases in speed as it moves from being to being.
And then you enter it in to the healing,
whether it is the earth or individual beings
that have been placed into the center of the circle.
And that wheel of Energy
has a vortex that affects those placed in the circle.
And the Light that filtered, that entered in to each being,
will bring peace to that being.

307 The earth body has a responsive mechanism
to the east ritual.[15]
The physical body responds to the vibration from the Farside,
from the Spirit, oft times even from Angel guides
and rarely from Essence of self.
Rarely, not because it is withheld
but because the Soul will not accept.
It is difficult upon the earth plane
to accept the glory of who you are.
When entering in to the east ritual, Souls of earth,
indeed, some beings find themselves
pushed back by the energy.
It is not that the energy is pushing you back
in your physical state,
it is that the body moves itself away
from the Energy being rained down upon you,
for it is not yet ready to release negativity.
And so, it pulls back.
When the Soul is pulled forward,
when the physical being is pulled forward,

that is the opportunity to transcendental travel.
You are being called, Soul.
If it was on your earth plane,
it would be, 'Come. Come here. We wait. Come'.
And so, when the being is, shall we say, in a neutral position,
the body neither moves forward or back.
It is so, because the mind is busy, thoughts broiling,
the being is not fully in the moment,
and so the fullness of what is available is ignored.
And so as you enter in to your east ritual,
we would have you understand,
you are not merely a cipher,
an inconsequential part of the ritual.
You indeed have the opportunity to partake fully,
or to refuse, or to only partially accept.
We would have you understand, the ritual is an offering
of communication between self and Farside self,
between self and Spirits of Farside.
It is a moment of communion.
It is a moment of Holy communion
but it is only offered, not forced.
When you are able to take full advantage
of that which is offered,
you will see exploding universes, stars of depth
and you will know, in a very minute form,
that which is ecstasy.

308 We would speak of the healing properties
of the color green,
of the various modalities of healing
with the color of green.
You may look to nature for the enormous variety,
the incredible variety of shades of green,
and know that with your earth eyes,
you see only a fraction
of these permutations of color.
Using the third eye,
there will be many more gradations of color
than you can imagine is possible with your earth eyes.

You will use the color of the palest of greens upon the temple,
in a circular motion, for instant relaxation of your being,
of the physical being.
Those who see with the third eye
will see the vibrant intensity of the color.
They will see the vibration and its effects upon the body.
Those who use only the earth eyes will not see this,
but they will sense and feel their relaxation,
for your form reacts to color.
You, Soul, are designed to react to color.
The very pores of your skin react to color.
The very blood within you,
the very bone and sinew of your being react to color,
and your mind is color, as is your will and your aura.
The gentle massaging with the palest of greens requires
only a minimum expenditure of physical energy.
You may use the first two fingers upon another
who cannot reach the temples of their being.
And in the same circular clockwise motion
you may grant them the relaxation.
Very gently, there is no pressure required,
only the feathery touch of compassion and Love.
Know that even unto thy cats and dogs
the same will work for them.
When they are agitated, Souls, merely a little feather touch.
The same color may be used as a massage
for tired sore muscles.
Always, feathery light touch in a circular motion
and you will feel the aches and the pain recede.
And you will see the color gently enter in
and soothe the injured members of skin,
of muscle, of tendon.

309 We would have you understand the pressure points
within the head of your being that may be applied
pressure to alleviate glaucoma.

Step 1
Close your eyes.

Step 2
Take both the thumb and the forefinger,
placing one thumb on each side
underneath the jaw line to the extent
that you may reach the forefinger to the temples.
For some, it may be a longer for their hands are wider.
For others, it would be shorter.
Hold this position, gently pressing upon
the four points for fifteen seconds.

Step 3
At the end of the fifteen seconds,
slowly release the forefingers from the temples,
maintaining the thumbs touching the jaw line.

Step 4
Move the forefingers and press them into the position
in the top of the earlobes,
in a direct diagonal to the previous temple position.
Bring your forefinger down
until it touches your earlobe.
Your fingers, except for the forefingers, are to be held
lightly against the palm of your being.

Step 5
Press lightly the earlobes and hold that position
for a further fifteen seconds.

Step 6
Move the forefingers down to the middle portion of the ear,
but not inside the ear.
Pressing inward the skin,
not pressing inward into the ear with the fingers,
but pressing that flesh inward,
until it is as you have closed your ears.
Hold for five seconds.

Step 7
Gently, slowly, release the forefingers and release the thumbs.

This, in the beginning stages of glaucoma will need to be done
at least thrice daily.
If you have entered into glaucoma further than the beginning,
then we would suggest this be done
a minimum of five times per day.
If you have reached the stage of glaucoma in its entirety,
you would be required to do this exercise twice an hour
each day until it receded from your being.

310 We bring unto you an exercise designed
to soothe any being who is unable
to communicate, even unto an adult,
that is in pain but unable to express
in a language the pain.

Step 1
Place the thumb and forefinger of each hand touching:
the thumb touching thumb,
forefinger touching forefinger
and the finger next to the forefinger touching
the same finger on the other hand.
The other fingers are loosely held.

Step 2
Place this pyramidal shape over the third eye of the being
and make a circle in front of the eye.

Step 3
Make a circle thrice, and pull from the being the pain.

Step 4
As you pull, bring your hands up, up, up past your third eye,
and then open up your hands, palm up.
Allow that energy to leave that you have pulled from the being.

Step 5
Cup your hands with the edges touching, receiving Energy.

Step 6
Place the Energy above the third eye
letting it flow into the third eye.

Step 7
Repeat this procedure thrice
and you will begin to see a lessening of the pain.

311 Settle down.
We ask you to settle down your being, literally, Soul.
Do this thrice each time you sense a tenseness
within your being, a frustration.

Step 1
Spread the hands wide open and place them
on either side of the top of the head.

Step 2
Slowly bring them, down, very slowly.
Settle them down and down and down unto your shoulders.
Allow your shoulders to relax.

Step 3
Place your left hand upon your right shoulder
and the right upon the left.

Step 4
Let your head slowly drop and
relax the shoulders.
Melt into the embrace.
Feel the relaxation.
Let go of the tension.

Step 5
Slowly move your hands, placing them in front of you.

Step 6
Turn them over, palms down and deep breath in,

breathe out: ahhhhhhhhhh,
and allow the tension to flow from you.

Healing Chapter Three
Color

312 We speak of the dimensional Energy.
We would have you understand dimensional Energy.
It is the colors of the rays of Light intermingled with the sound.
It is as if you looked upon a ray of light
coming in from your window,
and within that ray of light are motes of dust.
But, if you looked closer with your science's magnification,
you would see all sorts and manners of energies.
These Light rays, these colors emit sound;
they are identifiers, and each color,
as we have stated previously,
are not intermingled but cooperate.
Each has a specific intentionality for your being.
Each is formulated to assist
in the altering of matter unto wellness,
unto the perfection of that which is meant to be.
Not perfection judged by earth eyes,
but the perfection of wellness which is seen by the eye.
Understand the difference;
understand the Eye does not judge.
The eyes judge,
and when there is judgment it interferes,
it is a barrier that you choose
between the consciousness of your being and the colors.
Reaching unto high consciousness,
you instantly are aware of the color, or colors
that will bring that being unto perfect wellness,
unto a vibrational harmony.
All the cells, all the billions of cells within that being,
in perfect harmony,
resonating unto High C in their perfection.
Can the being who is lame be in perfect wellness?

Indeed, Soul.
With your earth eyes, you judge them as being unwell,
but the Eye would know,
would discern the wellness of that being.
Look with your eye, not your earth eyes.
The colors vibrate with an intensity of motion
and motion that is not discernible to the earth eyes.
That is not to say that you may not heal, or assist in the healing,
we speak of healing potential,
possibility of the Light rays of Creator.
They have a density, a density you may see with the eye,
feel with the chakras of your palm.
It is a weight upon your palms.
It is not lifeless; indeed they are filled with life,
and the promise of more life.
Anticipate joyousness, anticipate healing as miraculous
in its instantaneousness; for this you will do.
You will hear when in the dimensional reality of the colors,
the glory chimes.
You will be uplifted in sound vibration.
You will walk above the earth, not in vainglory, but in ecstasy.
For you will leave behind the flesh
and enter in to pure consciousness,
and there you will find Color and Sound.
And so, beloved Souls, to the dance of colors.
To each and every one is granted, is built in, is in thy Soul,
the knowing, the recognition,
the awareness of the dance of colors.
It matters not if you have one foot or no feet,
for the dance of colors is not upon the earth.
It is, when you leave behind that earthly being.
And thereupon when your consciousness,
when your awareness implodes,
you begin the dance of colors.
Each being has this ability.
For it only takes leaving behind all that is earth
and becoming aware of your Lightness of being,
becoming aware that you are Light,
that you have within and without Light,
that your consciousness began at Light and so continues.
Enter in to the dance of color.

Reclaim that which you are, Light, and dance, Souls, dance.
Your Purity is of your being, is of your aura,
    flows and swirls constantly about thy being.
There is no magic word,
    there is no magic gesture that will free your Purity
    to cloak the land, to care for your fellow beings.
It is you, Soul, and you, Soul, and you, Soul,
    who choose to reach and open thyself and open
    thy Purity to let it flow through thy earthly being.
Vision the Purity of your Soul being,
    a funnel of Light; brilliant, coruscating, warm Light
    flowing into thy being.
As you open to the flow, the flow becomes greater.
And hence, it becomes the fountain that can gush forth
    for those who thirst about thee,
    for those who sorrow about thee,
    for those in pain about thee, for those in agony,
    for those in negativity.
And, Souls, when we speak about those about thee,
    there is no distance,
    we speak of the planet,
    not your street, not your city,
    not your country, but the planet.
You have great responsibility, Souls,
    and we applaud your courage.
Know that our wings are always about thee.

313 Souls of earth, we speak of color
    and the effects of color upon your being.
Why would color have an effect?
It is because it is hard wired into your mind,
    into your consciousness,
    into indeed, even the brain and the cells of your body.
For you understand, you have come from color.
When you entered in to the earth,
    you brought with you the knowing of color,
    you brought with you the ability to respond to color
    indelibly marked into your aura.
All moods may be affected by color.
Color is who you are.
Your aura vibrates, pulsates with color.

All color has vibration.
All color has sound.
All color affects your being in some way.
You have research to prove the effects of certain colors
upon the mind set of a being.
And we would have you understand each color,
each phase of color has a particular property to it,
has a particular vibration,
has indeed, its own unique sound
that your being responds to.
It is the sound and vibration of the color
that the cells of your body respond to.
It is the color itself that your Soul recognizes,
that your aura throbs with
and may expel in a thrum unto another.
A thrum of healing with color,
for the color that throbs within your aura,
that from which you have come, is Holy,
has power to heal, to alter.
But the aura must be in wellness to do this,
for the aura that has rents and cracks
cannot function fully with the power of its potential.
Indeed, the aura of your being
may embrace the aura of another being, healing,
but a rend, a tear in the aura
prevents the fullness of healing potential.
It is as if instead of your arms being wide open
to embrace another, they are almost closed,
and so the embrace is quite limited.
The same with the aura that is broken, has tears and rents.
It is quite limited in comparison to one in wellness,
to an aura in its earth perfection
that may entertain healing of the Essence of being.
The color that may envelop your being
at the level of Essence healing
has little relationship to the vibrancy of earth color,
for it is so much more.
You may in the wellness of your being, feel the color
by simply placing your hands outward,
open palm facing open palm,
your arms spread to the width of your shoulders.

You may hear the color and see the color with the eye,
and you have all potential
to heal with this color.
For when your aura is in wellness
and it has reached unto the Light of your origin,
the healing may be instantaneous,
may be fermented within the psyche of another being.
Not forced, Soul, never forced.
For within the wellness of an aura,
only total compassion and Love.
You have all this potential,
heal thy aura and heal mankind.

314 We would have you understand you are color.
Your aura is color.
It is your identification.
Within that color is sound and vibration.
All that you have been,
all that you have done, all that you are,
all that from which you have been formed
is visible and readable with the eye.
Understand because you are color,
your psyche is affected by earth color.
You have an affinity and thereby a connection to,
and thereby a reaction to.
When the eye is opened, the veils removed,
then you are consciously aware
of the effect of color upon the being;
upon the mind and upon the body and the heart.
The heart takes precedence
when you are in the unconscious state
and unaware of the effects.
The heart will feel cold to a certain color.
The heart will know that that color is helpful.
The heart will know to shy away from that color
that brings forth negative vibrations.
But the heart working on its own,
without the cooperation of the eye and the mind,
cannot process and you stumble, as it were,
in the darkness of unconsciousness.
When your mind is full partner with the eye of your aura

and the heart of your being,
you have a knowing as a healer
which color and which shade
will assist the being upon the earth plane.
You will know what color to enter in from your sacred self
to help balance the being.
Understand, whether in the unconscious or the conscious,
all color affects each and every being,
in its collectiveness, affects all about thee.
For as you stumble forth in your unconsciousness you may,
inadvertently stumble into another,
but in your consciousness
you walk forward confidently and stumble not.
Color, Souls of earth, was placed upon the earth
to assist you in your purpose of humanity.

315 All colors upon the face of your earth are a dim
reflection of the color of Farside healing,
of Essence healing.
Colors upon the earth remind your Soul of home.
The Soul reacts to color.
The mind reacts to color.
The heart reacts to color.
The reaction of each of the three to a particular color
will depend upon the growth of Purity.
If you are attracted to green at a particular period
in your existence upon the earth plane,
it is because the body requires healing.
If you are attracted to red,
in a particular time upon your existence,
you have a great need to ground thy being,
to recognize the path you have taken,
to find within yourself the recognition
and the knowledge of negativity.
If you are attracted to the color of blue,
it is not for the body, it is for the earth mind.
It is to provide clarity to the earth mind
when you are struggling with an issue.
And the struggle may not even be readily apparent to thy being.
The blue is an indication of struggle of the mind.
Violet, when you are attracted to the color, violet,

you have a deep need of your Soul and heart
to engage in spiritual growth,
to welcome spirituality into your life.
It is an indication you need to become aware,
to recognize, to understand your higher self,
that you are not here only upon the earth,
but you have a Farside being Spirit and Essence.
Orange, the attraction to orange is to get busy.
It says to you that you have stilled your walk,
that you need to pick up the pieces of your life
and enter in to your walk.
An attraction to yellow is a literal reminder
to bring sunshine and joy into your life,
for you have too long resisted joy,
you have too long muddied thy being
with cares and concerns;
let the Light enter in.

316 We would speak with thee on the properties
of color that you can access from the Prism of healing
to give forth to all the Balm of Gilead.
Within the properties of color
there are turn upon turn upon turn.
No color is static, no color remains still.
There is movement,
there is constant swirling movement of a vortex.
Each color creates its own vortex,
each color blends into the vortex,
into the Flow of Creator,
and you can bring those colors into healing.
Know ye that colors are a gift of healing from your Creator,
and we ask that the gift be used widely and wisely.
Within each color there is an ionization that takes effect
when it is joined with your Energy, with your Purity.
It activates the color, it activates the force of the color,
it activates the flow of the color,
it activates the vortex of the color.
Color in itself is a gift of beauty, is a gift of soothing,
is a gift of joy, is a gift of calm, a gift of healing,
It must be combined, it must entwine.
It must flow within each other.
Your Purity and color bring forth healing together as a flow,

a swirling, whirling vortex of Energy.
Combine the Energy,
bring it in and know ye that you have begun to heal.
Build that vortex, build that Energy
and bring forth to all of mankind,
to all of the planet, to all of the life forms, to all that is.
Beloveds, see with thy Eye the Prism,
beloveds, use thy Eye to visit, to come to Farside.
Use thy Eye to travel through the Prism and bring forth,
into thy Purity the healing colors.
Oh, how powerful is the joining of thy Purity and color!
How wondrous, what a gift from thee to Creator!
What a gift from thee to humanity!

317 We would speak to thee of vibration, beloved Souls.
Know ye, that in every moment your energies vibrate,
they vibrate throughout the land,
they vibrate throughout mankind,
reaching each and every Soul.
From every Soul comes vibration.
We speak to you of the oneness.
Know ye that, in the fullness of vibration,
in the fullness of vibrational time within the earth plane,
healing can be yours.
Know that within the vibration of the Soul
are the colors gifted to mankind.
Know that each color has its own features of vibration.
Know that in the pearlescent pink is Love,
unconditional Angelic Love.
Allow it to warm thy being.
Allow thy being to feel Love.
Know that you, too, can express this warmth,
this unconditional Love to all.
Know that your thoughts have vibration.
Know that your thoughts can be focused,
know that all beings are receptors.
Be careful of the emittance of thy vibrational thoughts.
Take loving care of the reception of thoughts.
Within thy core is Love.
It is not meant to be hoarded.
It is not meant to be hidden!
Give all you can to be shared.
Give out thy Light, thy Love and gift it to the world,

to all of mankind.
Open thy being, open thy Soul's core of Love.

318 We bring unto you knowledge of the earth color pink.
We would have you understand the color of the pink
is most efficacious to beings in distress,
whether that distress be from grief or worry
or angst and anxiety of any kind.
Merely placing over the shoulders
of the being the softest of pink,
placing this soft color of pink over the being,
will begin to initiate a relief of the symptoms.
The being will have the impetus to ease the pain within.
It is preferable that the pink cloth used
be that which is not manmade,
for if it is not a natural cloth,
it will lose some of its efficacity.
A child crying, restless, feverish,
will also benefit from this color of cloth
laid upon its being.
A Soul may also, to stimulate the innate healing internally,
the innate need to comfort self,
may also gaze upon this color and increase its efficacy.
You may indeed also place a light of this color
to beam upon the being in distress,
for no more than three of your earth minutes at a time.
Longer than that will not increase its value.
We would recommend to any being
to replace worry in their mind
with this color and see that worry begin to fade.
It is a tool, Souls of earth, that we give unto you.

319 We would speak with you upon the properties
of the color green.
It is no accident that upon the face of your earth you have green,
various shades in your plant life.
For each shade of green has a definite movement,
a vibration, a vibratory propensity.
And each vibration, has a propensity to heal a certain ailment
whether it be an ailment of the mind or the body.
The deepest shades of green almost into the black,
which you may find in nature in the forest deep within
and you may find within some places in the ocean floor

and you may find beneath which you call pond scum.
We would have you look for the shade of this particular green
with the eye, not in your palettes of color.
Souls of earth, to bring forth a particular vibratory propensity
of a shade of color you must use the eye not the eyes.
For those who suffer from palsy of any type
brought on by varying types of ailments,
this deep shade of green will be most efficacious.
You may place it upon the body, head to toe,
each day until improvement is noted.
Each day a reduction,
place six times per day until improvement is noted
and then five and four and three
and two and one until the being is healed.
It matters not whether the palsy, the tremors
are slight or vigorous,
the color is of great healing in that ailment.
And now we enter in to the very palest shade of green,
almost unto a white with just a hint of the green.
All Souls afflicted with carbuncle, whether it be one or many,
whether it be on face or leg,
they will benefit from the use of that shade of color
for it will absorb the bacteria that causes the carbuncle.
It will provide surcease from pain and itching of the carbuncle,
you will see daily a decrease until it disappears.

320 We would have you understand the color olive green.
We speak of the olive green found in the Prism.
It bears some resemblance to that of your earth olive green,
but it has a vibrancy, a transparency, a stimulus
well beyond that of the earth color.
Many upon your earth see olive green as drab, as uninteresting,
and yet, even upon the plane of earth,
the color has an effect upon the mind.
Olive green is especially helpful for the being caught
in the throes of your breast cancer,
whether it be male or female.
Wearing the color olive green upon your earth,
you will find it stimulates the healing process.
This color is a neutralizing factor.
When from the high mind,[16]
given unto a being lost in the throes of cancer,
it will immediately neutralize, halt the spread.

And then, Souls of earth, you will be given the color of purple
to complete the healing while the olive
holds the negativity at bay.
The olive upon your earth will also assist, but,
understand to a lesser extent.
And yet, it will have an effect upon the mind.
The olive of the Prism is pure in its own state of being.
Upon your earth plane, we would recommend
the very lightest of olive shades, not unto the dark olive,
maintain the light olive.
Wear it as a covering about the affected body.
This, we give unto you.

321 We speak on the color orange.
There are layers and layers and layers
of possibilities of the color orange.
You will understand that the very palest of orange,
lacking the vibrant hue of red may be soothing,
may be in effect calming,
especially to the elderly afflicted
with the senility of the Alzheimer,
also effective for the young child
afflicted with hyperactivity.
The less the red is involved in the orange,
the more soothing the color upon your earth plane.
Understand all are affected by the vibration of the color.
We would speak on the properties,
on the color orange,
from the very palest of orange
unto the very deepest orange,
the very darkest orange entering almost into a brown.
The very palest orange will have a light tinge of gold.
The medium orange will have a deeper tinge of gold
and will be lighter than the color
of your deep orange, navel oranges.
And then, the darker phases will be as those orange color,
but with a deep golden tinge.
This is already known upon your earth.
We will speak on the properties of the color orange
that may be used in a healing modality.
The very palest of orange,
will be as a soother to the infant
who cries from loneliness and pain.

Those infants abandoned would benefit
        from being bundled in this color.
Those infants who are premature would benefit from this color.
Those infants who have had a surgery
        would benefit from this color.
The cloth of this color, to be most efficacious
        would be in a natural fabric, not manmade fabric.
Optimally, for the infant, it would cover most of the body.
For the very elderly who have had the feeling of abandonment,
        whether it is caused by loss of family,
        or whether it is caused by the imagination,
        will benefit from a covering of this color.
It will also soothe to have nearby this color,
        whether it be in a painting or in a furniture accouterment
        or even a pillow to rest the head on.
This color in the very palest of shades with the tinge of gold,
        speaks to the Soul.
The vibration of this color tells the Soul they are not alone.
They are in care.
Those who are autistic would benefit
        from wearing clothes of this color.
This color placed upon the wrists of the autistic will soothe,
        will allow the being to feel safer
        to enter back into the world.
It need not be cloth.
It may be paper but not leather
        or other manmade material, not plastic.
A braided thread would be acceptable.
Entering in to a more prominent orange,
        beyond the pale but not yet in the medium;
        this color is helpful to place underneath or on top
        of an ailing animal.
The vibrations will soothe the animal and assist in the healing.
This color may also be used for those who suffer
        from the arthritic array of disease,
        especially the area of the rheumatoid.
Place about thy being this color.
Meditate upon this color.
Let this color enter in to every pore of your being
        and it will soothe and it will help
        straighten the affected members of your body.
And it will repress that bacterium responsible.
This color is also efficacious for those

who have large areas of the body burned,
but only first and second degree burns.
To have this color nearby
or placed upon the portion of the body not burned
will assist the body in responding to healing.
For those places that have burn units,
the rooms painted in this color,
with white upon the ceiling,
and stripes of the orange across the ceiling
of a width of at least ten centimeters,
will be helpful to those burn patients.
Entering in to a very deep orange
with a quite visible tinge of gold;
this is for those kept locked in institutions,
prisons you call them.
This color will assist these beings to focus
on the positive of their particular station.
It will also be efficacious for those who have the position of guard
or any other employment in contact with these
behind your bars.
Even foods of this color will soothe
even unto your other barred places
for mental instabilities.
This color needs to appear everywhere,
the walls, the furnishings, the food, even the paper.
This will help in the healing process,
for it is a color that appeals to the mind,
that brings the mind
out of the deep doldrums of pain and despair.
Cancer patients, beings afflicted with cancer,
will also benefit with this color.
Gaze upon it.
Meditate upon it.
Cover thy being with this color.
Wear it on the pulse points of the body,
even around the knees and the ankles.
Allow it to permeate thy being
for it will enhance your ability to overcome this disease
and its resulting emotions.
The very deepest shade of orange
will ameliorate the tendency to violence,
for it sets up within the mind
a possibility of reconciliation

that did not previously exist,
and there is choice where there was no seeming choice.
Those too whom are caught in the throes
of degradation of drug addiction
will be helped by this color.
For they are doing violence to selves
and this may assist in the amelioration, in their choice.
And so places where they congregate
would benefit from this color.
Place upon thy wrist this color to remind you,
if you enter back into the deep darkness,
of the possibilities of resurrection.

322 We speak of the color orange.
We speak of the vibrant color orange
that you see in the fruit you call orange.
You have, Souls of earth, a Pillar of Light about your being
that you may access at any moment.
Within that Pillar of Light are all color,
and each has a particular strength
as a component of its being.
For colors are Energy.
Colors have being.
Colors are.
In your high consciousness you will recognize
the colors in the Pillar of Light, and you will know,
that which is enhancement of the goodness of your being.
Enhancing the Love and compassion,
the goodness of your being,
gives the impetus to the vibration of that Energy
so that it expands outward from your being
in ever widening, in ever greater vibration.
The color orange is particular to those beings
who have disorders of the nervous system.
Whether those disorders of the nervous system
be emotional, be a damaged brain, or be it physical,
the color of orange brought to bear upon that being
with your high consciousness,
and in Love and compassion,
will bring about a miracle of wellness.
The being will physically alter.
The cells will physically alter.
The brain will physically alter,

for you will have touched the Soul of this being.
And as you reach out with that color,
if the being tremors, the tremors will ease,
if the being has fear, the fear will ease,
if the being has due to nervous disorder,
a mental aberration, that too will ease.
Understand the color of the orange from the Pillar of Light,
has within it a palpable, tangible Energy
that you may share and heal.

323 We have for you the color blue.
We have for you an understanding
of the gradations of the color blue,
and an understanding of the energies
of the gradations of the color blue.
We speak simply of blue at this point,
not the blue green, not the blue purple;
as close as you may come to
upon your earth plane of the pure blue.
You will understand all colors have energies.
All colors stimulate in the human psyche
and in the human body.
They may stimulate healing.
They may stimulate relaxing.
They may stimulate the mental faculties.
They may stimulate
even the movement of consciousness
beyond the earth plane.
Blue has great vibrational qualities.
In the very palest of blue
you will find the gentleness used especially
for the newborn, for the very, very young
in any area of congestion, croup, cold, cough, fluishness.
The most gentle of blue placed upon the babe
will stimulate within the babe a rejection of this illness.
It will calm the croup.
Some will only accept simply laying the cloth on them.
Others will appreciate being held closely within the cloth.
This same color may be used for those Souls
who have a restless mind,
who are unable to cease their compulsions,
those who are obsessive
and continuously, repetitively repeat an action.

Wearing this color twenty four hours a day
for three days, indeed, even in the sleep,
will assist in beginning to calm their being
and break the cycle.
And we speak of both top and bottom; a full covering.
Thereafter, the color is to be worn
a minimum of twelve hours per day
until they have ceased their obsession.
For those being racked with the withdrawal of drugs,
this color may also be of assistance
to aid in their rejection of their habit.
It will especially assist in the frenzy of withdrawal
and help the being through that particular period
of the progression of withdrawal.
This color may also be used for those beings
who have been burnt to the extent of the third degree.
You will make a tent over the being allowing, of course, the air.
The tent will remain for a period of five earth days,
twenty four hours each day
except when procedures are being done.
This color will do much to help
those in the final stages of Alzheimer,
who have frenzied thoughts and actions.
It will calm their being.
In this case, you will need to place the cloth around the head
and ensure that the gowns and the cloths are this color.
This will assist in calming the being.
The blue is active; it is not stationary.
It has movement, it has flow, it has color,
it has sound, it has vibration.
In its positive mode, it has total receipt.
There can be no stagnation within the movement of blue.
Wrap thyself in blue, be a veritable veraugo[17] of blue,
send the energies of blue to swirl about their being.
Choice is then theirs.

324 Souls of earth, we speak to you of the color yellow.
The pure yellow, not tinged with the brown or green or purple,
only in itself the color of the sun,
of the color of the dandelion,
of the center of the daisy, of the evening primrose,
all variations of the color yellow.
We give you these variations, so that you may picture the color

of which we speak for earth.
The delicate yellow shade of the evening primrose
is most efficacious
for the croupy child; worn about the neck, the chest,
covering the area of the chest.
Held in place by the Love of the parent
or the caregiver will soothe and ease the young one.
For the elderly, the frail elderly,
this color placed about their shoulders
brings comfort to the lost Soul,
lost in the agonies of the mind,
in a forever place of forgetfulness it will comfort.
For they may seem to the caregiver as catatonic,
as unfeeling, as unknowing, but that is not the case,
and this will soothe their being.
The yellow evening primrose color placed upon a table,
even a small scrap of color
will bring to a table of dissension, calm.
Even at the highest levels of your earth leaders, it would behoove
your earth leaders to carry with them
a small scrap of this color.
The yellow evening primrose color placed about the skull
of a being lost in the beginning stages
of the Alzheimer will temporarily
bring surcease, providing clarity.
The evening primrose color about the being of a burn victim,
as a tent over the burned area,
will absorb much of the pain.
Do not place directly upon the burn, for that is not the purpose.
It is to be tented over the burned area.
For the being lost in the throes of hatred, of uncontrolled anger,
a scrap of this color held to your being with your arms
crossed over your chest,
the left over the right and held in place,
will soothe, will bring momentary release
and clarity of intent.
The bright yellow of the dandelion
will lift the sorrow of a grieving Soul.
In this case the color is placed upon the wrists of the being and
fastened in some manner to hold it in place.
It will not remove the grief,
for that is your choice to do so or not to do so,
but it will provide a moment's release, a clarity.

It will penetrate the fog of sorrow.
To the depressed being this particular shade of yellow
will bring anger,
but out of that anger the depression will alter.
Gaze upon it and alter thy perception.
The bright yellow of the dandelion,
for the child receiving the chemotherapy,
will be most gratifyingly comforting.
Allow the child to wear this color during the process.
It will also to some extent soothe the adult
receiving this treatment.
It will be enough for the child to cover
the upper portion of the body.
The adult will require a full suit of this color to be efficacious.

325 We speak on the color lavender.
In your world,
lavender is a variation of the color you call purple.
We would have you understand,
lavender is a very definitive tone, shade,
on its own within the Prism.
Lavender, what you call lavender upon your earth plane,
bears a minuscule resemblance
to that of the Prism.
When we say minuscule,
we speak of the vibrancy of the color,
we speak of the sound of the color,
we speak of the shading of the color.
It is not to limit your earth creativity that we tell you this.
It is so that you understand that to see with the earth eyes
and to see with the third eye and the Eye of Beholding,
has a vast chasm of difference.
To use lavender upon your earth plane when healing,
indeed, has an effect upon a being from the healer.
But we would have you understand,
when using the color of lavender from the Prism,
using it with your sacred self,
reaching onto the Crystal Cave,
it is as if the healer on the earth,
using lavender on the earth plane,
places a little bandage upon a great gash;
using the lavender from the Prism closes the gash
as if it had never been.

A great chasm of difference.
One not meant to denigrate the other,
only allowing you to understand
the possibility that you have in your sacred self,
the possibility of healing
from the very Essence of your humanity,
You all have the possibility of reaching unto your high self.
You all have the possibility of operating with high consciousness.
You all have the possibility of using the Eye of Beholding.
You all have the possibility of the absolute knowing of Truth.
Lavender is of great benefit
in healing the desiccated areas of the earth.
It is a great benefit when reaching for both Sound and Color.
We would have you understand,
the greatest benefits are using the Eye of Beholding,
and encourage you to reach unto your high consciousness,
to reach unto the very Essence of your humanity.
When you reach unto the sacred self
and heal from the Crystal Cave,
you will note a particular form of violet
that is healing for the earth.
It is in the very most gentle of lavenders.
It has within that gentleness a density, an Energy of color
within a myriad of spirals moving,
affecting the cellular level,
defined and concentrated, all with purpose.
The color has consciousness, knows healing,
knows what is needed to heal,
permeates the ground of mother earth,
permeates the landscape,
permeates all Souls within its perimeter.
As humanity in your oneness,
you may circle the globe of mother earth with this color.

326 We would have you understand,
when you reach unto the Essence of being,
you place within the palms of your hands
great healing remedies.
When you have entered in to the sacred self,
you will see with the Eye,
that which requires the Prism of color.
Each being, will begin with
the crystalline White Light of your Creator.

That White Light surrounds the being
in an envelope of cloud like softness,
of warmth, comfort and Love.
The Flow of Creator, Truth, Love, Purity;
and from that Flow flows the great Love
of your Essence self,
for it is akin to the great Love of Creator.
No negativity, no pain, no trauma will gainsay that Love
if the being accepts.
There is naught that cannot be healed,
even unto another new limb being grown,
an eye being replaced,
the severed neck now whole.
Once you have placed the White Light,
you will enter in next to purple,
for purple is mandatory to prepare the being
for the great healing to occur.
And then you will discern with the Eye any other color
that is required to complete the triad of healing.
Always, Soul, three, always a triad of color
discerned with the Eye.
Know this is available to any being who reaches
unto the sacred self.
We bring unto you a teaching on the color purple.

327 We speak not of the earth color purple,
for it lacks the puissance of the purple
from the Crystal Cave.
You may reach unto the Crystal Cave in less than an instant.
You may know in less than an instant
the melding of Soul, Spirit and Essence,
enabling you to wield the power of purple.
All Energy sessions begin and end with this color,
for it is healing, but also it is cleansing.
And so you enter this color into the being,
you wash the being in this color.
Not just where the being is maimed physically,
but you wash the Energy field,
the aura of this being to be healed.
The purple cleanses and instigates,
is the catalyst to begin the process of healing.
Use the color purple to seal in the healing
within the aura and within the physicality of the being.

as the Energy field is altered by your healing.

328 We would have you flood your being with the color red.
We would have you saturate your being with the color red.
We would have you understand, the red we speak of is vibrant.
It pulsates within your being.
It causes vibration to emanate out from your being.
And we would have you catch this vibration before
it enters fully from the space of your being outward.
Catch it, Soul,
and in your generosity of Spirit offer it unto Creator,
for the red we speak of is that negativity
that abounds upon your earth.
For if you do not release it from your being,
it cannot be altered.
If you do not embrace this color, you cannot offer it.
We do not suggest that you embrace and hold
and refuse to release.
Indeed not! For you have come to embrace and release.
When you release negativity, you become buoyant in your being,
and may rise to high consciousness.
If you carry negativity it weighs you down.
It bogs you down.
It stills your being.
Soul, we would request that you release from you, negativity,
and offer it unto your beloved Creator.
There is upon your earth planet,
an infinite variety of shading of red.
but a particular shade,
a red that is not mixed with any other shading,
a red that comes direct from the beetle
is most perfect in its vibrational tone,
for each color, even in its muted form on the earth,
has a vibrational tone that affects the viewer,
Color, whether you see it with your eyes
or merely are in its nearby vicinity, affects your being.
Your science is beginning to unravel this mystery.
They have not yet understood the depth to which the vibration
affects the being,
for your body, your being, came from color.
It is attuned to color.
It recalls within the very cells of its being,
the color from which it came.

And so it is affected
within the very cellular memory of your being
by any color.
This is an indication to your being of your state of being.
In your positive ego you will vibrate,
gravitate to the pureness of the color.
And in your negative ego you will vibrate, gravitate,
to color that is muddied, dimmed.
Those who have chosen to use the eye,
will know instantly from the aura of the being,
the state of that being.
When a being is in the negative ego state,
it is imperative to place before that being,
within five inches of that being,
the pureness of the color.
You may also drape a natural cloth of that color about the being.
This is especially helpful for the mind.
It will assist in soothing the mind,
enabling the healing vibration
of the pure color to enter in.
You may use for the pure color any natural fabric.
The being in a state of negative ego
will require the placement of the true color
for fifteen of your earth minutes, thrice daily.
And you will see as will the being,
a revolution within of the state of the mind.

329 We would speak of the color black.
To describe black, the words of dark are used,
the words of midnight, no light are used.
And we would have you know, Souls of earth,
that black is a reflective color.
The very deepest of black will have a shine to it.
We speak of the color that you see with your earth eyes.
Black always used with another color
will highlight that other color.
Place a stripe of black next to it,
place a stripe of another color, even of brown,
and that color will be highlighted against the black.
And so black is used upon the earth plane
as an adjunct to other colors.
Always, in wearing black or in having furniture that is black,
or even in a darkened room,

always have another color present.
When in sorrow,
upon your western world you wear the color of black:
to show bereavement, to show bereftness,
to show the deep sorrow within,
to show that light, life, has left you.
To relieve the sorrow, use pink,
a soft pink placed against the black,
it will encourage the mind to think of the joys of life,
not the sorrows of life.
It will help the being to overcome the sorrow
that surrounds them.
The same goes for those cultures
that use another color to express sorrow.
Always have, also upon thy being, the light pink, the soft pink,
to help overcome that sorrow.
Not to repress it, Souls, to overcome it with the knowledge of joy.
The painting of black to indicate death is erroneous,
for it is the black that brings others to life.
For Souls who are drawn to black and only black,
recognize the illusion you are in.
Recognize that you are repressing the fullness of this color.
It was not given to earth accidentally, indeed not.
It was to show the rising of life, indeed!
Your volcanoes, the ash that spews from them and turns black,
nourishes the ground
and you will come to find healing properties
within that lava that has turned black.
The coal that is within your earth is black,
and yet it gives forth light and heat and warmth.
Look beyond the flatness that you see as black
and embrace the life therein.

330 We will speak of brown.
Brown can be a miraculous healing color
when used for healing, for life.
Those beings having problems with feet,
it would be advantageous
to place upon the feet cloths of brown,
tied with a green ribbon.
The combination provides the healing.
Those who have bones needing healing,
we would recommend

the placing of a brown cloth around the bone,
and tied with a green ribbon and yellow,
the triad would be most efficacious.
For those who have the schizophrenia, gazing upon brown
with a stripe of three quarters of an inch
of pristine white placed across the color brown,
will help the being bring forth lightness into self.
The brown will stabilize, the white will enhance the balance.
Also, wearing a cloth, a natural cloth of brown and white
will be efficacious for the schizophrenic person.
It may be worn as a neck cloth, a scarf, as a dress full, as a shawl,
even as ribbons about the being, about the wrist, the arm.
But it must be the brown and the white.
And the shade of the brown must be a deep brown
so that the contrast of the white is readily apparent.
For those who have difficulty staying grounded,
we would suggest a cloak of brown, of the color brown.
with streaks of gentle blue,
and this placed upon thy being daily
will ground the being, will stabilize.
In the dead of winter, brown will bring a soothing warmth
to fight off a winter's chill.
Place it in a corner of the room,
the north corner or northeast corner.
Place ribbons of brown to help with the chill,
place a pillow or a cloth of brown
here and there in your cold room, to help bring warmth.
For those who must work in the out of doors
or in any frigid place,
wearing of a brown cloth of some type, natural,
will assist in keeping the warmth within.

331 We would have you understand all gems, stones, rocks
were placed upon the earth for mankind.
All have Energy, all have Soul.
You may, Souls of earth, access the Energy
of any stone, gem, rock; we will call them all rocks.
All are available to you.
Amethyst enhances the healing of bone.
It is the vibrational property of the amethyst that will initiate,
that is the catalyst to heal very quickly
the fracture, the broken.
The size is not important;

neither the size of the break nor the size of the amethyst.
We would have you wrap it so that it is held in place
upon the broken area,
no matter where it is upon the body,
and that it is there for at least a seventy two hour period.
You may cleanse the amethyst with the cho ku rei thrice,
or you may place it in salt water,
sea salt, to those who have it available.
simply to rinse it in the water and it will be cleansed.
The emerald, and again, the size is not important,
and it does not need to be polished and shone;
in its natural state it is perfectly acceptable.
Placed at the third eye chakra
and held in place for twenty four hours
will relieve migraines, will relieve headaches of any kind.
For some you will not require the twenty four hours;
it may be less.
Then remove, cleanse, with either
the cho ku rei or the salt water.
We would bring you the sapphire.
Size is not important, cut is not important,
in its natural state is best.
And you will take and hold that against the stomach
for those who have heartburn,
for those who have gastric distress;
you will hold it there in place until the pain is gone,
until it is absorbed.
You will then cleanse the stone in the manner given.
For colds, for sinus we would have you place the topaz
just below the third eye
and hold it there until you find relief.
And then move it away and cleanse as given.
The basalt rock, even a small sliver
is an excellent Energy conductor for beings
who are exhausted by lack of sleep.
Place in your hand a sliver of the basalt ten minutes
before you enter in to bed, into your reclining mode,
hold it for a minimum of thirty seconds
in the palm of your hands.
Deep breath, release the basalt and you will find within four days
your sleep will have improved each day
until you have a restful sleep.
You may also place the piece of the basalt above your bed

near your head area.

332 We would have you understand the properties of garnet
to assist in the calming of a toothache.
You will place the garnet above the lip, in the center
between the nostril and the beginning of the lip.
And you will lightly press the garnet in and you will feel
within a few moments a lessening of the toothache.
You will then hold it until the toothache
has receded to a manageable level of pain.
Once it has receded somewhat you will then take
and place the stone inside upon the gum,
in the same area but on the gum.
And you will hold the stone until the pain has gone,
and then remove it and cleanse the garnet.
It need not be directly upon the ache area.
The size is not mandatory for any particular size,
but we would suggest that it be smoothed,
that it have no sharp edges.
It does not have to be of perfect gem quality.
There are many garnets in their original state.
Ensure, Soul, that if you do this for a child,
the stone is of sufficient size that you may
easily grasp it and not allow the being to swallow.
We ask that you rinse it with salt water;
one teaspoon of salt to one pint water will be sufficient.
Simply a rinse in the mixture of salt and water and then dry.
Souls of earth, we would have you understand
the properties of the stone, Chrysoprase.
It is the smooth stone that will enable you
to hold it in your left hand.
Place upon it the first three fingers of the right hand
and rub the stone.
This will bring immediate relief of itching in the hands
for those who have the diabetic itch or the rash itch.
It will in essence absorb the itch.
You will continue to rub it,
to massage the stone with the fingers of the right hand
until the itch has subsided on the left hand.
You will then move the stone into the right hand
using the three fingers of the left hand.
You will massage the stone
until the itching has ceased in the right hand.

You may also move the stone onto any area
you have been plagued with an itch
and rub the actual stone upon the itch and feel relief.
Always make sure the first three fingers
are the ones used to rub the stone
onto whatever area you are attempting to alleviate an itch.

333 Beloved Souls, we would have you know
that in the twinkling of an eye,
all that is illusion can vanish.
We would have you know that in the twinkling of an eye
all that is illness, all that is dis ease would, can vanish.
We would have you know when we speak of twinkling of an eye,
we speak of the orb, the orb that sees all,
that knows all to the level to which it has attained.
Understand, the complexities of your universe
are as a child's toy to the orb, to your eye.
There are no mysteries to the eye.
All answers to your earth questions are available to the eye.
It is only a twinkling away.
We await to greet thee, to welcome thee.
Souls, twinkles can come to the will of the mind,
the wish of your heart.
The burden, it is of earth.
Release the burden
and open thy being to the twinkling of an eye.
Beloved Souls, to access the eye,
clearing, cleansing must be done within the solar plexus.
It is necessary to remove the mass
that masks the clarity of the eye.
It is necessary to remove the pain to free the eye.
Vision the inside of the solar plexus.
Vision the gelatinous mass of grey matter
prevalent in many Souls,
preventing access to the eye,
preventing the freeing up of the mind's eye.
Understand this gelatinous mass is not in physical form
but it is matter and it is a barrier.
Vision often, beloved Souls, the power of thy mind's eye
and know you can clear that which prevents the vision.
Take the color yellow, mix within green,
bring forth the blue, brown and lavender,
form within the solar plexus a swirling vacuum of Energy,

absorbing the gelatinous mass.
Vision it, see it entering in to the swirl,
to the vortex and being released
and releasing from thy body all barriers to vision.
We urge the cleansing whenever you have difficulty and
you believe you have problems accessing the mind's eye.
Release, know the problem is unnecessary and need not be.
We urge you, urge all Souls, remove the mask.

Healing Chapter Four
Sound

334 We would speak of the sound of colors.
Put your mind to rest
and know within thy being that each color has sound.
The sound of color is an identifier.
Each sound has an identity.
Each color has an identity.
That is your healing color.
That is your armor to share unto all of humanity.
When you give forth energies of goodness,
there is a tone that heals.
Within the tone is an identifier of Sound and Color.
All movement has Sound and Color
if you see with the Eye.
But know, even though many eyes are veiled,
that does not alter the truth
that all energies of goodness have Sound and Color,
and are identified and are recorded,
for we hear within that note the pain,
the longing for surcease,
the longing for comfort and compassion,
the longing for Love, unconditional.
For when that is given forth,
the tone is altered and becomes calm, serene.
And you have all possibility, have all capability to alter.
We would address toning.
Many upon your earth have an inkling
of what sound is able to accomplish,
and they have ascribed various cures,
various states of well being to a particular note.
We would have the toners understand that the note to tone
is not particularly tied to an earth note.
The toning to be fully efficacious must be done with the eye.
For only the eye will ascertain the vibrational tone
that will bring about an alteration within the being.
It is the desire and the knowledge of the eye
that brings about the pure note of alteration.
It matters not whether in earth voice you can carry a tone
or have any sense of harmony.
What matters is the tone from the eye.

And when you are toning with sound,
 and out of the goodness of your being,
 toning to heal another, it is advantageous
 to place together the thumbs and forefingers,
 and to hold outward the palms of thy being,
 outward and palm up.
And then, tuning yourself to the Eye,
 utilize the tone given from thy high self unto the being.
And they will feel a vibration,
 a tingling within that part of the body to be healed.
Understand the tone you hear with your earth ears
 is not the tone heard with the physical cell body
 or the mental emotional body.
For when you heal with the Eye, when the tone is from the Eye,
 then that affects internally at the very nucleus of the cells.
While you are toning,
 maintain the thumbs and forefingers together
 and the palm up in the receiving mode.
For that, in conjunction with the eye, sets up a triangle.
The line goes from the eye to the palm, to the other palm,
 and back to the eye.
And within that triangle, the healing vibrations take place

335 Souls of earth, we speak of sound.
We speak particularly of your earth sound.
We will not limit sound
 to that which is made by your instruments,
 to that which is made by your voice,
 to that which is made by your machines.
We speak of the sounds of nature.
We would have you understand, all sound has healing capability.
But the sound made by man has within it an impurity.
That which is made by earth flora and fauna has Purity of tone.
You will understand
 that even the shrub, the tree, the bush has sound.
Indeed, they vibrate.
All plants to varying degrees have sound and vibration.
All animals and mammals of the sea have sound and vibration.
Your fish has sound and vibration
 you may not hear with the earth ear,
 but indeed, were you to listen with the eye,
 you would hear and you would know the language spoken
by this sound vibration.

Indeed, a plant can speak.
It does speak,
but you do not hear with the earth ears.
Each plant, each tree, each rock, yes, even rocks have sound.
All the denizens of the ocean, of the rivers,
has sound that could inform you of their healing abilities.
Even the most lowly of insects has sound vibration.
The ant can speak if you would but listen to its tonality.
Souls of earth, we have given to you the possibilities.
For within each being, within each humanity
is indeed the possibility to speak,
to hear with the eye of which is around your being,
indeed, of that which is on your being,
for you know you carry many microbes.
They too have sound vibration.
You understand all has purpose upon the earth.
You understand all came forth to assist mankind
in its growth and resolution.
And you may discover the purpose of each individual Soul:
the Soul of the rock, the Soul of the microbe,
the Soul of the whale, the Soul of the petunia.
All for the benefit, for the growth of mankind.
You have many creatures upon your earth
that you may hear with your earth ears,
but you cannot translate unless you listen with the eye.
The eye will translate the sound into words,
into meaning decipherable to your mind.
Your eye is vibratory.
It hears and it sees and it feels.
It sees the aura.
It sees beyond the earth unto Farside and beyond.
It hears the sounds of the earth
which you cannot hear with your earth eyes
or indeed your scientific instruments.
It hears the sound of glory of Farside.
It feels the pain of all mankind.
For all is connected through the vibratory sense of the eye.
And all humankind upon the earth may freely utilize the eye
to the level of their Purity.
Your eye is that which takes you beyond the bounds of earth
without a vehicle, a ship.
Indeed, Souls.
You may travel unto the Farside, return with healing.

You may travel to the psyche of the planet
and return with the knowledge of healing.
All is available.
You do not have to pass an exam or a test of fortitude.
Accept and allow the sound vibration to enter in
to the consciousness of your being.

336 Souls of earth, we would have you understand
the sounds you utter have great power
when combined with will and intent.
You have the ability, indeed,
to soothe what you call the savage beast,
whether in creature or in human form.
The mere utterance from your vocal chords,
combined with the will and intent
to place gentle calm upon a being,
will alter the actual cells involved within the being.
You alter the mind with your sound.
The sound that you utter forth
need not be especially melodic or even rhythmic.
It matters not whether you can carry a tune.
It is the combination of will, intent and syllabication
that will cause the alteration,
for you then have placed Energy upon the other being.
Often you croon to a babe and your soothing voice
calms the babe, calms the crying, calms the creature.
Again, it matters not how well you sing.
It matters, Soul, the Energy.
For in the crooning, the attempt to comfort the child,
the attempt to calm the puppy,
the attempt to soothe the thrashing elder,
the child with fever,
with the will and the intent and the voice,
the Energy from you enters in pure unto that being.
And in their acceptance of that pure Energy
a calmness descends.
It is not the voice, not just the will, not just the intent,
but it is the Energy engendered
by the combination of the three.
The sound could even be guttural and it would calm
if done with will and intent of goodness.
We would have you understand
that you may calm with the intent of goodness

but you may also negatively affect another being.
If your intent is to harm, to wound the other being with words,
then you have a triad of negativity: will, intent and sound.
And you will many times see a visible reaction
from the other being,
as they back away, or as they cower, or as they cry.
Understand your powers and understand the choice you have.
Understand that you may also
overcome another's negative darts of energy
by your calm of sound, will and intent.
In effect there is an Energy barrier that is created
so that the being must pause in their negativity
and may choose to re evaluate their actions.
But, if you retaliate with the same negative will, intent, and sound,
then you are at war and the negativity grows and grows.
Understand, even in a crowded room, uttering in goodness,
sound with willing intent may calm a fevered crowd,
may calm the raucous meeting.
It may also, on a battlefield when three or more join together
with will, intent and utter sounds;
you may certainly affect
a very large area around your being, making calm.
Be aware, Souls of earth, of the effects of your power.

337 Listen to the howling wind.
Hear it carefully, for it carries a message.
The message is not in earth words.
The message is in the motion, in the vibration.
The howl is the sound of the vibration
of the movement of the wind.
You, too, Souls of earth, have a howl,
individually and collectively.
Each being has Energy.
Ergo each being has motion.
Ergo each being has sound.
The sound is unique to each individual.
It ranges through all the tones
that you know upon your earth plane
and beyond to tones you have yet to discover.
When you access, when you reach unto your sacred self,
you hear and know and become
for that moment in time, High C.
Your being resonates, vibrates, to High C.

Your being is altered in that moment,
and you may as you reach unto High C
alter the very matter of another being.
You may alter the very cells of that being.
High C dispels negativity,
for it cannot maintain its presence
within the same Energy space as High C.
High C allows the being to heal in its perfection.
You are perfection in the reality of your sacred self,
Your Energy responds to that perfection
and you become that perfection.
How great thou art, Souls of earth, to reach unto the sacredness,
to reach unto that which is Creator,
that which you have all possibilities to be.
High C is movement, is vibration, is Energy,
Energy of sacredness,
connected to the humanity of your being,
connected to the Crystal Cave,
to that level of holiness, of glory.
And you vibrate upon the earth plane with that glory
and in your Love and compassion,
you heal and bring forth
joyous recognition of the Soul self.

338 You will understand, Soul,
all the positions of the hands and of the body
are designed to form a pattern of sound and vibration.
Within that pattern of sound and vibration,
each movement is as the instruments in a symphony.
You need all of the instruments
to have a full symphony of sound, of music.
If you were missing the violins would that not
impact upon the symphony?
Would that not give you an incomplete sound
of what Mozart intended?
And so it is with the Mudras, all must be in play.
At the beginning it is important, not only the position
of the hands and the body,
but the focus you give to the position
so that the mind becomes actively engaged in the process.
For it is the mind that must have the intent
and the will to carry out the symphony.
Without the agreement of the violinist to play

or the conductor to conduct and coordinate,
the symphony would not happen.
And so it is that the mind,
the intent and the will must come together.
And so you begin with focusing on your initial position,
as it is in the end.
The end positions signify,
signal to the brain, that healing is available,
that this symphony has completed its song.
Not its healing, only its song.
For as in when you hear a symphony,
when the symphony is finished,
you retain in your mind what you've heard,
what you've seen, what you've felt.
Even though you enter in to the finish,
your brain retains its memory,
and, indeed, the cells of your body retain the memory.

339 We will speak of the arc of cleansing.
Always cup left over right, right is also cupped,
but in the beginning they are not connected.
You do not place the left directly upon the right,
it is held slightly above,
both palms down.
It is the infusing of Energy into the chakra.
When cupping downward,
the Energy may be directed in various directions
about the body or the eye, and so it has reason.
All of the movements of the Mudras are symbolic
beyond that of the earth plane.
Often we give you the placement of palms facing palms.
This is indicative of the mirror of which you have been taught.
The palms up, often given, are indicative of all receiving;
upon the earth you receive,
upon the Farside they receive,
beyond the Farside they receive Energy.
You may not within your earth consciousness recognize this,
but indeed, your higher consciousness does,
and the cells of your being, recognize the symbolism
and respond to it.
The hands, the fingertips touching the other fingertips,
the thumbs touching thumbs, form a triad, Soul,
reminding you of heart, mind and body;

reminding you of the Creator Triad.
When the thumbs are upon the flesh of the forefingers,
and the rest of the fingers are touching,
you have the symbolism indicative of the separation,
willingly separated unto the earth from the Farside.
The forefingers touching and the thumbs touching the pads
form a pyramid of Energy, a base and three sides.
This is to remind you that all triads have a base.
When we place ending, it is not your earth ending, it is symbolic.
When we place the hands palm down upon a surface,
it is symbolic of your landing,
your grounding upon the earth,
is symbolic of your earth consciousness.
When we connect the fingers and the thumbs;
symbolic of your connections to the Farside,
to your High Self.

340 What is the purpose of Mudra?
Are there not, Soul, many rivers,
many types of rivers all leading to the same end?
Indeed!
There are many modalities of healing,
of support, of amelioration for humanity.
Many are drawn to varying types of modalities.
Many are drawn to this type of healing or that type of healing.
Many are at a level where
they may only accept a certain modality.
Others are at a level free to explore, free to access the higher self.
And so it is offered to the earth,
and it has been so for thousands of years
offered to the earth, varying ways of healing the mind,
the body, and, indeed, the spirit of man.
We would have you understand Mudras
composed of sound, of vibration and of will.
Your will is imperative in the accomplishing of the Mudra,
It is your intent, focus, on the movements given
that will assist you in success.
It is the triad that will ensure your success.
Understand that whether it be breath, whether it be vocal,
whether it be vocalized in the mind,
it is the sound which brings forth the vibration
which then alters the cells.
Understand the motions

engendered by the syllabication that we have given,
instills within your being a vibration.
Each syllabication designed to alter a particular cell
or group of cells.
Each vibration designed to connect to the brain, to the mind,
so that the synapses are in balance.
So that you work together; Soul, mind, body, Spirit.
So that you work together; Soul, will, sound and vibration.
Each that we have given you has been, in effect,
designed to affect a particular ailment.
And each step given designed for the ultimate goal
of overcoming the ailment.
Souls of earth, pay particular attention.
Focus your entire being on each step for ultimate succeeding,
for ultimate overcoming, for ultimate accomplishment.

341 This is not an earth translation.
It is not translatable.
It is the vibration that is the crux,
and it does not matter the language.
It is as the syllables given,
for if it was translatable,
then each language would be different
and the vibration would be different.
Hence, there is no earthly translation.
And this may be spoken, it does not need to be sung.
The words are sufficient.
It is the syllables joining together that enhances,
indeed, encourages the vibration along with
the movements of the body.
The two entwined become the third,
which is the outcome suggested at the beginning,
whether it be joy, or healing or relaxation.
There is no harm in any of the Mudras.
There is only assistance.
You will understand,
Mudras provide balance, vibration of the movements.
The combination of the movements
and the utterance come together;
along with the breath work,
you have a triad of balance assisting the being to wellness.
We would have you understand,
when engaging in Mudras, they must,

for most efficacious application,
be done as given in the instructions.
Variations of the instructions will cause a lack of efficacity,
they will not be as effective.
All Mudras are to be done slowly, in slow motion.
Mudras are designed to bring together
the physical movements of the body
and the patterning of the brain cells.
Each has an effect.
The patterning of the movement
given to the muscles that interact within your being
affect the pattern in the brain.
They alter.
And therein lies the efficacity of the Mudra,
for it engages the brain and the body in concert.
The brain has patterns deeply ingrained in some cases,
so that if you were to look inside
you would see them as ruts.
And often times you will fall in to these ruts, Soul.
And so, the interaction of the body and the brain
will repair in many cases the rut
and develop a new pattern.
The body, brain connection and the mind are triad.
The mind instigates and says, "We will do this Mudra."
and then the body comes into play and the brain.
And thereupon you have the results
in a most efficacious manner done as instructed.
You will also understand that Mudras,
when in the combination
of the triad of mind, body and brain,
have a movement, an Energy movement, a vibration.
And it is a sound that you do not hear with your earth ear
but you may hear with the Eye.

342 Decibel refers to the sound
that is prevalent within all universes, all existences.
It is the level of sound, the tone of sound.
The decibel of your earth is so low as to be almost unheard
even by the acute hearing of your animals.
It is a decibel, a tone
that is smothered by the negativity upon the earth.
It is an energy of sound, an energy
that can be distorted as it is upon the earth, muffled.

We would give you an example:
sound of a loud clash of cymbals
in a hall for orchestration is loud and meant to be.
You may take that same sound, the same cymbals
and place it in a acoustically soundproof room,
and those outside the room cannot hear.
And yet that sound exists.
And so it is with earth, the decibel is buried, muffled,
only not by an acoustic room, soundproofed;
it is muffled by negativity.
And you, humanity, have the power to free the sound,
to free the decibels of earth unto all existence.
Understand, you all have come from other planets.
You are the alien.
Indeed, you are.
But there are also Souls in other galaxies, in dimensions,
other dimensions, billions, trillions.
There are no numerical values in the earth language
that would encompass the myriad of beings that exist,
the myriad of galaxies, of cosmoses.
There are four particular alien groups who have
dedicated themselves to assisting humanity
in the gathering of oneness.
They are the Jinn, the Gummerians, the Lemurians, Pleiadians.
They have made their appearance for thousands of years,
even before record keeping.
Iin the stones buried in caves,
are records of what you would call prehistoric.
These four alien nations assist in helping the earth maintain,
in spite of the toxins, the poisons that are poured in,
and the negativity that is left in the earth.
And there will come a gathering time,
for you will gather as one and you will heal this planet.
And you will all, as the Soul of Creator,
enter back from whence you came.
The Jinn often appear out of the corner of your eye,
you'll see a movement and you look.
Nothing there.
But there is.
They move like this, not straight.
They have a negative reputation, the Jinn,
in many cultures, as mischievous,
but only because they do not walk

the straight line and so are blamed.
The Pleiadians speak unto many.
Their words are channeled.
The Gummerians
pay particular attention to the children of the earth.
The Lemurians
pay particular attention to the aged and the infirm.
These are, Soul, additional to the Angels.
Each of you have come from a planet
and offered yourself unto Creator;
all from various planets and all gifts to Creator.
How blessed you are Souls!

MUDRAS

The Mudras are arranged sequentially: Mind, Head, Upper Torso, Lower Torso, Full Body, and Emotions.

MIND

343 We would speak of the sound of the human voice.
We would have you understand, Souls of earth,
that you can control, that you can modulate
the pitch and the tone of your voice,
not so the voice is pleasant to the ears
or strident to the ears
but so that the voice embodies Love.
Indeed, your voice may embody Love,
may communicate Love unto another with the voice.
And we speak not of carnal love,
we speak of the unconditional Love of one of mankind
to another of mankind;
recognizing within the Love of the voice
that all are your brother, all are your sister.
Embodied within the tone of the voice,
the Love speaks loudly and clearly
to all who are in distress.
Understand that with the proper tone of vibratory Love
coming from your voice from your vocal chords,
you may soothe the demented Soul.
You may soothe the frightened being.
You may quell angst in a riotous crowd.
You may soothe the fevered thrashings of a being.
You may soothe the agony of a burn victim.
You may gently place calm upon an animal in distress.
You may break through the depression
of a being lost in the throes of deep suicidal thoughts.
Understand,
you may embody unconditional Love and bring it forth
with the connection of the vocal chords
to the mouth and to the eye; the triad.
To do this, you must practice.
And we give unto you a Mudra for this,
should that be your intention.

Step 1
Feet towards the ground or flat upon the ground,

hands placed flat upon a natural surface.

Step 2
All fingers of the right hand touching each other,
thumb against the forefinger of the right hand.

Step 3
All fingers of the left hand touching each other,
thumb against the forefinger of the left hand.

Step 4
Endeavor to sit up as straight as possible,
bring your head upward, so that the throat is exposed
and open your mouth.

Step 5
For as long as you are able, pronounce the word, hum.
Huummmm.
Begin with the mouth open on hu
and upon the m close the mouth.

Step 6
Head straight,
bring your hands up and turn the hands over, palm up.

Step 7
Bring your head up so the throat is exposed.
Express the word, hum for as long as you are able
with the mouth open on hu and closed upon the m.

Step 8
With the mouth still closed, deep breath through the nostril,
then open the mouth and exhale in a controlled manner
five times: wh wh wh wh wh.

Step 9
Bring your hands together,
with the fingers touching in front of the throat chakra,
expose the throat and once more
express the word, hum
for as long as you are able
with the mouth open on hu and closed upon the m.

Step 10
Move your hands upward and place them in front of
and slightly above the third eye, throat exposed.

Step 11
Express the word, hum with the mouth open on hu
and closed upon the m.

Step 12
With the mouth still closed, deep breath through the nostril,
then open the mouth and exhale in a controlled manner
five times: wh wh wh wh wh.

Step 13
Bring the hands down slowly in front of the throat,
expose the throat
and hold that position for twelve seconds.

Step 14
Maintaining the position of the hands,
bring them slowly down and lay them upon the surface.

Step 15
Remove the fingers from touching, turn your hands over
and you have completed.

344 Souls, we have for you a Mudra to assist
in the formation of intention.
For there is indeed for many upon the earth
difficulty in forming an intention,
one that will embed itself in the psyche, in the brain,
one that will connect with the Soul.
This is to be done daily until your intention is realized.

Step I
Feet on the ground or toward the ground; your hands flat
upon a surface, fingers spread wide, thumbs not touching.

Step 2
Deep breath.
Hold for the count of three and exhale
slowly and controlled

to the count of five: wh wh wh wh wh.

Step 3
Slowly raise your hands upward, approximately three centimeters.

Step 4
Deep breath.
Hold for the count of three and exhale
slowly and controlled
to the count of five: wh wh wh wh wh.

Step 5
Slowly raise your hands upward another three centimeters.

Step 6
Deep breath.
Hold for the count of three and exhale
slowly and controlled
to the count of five: wh wh wh wh wh.

Step 7
Turn your hands palm over, intertwine fingers of both hands,
place as far as you are able,
your fingers toward your palms.

Step 8
Bend your head forward as if you were looking
at the formation of the fingers
and focus with your eyes closed
on forming your intention.

Step 9
Place the intention in the formation of the fingers.

Step 10
Thrice, gently rock forward and rock back,
and forward once more.

Step 11
Express ohhhh laaaaaaaah [long o, a as in ah],
extenuating the 'la' as much as you are able.

Step 12
Maintain the forward position,
close the fingers and close the thumbs.

Step 13
Slowly take your fingers and move them apart,
then move the thumbs apart.

Step 14
Place both hands palm upward, unto the third eye,
the palm facing the third eye, but not touching.

Step 15
Deep breath.
Hold for the count of three.
Controlled exhalation to the count of five: wh wh wh wh wh.

Step 16
Bring your hands downward,
turn them over and you have completed.

345 There is, Soul, one Mudra that is for universal Love.

Step 1
Hold forth thy hands, palms up.
Head tipped back.

Step 2
Allow thy breathing to calm.

Step 3
Take your hands, palms up and gently raise them
unto the position of the eye,

Step 4
Hold them on either side of the third eye,
palms facing out, fingers touching each other,
thumbs touching flesh.

Step 5
And know that you will radiate Love,

healing Love unto all of humanity.

Step 6
Do three Aums.
As you do your aums, move thy body in a spiral[18] clockwise,
three times for each aum.
And so, you have a total of three aums and nine spirals.

Step 7
Bring your hands together, palms touching at the edges.

Step 8
Cup the palms and you will bring them forth unto the eye.

Step 9
Hold for a count of three.

Step 10
Place the palms together in the prayer position.

Step 11
In slow movements place the palms outward and then down.
And you have sent out Love unto all.

346 We present to you a Mudra
to ameliorate diseases of the mind.
This may be done on a daily basis
to assist in the balancing of the mind
who is on the verge of derangement.
Once the mind has entered in to full derangement,
this Mudra will not be applicable,
for it requires a focus
that the being will be unable to maintain.

Step 1
Place the palms face down upon a natural surface,
fingers spread as wide as possible but not touching.

Step 2
Bring your head downward,
looking into the form between the hands,
focus on that form for the count of fifteen.

Step 3
Raise your head back into its center position,
turn your hands over,
palms facing upward, elbows at your side.
The eyes are closed.
Hold this position for fifteen seconds,
keeping your head straight up,
neither down nor back.

Step 4
At the end of the fifteen seconds, repeat three times:
take a deep breath, hold for the count of three,
exhale gustily.
The arms are in the position of elbows at the side,
palms upward.

Step 5
Tilt the head back as far as is comfortable.

Step 6
Deep breath, hold for the count of three, exhale gustily once.

Step 7
Sing or chant while the head is in this tilted position:
aaaaaaa moe taaaa kaaaa
[long a, long o, a as in ah, a as in ah]
Repeat five times.

Step 8
Return the head to center position.

Step 9
Turn the palms facing toward each other
and bring them together slowly
until they meet, fingertip to fingertip, thumb to thumb.

Step 10
Maintain fingertip to fingertip, thumb tip to thumb tip and bring
your hands in this position up and over the crown chakra.
Hold for the count of five.

Step 11
Repeat thrice: aaaaaaa moe taaaa kaaaa

[long a, long o, a as in ah, a as in ah]

Step 12
Deep breath, gustily exhale.

Step 13
Begin slowly to move your hands down
until you have reached the middle of your chest.

Step 14
Remove the fingertips and the thumb
and turn the palms upward, elbows at your side.
Hold for the count of fifteen in that position.

Step 15
Deep breath, exhale gustily,
turn the hands over and bring them back down
into the starting position.

Step 16
Open eyes, look at the shape formed between the two hands,
hold for the count of five.

Step 17
Feel the body singing in its balance,
the mind refreshed, back into balance.
And you have completed.

347 We bring unto you a Mudra for the schizophrenic
who is caught in the throes of hearing voices,
of not sure of what is reality and what is illusion,
not knowing their place in the universe.

Step 1
Feet flat on the floor.

Step 2
Hands placed in the prayer position: palm touching palm,
fingers touching fingers, thumbs touching thumbs.

Step 3
Hands in this position in front of the face.

Step 4
Place the tips of the thumbs inside the lips,
    not fully into the mouth,
    not touching your teeth.
Hands held upright, fingers touching fingers,
    palms touching palms.

Step 5
Ten times, slowly and with firmness
    press the thumbs with your lips.

Step 6
Maintain the position of the hands,
    while moving them slightly away from the lips.

Step 7
Deep breath, hold to the count of three,
    release in a controlled manner
    to the count of three: wh wh wh.

Step 8
Deep breath, hold to the count of four,
    release in a controlled manner
    to the count of four: wh wh wh wh.

Step 9
Deep breath in through the mouth, hold for the count of six,
    release in a controlled manner
    to the count of six, wh wh wh wh wh wh.

Step 10
Place the tips of the thumbs back inside the lips,
    not fully into the mouth,
    not touching your teeth.
Hands held upright, fingers touching fingers,
    palms touching palms.
Hold for the count of three.

Step 11
Press down with your lips upon the thumb tips,
    once, twice, thrice.

Step 12
Move your hands apart, palms spread out and up,
but maintain contact with the little finger on each hand,
the thumbs touching the flesh of the forefingers.

Step 13
Thrice, inhale through the nostril, hold to the count of three
and exhale in a rush into the palms.
As far as you are able,
breathe out until you can breathe out no more.

Step 14
Move your hands apart slowly.
If you are dizzy, pause and wait until the dizziness passes.

Step 15
Bring your palms up, elbows out to the side of your being.

Step 16
Turn your hands over slowly, bring them down unto a surface
and you have completed.[19]

348 A Mudra for people lost in the throes of drug addiction
and yet having moments of sanity,
for those enthralled with the drug
who can not seem to get through a day or even hours
without the drug to mask, to hide their pain,
or to provide a false sense of ecstasy, of euphoria.
This we offer unto you as a way
of bringing your being back into balance.
We would suggest
no matter the level of addiction or the drug of choice,
that this be done a minimum of three times per day,
more if possible.

Step 1
Hands palm up above a natural surface.

Step 2
Bring the palms facing each other

Step 3
Move the palms, right above left.

Step 4
In the middle of the chest area,
rest the right hand on the left hand,
thumbs touching flesh, elbows at your side.

Step 5
Repeat thrice,
a deep breath as much as you are able,
hold for the count of five.
Release the breath gently, slowly in a controlled manner.

Step 6
At the end of the third exhalation,
extend the hands out from your body
as far as possible while maintaining the hands in position
of Step 3.

Step 7
Take the right hand and place it above the left hand,
touching the left hand,
palm facing inward toward your chest area,
fingers together, thumbs touching flesh.

Step 8
Repeat five times:
a deep breath as much as you are able,
hold for the count of five.
Release the breath gently, slowly in a controlled manner.

Step 9
Remove the right hand from the left,
and place palm facing palm in upright position,
fingertips touching, thumb touching flesh.

Step 10
Begin slowly to bring the palms toward your being.
Bend your elbows slowly and gently,
the palms toward your face.
Your eyes may be open or closed at this point.

Step 11
Sound forth five times: eeee naaaa waaaayyy taaaaaaaaaaaa
[long e, a as in ah, long a, a as in ah].

Step 12
Place the hands outward palms up, fingertips touching.

Step 13
Repeat thrice:
a deep breath as much as you are able,
hold for the count of five.
Release the breath gently, slowly in a controlled manner.

Step 14
Gently move your hands apart, palms still facing upward,
thumbs still touching flesh.
Move hands apart until even with elbows at your side.

Step 15
Place your hands palm down and back unto the starting position
and you have completed.

349 We give unto you a Mudra that will increase your understanding of a situation where all seems hopeless,
where you can not see an out,
where you can not see what your next move
could possibly be.
This Mudra will allow you to clear the darkness,
clear the cobwebs.
It will not miraculously remove the situation you find yourself in
but it will allow you to see a pathway.
This may be a situation where a member of the family
is involved in drugs or addictions of some manner
and seemingly is on a path of destruction.
It could also be a situation of a estrangement within the family.
It could also be an illness that overwhelms you.
It could be the illness off a child that you find overwhelming.
In all these cases, Soul, you will find a measure of relieve.

Step 1
Hold together the sides of the feet.

Step 2
Place your hands on a surface, bend the fingers and thumbs,
in the form of claws.
The hands are not touching.

Step 3
Three times gently move the hands up and down.

Step 4
Deep breath, hold for the count of three.
Exhale.
Keep your hands in the same position.

Step 5
Three times move your feet side to side, moving apart and back.

Step 6
Deep breath, hold for a count of three
and exhale in a controlled manner: wh wh wh.

Step 7
Sit in a relaxed manner.
Ensure that your shoulders are not tense,
that your head is not tensed,
that your body is not tensed,
that your spine is as straight as you are able
and your head is as upright as you are able.

Step 8
Maintaining the position of the bent fingers and the bent thumbs,
slowly bring your hands upward to the heart level.

Step 9
Deep breath, hold for the count of three.
Exhale in a controlled manner to the count of three: wh wh wh.

Step 10
Slowly bring your hands, in the same position,
in front of the third eye and hold for the count of five.

Step 11
Deep breath, slowly exhale for the count of five
in a controlled manner, wh wh wh wh wh.

Step 12
Deep breath, exhale once, gustily. Whooo!
So that your stomach is pulled inward with the exhalation.

Step 13
Move your hands down to the heart area.

Step 14
Separate your feet, turn your hands
toward your body in the claw position.

Step 15
Allow the mid knuckles of the fingers, to touch, left to right,
the thumbs to maintain an upright position.

Step 16
Thrice sing or chant
eee lala maaaaaaaaahhh [long e, a as in ah, a as in ah].
Hold the last syllable as long as you are able.

Step 17
Three times, a deep breath, hold for the count of three
and exhale for the count of five.
Maintain your hand position.

Step 18
Maintaining the claw position of your hands,
bring the hands downward unto the surface.

Step 19
Move the hands apart, turn them over, palms up,
but maintain the claw position.

Step 20
repeat once more,
eee lala maaaaaaaaahhh [long e, a as in ah, a as in ah].
Hold the last syllable as long as you are able.

Step 21
Deep breath, exhale and slowly allow your fingers to relax
and your thumbs to relax,
place palms flat upon the surface
and you have completed.

350 We bring unto you a Mudra for beings caught
in the web of negativity

and unable to bring forth a change in their being,
unable to bring forth an alteration
in the paradigm of the mind,
unable to see an alternative,
for those who lack knowledge there is no hopelessness.
Recognize, Soul, this exercise requires
your diligent application thrice daily.
And you will see, feel, hear results.

Step 1
Sit, the back straight, the neck straight and the head upright
feet flat on the floor or toward the floor.

Step 2
Your hands hover slightly above a surface.
The palms are facing each other
and the thumbs rest upon the forefingers.

Step 3
Fingers are not curled, they are straight.
Your hands are held closely together but not touching.

Step 4
In a rhythmic manner, move your hands, palm facing palm,
slowly toward each other, almost to the point of touching.

Step 5
Slowly move them outward to the far sides of your body
and bring them slightly toward each other,
however, not as close as Step 4.
Bring them in and out three times,
each time you bring them inward less than before.

Step 6
Extend the palms out to the full extension of your arms
on either side of the body.

Step 7
At the area of the heart, bring your hands slowly in
toward each other in the prayer position.

Step 8
As far as you are able bring the head down toward your hands.

Step 9
Touch the body at the level of the heart with the thumbs
and hold for fifteen seconds.

Step 10
Raise your head slowly as you open your hands, palms up,
palms touching side to side,
as if you were receiving at the heart level.

Step 11
Thrice sing or chant: leeee ree eee [long e, long e, long e].

Step 12
Deep breath, hold for a count of three
and exhale in a controlled manner thrice: wh, wh, wh.

Step 13
Close your hands, fingers to fingers, thumbs to thumbs,
palm to palm.

Step 14
Thrice sing or chant: leeee ree eee [long e, long e, long e].

Step 15
In the prayer position, bring your hands up to the third eye.
Your index fingers touch the third eye.
Ensure that your neck is straight.

Step 16
Thrice sing or chant: leeee ree eee [long e, long e, long e].

Step 17
Deep breath, hold for a count of three and release
in a controlled manner thrice: wh, wh, wh.

Step 18
Maintaining the prayer position, move your hands away
from the third eye to above the surface.

Step 19
Maintaining the palms facing each other, move them apart
to the sides of the body and back to the prayer position.

Step 20
Turn hands palm up and then over and you have completed.

351 Souls, you have upon your earth the many cultures,
in many ceremonies and rites,
indeed in some religions, meanings to various positions of the hands and the fingers.
We would add to this body of knowledge.
To enhance your decision to open the eye, to use the eye,
to remove the veils from the eye,
each day as often as you wish:

Step 1
On each hand, place the thumb and last three fingers together.

Step 2
Bring the hands up to the third eye.

Step 3
Place the forefingers against the eye,

fingertips touching each other,
the edges of the forefingers laying on the third eye area.

Step 4
Gently and slowly move the other fingers into a pyramidal shape
and hold there until Step 8.
Maintain the forefingers at the third eye.

Step 5
Move the thumbs down to touch the cheeks and rest there.
Hold there until Step 8.

Step 6
Deep breath, hold for a count of three, relax,
allowing the breath to leave.

Step 7
Hold the position of the hands for another seven seconds.

Step 8
And then, slowly, place three fingers
and the thumbs together as in Step 1.
Maintain connection with the third eye with the forefingers.

Step 9
Slowly move the forefingers
no more than one half an inch to either side of the eye,
keeping the thumbs and fingers together
at the level of your earth eyes.

Step 10
In a straight line, move the forefingers together again,
so that the tips touch.

Step 11
And then, slowly, to avoid dizziness, bring your hands down.

Step 12
Allow the fingers and thumbs to release.

Deep breath and you have completed.

352 A Mudra for the cleansing of the crown chakra.
Upon your earth there are many beings involved in negativity
and unable to cleanse their chakras to allow for a
precise connection to their higher being.

Step 1
Ensure that your feet are flat upon the ground
or toward the ground.
Your spine is as straight as possible
and your head is in an upright position.
neither drifting to the right or to the left.

Step 2
Place your hands in the cleansing chakra position:
left fingers over right fingers, left thumb over right thumb.

Step 3
Place the edge of the palm of the left hand upon a surface
and place right palm slightly cupped above the left hand.
Hold that position for five seconds.

Step 4
Place edges of both palms upon the table.

Step 5
Hold the edge of the palm of the right hand upon a surface
and place left palm slightly above the left hand.
The left hand is slightly cupped over the right hand.
Hold that position for five seconds.

Step 6
Return to the original position in Step 2.

Step 7
Deep breath in through the nostrils.

Hold for five seconds or as near as possible,
and exhale forcefully through the mouth.

Step 8
Bring the hands slowly upward, pausing at the third eye chakra.
Palms are now facing the third eye chakra.

Step 9
Continue moving the hands slowly upward
until they are above the crown chakra.
Hold that position for fifteen seconds.

Step 10
At the end of the fifteen seconds,
gently bring your palms in front of the heart,
ensure the palms are facing toward the heart chakra.

Step 11
Enter again slowly into the initial position of Step 2,
pausing at the heart chakra for fifteen seconds.
You will begin to feel the connection between the heart chakra
and the crown chakra.

Step 12
Deep breath in through the nostrils and exhale gently and slowly
through the mouth as you continue moving your hands
down back into the position on a surface as in Step 4.

Step 13
Bring your head downward as far as you are able
and hold for five seconds.
Remain gently breathing.

Step 14
Bring your head slowly back into the center upright position.

Step 15
Gently tilt the head back and hold for five seconds.
You will feel again, a tingling in the crown chakra.

Step 16
Slowly bring your head forward into the center position.

Step 17
Maintaining the center upright position, move your head slowly
over to the left, as far as you are able
and hold for five seconds.
Then bring it back slowly into the center position.

Step 18
Move your head slowly to the right, as far as you are able.
At this point you will breathe deeply in through the nostrils.
Hold for five and exhale gently out through the mouth.

Step 19
Bring your head back into center position,
spine as straight as possible.
Breathe deeply in through the nostrils, hold for a count of five
and exhale as forcefully as possible. Whoooh!

Step 20
Bring your head down toward the chest as far as you are able.
Move hands upward until the palms are above the crown chakra.
Hold for a count of six.

Step 21
Slowly bring your hands down,
back into the original position in Step 2.
Move your head back up into the center position, slowly.
Open your hands palm up and you have completed.

353 Souls of earth, we would take you now
to the cleansing of the eye chakra.

Step 1
Place at least six inches in front of your body,
left fingers over right fingers, left thumb over right thumb;
feet flat on the floor or toward the floor,

the spine as straight as possible,
the head in a neutral position.

Step 2
Hold this position for fifteen seconds, eyes closed,
your being focused upon the shape of your hands,
in their position.

Step 3
Deep breath in through the nostrils, hold for a count of five
and release, deeply, forcefully through the mouth.
Whoooh! Forcefully enough that you feel the warmth
within the sacral chakra.[20]

Step 4
Move hands up, maintaining position,
until they reach the heart chakra.
Hold for ten seconds.

Step 5
Deep breath in through the nostrils, hold for a count of five
and release gently through the mouth,
as far as you are able, all the air within your lungs.
Keep pushing out much as you are able.

Step 6
Deep breath in, hold for the count of five and exhale forcefully,
feeling the warmth moving up from the sacral.[21]

Step 7
Moving the hands upward to the third eye,
hold for fifteen seconds, or as long as you are able.
You will begin to feel an aliveness within the eye.

Step 8
Breath deeply in through the nostrils, hold for a count of three.
Gently release breath in short bursts, whoo whoo whoo whoo
Keep releasing in short bursts,
until you feel you have no more breath to release.

Step 9
Deep breath in, hold for a count of three
and then gently release.[22]

Step 10
Move hands apart, palm facing palm, at the level of the eye,
until just beyond the outer edge of your skull.

Step 11
Bring the hands inward to before the ears,
hold for a count of six seconds.
You will feel a tingling between the eye,
the back of the skull and the ears; a triad, Soul.

Step 12
Breathe deeply in through the nostrils and release gently.

Step 13
Bring your hands forward, palms facing the eye,
the edges of the palms touch and hold for six seconds.
Ensure that it is the palms at the level of the eye, not the fingers.

Step 14
Move your hands apart maintaining the palms facing your being.

Step 15
Bring hands out to the side of your being,
the palms be facing each ear.
Hold for five seconds,

Step 16
Bring your hands forward in front of the body,
left fingers over right fingers,
left thumb over right thumb.
Deep breath, hold for three, release gently.

Step 17
As you feel the warmth enter up through all the chakras
and out through the eye, deep breath.

Hold for three.
Forcefully expel, and you have completed.[23]

354 We give unto you a Mudra
for the cleansing of the throat chakra.

Step 1
Feet toward the floor or flat upon the floor.
Sit as straight as possible given any condition that you may have.

Step 2
Upon a natural surface, place your hands palm down,
fingers spread, thumbs spread apart.
head bent toward your hands, looking at the hands,
eyes are closed.

Step 3
Place the forefingers of each hand, slowly,
in front of your mouth,
the thumbs are not touching
and neither are the hands at this point.

Step 4
Deep breath in and hold for the count of five,
Release in a controlled breath to the count of five:
wh, wh, wh, wh, whhhh.

Step 5
You will begin at this point to feel
a vibration in the back of the head.
If you do not feel this vibration then continue to hold your hands
in the position given until the vibration begins,
for you can not go unto the next step
until you have attained the vibration.

Step 6
Bring your hands together in a prayer position
so that the fingers are touching

and the thumbs are touching.

Step 7
Bring your hands upward in front of the third eye.
Your thumbs pointed toward the third eye
but not touching, only in front of.

Step 8
Sound: keeeeeeeeeeeeeeeee [long e] for as long as you are able.
You will know the correct sound when
you feel a slight vibration within your hands.
If you do not feel any vibration at this point,
do not be concerned.
You will with practice attain the vibration.

Step 9
Bring your hands down into the prayer position

Step 10
Open the hands at the throat area, palms facing the throat area,
while the little fingers remain touching
as do the edges of the hands.

Step 11
Lift your head upward, open your mouth and breathe in
through your mouth, as deep a breath as you are able
and hold for the count of five.

Step 12
In a controlled manner above the hands
breathe out for five: wh, wh, wh, wh, wh.

Step 13
Sound once again: keeeeeeeeeeeeeeeee [long e]
for as long as you are able.

Step 14
Move your hands apart and place the palms facing each other
fingers together, thumbs touching the flesh.

Step 15
Slightly cup your fingers and once again sound:
keeeeeeeeeeeeeeeee [long e] as long as you are able.

Step 16
Move your hands in a slightly cupped position,
the right in front of the left.

Step 17
Sound once again: keeeeeeeeeeeeeeeee [long e]
for as long as you are able.
Step 18
Move your hands apart, palms up in a slightly cupped position.

Step 19
Deep breath, hold for the count of five and release in a controlled manner seven times: wh, wh, wh, wh, wh, wh, wh.

Step 20
Bring your hands down to the surface with the palms up,
Slightly tilt your head toward your hands
and sound one final time:
keeeeeeeeeeeeeeeee [long e] for as long as you are able.

Step 21
Deep breath, hold for the count of three,
release to the count of five
in a controlled manner: wh, wh, wh, wh, wh.

Step 22
Slowly release the fingers and the thumb.
Slowly bring your head upright.
If you become dizzy, pause, allow the dizziness to pass,
and then resume.

Step 23
Turn your hands over, palm down and you have completed.

355 We now bring you to the vibratory cleansing
of the fourth chakra.
Understand the movements of the body in conjunction with the concentration of the eye set a particular vibration that is felt within that chakra.
Recall, that at any time during the process if you feel dizzy, stop and hold that position until the dizziness passes and then resume.

Step 1
Ensure that your body is relaxed, releasing all tension, your feet flat upon the floor if possible or pointing to the floor.

Step 2
Left fingers over right fingers and left thumb over right thumb holding it away from the body.

Step 3
Eyes closed, maintain a straight posture of the spine, as well as you are able.

Step 4
Tilt your head gently upward to the left, hold for five seconds.

Step 5
Deep breath in through the nostrils.
Hold for three seconds, exhale gently.

Step 6
Move your head to the center upright position, and hold for five seconds.

Step 7
Deep breath, hold for five, and exhaling forcefully, so that you feel the fire in the sacral. Whooooh!

Step 8
Tilt your head gently upward to the right

and hold for five seconds.

Step 9
Twice, breathe in through the nostrils and exhale gently.

Step 10
Slowly bring your head back into the center position.

Step 11
Tilt your head back from the center position,
hold for five seconds.

Step 12
Three times, breathe gently in through the nostrils,
exhale forcefully. Whoooh!
Each time feeling the fire in the second and third chakras
and up into the heart chakra area.
Your whole body concentrated upon the feeling
of warmth nearing the heart chakra.

Step 13
Maintaining a straight posture, as far as you are able,
bend your head down from the center position.

Step 14
Maintaining the position of the hands,
move them unto the heart chakra area.

Step 15
Press the hands gently upon the heart area,
holding for a count of five.

Step 16
Breathe gently in through the nostrils,
breathe gently out through the nostrils.

Step 17
Maintaining the position of the hands,
move your hands slightly away from the body.

Step 18
Bring your head slowly upright into the center position,
with the spine as straight as possible,

Step 19
While maintaining your head in the center position,
move your hands unto the heart area.
Hold for the count of five and while holding this position
for the count of five,
gently breathe in through the nostrils
and gently breathe out though the mouth.

Step 20
Breathe in deeply through the nostrils, hold for a count of five.
Exhale forcefully. Whoooh!
At this point, you feel the fire in through the first, second, third,
and now unto the fourth chakra.

Step 21
Move your hands away from the heart area, remove the fingers.
Place the hands palm up and you have completed.

356 We would provide a Mudra
for the cleansing of the third chakra.[24]
All movements are to be done slowly.
If at any point you feel dizzy, lightheaded, hold until it passes.

Step 1
Place the left hand over the right fingers in a cupped position.

Step 2
Place the left thumb over the right thumbnail.

Step 3
Place the soles of the feet as flat as possible upon the floor.

Step 4
Hold for fifteen seconds the spine as straight as you are able

and with the head bent forward as far as you are able.
You will notice your tension
will be withdrawn to the muscles in your back.
Understand, this exercise will also relieve back pain.

Step 5
Slowly rise your head upward into the center position.

Step 6
Move the left hand over the right fingers in a cupped position,
the left thumb over the right thumbnail,
until they touch just below the heart chakra

Step 7
Press inward firmly but not forcefully,
hold that position for five seconds.

Step 8
Deep breath in through the nostrils and push it forcefully out
through the mouth: Haaaahh![25]

Step 9
Holding the spine as straight as possible, move head back slowly
as far as you are able,
so that your chin faces toward the sky,
and hold that position for five seconds.

Step 10
Bring your head slowly upright, gently,
until it is in the center position.

Step 11
Deep breath, hold for three seconds
and exhale forcefully. Haaaahh!

Step 12
Move your head slowly downward as far as you are able,
without touching the chest and hold for five seconds.

Step 13
Move your head, still down, to the right, slowly,
as far as you are able and hold for three seconds.

Step 14
Holding the head down, bring the head back into the center.

Step 15
Breathe in through the nostrils, hold for three seconds
and exhale forcefully. Haaaahh!

Step 16
Move the head, still in a down position to the left
as far as you are able and hold for three seconds.

Step 17
Bring your head, still holding it down, back into the center.

Step 18
Holding your head down,
bring your hands again into the position
below the heart chakra.

Step 18
Press inward lightly and hold for five seconds.

Step 20
Breathe deeply in through the nostrils
and exhale forcefully, Haaaahh!

Step 21
Bring your head slowly upright into the center position,
assuring your spine is as straight as possible.

Step 22
Breathe deeply through the nostrils, exhale forcefully. Haaaahh!

Step 23
For the final time, bring your hands to just below the heart chakra
and hold for five seconds.

Step 24
Breathe deeply into the nostrils and exhale once more forcefully.
Haaaahh![26]

Step 25
Move your hands away, place the palms upright
and you have completed.

357 A Mudra for the cleansing of the sacral chakra.
All movements to be done slowly and gently.

Step 1
Place left hand over right hand in a cup formation,
the left fingers over the right fingers,
the left thumb on top of the right thumbnail.

Step 2
Place the hands upon a surface,
approximately six inches from your being
or further but no less.

Step 3
Sit as straight as you may, hold the head in the center position,
soles of your feel, if possible, flat upon the floor.
Hold this position for fifteen seconds
while maintaining comfort and ease of breath,
neither forcing it in or out,
but breathe as you do naturally.

Step 4
Deep breath in through the nostrils, hold for the count of five
and gently release.

Step 5
Move your hands inward maintaining the position in Step 1,
until they are touching the solar plexus.

Step 6
Press lightly inward and hold for a period of five seconds.

Step 7
Move your hands outward, back to the original position,
maintaining the fingers and thumb position.

Step 8
Move your head to the right, as far as you are able,
and hold for five seconds.

Step 9
Bring your head back into its center position,
hold for five seconds.

Step 10
Bring your head downward, as far as you are able,
without touching the chest,
hold for five seconds.

Step 11
Do not bring your head back up.
Move it to the left, as far as you are able, hold for five seconds.

Step 12
Keeping your head down,
bring your head back into the center position,
hold for five seconds.

Step 13
Slowly and gently raise your head up.
If you become dizzy, stop, hold for five seconds
and then continue back upward.

Step 14
Slowly tilt your head back
as far as you are able without discomfort.
Hold for five seconds.

Step 15
Move your head slowly, still tilted back, unto the right,
as far as you are able and hold for three seconds.

Step 16
Bring your head back into the center, still maintaining the tilt
and hold for three seconds.

Step 17
Slowly move your head to your left, maintaining the tilt,
and hold for three seconds.

Step 18
Bring your head slowly back into the center
so that your head is now upright
and the spinal column is as straight as you are able.

Step 19
Hold in this position for fifteen seconds,
allowing the Prism of Light
to enter in through the crown charka,
directly to the sacral.

Step 20
Move your hands apart, placing palms up

Step 21
Deep breath in through the nostrils, out through the mouth,
whooshing forcefully through the mouth
so that you feel at the very base of your being, the fire.
And you have completed.

358 We bring forth a Mudra
for the cleansing of the root chakra.
This exercise is to be done no more
than thrice a day at any one time.
And you will understand, when you bring your head back up,
you will do it slowly.
If you become dizzy, you will pause, allow the dizziness to pass
and then proceed.
You will know that you have attained
the correct rhythm of the exercises
when you feel a warmth streaming up from your toes
unto the root chakra.

Step 1
Feet toward the floor or flat on the floor if possible,
placing your hands flat upon a natural surface.

Step 2
Hands spread apart, no fingers touching, no thumbs touching.
Your head looking down at the hands.

Step 3
Take a slight breath in through the nostrils,
hold for a count of three
and slowly in a controlled manner
release for three, wh, wh, wh.

Step 4
Bring together without lifting from the surface,
the forefinger and thumbs,
and note you have formed a figure.

Step 5
While raising your head slowly,
raise also the forefingers and thumbs
in front of the third eye.
The other fingers remain untouching.

Step 6
Take another slight breath in through the nostrils,
hold for the count of three
and release in a controlled manner
to the count of four, wh, wh, wh, whhhhh.

Step 7
Place your thumbs so that they are touching
the very tip of the bridge of your nose.
Forefingers remain touching each other.

Step 8
Sound ohhhh laaaaaa maaaaaahhh. [long o, a as in ah, a as in ah].

Hold mah for as long as you are able.

Step 9
Bring together the forefinger and thumbs,
right to right, left to left.
Maintaining the position of the forefingers and the thumbs,
bring your hands down to just below the heart chakra.
Allow the thumbs to touch the flesh.

Step 10
Sound ohhhh laaaaaa maaaaaahhh. [long o, a as in ah, a as in ah].
Hold mah for as long as you are able.

Step 11
Slight breath into the nostrils.
Hold for the count of three and release in a controlled manner
to the count of five, wh, wh, wh ,wh, whhh.

Step 12
Sound ohhhh laaaaaa maaaaaahhh. [long o, a as in ah, a as in ah]
Hold mah for as long as you are able.

Step 13
Bring your hands downward to in front of the root chakra
or as close as you are able
without taking the thumbs and forefingers apart.

Step 14
Sound ohhhh laaaaaa maaaaaahhh. [long o, a as in ah, a as in ah].
Hold mah for as long as you are able.

Step 15
Slight breath into the nostrils.
Hold for the count of three and release in a controlled manner
to the count of five: wh, wh, wh ,wh wh.

Step 16
Maintaining the position of the forefingers and the thumbs,
bring your hands slowly to the third eye again.

Step 17
And once more the thumbs will touch the bridge of the nose,
while at the same time, repeating three times,
each time with a short pause in between:
ohhhh laaaaaa maaaaaahhh [long o, a as in ah, a as in ah].
Hold mah for as long as you are able.

Step 18
Slight breath into the nostrils.
Hold for the count of three and releasein a controlled manner
to the count of five: wh, wh, wh ,wh wh.

Step 19
Move your hands back to their original position upon the table,
your head slightly down.

Step 20
Slowly move your fingers and thumbs apart.
And you have completed.

359 A Mudra for a great level of relaxation
to the extent that it is beneficial
for the heart, for the lungs, for the throat,
for the eyes and the ears.
For the vibrations that you experience enter in
to the very flesh of your being
and they are of Purity, they are of healing.
The chakras of the palms
are indeed powerful in their sacredness.
You may do this thrice daily.

Step 1
Place the right hand upon the upper left chest,
hold for five seconds.
The other hand is flat, palm down upon a surface.

Step 2
Remove the right hand from the upper chest, slowly,
and as you are moving it,

you will feel a tingling or a heaviness
about your head, your face, your forehead.

Step 3
Bring your right hand palm down,
place left palm unto the upper right chest
and hold for five seconds.

Step 4
Slowly, very slowly, move the palm away from the chest.
And as you move it away, you will feel the tingling
or the heaviness around your head.

Step 5
Place your right hand, palm down.
You now have both hands flat down on a surface.

Step 6
Place the right palm on the left upper chest,
place your left hand on the right upper chest.
Hold this position with your neck as upright as possible
for the count of twelve seconds.
And you will begin to feel a warmth, a tingling,
from the palms of your hands onto your upper chest.

Step 7
While keeping your wrists crossed, the left over right, slowly,
move your hands away from your chest
and turn the palms upright.

Step 8
Move your hands away from each other slowly
and place them palms up upon a surface.

Step 9
Fingers close to each other on each hand
and the thumb of each hand will touch the forefinger.

Step 10
Your hands are at a forty-five degree angle toward each other
as you slowly move your head slightly down
toward your palms.

Step 11
A deep breath and let it out. Whooosh!
As you let it out, Soul, you will begin to feel
a further pressure around the top of your head
and forehead, even unto the face you may feel a tingling.

Step 12
Move your hands, palm up,
two middle fingers touching at the fingertips.

Step 13
Place these four fingers in front of your mouth, deep breath,
hold for the count of three seconds,
release breath gently, slowly to the count of three.

Step 14
Move your hands so that the center of the palms are
in front of each of the earth eyes.
Feel the tingling, feel the pressure
and hold for the count of three.
Breathe easy in and out, thrice.

Step 15
Move your hands slowly away from the eyes and unto a surface.
If you become lightheaded or dizzy, stop moving the hands away
and when it passes, continue until they have reached the surface.

Step 16
A further deep breath, hold for the count of three, exhale slowly.
Turn your hands over and you have through this exercise
attained a great level of relaxation,

360 Souls of earth, you have upon your earth many beings
who inflict upon themselves injury,

who in their mind have a desire to obliterate their being,
to punish their being.
Their minds, the brain has become distorted.
These beings may use sharp objects.
They may use fire.
They may use, attempt in various ways.
They may smash their heads against a wall.
These beings may be assisted, not, Soul, to prevent their walk,
but to calm their being by touching certain meridians
so they may make a choice
When they are in the throes
of insisting upon punishing their being,
they see no other alternative.
To them, there is no other vision.
It is closed.
And their whole being is dedicated to harming self.

Step 1
Hold their left forefinger between your thumb and forefinger
and press firmly.
This will catch the attention, minutely, understand,
but it will begin catching the understanding of the being.
You will hold this for as long as the being will allow
but no more than ten seconds.

Step 2
Move to the knuckle and again press, five seconds.

Step 3
Third pressure point,
at the top of the knuckle near the thumb nail,
press between the forefinger
and the thumb for five seconds.

Step 4
Move to the thumb nail, press firmly for five seconds.

Step 5
Move to the knuckle above the thumbnail,

press firmly for five seconds.

Step 6
Move to the final joint of the thumb and,
press and hold for six seconds,
or as long as the being will allow,
but no more than six seconds.
At this point, the being will begin
to focus their intention away
from the intended harm to self.

Step 7
Clasp the left hand of the being,
holding the palm of the being with your hand.
Gently, but enough so that the palms touch palm.

Step 8
And you will hold that while looking directly
into the eye of the being.

Step 9
As the being begins to calm,
and looks into your eyes, you will know
that the need to harm has passed.

Step 10
Ask the being to place their hands together:
right over left, palm to palm,
and close the fingers over the hands.
Hold that position for six earth seconds.
And you may point out to the being the beauty of their Soul.

HEAD

361 Any injury to the brain, to the mind,
whether it be by migraine, headache, or blow,[27]
for internal injuries and also for those victims of stroke
and as a preventative for the Alzheimer.

Step 1
Bend elbows, hands outward,

Step 2
Bring hands out to the side, palms up

Step 3
Three times bring the palms upward unto the ears,
as you sing wweeeeeeeeeeeeeeeeeee [long e]
and hold the sound for three earth seconds each time.

Step 4
Place the hands in the prayer position and
move slowly up above the head.

Step 5
Then move the hands in the prayer position above the third eye.

Step 6
Bring them further down to the front of the face,
holding the thumbs and the fingers together
of each hand.[28]

Step 7
Move the hands in the prayer position
to below the chin and the throat area,
and then you may slowly release the hands.

362 We present a Mudra to strengthen the eyes.
We recommend that this be done three times daily.
As you see improvement and your eyes see better,
you may then reduce to twice daily and continue
until your eyes have reached a state
that is agreeable to your being.

Step 1
Place the backs of the hands upon a natural surface.
Intertwine the fingers to the point of the first knuckle.

The thumbs touching flesh, eyes closed.

Step 2
Repeat slowly nine times: eelaaa eeelaaa eelaaa [long e, a as in ah]

Step 3
Retaining the position of fingers intertwined at the first knuckle,
thumbs at the flesh, bring your hands upward
in that cupped position up unto your eyes.

Step 4
Open the eyes, with the hands over the eyes.

Step 5
Bring the end of the palms against the sides of the eyes
and hold the hands in this position for fifteen seconds.

Step 6
Move your hands away from the eyes, closing the eyes,
unlocking the fingertips.

Step 7
Slowly move the hands apart
while maintaining the palms toward the eye area.

Step 8
Move the hands to the sides of the eyes at the temple.

Step 9
Place your fingers close, touching each other,
your thumbs touching flesh.

Step 10
Nine times in a clockwise motion,
massage gently each side of the temples
with the fingertips.

Step 11
Fingers again intertwined at the first knuckle,

hands in the cupped position,
move your hands back in front of the eyes.

Step 12
Hold for the count of nine.
Deep breath, exhale.

Step 13
Hands remaining in the position,
bring your hands down until they are again
touching a surface with the backs of your hand.

Step 14
Gently unlock the position of your fingertips and your thumbs,
turn your hands over and you have completed.

363 A Mudra for the problems with the ears,
whether hearing or infections.

Step 1
Hands palm up, elbows bent.
Swing the arms outward
until they have reached the sides of the body.

Step 2
Bring the hands forward slowly
in the front of your being in the heart area,
Cup your hands, palms facing each other until the fingertips
and the thumb tips are touching.

Step 3
Place the right thumb over the left thumb
and hold for a count of five.

Step 4
Release the thumbs, the fingers and move the hands apart slowly,
palms facing each other.

Step 5
Bring hands slowly out unto the sides of the body.
The upper arms do not need to be touching the body.

Step 6
Move your palms slowly upward unto the ears.
Hold approximately three inches from either ear
for a count of five.
The palm of the hands will be in direct line with the ears.

Step 8
Deep breath, exhaling gently

Step 9
Bring your palms directly over the ears.
Hold for a count of three.

Step 10
Deep breath, exhalation and slowly move your hands away
from the ears
to approximately six inches upon either side.

Step 11
Bring the hands upward to the top of the head
in the prayer position.
Hold for a count of three.

Step 12
Move your palms slightly apart
but with the fingers and thumb still touching,
and hold the hands over the top of your head
for a count of three.

Step 13
Starting with the thumbs then the fingers,
remove the hands from the top of the head,
gently bringing them down
into the beginning position in Step 1.

Step 14
Sing or chant three times: oooooooooooh [long o, in a low tone].

Step 15
As you feel the vibration enter the ears and the third eye,
enter in to the second ooooooh [long o, medium tone].

Step 16
As you feel the vibration enter in to the ears and the third eye,
enter in to the third,
sing or chant: eeeeeee [long e, higher tone].

Step 17
Hands together in a prayer position, bring them up to the eye,
gently touching the eye with your forefingers.

Step 18
Bring the hands back into the beginning position,
and then place palms facing down,
and you have completed the healing of your ears.

364 Souls of earth, for those who have ringing of the ears,
the tinnitus, the earache caused by pressure,
even that which is caused by infection.

Step 1
Place the forefingers at the ear lobe, not in the ear.

Step 2
Gently press in as if you were attempting to partially mute noise.

Step 3
Move your forefingers along your flesh
to the very tops of the ears.

Step 4
Gently press forefinger into the skull at the tops of the ears.

Step 5
Bring your fingers down the flesh unto and
behind the major portion of the ear.
And again press inward upon the skull.

Step 6
Gently press the ear lobes with your thumbs and forefingers.
Hold for a count of three.

Step 7
With the pads of your thumbs maintain contact with ear lobes,
while slowly releasing the forefingers.

Step 8
Move the pads of your thumbs in front of the ear canal.
Press gently in front of the ear canal, not into the ear canal.

Step 9
Bring the thumbs downward following the line of your chin
until they meet at the chin area.

Step 10
Press the thumbs together, press your fingers together and
hold that position for five seconds.[29]

Step 11
Move your thumbs upward unto just above below the lower lip,
maintaining your fingers together
and hold for three seconds.

Step 12
Slowly move your hands apart, place palms up and you have
completed.

365 A Mudra for those beings
who have often cricks in the neck,
or who have neck injury or who have stiff neck.
Note: repeat Steps 1 through 4 three times.

Step 1
Left thumb is over the right, intertwine the fingers.

Step 2
Palms down, place hands in this position underneath your chin.

Step 3
Slowly bring your elbows up.[30]
Hold that position for five seconds or as long as you are able.[31]

Step 4
Bring your elbows back in.

Step 5
Slowly remove the fingers from being intertwined,
thumbs remain touching the chin
as you move your fingers apart.

Step 6
Bring them upward unto the area at the edge of the eyes.

Step 7
With the first knuckles of the first two fingers, gently tap
the sides of the eyes five times.
Do not tap directly upon the eye.

Step 8
Bring the knuckles downward back underneath the chin.

Step 9
Have the knuckles of each hand
momentarily touch underneath the chin.

Step 10
Maintaining the touching of the knuckles of the first two fingers,
bring downward the hands to the solar plexus area.

Step 11
Release the knuckles and you have completed.

366 Souls of earth, we would give unto you
a Mudra for neck pains,
especially those pains caused by tension,
those pains caused by what you call whiplash,
those pains caused by beginning of stiffness
from the arthritic.
At no time, when you feel pain
do you continue with the movement.
You will only move to the extent there is no pain,
and you will find this extension will gradually increase.

Step 1
Arms bent at the elbow, palms upward, hands slightly cupped.

Step 2
Deep breath, hold for the count of three,
gently release and push out slightly for a count of three.

Step 3
While you maintain Step 1 position,
sing or chant: waaaaay [long a].
You will feel the tone ringing through the neck area.

Step 4
Move the arms slightly apart from the body
at a forty-five degree angle.

Step 5
Slowly bring them back in
as you repeat your song: waaaaay [long a].

Step 6
Maintain position for fifteen seconds.

Step 7
Palms facing each other and gently coming together
at the area in front of the throat.

Step 8
The fingers will touch in a pyramid like shape,
the thumbs will not.

Step 9
Touch your chin with your forefingers.
Arms held close to the body.
Hold that position as you breathe deeply for the count of three
and exhale for the count of three.

Step 10
Arms close to the body,
while your thumbs now rest against your chin,
your fingers in the pyramid shape, sing:
weee aaahhhhhhh [long e, short a].

Step 11
Release the thumbs from the chin.

Step 12
Bring your fingertips and hands forward until palms touch palms
and fingers touch fingers, thumbs touch thumbs.

Step 13
Gently lower the arms and the hands
until you have reached the solar plexus.

Step 14
Gently and slowly bring your hands apart
and back into the initial position of Step 1.
You will feel at this point, a tender stretching of the neck muscles.

Step 15
Move your head as far as you are able to your left slowly,
and slowly back to the center.

Step 16
Move your head slowly to the right as far as you are able,
and slowly bring the head back into the center position.

Step 17
Bring the head slowly downward as far as you canon your chest..

Step 17
Bring it slowly, very gently, back upward.
When the head is fully up again in the center of the body,
move your palms and turn them palm down,
place them upon your thighs and you have completed.

367 We bring unto you the Mudra for brain cancer.
Understand, Soul, this first one we give you is for stage one,
a cancer that has not spread beyond its nodule.
This is to be done a minimum of three times daily.
When you no longer feel the vibration mentioned in Step 4,
you will know you have conquered.

Step 1
Place your hands flat upon a surface, palms down,
your feet toward the floor or flat on the floor.

Step 2
Turn your palms up, intertwine your fingers.
Thumbs will hang loosely.

Step 3
Bring hands in this position up to your heart level.

Step 4
Thrice chant or sing slowly the following syllables:
aaaaa kaaaah naaay [long a, a as in ah, long a].
You will know, Soul, that you have the correct pronunciation
when you feel vibration in your head,
throughout your brain.

Step 5
Move hands up to throat chakra,
in the intertwined fingers position.

Step 6
Turn the hands in the intertwined fingers position
to face in front of your throat chakra

Step 7
Three times, chant or sing slowly:
aaaaa kaaaah naaay [long a, a as in ah, long a].

Step 8
Move the hands in the intertwined fingers position
to directly in front of the third eye chakra

Step 9
Three times, chant or sing slowly:
aaaaa kaaaah naaay [long a, a as in ah, long a].

Step 10
Move your hands in the intertwined fingers position
upward over the top of your head,
and bring them slowly down
to rest on the top of your head.

Step 11
Three times, chant or sing slowly:
aaaaa kaaaah naaay [long a, a as in ah, long a].
You must do this slowly.
If you feel light-headed or dizzy, stop, take a deep breath
and then proceed again where you left off.

Step 12
Move the hands above the head
in the intertwined fingers position.

Step 13
Bring the hands in the intertwined fingers position,
in front of the third eye, pausing momentarily

Step 14
Pausing momentarily at each chakra,
move the hands in the intertwined fingers position,
to the front of the throat and in front of the heart.

Step 15
Move the hands unto the surface, palms up, fingers intertwined
and tilt your head down, gently. Hold for a count of four.

Step 16
Three times, chant or sing slowly:
aaaaa kaaaah naaay [long a, a as in ah, long a].

Step 17
Move your fingers apart slowly and turn the hands over,
palm down upon the surface.
If you become dizzy, stop, take a deep breath.

368 A Mudra for a more advanced form of brain cancer,
even unto that which you have been told is terminal.

Step 1
Place your hands palm down, upon a surface,
your feet toward the floor or flat upon the floor.

Step 2
Slightly bend your head toward the surface where your hands are.

Step 3
Alternately, seven times slowly,
beginning with the right hand,
gently lift it up and bring it down.
Lift up the left hand and bring it down.[32]
Each right and left movement is one time.

Step 4
Place your palms up.

Step 5
Cup the palms and place your left hand
cupped within your cupped right hand, thumbs outward.
Your head has remained bent.

Step 6
Slowly raise your head as well as you are able,[33]
and slowly bring your hands in their cupped position up
until you can place the hands in front of your mouth,
but not touching the mouth.

Step 7
Five times chant or sing slowly:
leeee aaah oooh maaay
[long e, a as in ah, long o, long a].[34]
You will feel the vibration, Soul, in your brain.

Step 8
Move the cupped hands unto the third eye chakra.

Step 9
Five times chant or sing slowly:
leeee aaah oooh maaay [long e, a as in ah, long o, long a].

Step 10
Slowly move your hands above your head
and slowly place them down upon the top of the head.
The left hand is on the top of the head,
the right hand is cupped over the left.

Step 11
Head tilted downward as well as you are able.

Step 12
Five times chant or sing slowly:
leeee aaah oooh maaay [long e, a as in ah, long o, long a].

Step 13
Inhale, hold for the count of three and then exhale in a

controlled manner
for the count of five: wh wh wh wh wh.

Step 14
Slowly move your hands upward away from your head
and back down to your third eye, pausing momentarily.

Step 15
And back down toward your mouth, pausing momentarily.

Step 16
And back down, stopping at the heart level for a count of three.

Step 17
Place your cupped hands upon a surface,
slowly move your left hand away and then your right hand
turn them both over palm down and you have completed.

369 We bring forth to you a Mudra
for cancers of the nasal and the mouth.
This exercise is to be done a minimum of three times per day.
You may, Soul, certainly do it more often.
We would suggest that you continue to do this exercise
until you have conquered.

Step 1
Place your hands palm down upon a surface, fingers spread,
and your thumbs not touching the sides of your fingers.

Step 2
Feet pointed toward the floor or on the floor if possible.

Step 3
Place the hands so that you can move them back and forth
upon the surface, along with your body.
Five times slowly
move your body and your hands back and forth.[35]

Step 4
Move your hands upward slightly off the surface;
leave the fingers and the thumb apart,

so that you have a totally open space between each.

Step 5
Bend your head downward as if you were looking at your palms
and close your eyes.

Step 6
Maintain a rhythm as well as you are able,
alternating five times the left and right leg.
Stretch left leg out fully forward
and then bring it back down to the floor,
And the same with the right leg,
extend it forward and bring it down slowly.

Step 7
Place your hands together slightly up off the surface,
join the fingers and the thumbs.
The thumbs remain away from the flesh,
but touching each other as in a prayer position.

Step 8
Bring hands up to heart area, hold this position for five seconds.

Step 9
Bring your hands still in the prayer position
up underneath the chin,[36]
touching your chest with your thumbs.

Step 10
Sing or chant three times:
reeeeeee aaaah noh [long e, a as in ah, long o].
The emphasis, Soul, on the first syllable, the 'ree' sound.

Step 11
Move your hands apart, maintaining them at the heart level,
the palms facing each other.

Step 12
Sing or chant, three times, as well as you are able:
reeeeeee aaaah noh [long e, a as in ah, long o].

Step 13
Five times slowly move your hands together and then apart,
back and forth.
You will know you have attained a rhythmic vibration
by the pressure within the top area of your forehead,
of your head and your stomach area.

Step 14
Holding your hands in the prayer position,
bring up under the chin, take a deep breath,
hold for the count of three
and exhale as well as you are able,
in a controlled manner f
or the count of five: phh phh phh phh phhhh.

Step 15
Bring your hands up in front of your face
and open them toward your face,
maintaining the edges of your palms touching.
Hold for a count of five.

Step 16
Move your hands back into the prayer position
and bring them downward and then apart.

Step 17
Turn them over, palms down, place on the surface
and you have completed.

UPPER TORSO

370 Souls of earth, we give unto you a Mudra for cancer of the esophagus.

Step 1
In an upright position, feet toward the floor
or on the floor, hands placed on the surface, palms down.

Step 2
Establish a rhythmic movement of your feet slowly.
Three times slowly move your left and your right foot.
The left foot is to be brought up off the floor
and moved forward three inches and back three inches.
Follow with your right foot,
move forward three inches and back three inches.[37]

Step 3
Turn your hands palm up and raise them slightly off the surface

Step 4
Move your hands, slowly and gently, six times,
back and forth in tandem.

Step 5
Turn your palms toward your body, the left below the heart,
the right above the heart.
Hold for twelve seconds,
while either mentally or physically humming.
If at all possible, hold the hum for six earth seconds
while you are holding your hands in this position.
Hummmmmmm.
You will feel the vibration in your esophagus.

Step 6
Continue holding the palms toward you
and six times[38] rhythmically
move your hands slightly away and bring them back.

Step 7
Place your left hand on the esophageal area,
your right hand over your left hand, thumbs upward,
Hummmmmmm for six seconds.

Step 8
Maintaining the right over the left, the thumbs upward,
three times rhythmically move your hands slightly away
from the esophageal area and back again.[39]

Step 9
Maintaining the right over the left, the thumbs upward,
move your hands down onto the surface.

Step 10
Move your left hand away first, then move your right away,
place palms down and you have completed.

371 We would give unto you an alternative
for reducing and eliminating high blood pressure.
Done thrice daily, the blood pressure will return to normal.
And thereafter, to remain normal, you may do so
once every three daysand this will contain.

Step 1
Place together the fingers and the thumbs,
but hold the palms apart.
Your feet flat on the ground, your back as straight as possible.

Step 2
Maintaining the position in Step1,
bring the hands up unto the eye.
The fingers pointing outward.
Hold for a period of seven seconds.

Step 3
Deep breath in through the nostrils
and exhale gently out through the mouth.

Step 4
Move the hands in an upright position to the third eye.

Step 5
Deep breath in through the nostrils,
exhale slowly out through the mouth.

Step 6
Bring the hands still held together down unto the heart area,
holding that position for seven seconds,

hands pointing outward, but hold the palms apart.

Step 7
Deep breath in through the nostrils.
Hold for a count of five and release forcefully, whoooh!

Step 8
Release the touching of the fingers and the thumb,
moving your hands away, side to side,
in the area of the heart.

Step 9
Palms facing each other, the thumbs touching the fingers,
the fingers held close together.
Hold this position for seven earth seconds.

Step 10
Deep breath in through the nostrils.
Hold for five and gently release.

Step 11
Bring together the hands at the heart level,
fingers touching fingers, thumbs touching thumbs.

Step 12
Close the hands so that the palms are also touching,
and hold the hands at a forty-five degree angle upward
for at least three earth seconds.

Step 13
Release the hands and you have completed.

372 A Mudra for the heart health.
This may be done sitting, standing or laying.

Step 1
Place thumb and forefinger together, palms upward, elbows bent.

Step 2
The tops of your arms from the shoulder to the elbow
are held close to the sides of the body
as you breathe deeply, as deeply as you can.
Hold for a count of three and breathe out for a count of three.
A gentle breath out will be sufficient,

Step 3
Move your arms away from your body, elbows bent outward
maintaining the thumbs and forefingers touching.

Step 4
Maintaining the thumbs and forefingers touching,
bring your hands close at the level of the heart area,
placing fingers of the left hand
over the fingers of the right hand.

Step 5
Three times voice the sound: woooooooooooooooooo [long o]
in the tone of C as well as you are able and it will be held
for as long as it is feasible for thy physical being.
In between each sounding, hold your position quietly
for a period of five seconds.

Step 6
Release the left fingers from the right fingers,
maintaining the thumb and forefinger together.

Step 7
Gently begin to move your hands away from your chest,
maintaining the position
of thumb and forefingers touching.

Step 8
Bring the hands up unto the third eye.

Step 9
Release the thumb and forefingers and bring the palms upward.
Hold for a count of three.

Step 10
Turn the palms over, bring them down and you have completed.

373 We bring unto you a Mudra
for the strengthening of the heart muscle.
It is particular to the heart muscle that has become flaccid
through disease or through overuse, or even genetically.
If you are unable to fully complete the exercise physically
due to the flaccidity of the heart muscles,
you may do the exercise within the mind.
This exercise may be repeated daily as often as required,
until you feel the strength returning to your being,
until you can breathe easier, walk easier.
And then maintain once daily.

Step 1
Feet flat on the floor or at least toward the floor.

Step 2
Lay your hands palms down upon a surface.

Step 3
Lean forward so that your head is bent toward your hands.

Step 4
Relax your body as much as you are able.

Step 5
Turn your hands palm up and rest them upon the surface.
Fingers spread apart, thumbs spread apart,
remain looking down at the palms.

Step 6
Slowly intake five controlled short breaths:
wh wh wh wh wh, as if you are sipping from a straw.

Step 7
Rest your being for a count of ten.[40]

Step 8
Slowly intake five controlled short breaths:
sh sh sh sh sh - as if you are sipping from a straw.

Step 9
Rest your being for a count of ten.

Step 10
Slowly intake five controlled short breaths:
sh sh sh sh sh - as if you are sipping from a straw.

Step 11
Bring your hands up, fingers and thumbs spread apart,
raise your head very slowly and bring your hands up.

Step 12
With the neck straight, place your hands underneath your chin,
maintaining spread apart fingers and thumbs.

Step 13
Slowly intake five controlled short breaths:
sh sh sh sh sh - as if you are sipping from a straw.

Step 14
Rest your being for a count of ten.

Step 15
Slowly intake five controlled short breaths:
sh sh sh sh sh - as if you are sipping from a straw.

Step 16
Rest your being for a count of ten.

Step 17
Slowly intake five controlled short breaths:
sh sh sh sh sh - as if you are sipping from a straw.

Step 18
Three times, gently, as if you were sipping,

intake one short breath, sh, and exhale,
pausing slightly between each sip.

Step 19
Move your hands out and up unto the third eye.

Step 20
Place the left hand over the right.
The right will be in front of the third eye,
the left palm will be
behind the right palm but not touching.
Hold[41] as well as you are able during Steps 21 and 22, 23.

Step 21
Hummmmmmm for as long as your breath will hold, Soul,
even if it is only a momentary Hummm.

Step 22
Slowly, if you are resting your elbows upon a table,
slowly come back up into the sitting upright position.
Step 23
Move your hands from the third eye, left hand first.
and slowly bring them down back unto the surface.

Step 24
Deep breath, as well as you are able and hold for a count of three.
Thrice exhale gently: wh wh wh.

Step 25
Turn hands palm over and you have completed.

374 We give unto you a Mudra
for the severe palpitations of the heart,
the severe anxiety that comes with the palpitations
that can not seemingly be controlled.
The heartbeat that is irregular will also be assisted
by this Mudra to regulate itself in a more normal manner.
And we would suggest that you do this often throughout the day.

When you become dizzy, stop,
hold for a moment until the dizziness passes,
and then resume where you left off.
You will find the heartbeat will become regular.
Step 1
Feet toward the floor or directly upon the floor,
legs not touching.

Step 2
Place the backs of your hands upon a surface,
palms cupped upright in a receiving position,
thumbs touching the flesh of the forefingers,
the forefingers and the other fingers held closely together.

Step 3
Bring your cupped palms close together,
as if you are holding water within your hands.

Step 4
Bring the cupped palms up to the level of the heart,
ensure your elbows are tightly against
the sides of your being,
and slightly bend the head toward the cupped palms.

Step 5
Moving only the forearms and hands,
bring them up in front of the throat chakra,

Step 6[42]
Three times express, chant or sing:
aaa eee yaaaah [long a, long e, a as in ah]

Step 7
Deep breath, as well as you are able, hold for the count of three
and exhale to the count of four, gently and slowly.

Step 8
Deep breath, as much as you are able in your condition,
and expel again slowly.

Step 9
Deep breath in, as much as you are able,
hold for the count of three and expel to the count of five
in a controlled manner: wh wh wh wh wh.

Step 10
Move the palms upward in front of the third eye,
maintaining the closeness of the elbows
to the sides of your being.

Step 11
Three times express, chant or sing:
aaa eee yaaaah [long a, long e, a as in ah]

Step 12
Deep breath, hold for the count of three,
and expel for the count of three
in a controlled manner, wh wh wh.

Step 13
Deep breath as well as you are able to the count of three,
expel your breath, gustily; whhsssssh.
Make the sound, whhssssh.
When you exhale in a gusty manner
you will feel in your stomach area
a contraction and that will tell you
that you have entered in correctly the breath.

Step 14
And once more, slowly, gently, deep breath in,
hold for the count of three,
exhale in a gusty manner, whhsssssh.

Step 15
Bring your cupped hands down, directly in front of your mouth

Step 16
Three times, express, chant or sing:
aaa eee yaaaah [long a, long e, a as in ah]

Step 17
Three times, take one deep breath in, as deep as you can,
and hold it for the count of two,
and then exhale directly into the palms
as gustily as you can, whhsssssh.

Step 18
Bring your cupped hands down back unto the surface
and rest the backs of your hands upon the surface,
thumbs against the forefingers,
head slightly bent downward

Step 19
Express the sound once more, chant or sing:
aaa eee yaaaah [long a, long e, a as in ah]

Step 20
Deep breath, hold for the count of three
while turning your hands over
and spreading the fingers and the thumb wide,
then expel your breath and you have completed.

375 A Mudra for the areas of lung damage
or disease internally.
You may sit or stand or even lay during this Mudra.

Step 1
Begin in the position of elbows bent, palms up.

Step 2
Cup your hands.

Step 3
Bring them forward unto the area of the chest.

Fingers will be close together, one touching upon the other
and the thumbs held gently within the hand.

Step 4
Sound three times: raaaaaaaaaaaaaaaaay [long a].[43]

Step 5
Deep breath, hold for the count of three,
releasing unto the count of three.

Step 6
Continue to hold the position for one earth minute
and you have completed.

376 Souls of earth, for chronic inflammation of the lungs,
we would give forth a Mudra to break the cycle of illness.

Step 1
Sit, feet upon the floor or as close to the floor as possible,
with the legs not cramped in any way.

Step 2
Place your hands, palms facing palms upon a surface.

Step 3
Thumbs touch the forefingers, right to right, left to left
and the other fingers held close together.

Step 4
Hold the hands apart for as wide as you are comfortable
upon the surface,
yet, not beyond the sides of your being.

Step 5
Move the hands toward each other, just above the surface,
until the palms touch.

Step 6
Twice move the hands outward again to the same space as before
and bring them back in palm to palm.

Step 7
Move your hands upright in the prayer position
in front of the heart.

Step 8
Repeat thrice as well as you are able:
ha lay lu yaah[44] [a as in ah, long a, o as in oo, a as in ah].

Step 9
Bring the hands back again into the prayer position,
but facing outward,
not upright and hold for the count of six.

Step 10
Move your hands upright in the prayer position
in front of the heart and repeat three times:
ha lay lu yaah [a as in ah, long a, o as in oo, a as in ah].

Step 11
Move your hands outward, maintaining palm against palm
and once more repeat:
ha lay lu yaah [a as in ah, long a, o as in oo, a as in ah].
If you are doing this correctly,
you will feel the vibration in your chest.

Step 12
Move your hands apart to the original position in Step 1
and place them downward and you have completed.

377 We would give unto you a specific Mudra
for that which you call carpal tunnel.

Step 1
Raise your hands above the surface,
fingertips and thumbs touching.
The hands will be at least three inches apart.

Step 2
Hold them in this position with the elbows raised

on the same level as the hands, not below and not above.
Hold this position for fifteen seconds.

Step 3
Slowly bring your fingertips inward
until the first knuckle is touching the surface.
The thumbs remain in the same position.
Hold this position for twelve seconds.

Step 4
Deep breath in through the nostrils
and exhale through the mouth, gently.

Step 5
Move and curl your fingers further until
the second knuckle is upon the surface.
Your thumbs maintain their position.
Elbows are bent upward, forty-five degree angle.
Hold this position for ten seconds.

Step 6
Maintain the position in Step 5 while raising your thumbs.
Continue in this position for seven seconds.

Step 7
Deep breath in through the nostrils, exhale through the mouth.

Step 8
Slowly enter again into the position in Step 1.
Slowly allow your knuckles to raise up, while allowing
your elbows to stay on the same level as the hands.

Step 9
Deep breath, gentle exhale while laying your palms flat down
with the fingers spread,
the hands not touching each other.
Hold the hands in this position for a count of five,
and then you have completed.

378 A Mudra for those who have broken,
strained, or sprained the arms,
for those who have repetitive motion injuries.
For those who are without hands, use the Mudra
as if they were in physical form.

Step 1
Bend the elbows, hold the palms upward.

Step 2
The thumb and forefinger are held together.

Step 3
Hold together the other fingers and bring the thumb
and forefinger forward, touching the two center fingers.

Step 4
The small finger is bent inward.
Hold this position,

Step 5
Take a deep breath and slightly bend thy head
toward thy injured member
and sound: bah luuue[45] [a as in the ah sound, o as in oo].

Step 6
Pause, Souls, for a count of five seconds.

Step 7
Take a deep breath and repeat:
bah-luuue [a as in the ah sound, o as in oo]
using as close as possible, the tone of A
while expressing the color blue.

Step 8
Touch the injured member with the fingers
in the position given in Steps 3 and 4.

Step 9
Open the thumb and forefinger and your other fingers
and you have completed.

LOWER TORSO

379 A Mudra for beings lost in the pains of severe
digestive complications,
those who are riddled with parasites,
those who are riddled with cells of cancer,
those who are riddled with the decimation
caused by diseases such as Crohn's.
Faithful adherence to this Mudra will bring about relieve,
will alleviate the pains
and will allow the being to enter in to a state
whereby the mind becomes clarified of pain.

Step 1
Hands flat upon a natural surface,
fingers held tightly together, thumbs raised.
Neither hand touching.

Step 2
Ensure that the back is as straight as possible,
head upright, looking forward.

Step 3
Deep breath, hold for the count of five and gently release.

Step 4
Another deep breath, hold for the count of five
and breathing out with a little more gusto.

Step 5
One more deep breath,
hold for the count of five and gently release.
What you are doing, Soul, is setting up a rhythm

within your being,
calling the cells of your being to attention.

Step 6
In front of the breast area, bring your hands together,
palm facing palm
and hold that position for a count of five.

Step 7
Breath in, hold for a count of five and release gently.

Step 8
Bring together the fingertips of each hand
and the thumbs of each hand.
The thumbs are not to be resting on the flesh,
they are to be above the flesh,
pointing unto your chin area.

Step 9
Breathe in, hold for a count of two and release gently.

Step 10
Five times, sing or chant as well as you are able:
oh may re kah! [long o, long a, long e, a as in ah].
The end syllable is to be coughed, KAH!
This is to bring your being into alignment.

Step 11
Gentle breath in, hold for the count of three, breathe gently out.

Step 12
Gently and slowly move your hands apart,
keeping the palms facing palms,
until approximately six inches apart.

Step 13
Move your palms in an upward position,
place your head downward toward the palms

but not touching, and hold for a count of three.

Step 14
Raise your head, breathe in deeper than before,
hold for a count of three, release gently.

Step 15
Turn your hands palms facing down into the starting position
and you have completed.

380 Souls, a Mudra for the diabetes.

Step 1
Hands are to be held outward, elbows bent, palms up,

Step 2
Move fingers inward touching the palm,
thumbs held close to the flesh

Step 3
Bring hands together by touching the forefingers
and as much as you can the other fingers.

Step 4
Bring hands to the area of the heart, hold for five seconds.

Step 5
Take a deep breath, hold for count of three,
release gently and slowly for a count of five seconds.

Step 6
Bring the hands inward unto area of the heart
in the position given in Step 3.

Step 7
Sound three times:
aaaa maaaaah reeeeeeee [long a. as as in ah, long e]

Step 8
Bend forward from your sitting position, gently,
at a forty five degree angle,

Step 9
Bring the forefingers unto the third eye,
touching the third eye and hold for a count of nine.

Step 10
Remove the forefingers from the third eye,
slowly straighten thy being.

Step 11
Proceed to release first the forefingers,
then the thumb and the rest of the fingers,
leaving the hands in the upward position, palms up
for a count of three seconds.

Step 12
Bring palms down and you have completed.

381 We give unto you a Mudra to assist those beings
who are afflicted with veins who no longer
allow the blood to flow freely,
whose veins are in a state of collapsing,
whose veins are in a state of atrophy.

Step 1
Begin sitting, if possible, if not, the prone position is acceptable.

Step 2
Place hands palm down upon the solar plexus of your being.
Ensure that the forefingers are touching each other
and the thumbs touching each other.
The other fingers are splayed wide.

Step 3
Take a deep breath through the nostrils

holding to a count of three
and exhale gently through the mouth..

Step 4
Inhale again through the nostrils, hold for a count of four,
and exhale gently though the mouth.

Step 5
Inhale again through the nostrils, hold for a count of five
and when exhaling, push out your breath: whhhhhoo.

Step 6
Breathe in once more through the nostrils and exhale gently.

Step 7
While remaining with the hands in the position of Step 2,
close your eyes and move your head to the left, slowly,
until it can turn no more.
Hold for a count of six.

Step 8
Slowly bring your head back to the center,
hold for the count of three.

Step 9
Move your head slowly to the right as far as you are able.
Hold for the count of six, and then gently
move your head back to the center position.

Step 10
Ensure, if you are sitting up, your back is straight,
chin held forward.

Step 11
Open the eyes and blink six times, slowly.

Step 12
Close your eyes and move your hand away from the solar plexus,
maintaining the thumb touching thumb

and the forefinger touching forefinger.

Step 13
Bring palms upward in front of the center eye,
and pause for the count of six.

Step 14
Moving your hands downward in the position of Step 2,
bring them unto your solar plexus.

Step 15
Hunch your shoulders forward,
hold for a count of three,
and relax and hold for a count of three.

Step 16
Move the right shoulder forward in a hunch position.
Hold for a count of three.
And slowly relax.

Step 17
Move the left shoulder, forward in a hunch position.
Hold for a count of three and slowly relax.

Step 18
Maintaining the position of the hands, thumbs and forefingers,
thrice move your left foot upward[46]
and then, press it downward.
Do the same with the right foot. Press up then down.

Step 19
Take a deep breath,[47] entering in through the nostrils,
hold for the count of three
and expel forcefully though the mouth,
blowing, as if you were blowing out a flame.

Step 20
Release your hands from your solar plexus,
maintaining the thumb and the forefingers together

until you place your hands downward.

Step 21
Gently, slowly, slowly move them apart,
and you have completed.

382 Souls of earth, we give unto the pregnant mother
who has difficulty with nausea,
a Mudra to assist in calming the nausea
and releasing that symptom from her pregnancy.
You may do often as you will during the first three days,
thereafter, it should only require
a maintenance of once per day.

Step 1
Begin, dear mother to be, feet flat on the floor
or at least pointing toward the floor.

Step 2
Hold the four fingers together above a surface
where they may come down and rest.
Press the thumb against the four fingers.

Step 3
Move the little fingers slightly away
and holding the three fingers and thumbs
together on each hand,
bring your hands up unto the heart area

Step 4
Place against your flesh the fingers and the thumbs,
the fingers of each hand
touching at the knuckles of the other hand.

Step 5
Put your little fingers outward crossing the left over the right.
Holding this position, gently press inward.

Step 6
Deep breath, hold for the count of three,
gently and as slowly as you can
release in a controlled manner, wh, wh, wh,.

Step 7
Chant or sing three times:
ray me la ah [long a, long e, a as in ah, a as in ah].

Step 8
Move your hands away from your body,
releasing thumbs and fingers

Step 9
Hold hands palm up above a surface
and slowly bring your hands down
so that the backs of your palms are resting upon a surface.
Your fingers are held close together on each hand,
but the left and right hand are not touching
and the thumbs are held outward.

Step 10
Chant or sing three times:
ray me la ah [long a, long e, a as in ah, a as in ah].

Step 11
Deep breath, hold for the count of three,
release in a controlled manner
four times, wh, wh, wh, wh.

Step 12
Holding the hands as in Step 9, bring the palms upward,
facing in front of the third eye,
neither hand touching, but close together.

Step 13
Chant or sing three times:
ray me la ah [long a, long e, a as in ah, a as in ah].
You will note a heaviness,

a feeling of pressure around your third eye area,
and you will know that you have almost completed.

Step 14`
Holding your hands in the same position as in Step 12,
move your hands back and fourth slowly, thrice;
once in, once out, once in, once out, once in, once out.
Note, when you go inward, the tips of the little fingers will touch.

Step 15
Place the backs of your hands upon a surface,
maintain finger and thumb position.

Step 16
As you tilt your head down toward hands,
release fingers and thumbs, open palms.
Hold for the count of three.
Turn your hands over and you have completed.

383 We give unto you a Mudra to assist the pregnancy
to bring forth the healthy babe.
It is to bring forth calmness in the mother so that the babe
is not stressed and can develop in a peaceful atmosphere.
Your fetus will feel the vibration,
will feel the comfort and peace you have given.

Step 1
We ask that you sit and place your hands upon a surface,
feet flat on the floor or pointing toward the floor.
The fingers, spread wide apart.
The thumbs spread as far as possible
from the tip of the forefinger
and the thumbs pointing toward the womb.

Step 2
Maintaining the separate position of the hands
upon an flat surface
slowly move together the fingers of each hand.

Step 3
When they meet, lightly press the thumbs
        unto the flesh of the forefinger.

Step 4
Raise your hands slightly up, turn them to face each other,
        the palm of the left facing the palm of the right.
Rest the little finger of each hand upon the surface.

Step 5
Slowly, six times, maintaining the palms facing each other,
        move the hands to either side of the body.
Bring them back to within three inches of each other.
When you move out and in, do not slide
        but lift slightly up and move your hands back and forth.

Step 6
Turn your palms up, the little fingers touching each other
        as the fingers next to the little fingers are held close.
Thumbs remains pressed against the flesh of the forefingers.

Step 7
Moving your hands up to the front of the mouth,
sing or chant: ooh may aaay laaaaaaaaaaaaah
        [long o, long a, long a, a as in ah].
Hold the last syllable for as long as you are able.

Step 8
Deep breath, as much as you are able
        depending upon your trimester.
Hold it for a count of six and
        release your breath slowly in a controlled manner
        six times: wh wh wh wh wh wh.

Step 9
Move your hands up to the front of the mouth, sing or chant,
        ooh may aaay laaaaaaaaaaaaah
        [ong o, long a, long a, a as in ah].
Hold the last syllable for as long as you are able.

Step 10
Deep breath, as much as you are able
depending upon your trimester.
Hold it for a count of six and
release your breath slowly in a controlled manner
six times: wh wh wh wh wh wh.

Step 11
Move your hands up to the front of the mouth, sing or chant,
ooh may aaay laaaaaaaaaaaaah
[long o, long a, long a, a as in ah].
Hold the last syllable for as long as you are able.

Step 12
Deep breath, as much as you are able
depending upon your trimester.
Hold it for a count of six and
release your breath slowly in a controlled manner
six times: wh wh wh wh wh wh.

Step 13
Move your hands upward unto the brow area
and move your fingers apart, no longer held close.

Step 14
Each palm held in front of your earth eyes,
as if you were covering them from the sun

Step 15
Sing or chant: ooh may aaay laaaaaaaaaaaaah
[long o, long a, long a, a as in ah].
Hold the last syllable for as long as you are able.

Step 16
Deep breath, as much as you are able,
hold it for a count of three,
exhale in a controlled manner
to the count of four: wh wh wh wh.

Step 17
Maintaining the position of the palms facing each other,
move your hands apart as far as you are able.

Step 18
Ensure that as well as you are able,
the spine is straight, the neck is straight.

Step 19
Bring your hands slowly back in toward the center
until the fingertips touch at the level of the heart area.
If you become dizzy, pause, and then, resume.

Step 20
Sing or chant: ooh may aaay laaaaaaaaaaaaah
[long o, long a, long a, a as in ah].
Hold the last syllable for as long as you are able.

Step 21
Deep breath, as much as you are able,
hold it for a count of three,
exhale gently, slowly, in a controlled manner
to the count of four: wh wh wh wh.

Step 22
Move your fingertips apart.
Turn your hands palm over and you have completed.

384 A Mudra to assist in calming the gall bladder.

Step 1
Place the last two fingers and thumb together.

Step 2
Move your first two fingers to the middle of your torso
below the heart and above the navel.

Step 3
Entwine the forefingers and the finger next to it.

Step 4
Press inward, Soul, once twice, thrice.
At the third press inward, hold for the count of three
and then release quickly.
You will feel a bounce as you do this.
The bounce stimulates the juices
and assists the gallbladder to return to normal.

Step 5
Gently repeat Steps 1 though 4 until the gall bladder has calmed.

385 We have a Mudra for the incontinent being that will strengthen the muscles of any bladder, be they male or female.

Step 1
Find a comfortable position,
feet flat on the ground or toward the ground.
Hands flat upon a surface.
As well as you are able, your spine is straight, neck is straight.

Step 2
Move the feet and place sole to sole:
the bottom of your left foot will touch
the bottom of the right foot as well as you are able.

Step 3
Three times move the soles back and forth:
together, apart, together, apart, together, apart.

Step 4
Once more move the soles back and forth
and then hold for the count of three.

Step 5
Move the feet apart and place toward or on the ground.

Step 6
Four times move the thighs back and forth:
together, apart, together, apart, together, apart.
On the fourth, hold for the count of four and release the thighs.

Step 7
Four times exercise your bladder muscles
bringing them tightly together,
as far as you are able; once, twice, thrice.
On the fourth time hold as long as you are able,
to a minimum of the count of four.[48]

Step 8
Elbows held close, one on either side of your body.

Step 9
And with your hands flat upon a surface,
four times move the elbows out and in.
On the fourth, hold your elbows out for the count of four.
And then, Soul, bring them back in.

Step 10
Place your hands in front of the heart area
in the prayer position, palm to palm.
The fingers are touching each other, the thumbs are touching
each other, but not the forefingers.

Step 11
Four times move your hands apart and back together;
the fourth time bring them back
and hold for the count of five.

Step 12
Deep breath, hold for the count of three
and release in a controlled manner five times,
wh wh wh wh wh.

Step 13
Palms facing each other, slightly apart,

thumbs pressed against the flesh of the forefingers,
the tips of the little fingers touching each other.

Step 14
Bring your hands up in front of your eyes.
Three times, open and close your eyes.

Step 15
Open your eyes for the count of three and close the eyes again.

Step 16
Deep breath, hold for the count of three.
Release gently in one breath.

Step 17
Move your hands apart from your eyes.

Step 18
Bring your hands slowly down to the surface,
with the tips of the little fingers touching, palms up.
Open your eyes.

Step 19
Deep breath, controlled release to the count of three, wh wh wh,
as if you were blowing into your hands.

Step 20
Move your finger apart, hands apart and spread your thumbs wide apart.

Step 21
Turn your palms over and you have competed.

386 Souls of earth, we give unto you a Mudra
for bladder infection.
At any stage of the bladder infection, this will be efficacious.
This is to be done, depending upon the severity of the infection,

as often as you may during the day,
however, a minimum of thrice each day
until the healing begins.
And then once daily until you are fully healed.
For those with the severity of the infection,
who experience the pain of urination,
you will have a minimum of five times per day.
And then, as the pain recedes,
three times, and then once per day.

Step 1
Feet flat on the floor or at least pointing toward the floor.
Your thighs apart, not closed.
Your hands flat upon a surface,
fingers spread wide, the thumbs spread wide.
The left hand will not touch the right hand at this point.

Step 2
Five times move your thighs inward and apart.
Begin by moving your thighs inward,
as close as possible without touching.
Hold that position for the count of five.
Move your thighs apart, hold for the count of five.

Step 3
Bend your head down looking toward your hands.
Your eyes may be open or closed.

Step 4
Move your hands into a slightly curved position
and bring them slowly up to just below the heart.

Step 5
Bring together the forefingers and the thumbs,
the other fingers remain spread as wide as possible.

Step 6
Bring your hands in this position unto the third eye,
thumbs resting on the bridge of the nose,

forefingers resting on the forehead.
The third eye will be in the center of this form
created with your hands.

Step 7
chant or sing: aaa laaaaaaaaaaaaah [long a, a as in ah].
On the syllable la, hold it as long as you are able.

Step 8
Maintaining the form, move your hands away from the third eye,
down unto the position of the naval area.

Step 9
The thumbs touching each other rest upon the naval.
The forefingers touching and held outward.
The other fingers point down toward the bladder.

Step 10
Thrice chant or sing: aaa laaaaaaaaaaaaah [long a, a as in ah].
On the syllable la, hold it as long as you are able.

Step 11
Three times take a deep breath, hold for the count of three,
each time release the breath
quickly in a controlled manner, forcefully: wh wh wh.

Step 12
Maintaining their position,
move your hands away from the naval area,
to up near the surface where you began.

Step 13
Deep breath, exhale and repeat once more the phrase:
aaa laaaaaaaaaaaaah [long a, a as in ah].
On the syllable la, hold it as long as you are able.

Step 14
Deep breath, hold for the count of three and release gently.

Step 15
Move your hands apart
and place them palm down unto the surface,
fingers spread wide,
thumbs spread away from the forefingers.

Step 16
Move your hands closer so that the forefingers
and the thumbs are touching,

Step 17
Repeat once more the phrase:
aaa laaaaaaaaaaaaah [long a, a as in ah].
On the syllable la, hold it as long as you are able.
And you have completed.

387 A Mudra for the colon.

Step 1
Palms open, elbows bent and held close to the sides.[49]

Step 2
Place the palms downward, but still facing outward,
hold for a count of three.

Step 3
Deep breath, hold for a count of three,
push it out for a count of three.

Step 4
Turn hands over, bring hands up as far as possible
to touch the front of the shoulder,
holding the arms close to the body,
hold for the count of three.

Step 5
Bring hands back down, small fingers bent inward
as you close thumb and forefinger

and hold curved with the fingers touching at the belly.

Step 6
Breathe deeply, release gently

Step 7
Three times, sing or chant:
ohhhhhh laaaaaa leeeeee [long o, a as in ah, long e].

Step 8
Deep breath in, hold for a count of three.
Exhale for the count of three, forcefully.

Step 9
Unlock your fingertips, your thumb and forefinger,
your small finger,
open your palms outward, hold for a count of three

Step 10
Place hands downward and you have completed.

388 Souls of earth, we bring unto you a Mudra
for those beings afflicted with prostrate cancer,
cancer of the rectal area.
This exercise may be done three to five times a day
until you feel a release from any problem.

Step 1
Feet firmly on the ground, if possible,
or at least pointed toward the ground.

Step 2
Hands flat upon a surface, fingers close together,
thumb pads touching each other.

Step 3
Twice raise your hands up,
no more than four inches above the surface,
holding the thumbs together,
then bring them down firmly upon the surface
as if you were beating a drum.

Step 4
Then three times raise your hands up,
no more than four inches above the surface,
holding the thumbs together,
then bring them down firmly upon the surface,
as if you were beating a drum.

Step 5
Moving the palms to face each other, three times,
bring your hands upward,
then bring them down, rhythmically.

Step 6
Position your hands so that the left hand
is just above the prostate area
and the right hand upon the heart area.

Step 7
Ensure that as well as you are able, you are sitting upright,
spine straight, neck straight, head straight forward
and then cough three times.
The cough must come from the lower sacral.

Step 8
Position your hands, palms facing palms,
and thumb touching thumb.

Step 9
Three times repeat the drum motion as in Step 5.

Step 10
Place your hands palms down above the surface,
no more than four inches.
The thumbs will not touch.

Step 11
Alternate three times:
with your left hand, Soul, you will come down
as if you were beating a drum,
then down your right hand,
as if you are beating a drum.

Step 12
Bring your hands together in the prayer position,
head bent toward your hands.

Step 13
Once again cough from the sacral area.

Step 14
Open your hands, palms up.
Place the right at the heart area, the left just above the prostrate.
Hold that position for a count of three.
Cough, as in Step 7, once more.

Step 15
Place palms down upon a surface and you have completed.

389 We bring a Mudra to enhance the plumbing
within the human body,

the full measure of the plumbing from top to bottom.
Doing this exercise thrice daily
for a period of six days will greatly relieve
the problems of internal plumbing and thereafter
maintenance is necessary twice weekly.

Step 1
Place your hands palms down upon a flat surface.

Step 2
Bring your hands upright
with the edges of the palms touching the surface.
Palms facing each other about four inches apart.

Step 3
Slowly bring your hands together, fingers touching fingers,
thumbs touching thumbs,
palms touching palms in the prayer position.

Step 4
Maintaining the position of the hands,
move them above the navel area,
but not touching the body.

Step 5
Count to seven holding your breath and exhale,
but slowly in eight controlled breaths:
wh wh wh wh wh wh wh wh.

Step 6
Maintaining the prayer position, bring the hands to the chest area
and press gently against the chest.

Step 7
While pressing gently, hold your breath for the count of seven
and then release in a controlled breath
for the count of eight: wh wh wh wh wh wh wh wh.

Step 8
Maintaining the prayer position,
bring the hands to slightly below the throat,
but not touching the body.

Step 9
Move your elbows out to the side.

Step 10
Make the following rumbling sound:
rillllrll rlrlrlr rlrlrlrllrll.[50]
The third section is longest.

Step 11
Maintaining the prayer position,
move the hands upward unto the third eye area.

Step 12
Hold your breath for the count of seven and
release in a controlled breath
for the count of eight: wh wh wh wh wh wh wh wh.

Step 13
Bring your hands downward back unto the chest area,
press lightly for a moment.

Step 14
Move your hands back into the original position
and you have completed.

390 For those who currently are afflicted
by the pain of hip difficulties,
we have for you a Mudra to assist in calming
the pain of your being.
Doing this Mudra as often as possible will alleviate hip pain
from arthritic or rheumatic disease.

Step 1
Begin with hands palm up.
The fingers and the thumbs are not touching.

Step 2
Thrice, slowly take a deep breath in through the nostrils
and hold it for a count of six.
Release it though the mouth.

Step 3
Move your hands to the side of your being
in a line with the hip bones on the side, palms facing hips.
Hold your hands in that position
approximately three inches from your body.

Step 4
Ten times picture electric blue Light
going from the left hand palm
to the other palm, back and forth through your being.
To go from your left hand to your right,
and from your right hand to your left is one time.

Step 5
At the end of the ten times, bring your hands back up,
keeping the palms in the upright position.

Step 6
Place together the right hand and the left hand,
all the digits touching at the tips, but not the palms.

Step 7
Bring that hand position up unto the third eye,
not touching the flesh, but holding it in front of the eye
and thrice breathing in through the nostrils
and out deeply through the mouth.
You will feel a pull of the hips in a line with the eye.

Step 8
Move the hands down to the throat area,
and slowly bring together the palms and fingertips
in the prayer position.

Step 9
Move your hands apart and place them at the back of the neck,
the middle three fingers of the right hand
touching the middle three fingers of the left hand.
Straighten the spine as best you are able,
and hold that position for a count of three.

Step 10
Move your hands apart and back into the original position.

FULL BODY

391 Mudras always involve the sacred palms
and they may be in various positions
and they are, indeed, accompanied by a chant
or a particular blend of wording,
and that particular blend of wording has a vibration
that becomes a synchronization
with the Energy from the sacred palms.
And for general well being we give unto you this Mudra.

Step 1
Place thy palms out, arms bent from the elbow, palms upward.

Step 2
Place right over left arm, bring the palms unto the shoulders.

Step 3
Deep breath and sound thrice:
ah laaaaay ooooo [short a as in ah, long a, long o].

Step 4
Uncross the arms, bring the palms upward again and then down,
and you have completed.

392 A Mudra to calm the palsied being.
All beings who have some form of palsy
will be assisted by this Mudra.
We ask these Souls to understand,
they may not be able to, at first,
have a smooth operation of the process.
You will do what you can with the instruction,
but know over time, repetition
will bring about the calming of the palsy.

Step 1
As much as you are able, place your hands face down
upon or near a surface that is not manmade.

Step 2
As much as you are able, place together the four fingers
and the thumbs touching each other,
the right touching left, the left touching right,
in an open pyramid position.

Step 3
Bend your head, as much as you are able, toward the shape
you have made with the thumbs and forefingers,
with the eyes looking downward into the shape,
for a period of twelve seconds.

Step 4
Holding that position in Step 3,
begin to rock your body back and forth, back and forth
for a total of fifteen rocks back and forth.

Step 5
Remove your fingertips and thumbs

and place your palms in an upright position,
continuing to hold the head
looking downward unto the hands.

Step 6
Five times sing, chant slowly:
lo no mo rah [long o, long o, long o, a as in ah].
Gently allow the syllables to enter in to your being.

Step 7
Again move your hands together, the fingertips of each hand
touching the fingertips of the other hand
and the thumb touching the thumb,
as much as you are able,
the eyes looking downward into the shape.

Step 8
Rock your being fifteen times, back and forth.

Step 9
At the end of the fifteenth rock, thrice slowly repeat the phrase:
lo no mo rah [long o, long o, long o, a as in ah].

Step 10
At the end of the third repetition move your hands outward,
palms up, take a deep breath as much as you are able,
and exhale gently.

Step 11
Turn your hands over, the palms facing downward and back into
original position and you have completed the Mudra.

393 For those afflicted with the Muscular Dystrophy:
it is important to do these exercises slowly,
for they increase the vibratory nature of your being,
and therefore may evidence itself in physicality
as lightheadedness.
The slowness will keep that to a minimum.

Step 1
Place the hands, as well as you are able, upon a surface.

Step 2
Curl the fingers inward, as much as you are able.

Step 3
Allow the thumbs to be outward,
away from the fingers as much as you are able.

Step 4
On your own or with the help of another,
slowly bring together the two thumbs, touching,
maintaining the curled fingers.

Step 5
Roll the thumbs around each other
in a circular motion seven times.
Ensure that the head is downward,
the neck is bent as much as you are able,
the eyes open,
watching the thumbs curve about each other.

Step 6
Move your thumbs gently apart keeping the head down.

Step 7
Gently uncurl the fingers, as much as you are able,
place hands palm up on a surface.

Step 8
Hold that position for at least three of your earth minutes.

Step 9
At the end of the three minutes, slowly, as much as you are able,
raise the head until it becomes as straight as you are able.

Step 10
Deep breath, through the nostrils, hold for a count of three.

Release as much as you are able.
And you have completed.

394 Souls of earth,
we bring unto you a Mudra for Multiple Sclerosis.
This sclerotic disease is debilitating,
but it is not necessarily the case.
We give you this Mudra in two stages.
We would have you understand the first stage
is for the newly discovered disease,
one that has not yet claimed
total domination over the flesh.
You will begin once a day for the first week.
You will then, increase to twice a day the second week
and three times a day the third week
until you have overcome.
For those who are in the more advanced stages
of this sclerotic disease,
we would have you repeat Step 6, three times
before moving unto Step 7.
And you will, Soul, perform the Mudra thrice daily at least,
until you have overcome.
Even as you improve do not relax your vigilance.
It is only when you have totally overcome
that you may release the ritual.

Step 1
Feet flat upon the floor or at least pointed toward the floor.
Hands on a surface.

Step 2
Place the pads of the thumbs together with the pads
of the first two fingers.
The last two fingers are held closely together.
The hands, a minimum of three inches apart at this stage.
Until you are given instruction otherwise, Soul,
maintain the position with the thumb and the fingers.

Step 3
Bend your head, as well as you are able,
toward your hands resting upon the surface.
Gently close your eyes.

Step 4
Three times, alternating the legs,[51]
begin first to slowly move the right leg.
Bring it upward, as far as you are able, without strain
and slowly bring it back down to the floor.
Proceed to do the same with the left leg.

Step 5
Three times bring the sides of the feet together slowly
and slowly push out to either side,
as far as you are able in comfort.

Step 6
Slowly raise your head upright.

Step 7
Maintaining the position given of the thumbs and fingers,
maintaining the depth apart given in Step 2,
bring your hands up to in front of the throat chakra.
The thumbs close to the throat but not touching the throat.

Step 8
Slowly move the hands apart, to the edge of your shoulders
and slowly back to in front of the throat chakra.

Step 9
Five times slowly move the hands
a minimum of three inches apart
and enter back together in front of the throat chakra.
If you become dizzy, stop,
and as the dizziness passes you may resume

Step 10
Place together the very tips of the fingers of both hands

in front of the throat chakra, as well as you are able.
Head will again be bent.

Step 11
Sing or chant or voice five times slowly and gently:
yaaaaay yaaaaay yaaaaaaaaay [long a].
Hold the last syllable as long as you are able.

Step 12
Maintaining the position of the fingers,
slowly move your hands up unto the third eye.

Step 13
Sing or chant or voice three times slowly and gently:
yaaaaay yaaaaay yaaaaaaaaay [long a].
Hold the last syllable as long as you are able.

Step 14
Deep breath, hold for the count of three
and in a controlled manner,
exhale to the count of four: wh wh wh wh.

Step 15
Move your hands apart slightly
and bring them up over the top of your head,
the hands are palm down above the top of the head.
If you cannot do this physically, do it mentally with the mind.

Step 16
Sing or chant or voice twice slowly and gently:
yaaaaay yaaaaay yaaaaaaaaay [long a].
Hold the last syllable as long as you are able.

Step 17
Move your hands apart, and as you are moving your hands apart,
take a deep breath, hold for the count of three.
And then a controlled exhale to the count of four: wh wh wh wh.

Step 18
Bring the hands down to the front of your mouth.
And once more sing, chant, voice:
yaaaaay yaaaaay yaaaaaaaaay [long a].
Hold the last syllable as long as you are able.

Step 19
Bring the hands in front of the throat chakra,
repeat once more the sound given:
yaaaaay yaaaaay yaaaaaaaaay [long a].
Hold the last syllable as long as you are able.
Breathe normally.

Step 20
Maintaining the position, move your hands between
the heart chakra and the lower chakra.
Deep breath, hold for the count of three,
exhale for the count of four.

Step 21
And once more sing, chant, voice:
yaaaaay yaaaaay yaaaaaaaaay [long a].
Hold the last syllable as long as you are able

Step 22
Maintaining the position, move your hands away from the body,
and then down, back upon the surface.
Turn your hands over, release the fingers,
palms upward in the receiving position,
thumbs spread wide apart.

Step 23
Bringing the palms together, clap gently, once, twice, thrice.
Turn your hands over.
Deep breath.
Release the breath and you have completed.

395 We give unto you a Mudra

for the healing of bone cancer,
for wherever it is in the body.
This will assist in not only the healing of the cancer,
but in the mending of the bone that has been attacked.
This exercise may be done as often as possible during the day;
preferably upon arising, at midday and before night sleep.

Step 1
Feet flat on the floor or at least pointing toward the floor.
You may, Soul, also proceed with this laying down.

Step 2
Neck, if at all possible, held as upright as you are able.
Hands flat upon a surface.

Step 3
Take in three breaths slowly: wh wh wh
and hold for a count of three.
Release in a controlled manner: wh wh wh.

Step 4
Turn palms upward and hold at the level of the heart,
fingers not together nor the thumbs touching flesh.

Step 5
Now, touch the fingertips of the two middle fingers
at the level of the heart.

Step 6
Head partly bent looking toward the fingers
as much as you are able.

Step 8
Five times slowly, gently move the two middle fingers apart,
no more than three inches and bring them back together.

Step 9
Move your hands into the prayer position
in front of the heart area,

thumbs touching and upright,
separate from the forefingers.

Step 10
Ensure as much as you can to hold your elbows
close to your being.

Step 11
Chant five times:
hay lah ma kah [long a, a as in ah, a as in ah, a as in ah].
The end syllable is held a for as long as possible.

Step 12
Deep breath, hold for count of five or as long as you are able.
Release in a whoosh, all at once,
push it out as best you can given your condition.

Step 13
Move your hands apart, place the palms up and facing
toward the third eye.

Step 14
The little fingers touch each other,
the forefingers touch the third eye area.
The rest of your fingers touch the tips together.
Hold that position for fifteen seconds.
You may, if you require, rest your elbow
upon the surface in order to accomplish this.

Step 15
Three times take a controlled breath in.
Hold for the count of three and release gently and slowly
in a controlled manner
for the count of five: wh, wh, wh, wh, wh.

Step 16
Remove your forefingers from the third eye,
move apart the other fingers.

Step 17
Bring your hands palms upward, move them apart,
then turn the palms over,
bringing them down upon the surface.

Step 18
Repeat the chant five times:
hay lah ma kah [long a, a as in ah, a as in ah, a as in ah].
The end syllable is held a for as long as possible.

Step 19
Place palms up slightly above the surface,
touch the fingertips of the two middle fingers.

Step 20
Five times move the hands slowly back and forth
while maintaining the connection
of the fingertips of the two middle fingers.

Step 21
Move your fingertips apart,
turn your hands palm over and you have completed.

396 Souls of earth, we give unto you a Mudra for leprosy,
to stop the progress of the disease.
Even the most disformed hands are to be utilized in this Mudra.
If you have lost a limb, understand you may use the mind.

Step 1
Sit as well as you are able in an upright position,
feet toward the floor or on the floor.

Step 2
Hands placed palm down in front of your being.
It may be on a surface if at all possible, or held above your knees.

Step 3
Place your hands together, raising them from the down position

into a prayer position.
The thumbs are not to be touching the forefinger,
they are to be held upright and away.

Step 4
Move the hands in the prayer position toward your heart chakra,
while lifting your head upward at a forty five degree angle.

Step 5
Deep breath as well as you are able, hold for the count of four
then release your breath forcefully, 'whoosh'.

Step 6
Move your hands apart, palms up,
but with the small fingers touching.
Keep them in front of the heart chakra.

Step 7
Move the hands back and forth five times,
along the side of the palm,
starting with the right and then the left,
back and forth, back and forth,
recognizing that each back and forth is once.

Step 8
Place your hands back in the prayer position and
bring your head upward to the forty five degree angle.

Step 9
Deep breath, hold for a count of four
and controlled exhalation as well as you are able
to the count of four: wh wh wh wh.

Step 10
Move your hands upward in the prayer position
in front of the third eye,
the thumbs in front of the third eye,
but not touching the eye.

Step 11
As well as you are able, sound out three times:
keeeee maaaaaaaaaaaaaaa [long e, a as in ah].
You will hold both syllables as long as you are able, Soul.

Step 12
Deep breath, hold for the count of three
and exhale in a forceful whoosh.

Step 13
Bring your hands downward from the third eye to the heart area,
maintaining the prayer position
as you slowly move them down.

Step 14
Open hands, palms upward, with the small fingers
touching each other.

Step 15
Move the hands back and forth five times,
along the side of the palm,
starting with the right and then the left,
back and forth, back and forth,
recognizing that each back and forth is once.

Step 16
At the end of those five repetitions, hold your hands palms up
while sounding:
keeeee maaaaaaaaaaaaaaa [long e, a as in ah].
Again, hold both syllables as much as you are able.

Step 17
Turn the hands palm down to where you began.

Step 18
Sound once more:
keeeee maaaaaaaaaaaaaaa [long e, a as in ah].
Again, hold both syllables as long as you are able.

And then, Soul, you have completed.

397 We give unto you this Mudra to alleviate
a being afflicted with intense pain of unknown origin.
You may do this exercise at least three times a day.
As your pain leaves,
you may consider a maintenance of once daily.
And there will come a time
when the pain will be totally gone and not return,
and you will no longer require this Mudra.

Step 1
Feet apart, flat on the ground
or at least pointing toward the ground.

Step 2
Ensure your legs and your thighs are apart.

Step 3
Hands palms down, flat upon a surface.
The fingers and the thumbs of each hand spread wide.

Step 4
Bend the head looking toward the hands upon the surface.

Step 5
Three times, a deep breath, hold for the count of five,
and then slowly, gently exhale to the count of five

Step 6
Maintaining the position of the hands palms down,
slowly bring the hands up
until they are at the level of your ears,
but not touching the ears.

Step 7
Turn the palms facing forward.

Step 8
Deep breath, hold for the count of three,
exhale in a controlled manner
for the count of three: wh wh wh.

Step 9
Inhale, hold for the count of three;
exhale in a controlled manner
to the count of four: wh wh wh wh.

Step 10
Deep breath, hold for the count of three,
exhale slowly and gently to the count of five
in a controlled manner: wh wh wh wh wh.

Step 11
Maintaining position of the hands at the level of the ears,
seven times sing or chant:
ooooooh maaaay [long o, long a].
Hold the first syllable as long as you are able.

Step 12
Move your hands so that the palms are now facing your ears,
fingers and thumbs spread wide
and not touching the ears.
You will feel at this point a tingling,
a pressure within the head area, especially near the ears.

Step 13
Three times sing or chant the syllables:
ooooooh maaaay [long o, long a].

Step 14
Turn your palms outward at the level of the ears,
keeping the fingers and thumbs spread wide.

Step 15
Five times sing or chant the syllables:
ooooooh maaaay [long o, long a].

Step 16
Deep breath, hold for the count of three,
exhale in a controlled manner
slowly and gently to the count of five: wh, wh, wh,wh, wh.

Step 17
Move your hands in front of your face, palms facing palms

Step 18
Slowly move the hands toward each other
at the level of the nasal area and the eyes
almost to touching each other in a prayer like position,
but keeping the fingers slightly apart
and the thumb slightly apart from the fingers.

Step 19
Sing or chant the syllables:
ooooooh maaaaaay [long o, long a] once.

Step 20
Deep breath, hold for the count of three,
exhale for the count of four,
slowly in a controlled manner: wh wh wh wh

Step 21
Move the palms of the hands apart
bringing only the palms of your hands to cover your ears.
The palms will be touching the ears, but not pressing into the ear.
You will hear a sound as of the ocean,
and you will know that you have connected
and the pain, if not already relieved, will soon relieve.

Step 22
Once more expressing the sound,
sing or chant the syllables:
ooooooh maaaaaay [long o, long a].

Step 23
Deep breath, hold for the count of three,

exhale in one breath forcefully to the count of three.

Step 24
Bring the hands down to in front of the heart area.

Step 25
Move the hands together in the prayer position,
but the fingers and the thumbs
are not touching each other.

Step 26
Turn the hands over, palms down, back onto the surface
and you have completed.

398 We bring unto you a Mudra,
one that would be applicable to all Souls
infected with bacteria that may cause gangrene.
When you notice the sore becoming an angry red
around its edges, then this Mudra must be begun.
You will understand these bacteria
are increasing in numbers to the point
where they will be resistant to known antibiotics.
This Mudra is to be done a minimum of three times a day,
preferably five.
If you are unable to complete this exercise due to fever or
disabilities, it may be done for you.
You will have another being place your hands in
the positions given and help you with the breathing given.

Step 1
Sitting if at all possible, feet on the floor
or pointed toward the floor.
Hands, palm up, elbows close in to your sides.

Step 2
Palms up, cupped as if to hold water,
fingers held close to each other.
Head bent toward the palms.

The thumbs will not be touching.

Step 3
Move your slightly cupped left hand above
the slightly cupped right hand
in front of the perimeter of the heart,
and hold this position for the count of seven seconds.

Step 4
Deep breath, hold for the count of three,
and exhale directly into your palm: whhhhh.
Ensure the breath leaves fully from your being.

Step 5
Move the left hand below the right, deep breath in,
hold for the count of three and exhale, whhhh,
into the hand.[52]

Step 6
Once you have attained the feelings given,
the next step is to slowly bring your head upright.[53]

Step 7
Move your hands slightly apart,
the thumbs touching the side of the forefingers.

Step 8
Maintaining the cupped position of the hands,
slowly bring together the hands
in a partial prayer position;
palms touching only at the bottom of the hands,
fingers touching, thumbs touching.

Step 9
Move the hands in this position to the front of the heart area

Step 10
Bend your forehead down
and touch the index fingertips to the third eye.

Step 11
Maintain the position of the hands.
Picture in your mind the sore that is to be healed
and place the sore within your hands with the mind.
Hold it for a period of fifteen seconds.
At the end of the fifteen earth seconds,
you will notice again a heaviness,
a weight that descends upon the back of the head.
This is your indication that the healing has begun.

Step 12
Slowly bring your head upright.
If you become dizzy, pause and then continue
until your head is in the upright position.

Step 13
Open your hands, palms up,
the sides of the little fingers of each hand touching.

Step 14
Bring the hands unto in front of the third eye.
Deep breath, hold for the count of three, exhale slowly, gently
until there is no more breath that you can push outward.

Step 15
Move your hands apart, slowly, or you will be dizzy,
and then bring them down to just above the surface.

Step 16
Turn the hands over and you have completed.

399 We give unto you a Mudra to increase the circulation within the body,
the circulation of the blood that can affect the heart,
the legs, the mind, the brain.
This will strengthen the arteries that have become flaccid,
or that are closing.
This must be done thrice daily to stimulate the flaccidity

of the arteries so that the circulation
is no longer impaired.
It will also assist in cleansing of the arteries. .

Step 1
Feet flat on the floor if possible or feet toward the floor.

Step 2
Hands apart and at either side of your being,
the right palm facing the left palm.
The sides of the palms resting on a surface.

Step 3
Slowly move your hands toward each other
until they are in the prayer position.
The thumbs are held upright.
Maintain this position until Step 6.

Step 4
Hold the hands in front of the sacral chakra area
for a period of five seconds.

Step 5
Bring your hands up unto the heart area, hold for five seconds.

Step 6
Holding the hands at the heart area.
bring your thumbs down touching the forefingers.

Step 7
Five times slowly chant or sing:
lee nah kaaaaaaaaah [long e, a as in ah, a as in ah].
Hold the last syllable for as long as you are able.

Step 8
Move your hands in the same position as Step 6,
up unto the area of the third eye.

Step 9

Thumbs move from the forefinger and touch the third eye.

Step 10
Five times slowly chant or sing:
lee nah kaaaaaaaaah [long e, a as in ah, a as in ah].
Hold the last syllable for as long as you are able.

Step 11
Maintaining your thumbs against the third eye area,
and your hands in the prayer position,
deep breath in, hold for the count of five,
and release in a controlled breath,
for the count of five: wh wh wh wh wh.

Step 12
Deep breath in, hold it for the count of five,
and in a controlled manner
release your breath to a count of five: wh wh wh wh wh.

Step 13
Move your thumbs away from the eye,
move your hands to the heart area

Step 14
Three times slowly chant or sing:
lee nah kaaaaaaaaah [long e, a as in ah, a as in ah].
Hold the last syllable for as long as you are able.

Step 15
Move the hands in the prayer position unto the eye

Step 16
Three times slowly chant or sing:
lee nah kaaaaaaaaah [long e, a as in ah, a as in ah].
Hold the last syllable for as long as you are able.

Step 17

Deep breath, hold for the count of three and release in a controlled manner for the count of three: wh, wh, wh.

Step 18
Maintaining the positions of the hand,
bring your hands slowly back onto the surface
and turn the palms up.

Step 19
Move the fingers and hands apart, turn the palms over and down.

Step 20
Repeat once: lee nah kaaaaaaaaah [long e, a as in ah, a as in ah].
Hold the last syllable for as long as you are able.

Step 21
Where, Soul, it is specific to the circulation of the carotid artery,
there is one further step:
Place your hands, palms down and bring them up
unto either side of the neck, and hold gently your neck,
repeating the phrase once more, slowly:
lee nah kaaaaaaaaah [long e, a as in ah, a as in ah].
Hold the last syllable for as long as you are able.
Then, move your hands away, bring them down,
and you have completed.

400 A Mudra to assist in the quick knitting of broken bones.
You will recall that even if one of your limbs
that is required in this Mudra is broken,
in the mind there is no broken limb,
and so it will not prevent you
from completing the exercise.
For the whole body is synchronized
with the phraseology of the syllables
and with the movements of the hand,
for the eye connects all.

Step 1
Feet flat on the floor or at least, pointed toward the floor.

Step 2

The hands are palms down upon a surface.
The fingers spread as wide as possible
without touching the other hand,
the thumbs are not touching.
Ensure the elbows are held close to the sides of the body.

Step 3
Slowly raise hands upward slightly above the surface,
and turn the hands so the palms are facing each other,
fingers and thumbs are wide apart.

Step 4
Twice take a deep breath as well as you are able,
and hold for the count of three.
Gently release the breath in a controlled manner: wh wh wh.

Step 4
Take a deep breath as well as you are able,
hold for the count of three,
Gently release the breath in one breath and exhale until
you can not breathe out any more.

Step 5
Bring the hands together, palm touching palm,
the fingers are not touching yet, nor are the thumbs.

Step 6
Deep breath, hold for the count of five,
release in a controlled five: wh wh, wh wh wh.

Step 7
Join the thumbs and the fingers in the prayer position,
the thumbs held upright, not touching the forefingers.

Step 8
Bring your hands up unto your nose area.
The fingers are above the nose, the thumbs below.
The hands are not touching the face but are in front of it.

Step 9
Four times chant or sing[54]: raaah naay laah ti ah,
[a as un ah, long a, a as in ah, long e, a as in ah]

Step 10
Maintaining the position at the nose area, move your hands apart,
unto the farthest point of your cheeks,
directly in a line with the nose.

Step 11
Thrice chant or sing: raaah naay laah ti ah,
[a as ah, long a, a as in ah, long e, a as in ah].

Step 12
Deep breath, hold for the count of three.
Release slowly in one breath.

Step 13
Bring your hands up in front of the third eye
in the prayer position,
the thumbs resting against the forefingers.

Step 14
Deep breath, hold for a count of three, release in one breath.

Step 15
Repeat the phrase once more: chant or sing:
raaah naay laah ti ah,
[a as ah, long a, a as in ah, long e, a as in ah]

Step 16
Maintaining the fingers touching and the thumbs touching,
move your palms apart and the thumbs and fingers.

Step 17
Turn the palms down toward the surface
and slowly bring the hands down to rest upon the surface.

Step 18

Deep breath, hold for the count of five,
release in a controlled breath five times,
wh wh wh wh wh.
And then, you have completed.

401 We give unto you a Mudra for the atrophied limb,
whether it be the arms or the legs.
This is to be done as often as possible,
no less than three times per day.
When you begin to see and to feel results in the withered limb,
you may then go to twice a day,
and stay at that until you have accomplished your goal.

Step 1
Place yourself in a chair,
your back straight as far as you are able,
feet on or toward the floor.

Step2
Your hands flat upon a surface.
The fingers spread as wide as they are able.
The thumbs spread apart from the fingers.
Hold the hands thus until Step11.

Step 3
Lift your head up as far as your neck will allow,
while maintaining a straight position.

Step 4
Five times sing or chant: eeeee naaah laaah haayyyy
[long e, a as in ah, a as in ah, long a].
The last syllable is strung out for as long as you may.

Step 5
Move your head slowly back into the upright center position.
If you become dizzy, stop, and then continue when you are able.

Step 6

Move your head slowly to the left as far as you are able,
while maintaining the head in the upright position.

Step 7
Move your head slowly back into the upright center position
and hold for the count of three.

Step 8
Move your head slowly to the right as far as you are able,
while maintaining the head in the upright position
and hold for the count of three.

Step 9
Move your head slowly back into the upright center position
and hold for the count of three

Step 10
Bend your head down as far as you are able,
allow your chin to touch your upper chest if you are able.

Step 11
Turn your hands over, palms up, intertwining the fingers.
The thumbs will remain untouching.

Step 12
Three times sing or chant: eeeee naaah laaah haayyyy
[long e, a as in ah, a as in ah, long a].
The last syllable is strung out for as long as you may.

Step 13
Move your hands apart,
turn them back into their original position
Step 14
Sing or chant once more: eeeee naaah laaah haayyyy
[long e, a as in ah, a as in ah, long a].
The last syllable is strung out for as long as you may.

Step 15

Raising your head slowly into an upright position,
bring your hands together in the prayer position,
upright thumbs touching each other,
but not the forefingers.
Place the hands, in this position, in front of the heart area.

Step 16
Sing or chant once more: eeeee naaah laaah haayyyy
[long e, a as in ah, a as in ah, long a].
The last syllable is strung out for as long as you may.

Step 17
Deep breath, hold for the count of three, release gently.
Move your hands apart, turn the palms them over and down
and you have completed.

402 We give unto you for the withered limb a Mudra.
The limb may be any one of the four.
It will be the same for each.
This will stimulate the withered limb to function again.
You will understand, always, when you cannot physically
follow the directions you may do them mentally.
But they must be in the same order
and for the same amounts of time.

Step 1
Sit as upright as possible.

Step 2[55]
Join the thumbs and the forefingers together of both hands,
right to right and left to left.
Place upon a surface.
The other three fingers on each hand held loosely,
little finger resting on the surface.

Step 3
Inhale as far as you are able for the count of four,
exhale for the count of four.

This is to be done slowly, there is no rush,
you have all the time necessary.

Step 4
Inhale for the count of five, exhale for the count of five.

Step 5
Inhale for the count of four, exhale for the count of four.

Step 6
With your mouth closed and for as long as you are able,
begin to hum:[56] hmmmmmmmmm

Step 7
Maintaining the thumb and forefinger together,
bring both hands to the level of your heart

Step 8
Cross in front of your heart, the right wrist over the left wrist,
maintaining the thumb and forefinger together.

Step 9
Inhale as far as you are able for the count of four,
exhale for the count of four.
This is to be done slowly, there is no rush,
you have all the time necessary.

Step 10
Inhale for the count of five, exhale for the count of five.

Step 11
Inhale for the count of four, exhale for the count of four.

Step 12
Change position, cross left wrist over right wrist
in front of your heart,
maintaining the thumb and forefinger together.

Step 13

Inhale as far as you are able for the count of four,
exhale for the count of four.
This is to be done slowly, there is no rush,
you have all the time necessary.

Step 14
Inhale for the count of five, exhale for the count of five.

Step 15
Inhale for the count of four, exhale for the count of four.

Step 16
Uncross arms and hands, place upon a surface
the thumb and the forefinger together on both hands,
right to right and left to left.
The other three fingers on each hand, held loosely,
little finger resting on the surface.

Step 17
With your mouth closed and for as long as you are able
begin to hum: hmmmmmmmmm.
It is not necessary to take a deep breath and then hum;
simply, Soul, begin to hum with your mouth closed.

Step 18
Take a deep breath, hold for the count of four, release to the count of four.

Step 19
Take a deep breath, inhale to the count of four
and when exhaling push the breath out
in a controlled manner four times: wh wh wh wh.
If you are doing it correctly, you will feel it in your stomach area.

Step 20
Take a deep breath, inhale for the count of five and exhale
to the count of five
in a controlled breath: wh wh wh wh wh.
If you are doing it correctly,

your stomach will naturally become flatter, it will inhale.

Step 21
Turn your hands palm up and release the thumbs and forefingers.

Step 22
Cross in front of your heart, the right wrist over the left wrist,

Step 23
Three times: press inward lightly with the crossed wrists
and release,
press lightly, release, press lightly, release.

Step 24
Move your hands, your arms apart, palms over and down
and you have completed.

403 A Mudra for external diseases of the flesh,
for the external rashes, eczema, leprosy,
any place where the disease erupts upon the skin.

Step 1
Elbows bent, palms up,
the forefingers and the thumbs are placed together,
right to right, left to left.
Hold this position for a period of thirty-two seconds.

Step 2
At the end of the thirty-two seconds,
slowly raise your arms slightly,
continuing to hold the forefingers
and the thumbs together.

Step 3
Three times, taking a deep breath chant or sing as you exhale:
aaaaaaaaaaaaa [long a].
As you are chanting or singing, take the right hand
and bring it inward in an arc

from the chest unto the third eye and out again.

Step 4
At the end of the third time, place your hands together:
maintaining forefingers and thumbs pressing together,
the other fingers touching each other,
right to left, left to right.
Palms are not touching each other in this position.

Step 5
Slowly bring your hands down to the throat chakra,
and pause to a count of six seconds.

Step 6
Continue moving the hands slowly down unto the chest area,
slowly release the hands from their position.
And you have completed.

404 We give unto you a Mudra for the scourge of shingles.
This exercise may be done as often as you wish but,
no less than three times daily.
Improvement will be yours.

Step 1
Feet on the floor, flat, or at least pointing toward the floor.

Step 2
The back of your hands resting upon the surface,
palms up, fingers spread apart, thumbs spread apart.

Step 3
Elbows against your body.

Step 4
The eyes are closed and neck slightly bent toward your hands
as if you were looking at your hands.

Step 5
Move both hands at the same time slowly up to the heart area.

Step 6
Bring together your fingers and your thumbs,
but leave your palms apart.

Step 7
Move your elbows away from the sides
as you maintain the heart position.
Your head bent toward the hands.

Step 8
Holding the hands in the same hand position as in Step 6,
move the hands outward from your being
unto their furthest extension of your arms.

Step 9
At the furthest extension, lift your head up slowly into
the upright center position and hold this position.

Step 10
Three times inhale and exhale: deep breath in,
hold for the count of five,
exhale gently but controlled
for the count of five; wh wh wh wh wh.

Step 11
Maintaining your hands and arms in the same position,
thrice sing or chant:
aaaaaa maaaaaaaaaah [long a, a as in ah].
You will feel the sound reverberate to the inners of your being.
This will stimulate the healing of the shingles.

Step 12
Maintaining the hand position,
bring your hands back to the heart area.

Step 13
Your elbows are touching the sides of your being.
Your head is bent downward.
You will at this point feel a tingling in your fingertips

and in your palms.
This is an indication that the healing has begun
and that your intent has been focused on the healing.

Step 14
Maintaining your hands and arms in the same position, thrice
sing or chant: aaaaaa maaaaaaaaaah [long a, a as in ah].
You will feel the sound reverberate to the inners of your being.
This will stimulate the healing of the shingle.

Step 15
A deep breath, inhale for the count of three and exhale
between the hands, through the hands,
a controlled breath, for the count of six;
wh wh wh wh wh wh.
On the sixth exhalation permit all the air
that you can muster to leave your body.

Step 16
Close the hands in the prayer position,
bring the head up, move your hands under the chin.

Step 17
Maintaining your hands and arms in the same position,
repeat once: aaaaaa maaaaaaaaaah [long a, a as in ah].

Step 18
Move your hands apart, turn the palms up,
place them back on the surface
turn your hands over, palm down
and you have completed.

405 We give unto you a Mudra for scabies.

Step 1
Bring your hands close together,
palm toward palm, fingertips touching fingertips,

thumbs touching thumbs.
But, Soul, do not place the palms together, hold them apart.

Step 2
Bring your hands up in front of the third eye,
thumbs held at the bridge of the nose; one on either side.

Step 3
Bring your elbows in as far as you are able,
continue to leave the hands apart,
only the fingers touching.

Step 4
Twice, take a deep breath,
hold for the count of three, exhale gently.

Step 4
Deep breath, hold for the count of five,
and exhale in a controlled breath of five;
wh wh wh wh wh.

Step 5
The forefingers will now touch the top of your forehead,
while the thumbs remain at the bridge of the nose.

Step 6
Three times gently press your forefingers
at the middle of your forehead.

Step 7
Three times press the thumbs firmly
at either side of the bridge of the nose.

Step 8
Deep breath while gently pressing your forefingers
at the middle of the forehead,
holding for the count of three,
and controlled exhaling to the count of three: wh wh wh.

Step 9
Slowly, for you may become dizzy if you do this quickly,
slowly move the thumbs away
from the bridge of the nose,
the fingertips away from the forehead.

Step 10
Bring your hand down into the initial position,
open your hands palm up,
separate the fingers and you have completed.

EMOTIONS

406 We give unto you a Mudra for the being
in mental, emotional shock.
It is especially helpful in those times of great disasters,
whether they be of a whole nation
or only a small neighborhood,
or even one particular area, a home.
This exercise may be done up to five times a day,
And harken, Soul, to the instruction
of all movements to be done slowly.
If you become dizzy, hold, allow the dizziness to pass
and then continue.

Step 1
Place the hands in front of the third eye.
The hands are to touch at the smallest finger
and at the finger next to it.
The rest of your fingers are close to each other, but not touching.
The thumbs are held outward.

Step 2
Place your head slightly downward toward the hands
and hold this position for a period of fifteen seconds.
You will begin to feel an Energy,
a heaviness about the eye, about the head and a tingling.

Step 3
At the end of the fifteen seconds slowly move your hands apart,
no more than six inches,
and hold the palms facing toward the facial area.

Step 4
A deep breath, hold for the count of seven,
slowly release the breath
in a controlled manner, five times: wh, wh, wh, wh, wh.
The initial four will be short breaths out
and the fifth controlled breath outward will be longer.

Step 5
Repeat Step 1.
Place the hands in front of the third eye.
The hands are to touch at the smallest finger
and at the finger next to it.
The rest of your fingers are close to each other, but not touching.
The thumbs are held outward.

Step 6
Place your head slightly downward toward the hands and hold
this position for a period of twelve seconds.
You will feel an Energy, a heaviness about the eye,
about the head and a tingling.

Step 7
At the end of the twelve seconds slowly move your hands apart,
no more than six inches,
and hold the palms facing toward the facial area.

Step 8
A deep breath, hold for the count of five,
slowly release the breath
in a controlled manner, five times: wh, wh, wh, wh, wh.
The initial four will be short breaths out
and the fifth controlled breath outward will be longer.

Step 9

Place the hands in front of the third eye.
The hands are to touch at the smallest finger
and at the finger next to it.
The rest of your fingers are close to each other, but not touching.
The thumbs are held outward.
The head tilted slightly forward toward the hands,
and hold for the count of ten.

Step 10
Slowly move your hands apart again, no more than six inches;
and take another deep breath.
Hold for the count of three and release the breath,
in a controlled manner five times: wh wh wh wh wh.
The initial four will be short breaths out
and the fifth controlled breath outward will be longer.

Step 11
Raise your head, straighten your spine as well as you are able,
and place your hands palm facing the chest area.
The right hand on top, the left hand below,
the hands not touching.

Step 12
Hold the Energy and allow it to radiate toward
the heart of your being.
Hold this position for the count of fifteen seconds.

Step 13
Deep breath, hold for the count of three
and exhale fully and forcefully.
Breathing outward until you have no more breath left.

Step 14
Move your hands apart, place your palms up,
fingers held closely together, the thumbs still separate, and
bring them in front of the third chakra.

Step 15
Head down toward the hands,

hold for the count of seven, and deep breath out,
whoosh until there is no more breath left.

Step 16
Move your hands palm downward and you have completed.

407 Souls of earth, we would give unto those who feel imprisoned a Mudra of freedom to alleviate the emotional chaos, the emotional trauma
of the feeling of restriction.
It will in addition assist in clear thinking,
assist the mind to clarify courses of action.

Step 1
Place the hands flat upon a natural surface,
as much as possible maintain
a straight position of the spine.
The head will remain upright except for one step in the process.
The feet are to be kept separate throughout the process.

Step 2
The hands, palm down, have the forefinger tips touching
and the tips of the thumbs touching.

Step 3
Close the other fingers and hold them tightly together.
You have formed the shape of a diamond
within the space between the hands.

Step 4
Thrice, inhale deeply, hold for a count of three seconds,
exhale mightily, gustily

Step 5
Ensure that your spine is straight and your head is straight.
Lift the hands without breaking contact
between forefingers and thumbs,

rising the hands slowly upward until reaching the area
between the heart and throat chakras.

Step 6
Deep breath, gentle exhalation and chant or sing five times:[57]
ree ooh lah [long e, long o, a as in ah].

Step 7
Open the thumbs, open the forefingers and bring the hands,
palm facing palm,
to each side of the head unto the position of the ears.
Right palm facing right ear, left palm facing left ear.

Step 8
Hold the palms about three inches from either ear
for fifteen seconds.

Step 9
Deep breath and exhale gently,

Step 10
Bring your hands unto the front of your forehead,
The sides of the palms of the hands touching,
the thumbs lightly pressed against the flesh,
the palms facing the third eye.
Maintain a distance of three inches and hold for the count of six.

Step 11
Bring together your hands palm to palm,
thumbs touching, all fingers touching.
Deep breath, exhale, pushing out the exhalation.

Step 12
Gently, slowly, bring down your hands down
upon a natural surface, maintain fingertips touching,
thumbs touching, all fingers touching
until you have again the shape of the diamond.

Step 13

Deep breath, a gentle exhalation and you have completed.

408 We present you with a Mudra to assist in the alleviation
and overcoming of depression.
For those who find themselves in the beginning stages
of the throes of depression,
the Mudra will be required once per day.
For those who have sunk deeper into depression,
then we recommend the three times per day.
For those who find themselves in the severe depression,
contemplating suicide, and refusing all help,
all interconnectedness with another,
then, Souls, five times per day.

Step 1
Hands lightly cupped, palms up, thumb against the flesh.

Step 2
Reach out, Soul, straight forward
so that there is no bend in the arms,
maintaining the palms up.

Step 3
Hold this position for a count of ten.

Step 4
Turn hands so they are facing palm toward palm.
Maintain the thumb against the flesh.

Step 5
Maintaining your extension of your arms,
bring hands slowly together.
Entwine the fingers and the thumbs, right thumb over left thumb.
Hold that position for a count of ten.

Step 6
Move your fingers apart.

Step 7
Then slowly bring them together,
facing upward with the fingers entwined
and the thumbs upright away from the flesh.

Step 8
Bring the forefingers together, the right over the left.

Step 9
Bring the hands in this position, up to the third eye.
Hold that for ten seconds.

Step 10
Deep breath, release with the whoosh.

Step 11
Maintaining the intertwined, locked position,
slowly bring your hands down unto the heart area.

Step 12
Hold near the heart position,
but away from the body for ten seconds.

Step 13
Deep breath, release with the whoosh.

Step 14
Maintaining the intertwined, locked position,
move hands downward unto the area of the solar plexus,
but held away from the body.
Hold this position for fifteen seconds.
And you will feel a tingling of movement, a warmth,
within the top of your head.

Step 15
Deep breath and whoosh it out.

Step 16
Unlink your fingers, holding your palms upright near the body,

thumbs touching the flesh.

Step 17
Three times, sing or chant: aaaaaaaa [a as in ah]
The sound is guttural
and comes from the very depth of your being.

Step 18
Hold the warmth that you will feel in the front of your being.
When the warmth in the front of your being
begins to leave, the ritual is done.

Step 19
Place your hands over and down. And you have completed.

409 We bring unto you a Mudra
to alleviate great feelings of sadness.
This sadness goes beyond sorrow.
It is a deep grief of being and requires a variation in the Mudra
given for sorrow or depression.
You may sit or lay or stand while doing this exercise.

Step 1
Place together the forefingers and the thumbs
right to right, left to left
so that you have created the shape of a diamond.

Step 2
Place that shape in front of your face, not touching the face.
You will, Soul, begin to feel a warmth.

Step 3
When you feel the warmth, keep the thumbs together,
but push your thumbs up
and notice you have created a triangle.

Step 4
Move the triangle up in front of the third eye,

not touching the eye.

Step 5
You will feel a pull toward the triangle.
As you feel that pull, bring the triangle close
until you have touched the forehead of your being.
Hold for a count of five seconds.

Step 6
Maintain the shape of the triangle,
bringing your hands outward from the forehead
and down unto the front of the solar plexus.
Hold in place for a count of twelve seconds.

Step 7
Bring your thumb and forefinger together on each hand.
Maintain a touching of the thumbs and fingers,
pressing them together, right forefinger to right thumb,
left forefinger to left thumb, both hands touching.

Step 8
Bring that position, in front of the heart area.
Hold for five seconds.

Step 9
Move this same position of hands in front of the throat area.

Step 10
Release the thumbs and forefingers
and bring together the fingers of each hand touching.
Thumbs are in an upward position.

Step 11
Move your hands inward toward the throat area,
not touching, but in front of.
Hold this position for fifteen seconds.
You will feel a tingling,
a pressure about the top of your skull,
But do not be concerned if you have no such feeling,

know it is there.

Step 12
Move your hands outward with the fingers still touching
and slowly move up to the top of your skull,
over the top of your head and hold for five seconds.

Step 13
Thrice: deep breath in through the nostrils and whoooo,
pushing the breath outward through the mouth.

Step 14
Release the fingers touching fingers.
Pull your hands apart and place them, cupped, beside your ears.

Step 15
Bring hands inward toward the ears,
cup hands around the ears, gently, five seconds.
Fingers gently touching behind the ear lobe as well as the thumb.

Step 16
Move your hands away from the ears,
bringing them back to the front of your face.

Step 17
Place all the fingers and thumbs together
without closing the palms.
Hold for five seconds.

Step 18
Deep breath, exhale.

Step 19
Bring the hands down to the solar plexus, slowly move them apart.

Step 20
Palms up and you have completed.

410 To assist your being in times of stress:
stress of movement, stress of change, stress of death.

Step 1
Sitting upright, place your hands palm down upon a surface
that is not manmade.

Step 2
Your fingers spread apart with the thumbs touching
and the forefingers touching, right to left, left to right.

Step 3
Maintaining the shape of the hands,
slowly bring your hands upward unto the third eye
and hold in front of the third eye for fifteen seconds.

Step 4
Maintaining the shape of the hands, slowly bring the hands down
and place them again on the surface.

Step 5
When they reach the surface,
thrice inhale deeply through the nostrils
and then out the mouth, whoosh, strongly, whoosh!

Step 6
Place your fingers together and bring your hands together
palm touching palm in the mid-chest area.
Your elbows, as far as possible, flat against your being.

Step 7
Thrice inhale deeply through the nostrils
and then out the mouth, whoosh, strongly, whoosh!

Step 8
Move your hands apart slowly and bring those hands up,
touching the back of the neck.
The ends of the palms pressing against the bottom earlobes.

Step 9
Take the middle fingers and press lightly into that dent
in the middle of the back of the neck
and hold for fifteen seconds.
And then slowly release.

Step 10
Bring your hands once again together, mid chest
and thrice inhale deeply through the nostrils
and then out the mouth, whoosh, strongly, whoosh!

Step 11
Move the hands back into the original position:
Your fingers spread apart with the thumbs touching
and the forefingers touching, right to left, left to right.

Step 12
Breathe deeply to the count of three in through the nostrils,
expel forcibly to the count of four
through the mouth.
And you have completed.

411 We present a Mudra for those who experience severe
anxiety, what you call panic attack,
for those who have severe incapacity
to enter out of the home due to fears,
fears of any type incapacitating their ability of movement.

Step 1
Place your hands upon a surface.
The surface, not manmade, only what was given by nature.

Step 2
Place the thumb and forefinger of each hand together,
resting the other fingers flat upon the surface.

Step 3
Five times lightly take a breath, hold for the count of three

and release gently.

Step 4
Maintaining palms down,
maintaining the thumb and the forefinger together,
move your hands upward
about four inches above the surface.

Step 5
Turn hands over, palms up,
maintaining thumb and forefingers together.
Hold for the count of three, breathing normally.

Step 6
Place your hands palms facing each other
and begin gently, slowly to move them together.

Step 7
At the point where the hands have moved together
and the fingers are touching,
release the thumbs and forefingers.

Step 8
Place the hands in the prayer position,
all fingers and thumbs touching.

Step 9
Moving the hands in position near your solar plexus,
fingers pointing outward and thumbs facing inward,
you have established a pyramid shape.

Step 10
Five times breathe as deeply as you can,
hold for the count of three, release the breath.

Step 11
Move your hands and fingers apart and hold your palms upward,
allow the smallest finger and the one next to it

to remain joined at the tips.
As you hold your palms up,
the thumbs touch the side of the forefinger.

Step 12
Feet flat upon the ground or pointing toward the ground.

Step 13
Three times chant or sing: yay loo too nah way
[long a, o as in oo, o as in oo, a as in ah, long a].
Hold the last syllable for a count of three.

Step 14
Five times breathe as deeply as you can,
hold for the count of three, release the breath.

Step 15
Place your hands palm to palm, finger to finger, thumb to thumb,
again in the area of the solar plexus.

Step 16
Deep breath, hold for the count of five, exhale.
Take your hands apart.
Place them palm down back on the surface.

Step 17
Bring your thumb and forefinger together,
one more breath, release and you have completed.

412 For beings assailed with anxiety, anxiety strong enough
to impede any decision making or action.

Step 1
On a flat surface place together the two forefingers,
the thumbs, left to right, right to left.

Step 2
Your eyes will be open, your head slightly bent.

Focus your earth eyes upon the form
between the forefingers and the thumbs.

Step 3
Raise the forefingers up, the others remain flat and spread apart.

Step 4
Holding the pads of the thumbs together,
keep the forefingers up for a minimum five seconds.

Step 5
Deep breath, hold for a count of three, release.

Step 6
Move the forefingers down and hold close to the he next fingers.

Step 7
Slowly pull apart the thumbs, the fingers.

Step 8
Rest hands flat upon a surface.

Step 9
Bring together the fingers, touching each other.
Keep the thumbs apart.

Step 10
Turn the hands over palms up and you have completed.

413 We give unto you a Mudra
to assuage the desolation of separation.
Understand, Souls of earth, you see it, you feel it as separation,
as pain.
We do not see separation from earth as pain,
but welcome home the being.
The pain that you feel is as a wrenching from your being.
We would give unto you a Mudra that will assuage that pain
and assist you to enter back in

to the flow of positive Energy.
This Mudra holds true for all types of separation
that become negative pain upon your being.

Step 1
Hands palm down, fingertips of the forefinger
and the thumbs touching,
right to left, left to right.
You will create, Soul, a vortex of Energy.
The other fingers are to be separate at this point.

Step 2
Bend your head, so that your forehead
is in a line with this vortex you have created.
Hold that position for fifteen seconds
and allow the Energy to flow
between the eye and the hands.

Step 3
Deep breath, while raising your head into the upright position
and release the breath, gently.

Step 4
Two more deep breaths and gently push them out.

Step 5
Without breaking contact of the fingers and the thumbs,
bring hands in front of the third eye.
Bring the hands close, but do not touch the forehead.
Hold for fifteen seconds.

Step 6
Deep breath, push gently out.

Step 7
While maintaining the position at the third eye,
chant or sing three times: nooo men naaay yaah
[long o, short e, long a, a as in ah].

You will feel the vibration within the heart of your being.

Step 8
Maintaining the fingers and the thumbs together,
slowly move the hands back down to the original position.
Step 9
Deep breath, move the hands apart and you have completed.

414 We give unto you a Mudra for beings who are caught
in the throes of loneliness.
This will alleviate the loneliness.
This will give you a new perspective of belonging.

Step 1
Feet flat upon the floor if possible or pointed toward the floor.

Step 2
Place hands flat upon a surface, close but not touching,
fingers, thumbs spread wide.

Step 3
Seven times slowly, carefully begin moving your legs
forward and back,
forward and back, both at the same time.
Each movement forward, count to three,
as you move back, count to three.

Step 4
Thrice take a deep breath, as much as you are able,
hold for the count of three.
Controlled gentle exhale: hah hah hah.

Step 5

Ensure your head is in an upright position, as far as you are able,
spine as straight as possible.

Step 6
Slowly move your hands up from the surface
as if there is air pushing them upward.
Maintain the fingers and thumbs spread wide, not touching.

Step 7
Bring the hands in front of the heart chakra,
turn hands so the palm of the right hand
is facing the palm of the left hand.

Step 8
The fingers of the right and left hand will close,
your thumbs touch the flesh of the forefingers.

Step 9
Slowly move your hands together in the prayer position
in front of the heart chakra.

Step 10
Three times, deep breath and slow,
controlled exhalation: wh wh wh.

Step 11
Move your hands over the crown chakra,
maintaining the prayer position,
the spine as straight as possible.
Hold for the count of three.

Step 12
Breathe in and slowly exhale to the count to the three.

Step 13
Slowly move the hands in the prayer position in front of the eye.
You will at this point feel a tingling,
a pressure of some sort around the eye.

Step 14
Maintaining the thumbs touching the forefingers,
and the little fingers touching each other,
turn the hands palms up, so that in effect,
you have a bowl made from your hands.

Step 15
Deep breath, release slowly to the count of four: wh wh wh wh.

Step 16
Move this hand position in front of the third eye,
allowing the fingers, thumbs to touch in a prayer position
but the palms remain open
and hold for the count of three.

Step 17
Deep breath, exhale slowly for the count of three.

Step 18
Maintaining the position of the hands,
slowly bring them unto the heart area.

Step 19
Move your hands into the prayer position, palm to palm,
bring them down unto the surface,
turn your hands palm over
and you have succeeded in completing.

415 The Mudra for anger: excess emotions of anger,

anger toward self, anger toward others.

Step 1
Begin palms up, elbows bent, hands cupped.

Step 2
Bring together your hands, remain cupped until
the fingers are touching fingers,
the thumbs are touching thumbs.

Step 3
Holding this position,
bring your hands up unto the area of the mouth

Step 4
Sing or chant three times: aaaaaaaaaaaaaaaaa ree![58]
[long a and long e]

Step 5
Gently move apart the thumbs, each set of fingers,
in order from forefinger unto the small finger.

Step 6
Pulling your hands apart to either side of your body,
turn them downward and you have completed.

416 We continue with the Mudra
to bring into thy life, into thy being the emotion of joy.

Step 1
Palms up, elbows slightly bent, held away from the body,
at least two inches on either side.

Step 2
Bring the palms up and toward each other slowly
until you bring the hands together
at the level of the eye in a prayer position.

Step 3
Holding at the eye level, move the palms apart slowly,
keeping the thumbs touching one another
and all the fingers touching one another.
As you slowly move the palms apart,
sing or chant three times: aaaaaahh [a as in ah].
Stop quickly at the end,
no uplift of the voice at the end, merely a quick stop.

Step 4
Deep breath inward for a count of three,
gentle exhale for a count of three.

Step 5
Maintaining the position of the hands,
slowly bring your hands and arms downward.

Step 6
When you reach the level of the mouth area, smile in joy.

Step 7
Hold the smile for the count of three.

Step 8
Bring your elbows close to your sides,
and starting with the thumb,
move your fingers apart holding your palms upward.

Step 9
Deep breath, exhale, hands palm down
and you have completed the ritual
to bring joy unto thy being.

417 We bring forth a Mudra of happiness.
This Mudra will bring forth from your being a contentment
and within this contentment,
you will be able to see clearly your path

and that is why we would call it the Mudra of happiness.

Step 1
Place your hands face down, head bent, looking at your hands.

Step 2
Fingers held close to each other, but not touching the other hand.
The left thumb pad touching the right thumb pad.

Step 3
With eyes open, look upon the shape made by the hands f
or fifteen seconds.
That shape is a directional shape
encouraging your being to look outward, not inward.

Step 4
Move the hands up with the thumbs touching but the fingers not,
until the thumbs reach and touch the chin.
Close your eyes.

Step 5
Thrice, deep breath in, gently release.
The thumbs remain in contact with your chin.

Step 6
Move the hands to either side of your face,
palms toward your face,
thumbs touching the sides of the forefingers.
The palms are held slightly away.
Hold this position for fifteen seconds.

Step 7
Slowly breathe deeply three times and exhale fully.
You will feel a pressure,
a vibration and that is natural and as it should be.
It is part of the process.

Step 8

Move your hands outward
until you have reached the full extent of your arms.

Step 9
Bring your hands together slowly and gently
until the fingertips touch one upon the other.
The thumbs do not touch.

Step 10
Bring your hands inward toward your heart area,
the fingertips remain touching.
Hold that position for fifteen seconds.

Step 11
Three times, slow deep breath in and then exhale mightily.

Step 12
Sing or chant in a low voice: bo lo mo ka
[long o, long o, long o, a as in ah].

Step 13
Once more, slow deep breath in and then exhale mightily.

Step 14
Sing or chant in a low voice: bo lo mo ka
[long o, long o, long o, a as in ah].

Step 15
Bring your hands out in front of the heart area,
release the fingertips from their touching.

Step 16
Hold your hands palm up at the area of the heart,
deep breath in and exhale deeply: whoosh!
You will feel, Soul, at that point, heaviness in your head.

Step 17

Bring your head down, turn your palms down and you have completed.

Healing Chapter Five
Vibration

418 Souls of earth we would have you understand
all life is a song.
All life has existence in song.
Song, upon your earth you think of as a melody
strung together note by note by note.
And we would tell you, all is strung together note by note by note.
It is important to understand that all notes are connected,
except for one.
It is necessary to your understanding
for the oneness of humanity.
When we speak of as one, we speak of as one in a chord,
rising in a crescendo of sound,
sound that is replicated, echoed forth unto all that is.
Souls of earth, when you are separate and not in accord
as humanity in oneness, then you have a discord.
For it is not possible
to be in the oneness of humanity and have discord.
But it is entirely possible when not in oneness to be in discord.
One note clashing upon the other.
One note strung in discord to another,
crashing in sound waves upon your earth and echoing.
But the echo returns unto your earth,
for it cannot when in discord reach beyond.
We would have you understand
that each creation of negativity creates a discordant note.
Each creation of goodness has the possibility of
a chord of harmony, of oneness.
When in negativity, when in discordance,
the vibration of earth is as a jagged,
random forming line of energy.
When in goodness, when you are flowing out in goodness,
the line of Energy is not random.
It is, indeed, in a spiral of perfection
and that spiral of perfection notes a harmony of mankind.
We would have you understand

the vibration of the flow of goodness creates goodness.
It is a simple equation, Souls.
As the flow of negativity creates negativity,
it too is a simple equation.
It does not dissipate when it is a negative vibration,
for it randomly goes hither and thither,
and all in its path is touched.
When you flow in goodness,
the vibrations are as waves in a pond
when you throw a pebble in the water.
They form an arc and move out and out and out, and they, too,
touch all who come in contact with that wave of vibration.
Vibration causes the tone, the sound,
brings forth the notes of your being,
brings forth the notes of existence.
Understand, it is all existence that you know and beyond.
You cannot be in existence without vibration.
Vibration is more than motion,
for it is creation, also.
Understand that which you create, for indeed, you are a creator.

419 Beloved Souls, we would speak with thee
of the power of song,
the song that swells from the heart, from the inner being,
and bursts forth into the sound of humanity.
We would speak with thee of the songs of the crickets,
of the whale, of the fly.
Yes, even the fly and the song of the mosquito
is precious to our ears, to our sight.
Know that the songs of all those who populate the earth,
with the exception of mankind, are never discordant
but always a pleasure,
if one would listen with the heart and the Soul,
and not negativity.
Know mankind has the power,
the ability to make great songs of discord,
of disharmony, of dissonance,
of dissidence between one another,

between nations and individuals.
Songs can soothe, can comfort,
can bring forth images of Love and gentleness.
Songs can bring forth pain within the discord of harmony.
The gentle touch of a harp's string in full tune can bring a smile,
can bring a tear of joy and sadness, but not pain.
The song you croon to the little babe within thy arms,
within the crib, within the bassinet,
within the stroller, walking beside you,
conveys Love, conveys your Purity.
The strident voice, screeching, yelling in anger conveys discord.
This sound disrupts the chi within the being.
Think ye, Souls, how the chi of millions of beings
is disrupted in times of war:
the discordant whine of missiles,
the screaming of the bombs,
the impact upon the earth, the pain.
We would have you be aware that your voice is a song,
and we would have you be aware
of the power of your voice,
and we would have you be aware,
we would have you be careful
in how you use your instrument.
We would urge gentle speakings,
gentle songs uttering forth from thee.
We would urge that you speak and utter only Love,
and know there will be no disruption of chi
within the land, within an individual, within a country.
Know, instead, you provide soothing,
loving comfort and brotherliness.
So shall it be.

420 Souls of earth, you will understand vibration.
You will understand the effect a vibration has
upon the cells within the human body.
Indeed, within the cells of all that is upon your earth planet,
even the minuscule ant,
even the tiniest of flowers,

even the greatest of whales,
even from the smallest babe newly born
unto the babe still within the womb not yet born,
unto the child, unto the adult, all are affected by vibration.
You may vibrate your body, your voice, your mind,
your very thoughts at will, or you may,
unconsciously vibrate unknowingly.
You may vibrate negative and you may vibrate positive.
All the cells even unto the brain
may be penetrated by darts of negativity.
Be aware of the possibilities of your being.
Be aware of the power of your being.
Recognize you are not without Energy power.
Recognize you may direct the Energy of your being.
Your being is as a beacon emitting rays of Energy,
positive or negative.
Understand, emitting positive Energy has the possibility to heal,
has the possibility to alter the very cells of a being.
Souls of earth, you have great power, and yet,
you denigrate your beings.
"We are powerless to prevent, we are powerless to change,
we are powerless to alter, I am powerless."
Indeed, you are not!
What you are, when you believe you are powerless,
you are in a state of non recognition of the vibration
of your being, of its possibilities.
Take your step, Souls of earth;
recognize the possibilities of the power of your vibration.
Recognize you emit constantly, Energy.
Make a conscious choice of the energy
that you emit from your being.
You are Holy; Holy unto Holy.
In the very core of your being, you know your possibilities.
But you must, in order to know the possibilities,
to be aware of them,
you must remove the veil from your knower
so that you may will the vibration,
so that you may understand the consequences

of the vibrations you emit from your being,
so that you are aware of that which you do.
All Souls of earth enter in to the earth
with all possibility of their Creator,
all possibility of Truth, Love and Purity,
all possibility of compassion on Creator's Path.
It is when you deviate from the Path that you create negativity.
It is not, Souls of earth, imposed upon your being.
Mankind creates negativity.
Be aware of how you have all possibility to alter negativity,
by offering it unto Creator.
Offer it unto Creator
and Creator will alter the vibration of negativity.

421 Humanity has a propensity for self abnegation,
for self castigation, for self recrimination, for self guilt.
This propensity harms the individual.
This propensity inhibits positivity.
Those propensities are full of negative emotion,
are full to bursting of negative energy.
That energy bursts outward and affects all life.
Not just human, but also your animal life, your plants;
all are affected by the energy pulsating
from each human being, from each Soul of earth.
It pulsates outward,
and invades the space of other energy
and alters that space.
We do not say this in condemnation or judgement.
We only say it for awareness, for your understanding,
for your knowledge, so that you may understand,
that you may think upon, that you may ponder
the result of your choices.
For all choice is an opportunity to learn,
but we would have you aware of the effect
of the choices you make.
Positive Energy does not invade, but embraces and fulfills
and lends itself to the song of earth,
to the song of the Soul, to the song of Farside;

positive Energy that heals the varied of wounds,
the deepest sorrow, the most shameful act.
Positive or negative is yours to decide,
for there can be no neutral.
It is one or the other.
We would speak further on the vibratory being,
that which you are.
You come into the earth plane,
you enter in fully able to completely vibrate
your whole being, to energize your being,
to vibrate Energy that can arc unto another.
You come into the body, the flesh and blood, fully endowed
with all possibilities to vibrate the purest Truth,
the purest Love,
the purest compassion in the Purity of your being.
You may vibrate pure Love; Love without judgement.
You may vibrate the pure Love of your Creator!
You value little of the possibility of your being.
The vibration of your being can alter molecules,
the cells within the cells,
that you have not even discovered.
But the vibration works best and instantaneously
when combined with Sound and Color.
It is the triad, Soul.
Indeed, the Sound and Color of your being,
attained in your reach to the high self,
vibrates as an Energy, as an electricity.
for if you had a camera able to capture,
when you are in the midst of healing,
the vibration of your being would be visible as an action.
You shimmer in your vibration.
There are some few upon your earth plane
who see with the eye of that which we speak.
You will understand, the Pillar of Light is not just color.
It is sound and vibration.
When you fully accept the vibratory nature of your being,
you literally shake with the power of that triad.
For to be in that triad, you have already reached the Purity,

the pureness of Truth, the pureness of Love
and the pureness of compassion.

422 When we say vibrate,
we speak not just of the flesh and blood,
but we speak of the actual molecules
within the casing that you call brain,
for it has a part in the vibration.
When you are in the triad for healing,
the electrical stimulus of the brain is necessary
to work with the Soul's compassion.
All is triad.
When you are healing from the sacred self,
all parts of your earth being are synchronized,
are in synchronicity.
And all vibrates,
all is as a symphony of Sound and Color and movement.
Will you see that?
If you had such a machine, it would,
indeed, be visible on the screen of the machine.
When you vibrate to the sound of High C,
in that moment of your earth time, time ceases to be.
In your physiology, you will not notice this,
and you will see it as instantaneous.
We would have you understand
time has stood still during the healing
when you are in sacred self,
for your earth time is measured in moments,
and days, and hours, and years,
but the Time of Farside has no such barriers,
and time and space become irrelevant,
for you have crossed a dimensional border
and are no longer within the constraints of earth.

423 Souls of earth, we speak upon
the vibration of your whole being.
And we would have you understand,
your whole being encompasses the physical being,

that you may see, touch, feel and hear;
your auric being and beyond,
your connection to Spirit and Essence.
There is a connection that you may at any time access.
Understand, the connection to Spirit and Essence
may not be accessed without Purity of intent,
for negativity cannot pass beyond the curtain of care.
Upon the earth plane you vibrate at a level in physicality of being,
in the Energy field of being and in the Soul of being.
You have a triad.
When you vibrate in your physical being
this allows your science to test with their instruments,
to show you pictures of your inners.
It is vibration that allows this connection to science.
The vibration of your physical being
is intimately connected to your Energy field.
When you embrace negativity and hold on and internalize it,
the intent to dwell in negativity, to create negativity,
has a deleterious effect upon the physical body
and can be measured.
Science has already a prototype of this measurement
and it will become commonplace for home usage.
It also affects the mentality of your being,
holding within the mind negative thoughts,
negative intent, negative feeling.
Your Energy field is also affected by negativity,
not only the negativity that you create,
but that of others; for mankind is one.
Negativity held within your Energy field,
places that barrier to connecting to Spirit and Essence,
to passing beyond the curtain of care.
We would have you be aware of the insidious
contamination of being, of negativity.
We do not suggest you condemn negativity.
Indeed not, for it has great purpose,
for in overcoming the negativity
you scarify your being, you grow;
you have attained the purpose of your coming into earth.

We would have you understand
both the positive and negative effects
of entertaining and holding negativity.
And when you overcome, when you release,
we ask that you not release it into the earth.
But that you release it unto your Creator.

424 The mind comes to you in a fractalled state.
In its wholeness, it has power beyond that of your imagination.
The mind does not control,
the mind answers to the will of your being.
When the will of your being is clouded by negativity,
the connection to the mind is lessened,
never quite totally broken, but certainly fractured.
The power of the mind is directly linked to the clarity of the will.
When the will has been clouded,
the mind is powered by negativity for the most part.
When the will has no barrier, has refuted and released negativity,
then the power of the mind
becomes in its wholeness, upon the earth,
of goodness, of compassion and Love.
The Purity of the mind is allowed
to blare forth in its crystalline essence.
It is at that state of being
that you are enabled to reach unto the high self and heal.
Heal in sound, color and vibration.
The vibration of a being's mind caught in negativity is low.
It cannot reach high.
It is only the high mind that may reach high,
for when it is unclouded by negativity,
the mind is free to reach beyond the bounds of earth.
Hear what we say,
Cleanse the will of your being.
Allow the vibration to be pure, to resound in Purity.
Allow the vibration of your being to emit the sound of High C.
Allow the vibration of your being to color itself,
to acknowledge the color that is held within the aura.
All beings have aura.

All beings have color in the aura,
and all beings have the potential
to vibrate to the sound of High C.
Know that there is upon your earth plane,
no being restricted from entering in the Farside,
except by self, for negativity may not enter.
This is not wisdom that you come unto.
It is wisdom that you are aware of
before the decision to enter in to the earth plane.
Why would you need to leave the bounds of earth,
in your compassion and Love, to heal?
It is because the vibration of the earth plane
is affected by negativity
and it holds the vibration slow and low.
And only with the highest of vibration may you enter
in to healing with the sacred self.
Do not be dismayed that this is limited to a special few,
for it is not.
Indeed, not!
Any being, even the infant,
may reach out in its blessed state of sacred self
and bring forth healing.
It is the Purity, that level of Purity that is necessary,
and that level is indeed at the Crystal Cave.

425 Souls of earth, we would have you understand
the voice and vibration.
You will understand, even if you cannot make sound
with your vocal cords,
you may make the sound within your mind.
There is naught without vibration.
It is the combination of the sounds uttered forth
that attract the sounds of the body to pay attention,
to allow the vibratory electricity
to enter in to the affected cells.
You are not limited except by that limit that you place upon self.
It is the will that instructs the voice to pronounce the syllables,
to cause the vibration that alerts the body.

Your cells have intelligence, have an affinity for sound,
have an attraction to sound.
Each cell of your body has a role to play
in the overall well being of your body,
and it is in the oneness of wellness
that your body attunes itself and vibrates to the High C.
Just as within humanity there are individuals
and yet a oneness within the humanity,
so it is within the individual body and the cells
of the body.
And you may affect these cells,
understanding they are not independent of you,
they do not operate as a separate part of your being.
Indeed not!
You have within your being, a cell aura that contains
the operation, the optimal operation of each cell,
and when this aura becomes disjointed or torn,
the vibration of the voice
is one of the many methodologies
upon the earth plane, that may assist
in obtaining the optimal wellness of being.
You see a wound upon the hand
and you watch over days as the wound heals.
If you were to look below the wound
you would see the cells changing, altering,
moving in a constant circle, a constant ring of healing
until you see the wound is gone.
For the cells have achieved, ~~again,~~ optimal wellness.
You may do this, you may heal this wound by voice,
by the vibration of certain syllables.
And so we say unto you, treasure the voice,
understand its healing powers.

426 We would have you understand the vibrational throat.
It is in the vibration of the throat that you may heal
not only self, but others.
The throat has a connection to the voice.
You will understand that even if upon the earth plane

you see yourself as mute, you are indeed not mute.
For your mind may recognize the voice within your being,
and so it matters not whether you have a physical sound
or you use the mind to sound.
We would have you often
take and pull slowly forward at the throat chakra,
the flesh, once, twice, thrice,
using the pad of the thumb and the side of the forefinger.
This is to begin to attune your mind
to the possibilities of the toning of the throat, of the voice.
For seven days, minimum five times daily, the once, twice, thrice.
At the end of the seventh day you will prepare yourself
with a short meditation of no less than fifteen minutes,
and you allow your being
to be immersed in the color of blue.
And then on the eighth day you will take again the flesh
and begin as low as you may, the letter 'o' ooooooo.[59]
Simply, as long as you are able, hold the letter 'o'.
And you will feel,
you will know you have reached the correct tone
when you feel the vibration
upon the shoulders and your upper back,
and you will feel slight vibration below the throat.
You will practice for the next three days that letter and that tone
and more, if necessary,
until you feel the tingling vibration.
And we would have you understand
that when you reach that vibration, that tingling,
you will have begun to be healing any discrepancy
within the area from the shoulder,
top of the shoulders to the top of the head.
Whether it be the ears, the eyes, the mouth,
this will assist in the healing.
This vibration will actively enter in to the area
that is not in balance and assist in balancing.
And we would have you practice this
until you have attained the ability
to not only affect your own healing,

but affect that of another.
And how would you do this, Soul?
You would hold the flesh of the throat chakra gently
of the other being to be healed
with the thumb and the forefinger.
Do this physically or with the mind.
And then as you voice the tone given,
they will also feel the vibration
and know they have been assisted in their healing.
Always the triad: the will, the intent, and the action.

427 We ask that you allow your beings to thrum,
to vibrationally thrum.
Understand the higher the vibration of your being,
the more your consciousness lifts from the earth plane
unto a higher plane, even unto another dimension.
The thrumming of your being
lifts the consciousness beyond the bounds of earth.
You create a synergy of Energy that spirals faster and faster,
flings you forward out and beyond the bounds of earth.
You are a vibratory being.
But understand,
negativity may dampen the vibration of your being,
so that the vibration is tremulous in itself,
so that it cannot lift.
It is as a lead weight was holding you down.
Your consciousness is no longer
held in its minute cavity of the mind,
but is allowed to expand to beyond
and beyond and beyond.
You limit your high mind by holding it unto the earth.
By narrowing its possibilities, you place tethers upon the mind.
Free yourself.
Let there be Light.
Let your vibration lighten itself,
and allow the consciousness to raise to the high mind.
Hear the High C.
Know in your being that which you are.

For when you allow the high mind,
it imbues the mind of your earth being
with a greater consciousness, a greater awareness,
and a greater recognition of the purpose of humanity,
indeed of your purpose of being.
It is your choice to limit that which you are.
It is your choice to come into the fullness of your possibility.
We await your coming into the fullness of your possibility,
and we bless your beings in your great struggle to become.

428 We speak further on sound.
You have ability to access varying levels of sound;
you have the myriad of sounds of earth
that you may hear with your ear
or you may hear with your eye, the third eye.
You have a level of sound available to the third eye,
which is beyond that which you may hear
with your earth ears upon the earth plane,
and it is that which you may hear upon the Farside.
All sound upon the earth is available to your hearing.
Even if you have no hearing, you may feel the vibration
of the sound with the mind, with the eye.
You do not require ears.
The sounds you hear upon your earth, all have vibration,
all have meaning, all may be replicated by your voice
and the attending vibration to that sound.
You may also replicate this sound, this High C,
to heal upon the earth.
The sound of a plant; and you say, 'a plant has no voice',
ah, but it does, for it has a vibration
and that vibration is its voice.
And when you are attuned with the eye,
you hear this sound, you know this sound,
and may replicate this sound.
It is known upon your earth that as an aid to digestion,
the peppermint is often used.
But understand,
it is not merely the physical, mechanical peppermint.

It is the vibration of the peppermint that the cells react to.
And knowing the sound of the peppermint,
you may replicate without the actual
physical manifestation of the peppermint.
You manifest it within the cells of your being,
with the eye, with the voice.
And so you have available to you all manner of healing,
whether you may hold it within your hand
as a physical manifestation,
or whether you hear it with the eye
and use the voice to replicate the vibration.
For it is always the vibration that heals.
And it is the vibration,
for those who would access the Crystal Cave,
that heals, that alters
the physical composition of your being,
that alters the matter, that alters the ion,
because you cannot alter one without the other.

429 Mankind, in its individuality,
often has a gesture of the mind.
It is a universal across your continents,
and this is the shaking of the head in consternation,
in wonderment, in puzzlement, when confronted
with an enigma not readily understandable.
There is purpose to this gesture.
You will even see it in the very young child
who will shake their head when presented with something
that it can not understand,
that does not fit into their knowledge base,
their parameter.
It does not seem to be a square peg in a square hole,
rather, a square peg into a round hole.
This is a normal consequence of the thought process
of mankind in its individuality.
You will see it used when a behavior is seemingly unexplainable,
when a phenomena is seemingly unexplainable.
And we would have you understand

why this is associated with the unexplainable.
This gesture is an earth indication
of the need for vibrational harmony.
What do we mean by vibrational harmony?
Vibrational harmony is an acceptance of all that is,
to the point where no explanation is necessary,
for the knowing is in the eye and the heart.
In the state of vibrational harmony,
the conceptuality of the mind is available to all beings,
not limited by language or previous knowledge.
In vibrational harmony,
it is not necessary to know the basics of mathematics
to understand quantum physics and beyond.
You need not progress from A B C unto your Z.
You may leap from the A to Z.
Within the vibrational harmony all is open unto thee,
for you will then understand, there was no concealment.
There was not secrecy.
It was only your barrier, your individual barrier
that prevented you from seeing
and understanding all that is.
Vibrational harmony is the key to all understanding,
is the key to all healing, is the key to all oneness of being.
And we urge all of humanity, all of mankind in their individuality,
to enter in to vibrational harmony.
Enter thou in.
Enter in to the knowing of the heart and the mind and the eye,
a formidable triad of being.

430 We would speak further on the body.
The body is as a harp.
All the strings must be in proper placement
for the harp to bring forth its glorious sound.
To make the song pleasing to the earth ears,
the harp must be in tune, attuned in proper notes.
Your body is very much as a harp in vibration.
For if the body is not in its optimum attunement,
the song it sings is discordant,

not in voice, but in wellness.
The vibration of your body, when in wellness,
sings forth a glorious melody,
But, when it is out of balance,
any portion of the body out of balance,
then you have your chaos, your cacophony of sound.
For vibration and sound are entwined.
Your body, when in wellness, vibrates to a perfect pitch.
The vibration is visible to those who would see with the eye.
It literally sings in wellness.
It has a bloom, a luminescence visible to the eye.
When in discord, through illness,
through toxins, through disease,
the vibration is dulled, thuds,
and does not vibrate at the high level of Spirit,
but at the low level of earth.
Souls of earth, you are the master tuner
of the harp of your body.
You are the tuner of harmony.
You have all possibilities of high vibration of optimum being.
The mind is affected by the vibration of the body.
It is part of your triad.
When the vibration is low, the mind is dull, thinking is unclear.
You become a plodder rather than a strider,
for your vibration is thudding.
When you have balance and the strings are all tuned,
you then have clear mind, clear vision, quick thought.
You feel vibrant.
Bring unto thy being, balance.
Tune the strings and sing ye the High C of Spirit.

431 We would speak of the power
within the palms of your hand,
the sacred chakra within the palms of your hand,
no less sacred than the other chakras within your body.
Whether it be for the intention of purifying
your food, your water,
or whether it be with the intent to heal self or others,

there is within the palms of your hand a
vibration of Energy concentrated,
meant, placed there to give out.
Knowing that the reality is the Energy
is entering out and has a physicality.
You may not see with the earth eyes, but the eye
will see the Energy flowing out, flowing into.
When you have the intent to heal, to purify,
you have produced a vibration of intent.
And in the releasing of that intent, you have caused an alteration.
You have altered in some form or matter, negativity.
And so you have intent, vibration, alteration, a triad.
This Energy, this sacred Energy
is available to all beings, all Souls,
and, as in all things,
it is choice to give forth that which you have.
Know that the triad, when all three are together in unison,
has power to affect all humanity.
432 Beloved Souls, we would speak with you on the
maelstrom that we refer to as energy.
It has within its being, vibration,
consistent, constant
and convoluted complexities of sound.
Sound within the sound within a sound, echoing, vibrating.
It is as your earth gong when struck,
and you hear vibration upon vibration upon vibration,
echoing further and further and further.
And it is like your thunder,
when you hear that which is already sounded miles away
by the time it reaches you, your hearing.
Understand it is the vibration that brings forth the web,
that brings forth the Energy into all that we know.
It is the vibration of creation that creates.
It is why your vibrations create that which you do not even know,
that which you had no intent, consciously, to create.
And yet because you vibrate, you create.
It is the intensity of the vibration that accounts for the immensity,
the amount, the formation of any creation.

We would have you understand the tympani of sound.
Sound affects all beings, all life, all Souls,
even unto the rock, sound has an effect.
We would give unto you a simple exercise to calm your being,
using a sound.
You will place your hands, palm down upon a thick material.
It may be cotton, it may be wool, it may be silk
but it is to be thick in the matter of at least two inches,
for it will cause a sound that will assist your being.
Place your hands on top, palm down.
Lift your right hand first,
above to a height of four of your earth inches,
and bring it down slowly until just above the material,
and then let it fall so that it makes a sound.
And then the other hand, the same procedure;
when it gets close, let it fall.
And again.
It is important that you not move it one after the other quickly.
It is important that you raise it, bring it down slowly and let it fall.
And you will do this in a row, five times,
and you will find at the end of the repetition
your body moves in a rhythm,
and you may continue to do this
until you are in total relaxation.
This is also a very effective prelude to meditation,
a deep meditation.
It is the muffling that is the relaxing.
Doing this on a drum, even in the slow process,
would be more of an invigoration than a relaxation.
You will also understand,
in the process of moving the hands up and down,
your shoulders are also involved in the process,
and you have created a vortex
within the heart chakra area by the movement
and hence the relaxation and the calming.

433 Souls of earth, we would speak with you

on the power of the human voice, on the power of song.
Humanity has defined narrowly, song.
And yet, we would have you know
that the voice of humanity is a song heard,
not just around the world of your planet,
but beyond and beyond and beyond.
You limit, mankind, song and voice to what your ear,
your earth ear hears,
and we would tell you that the voice is so much more.
Each voice, whether heard with the ear or not, has vibration.
All vibration is a song,
in its broadest earth terminology and definition.
You know in your earth being how a song may touch the heart,
how a voice may touch the heart,
how a voice may be termed angelic
as it is discerned by the human ear.
And you have heard what the human ear discerns as false voice,
one that grates upon the human ear.
And we would have you understand that all voice is vibratory.
Whether the vibration speaks to and affects the heart,
or the mind, or the will,
is inherent within the particular being,
is inherent in the interaction
between the voice and the being.
We would give you example.
One human ear may discern
an operatic aria as uplifting the being,
as uplifting the heart, as uplifting the mind,
as bringing the being almost to a state of ecstasy.
For the vibration that is heard by that particular being
speaks to each cell within the body
at that particular moment.
Another being, discerning with their ear that same voice,
that same aria, hears it as if it is screeching
upon their being
and finds it almost hurtful to their ears.
And so each individual
is affected by voice and vibration in a different manner.

Understand, Souls of earth,
no voice heard beyond the earth plane is discordant,
no voice given in song is discordant.
Understand the vibration of your voice
has power to affect all other beings.
It need not be raised in song, what earth defines as song.
It may only be in conversation or in any verbalization.
The vibration of the voice of the mother speaking to the child,
affects the child.
The extent of the effect will depend upon the manner,
for a voice given in gentleness portrays to the child
the vibration of gentleness
and is felt within the cells of its being.
Your young ones, humanity, are vulnerable to vibration.
Know this when you choose how to speak to your young ones.
The vibration of the voice
has the power to alter the cells of a being.
Understand when you choose the manner of speaking,
you affect another being.

434 We would have you understand,
the sanctity of the most holy temples
is not due to the building.
It is due to the energy of those who enter in.
The brick, the mortar, the wood, the marble,
all the building materials absorb energy.
It travels to the being next to you, in front of you, beside you.
You cannot place yourself in a room
and not emit energy, for you are energy.
You vibrate with energy.
The extent of the duration, of the degree of, varies.
But not the truth that you are a vibrant being of energy,
and therefore emit a charge.
Emanating a negative energy charge from your being;
hastens to look for a place to strike.
Just as your lightning must find a place to lite,[60]
to enter in to strike,
so does the negative energy of your being.

You have, upon your earth, the example of the lightning strike,
 the zig zag, the flashing.
It is chaotic, and so is the negative energy that you emit chaotic,
 lites upon the vulnerability of another being.
A being who is not grounded in Purity is vulnerable.
A being who has not the wisdom
 to embrace the chaos and offer it unto Creator,
 will absorb that energy
 and it becomes a part of their being.
Understand the chaos.
We ask that you recognize, when your being is in chaos,
 it is as lightning ready to strike.
When you emit from your being the positivity of Purity,
 that, too, lites upon another, that, too,
 is absorbed in the bricks and the mortar of the building,
 that, too, may be accepted as Energy,
 to be taken in and embraced.
It is not chaotic as the negativity.
It is filled with Love and compassion, a calmness.
The chaos of the negativity is curious, and yet that curiosity,
 when embraced and held within,
 is detrimental to the growth of the being.
That curiosity embraced, and then overcome
 and given as gift unto Creator,
 fulfills the growth of the being.
We would have you understand in all places of gathering,
 whether they be temples or not, whether they be homes
 or just long houses, great houses, small houses,
 in any place of gathering, we would have you
 be conscious that you are a vibrational being.

435 We would speak of vibrational healing.
We would have you understand all healing is vibrational.
All energy is vibrational.
It is imperative to your understanding of the process of healing.
When the body is in a diseased state,
 or when it is in a state of dis ease,
 the vibrational tone of the body can be measured.

The vibrational tone can be measured with your instruments
and it can be seen with the eye.
Using the eye, you may look upon a being and literally
see the vibrational tone of that being expressed in colors.
You will see breaks in the colors and you will know
that that is the area where the vibrational tone
has been altered detrimentally.
You will see vacant spots of color, a darkness
and you will understand that is an indication
of the vibrational tone being distorted.
Some will see, within the vibrational tone, a discoloration,
a blemish, and that is their indication
of the distortion of the tone.
When the being is in full wellness,
there will be no distortions within
in the vibrational tone seen with the eye.
There will be not cracks.
There will be no dark spaces.
All will be in perfection.
All will shimmer with a sound,
with a tone pleasing to the ears of the eye,
indeed, the ears of the eye.
For the Eye discerns both Color and Sound.
You may see sound, indeed, and hear sound with the eye.
Each cell within your being has a vibrational tone,
vibrates visibly to the eye, the state of its health
even unto the very nucleus of each cell.
And having discerned where the vibrational tone
has been altered or distorted,
healing is then given a focus.
For the vibrational tone of each cell
of each being radiates a sound.
It is not self contained; it radiates outward,
so that when in illness, when in disease,
when in emotional crisis,
you broadcast that distortion as vibrational sound.
And when in wellness you also vibrate,
but you vibrate a pure note of joy and goodness.

You have within the ability to reach unto the Crystal Cave
 and heal self and others.
But to give out that goodness, to see with the eye,
 you have need to reach the level of manifestation.[61]
For otherwise, you have not reached
 the level of wisdom and knowledge
 to wield the sacred Energy in all its glory,
 in all its wellness, in all its pure tones of joy.
Souls of earth, we would speak on what
 we will call, waves, waves of light,
 waves of energy in your oceans,
 in your eddies, in your pools of water.
Even in the most minute pool of water
 you may physically see and feel
 vibration by the momentum of the waves.
The waves are caused by natural occurrences
 within the ocean, the tides.
Entering in to the water, you cause waves.
You see and you feel the physical manifestation of vibration.
And how did you do this?
You entered in.
You saw with your eyes, with your physical hand you felt.
When you see with the eye
 and you enter in to that which you are,
 to thy aura, to the extension of your being,
 you see the vibration of Energy.
You feel the vibration of Energy.
All sound is vibration.
All color is vibration.
Indeed, you are vibration.
You have come unto this earth for pain and growth.
You have come in to this earth with all choice.
Accept that you are a fragment of Creator,
 that you have within your very being of your body,
 mind, aura, the Energy of Creator.
It is Holy.
You are Holy.
Indeed, vibrate, but know you have choice in how you vibrate.

And know your aura is not the ephemeral construct,
    but it is, indeed, matter.
Your science knows this,
    have known of the existence of aura,
    and it will become a subject of great consternation.
It will be at the forefront of your news
    and man will know the aura exists and is palatable.

436 Beauty is indeed in the eye of the beholder.
For when you enter in to the Eye, you behold Farside,
    you behold to a level of Purity of being.
You may behold the Crystal Cave, the mighty Prism,
    and you know that the beauty of your earth,
    in all its grandeur is only a minuscule,
    infinitesimal portion of the beauty of beholding
    the myriad of colors round about thee
    as you enter in to the Farside,
    as you enter in to the Spirit of your being.
The variety of worlds available unto thee,
    each in its own individuality,
    brimming with Color and Sound.
The world of the whales, the crystalline blue,
    where you may enter in without thought
    for you have beheld,
    and you have all knowledge available.
And there is, we would say instantaneous, but it is even quicker,
    instantaneous recognition of other beings,
    instantaneous recognition of Angelic.
You may enter in to the worlds of reptile and be welcomed,
    for there are no barriers
    except for the level you have reached.
As you desire to enter in, so you are taught and so you expand,
    until you have reached the capability
    to enter in to another level.
Souls of earth, in comparison to the beauty of your colors,
    of your sound, of your nature,
    there is so much more awaiting you.
You do not need to wait to pass, you may enter in

with the eye at any moment of your choosing.
Reach for the triad of your being.
Reach unto your sacred self.

437 You have been taught all is vibration.
When the body is in its optimal vibratory mode,
it literally sings the sound of High C.
This vibratory mode is the sacred self.
It is entering in to and beyond high consciousness.
This vibratory mode is not available upon your earth.
It is only available as you reach unto the sacred consciousness
and there you have in abundance,
Energy, healing Energy that is full of radiant Love,
and that responds to illness, to disability within any being.
As Love, total Love, has within, no judgement,
has only the spewing out of compassion,
so does this radiant Love
have only compassion and sees the pain,
and reaches out to the pain to heal, should the Soul allow.
It is not a healing that requires months of daily application.
This radiant Love is in your earth time instant.
It has the power of your Creator.
It has, in your earth terms, the power of a mighty thunder clap,
for, as the thunder clap, it reverberates within the being.
Whether it is to do with the mind,
the emotions, or the physicality, it reverberates,
and the molecules, the matter within the being is altered.
A gaping wound will close, there will be no festering,
it will be as if it had never been.
The crippled withered limb will straighten,
the being will walk, even if the being has never walked.
The being afflicted with schizophrenia will become whole,
no longer split, no longer attacked by self.
All of humanity has the potential to be such vibratory healers.
Reach for that Love.
Enter you in to that which you came to do: to be in oneness,
to see all with no judgement, to see all with Love,
and seek to hold, within your arms of radiant Love,

all who are ill or troubled in spirit.
So be it.

438 We would speak on the Holy vibration.
Beloved Souls, recognize your holiness.
Know that each Soul is Holy, is treasured, is precious to Creator,
is unconditionally loved by Creator.
Know ye that each Soul has a singular signatory vibration,
and yet the vibration can be joined with another vibration
that in itself is unique and has its own signature.
And another Soul and another Soul can blend their vibrations.
This is what constitutes a vortex of Energy.
It is the commingling of vibrations,
it is the joining of each individual signatory in a wave,
in a flow, in a swirl that reaches beyond the earth,
beyond the planet, beyond the galaxy.
The vibration reaches unto the Farside.
And your intent as individual signatories,
and their joint signatories is heard.
Know ye that the vortex of the commingled energies resounds,
echoes throughout the universes.
The vortexes of Purity filter up unto the Farside.
And you lift our Spirits whenever you use your vortexes,
the commingling of your vibrations
into a vortex to send negativity home,
the vibrational level of your Purity joining together
in pure intent of Love.
Oh, Souls, the chorus that welcomes!

439 We would have you understand
you may heal with vibration,
you may heal in vibration and you may heal a vibration.
When you choose to heal with the Essence of your sacred self,
a vibration of Sound and Color enters in to thy being
and it flows out from thee in thy goodness.
It attaches to that which needs healing.
It takes the broken chord,
the broken note of discord and tunes it.

As a fine instrument is tuned by the expert, by the master,
so would you tune the discordant note within a being.
The discordant note, that break in the vibrational harmony.
All that is upon your earth has Soul
and you may heal, should you choose,
all that is upon your earth.
And in that healing you bring forth a harmony,
not just to that one being,
but that vibrational healing echoes forth
throughout the earth, reverberates
beyond the impact of the individual.
It is exponential.
Understand, you are great in your powers,
you are formidable beings
when you release from the bonds of earth
and enter in to Spirit and then unto Essence.
You have a direct line to the Crystal Cave.
The Crystal Cave is a vibration.
Indeed, the vibration of Color and Sound in harmony.
The triad of sound, of color, of vibration
are based in the oneness of the Flow,
the Flow of your Creator's Love.
When you are in your sacred self, there is not only a present,
there is all possibilities of what will be.
Enter in to the viscosity of color.
Each color and each shade of color upon your earth
has a measurable viscosity to it.
Science is experimenting already with this concept
and will eventually be able
to physically measure the viscosity of color.
The grain of color affects the viscosity of each color.
The grain has a physicality to it
that is not caused by what makes the color.
It is not caused by the pigment.
It is not caused by the oil or the water.
It is caused by the vibration of the color.
Within nature there are plants and barks
from which you may gain color.

All of these are alive, are vibrations.
The closer the pigment to the actual shade
of what you have found in nature,
the higher the vibration.
The viscosity of a color is affected
by the vibration of the intent of the being.
You may imbue a color with your vibration,
and it is the viscosity of the color that allows this to occur.
They have an affinity, and it is not one sided.
Indeed, not.
In the complexity of the molecular structure
of the viscosity of color, healing is found.
There is an interaction,
that the one affects the other in all forms of healing,
whether it be a human being, an animal,
a plant, or even the planet.
Understand you have the power, the vibrational wherewithal,
to align yourself with color to heal,
to imbue earth color with the vibration of your being.
It requires not the physical mixing of paints,
of compounds to bring forth healing colors.
It requires the mixing of your vibration,
of your Pillar of Light and the color.
You may take a ribbon, a form of material,
and it does give off a vibration,
it does encourage an affinity.
But when you imbue it with your Energy, it comes alive,
and has much greater power.
It is as if you increased the wattage of a twenty five amp bulb
to one that was one thousand amps.
And, so, in your healing process,
you understand that color affects.
And we would now have you understand
that you may affect the intensity,
the vibrational intensity of any color,
and thereby increase its effect upon the cellular being
to speed the healing.
We would speak upon the vibratory threads

that are a vibratory part of your being.
You will understand the threads are not static.
They are constantly in movement.
They can not remain still.
The frequency of the vibration depends upon the being's action.
Thought affects minutely, action has the greater deal of effect.
When the threads vibrate at a low, slow level,
the growth is minimal to nonexistent.
When the threads vibrate at a higher level, at a higher frequency,
then the growth takes place, then karma is repaired.
You came to vibrate those threads at a higher frequency.
You came of earth to have those threads
become glowing forms of Light,
to vibrate the Light outward unto all of mankind.
The higher the frequency of the thread,
the greater the growth of all mankind.
Vibrate thy being, vibrate the threads,
vibrate unto thy Holy self.
You have all possibilities.
You may enter in, in first life, as baby Soul
and vibrate to such an extent
that you become an aged Soul in one lifetime.

440 We would speak of your drums and drumming.
It is the vibration and the sound of the drum
that we would speak of.
The connection from one being to another is most apropos
when you look at and examine the drum.
The drum in its quiescent state, without any action,
has no seeming sound or vibration.
And yet when you lay upon the drum with hand or tool,
the sound appears.
And in that sound also appears a vibration.
The vibration is felt by other beings as the sound.
Hear this, Souls: the vibration is felt because of the sound.
Without the sound, quiescence takes place.
So, it is not only in your universe but all universes,
upon universe, upon universe.

You, individually, each being, may be likened to a drum.
Within your being you have sound, you have vibration.
And yet, until there is motion, until there is the tool of motion,
you are seemingly quiescent,
quiet, without sound or vibration.
Motion is necessary for the triad of sound, vibration and color.
All of humanity has a sound, a color, a vibration,
all of which, without motion, are quiescent.
Souls of earth, when you intend to heal,
when you have the intent of healing
and you reach unto the Crystal Cave
for healing of another,
then does the motion enter in,
then does the vibration alter,
then does the sound alter, then does the color alter,
not only in your own being
but in that of beings to which you intend the healing.
And those nearby sense or feel or see,
depending on their level of being,
that which you have become in the healing.
You are, Souls of earth, a sacred drum as humanity.
You are, Souls of earth, sacred being as humanity.
You are, Souls of earth, as Humanity the sound of High C.

The Mudras are arranged sequentially: Mind, Head, Upper Torso, Lower Torso, Full Body, and Emotions.

Hu Li

441 Souls of earth, we bring unto you for your learning,
techniques given to us by Master Twag.

MIND

442 Oft times, Soul, you will understand you will have a blockage in one particular chakra
and we would give unto you a quick unblockage.

Step 1
Cup the right hand, fingers held closely together,
the thumb touching the forefinger
and the finger next to it,
and place it in front of whatever chakra is blocked.

Step 2
Cup your left hand, fingers held closely together,
the thumb touching the forefinger
and the finger next to it,
and place it in front of whatever chakra is blocked.

Step 3
Place in front of the third eye your left cupped hand.
Thrice, slowly move the right to the third eye,
and the left to the blocked chakra
and back again to the eye.
Note: In the case where it is the third eye chakra that is blocked,
place both hands in front of the third eye
and three times pull them apart, bring them together.

Step 4
Take your cupped hands, open them, place palms up.

Remove the thumb from touching the forefingers
and you have completed.

443 For those who have been attacked
physically or emotionally,
and who are in the midst of a traumatic crisis,
repeat three times steps one, two and three.
This will enable the clarity to enter in to the chaos
and will soothe the trauma.

Step 1
Fold the right arm over the left arm.

Step 2
Place both arms over the area of the chest,
the left hand under the right arm and the right arm
under the left arm pit and hug yourself gently.
Hold for the count of six, release

Step 3
Deep breath, push the breath out and you have completed.

444 Souls of earth, for the stutterer who has difficulty
in speaking without a stutter,
practice this, daily as often as possible,
and you will find the stuttering eased
and then eventually disappearing.

Step 1
Place the thumb and the forefinger together:
the right thumb and right forefinger together,
the left thumb and left forefinger together.

Step 2
Holding the other fingers together,

place all the fingers and the palms in an upright position.

Step 3
Maintaining the thumb and forefinger closed,
press the pads of the first two fingers
after the forefinger together
in a rhythmic one and two, one and two, one and two,
one and two, one and two.
While doing this, the stutterer will vocalize:
one and two, one and two, one and two, five times.
Even, Soul, if it is stuttered, it is acceptable,
for you will soon find yourself able.

HEAD

445 We would bring unto you Mudras.
These are to be used in times of extreme stress.
For stress, Souls of earth,
that threatens the very being that you are.

Step 1
Intertwine the fingers at the initial first knuckle
closest to the nail bed, holding the thumbs apart.

Step 2
Place the hands in front of the solar plexus.

Step 3
Three times squeeze, release, and you have completed.[62]

446 For those Souls of earth
who have problems with sea sickness
or any like vertigo and need immediate relief
from the vertigo, from the nausea:

Step 1
Place the left thumb on top of the center of the right wrist.

Step 2
Fold the fingers as much as you are able around the wrist
and press the center of the wrist with the thumb
while gently folding in the fingers of the right hand.

Step 3
Softly squeeze the wrist with the fingers.

Step 4
Deep breath, hold for a count of twelve and then release.
You will feel in the stomach area the effects.

447 We would have you understand the pressure points
of the third eye for pain in the front of the head:

Step 1
Place the pad of the forefinger
upon the third eye and press firmly.

Step 2
Place the pad of the forefinger
in the middle of the back of your head,
center it between the neck,
the top of the head and the ears.

Step 3
Holding the head upright, hold the forefinger
at the back of the head until the pain eases.

Step 4
Slowly move the finger away from the head.
take a deep breath and release.

448 We would have you understand
the pressure point of the third eye
for headaches from the back of the head:

Step 1
Place the pad of the forefinger upon the third eye
and press to relieve.

Step 2
Hold a firm pressure until you feel the pain easing.

Step 3
Slowly release.
A quick release is not best for your being.
It is the slow release to allow the pressure point
to return slowly to its normalcy.

449 For pain on either side of the head:

Step 1
Place a forefinger just above the left ear
and place a forefinger just above the right ear.
Even if the pain is only on one side, Souls,
you will use both forefingers on either side of the ears.

Step 2
With the head upright, press inward firmly.
Hold that pressure until the pain eases.

Step 3
Once the pain has eased, hold for another five seconds
and then slowly release.

450 For the beings who suffer from the allergies
at various times of the year.
The tearing will ease, the congestion of the nose will ease.

Step 1
Place together on each hand your little fingers,

the fingers next to them and then the third fingers.

Step 2
Bring up unto the bridge of the nose,
placing the longest fingers at the bridge of the nose

Step 3
Three times, while lightly pressing,
slide your forefingers down the sides of your nose,
while taking a deep breath through the nostrils
and holding for the count of three.

Step 4
Exhale in a whoooooosh.
Exhale as long as you can,
pulling in your stomach as you do so.
And you will find that your allergies have been somewhat relieved.

451 We give you an exercise to calm the effects of allergies,
the runny eyes, the runny nose, the sneezing.
This will not cure for you must find the cause,
but it will stop the immediate effects.

Step 1
Palm up, cup the right or left hand, whichever you choose.

Step 2
Place thumb and forefinger of that hand
on either side of the bridge of the nose.
Gently pinch together the flesh.

Step 3
While maintaining Step 2,
gently pinch the flesh underneath the lips
with the thumb and the forefinger of the other hand.

Step 4
Maintain Step 2 and 3
while thrice, taking a slight breath in through the nostrils,
hold for the count of five, and then release.
You will find your eyes stop tearing, your nose stops running
and the tickle in your throat has ceased for the time being.

452 Souls of earth, for the tired, burning, aching eyes,
eyes that are blurred from tiredness.
Not the eyes affected by the allergy,
but the eyes that have been overworked.
You will need to repeat all these Steps thrice.

Step 1
Using the nail bed of the little finger
of the left hand and right hand
seven times on the right and seven on the left[63]
press in a rhythmic manner, one and two, one and two.

Step 2
Closing your eyes, place the little finger
in the center of each of your eyebrows and press inward
just beneath the eyebrow, but not in the eyes.

Step 3
Open your eyes.
You will notice that they feel better,
They are rested and not as blurred.

453 To stimulate the healing
for those who have aching sore gums:

Step 1
Press with the right thumb
the pad of the finger next to the right forefinger.
Seven times slowly, rhythmically press up and down on the pad.

Step 2
Press with the left thumb
the pad of the finger next to the left forefinger.
Seven times slowly, rhythmically press up and down on the pad.

Step 3
At the end of the seven,
move those fingers pads to either side below the nostrils,
between the nostrils and the lips.

Step 4
Press onto the gum lightly and rhythmically seven times.

Step 5
Pause and repeat the procedure three times.

Step 6
Continue to do the procedure until the gums are healed.

454 For the toothache[64] anywhere on the upper jaw:

Step 1
Place the right thumb in the spot
in the middle of and just beneath the chin.
Your left hand, forefinger and thumb touching,
the other fingers held close together.

Step 2
Place the forefinger of your right hand
at the indent on the upper lip
between the nose and the lip.

Step3
Three times at the same time,
press both right thumb and forefinger firmly
and then move the hands away.
Pressing for three seconds, moving away for three seconds.

Step 4
As the pain eases,
move only your thumb over to wherever the pain is,
and hold it, pressing gently for the count of three.
Move the thumb away for three and back again for three, thrice.

Step 5
Place the forefinger upon the pain,
and press, once, twice, thrice until the pain dissipates.

455 For toothaches upon the lower jaw:

Step 1
Place your right thumb beneath the chin in the center.
The fingers are lightly curled inward.

Step 2
With your left hand place your thumb and forefinger together,
the three fingers held close together.

Step 3
Without leaving the chin,
press the thumb in and out, in and out.
do not rub, do not circle, simply press in and out.

Step 4
As soon as you begin to feel an easing of the pain,
move the right thumb unto the area of the pain,
but still under the jaw line,
and press the thumb in and out, in and out
without leaving the flesh, until the pain has gone.

456 For the sore throat:

Step 1
Place your thumb and forefinger of the left hand together,

your three fingers held close together.

Step 2
Place the base of the right thumb into the crevice
just before the clavicles join,
the fingers of the right hand are lightly curled inward.

Step 3[65]
Once, twice, thrice, using the base of your thumb,
slightly press inward and release without leaving the flesh.
Pause.

Step 4
Once, twice, thrice, using the base of your thumb,
slightly press inward and release without leaving the flesh.
Pause.

Step 5
Once, twice, thrice, using the base of your thumb,
slightly press inward and release without leaving the flesh.

Step 6
Slowly move your thumb along the chin line,
moving up from the position on the throat
to the very center just below
the chin and press once, twice, thrice.

Step 7
Repeat the procedure until the pain has thoroughly dissipated.

457 For the sore throat which is irritated, ravaged, red.

Step 1
Place your thumb and forefinger
on either side of the middle of the throat and gently,
starting at the chin, bring your thumb and forefinger

down at the same time on either side.
Stop at the collarbone.

Step 2
Press gently inward to the width of your thumb and forefinger.

Step 3
Place thumb and forefinger
as if you were going to pinch the flesh,
but merely bring the flesh in gently
and hold for a count of seven earth seconds.

Step 4
Continue Steps 1,2 and 3 until you may swallow without pain.

Step 5
As you release the pain, place your forefinger
directly between the two collarbones
and press inward lightly and hold for the count of four,
and then release.
This will stimulate the healing of that which
caused the pain in the throat.

UPPER TORSO

458 For the pain in the neck.
You will understand, Soul, this refers to
injuries of the neck caused by strain or tension.
When sitting too long in a position,
this will relieve the pain of neck tension.

Step 1
Place thumb pad upon the right side of the neck,
place the pad of the forefinger
on the other side of your neck in the front.

Step 2
Press inward firmly and hold until the pain eases.
As the pain eases hold for another five seconds,
and then slowly release.

459 For pain in the neck caused by a vertebrae being misaligned.
This movement must be done in a sitting position.
It is not to be done standing.

Step 1
Place upon the back of the neck
the first four fingers of both hands.

Step 2
All four fingers are pressed inward firmly.
If you feel pain gently ease up a bit on the pressure,
otherwise hold the pressure until the pain eases.

Step 3
To help align the bones,
when the pain eases do not remove your fingers,
but move them upward unto the middle of the skull.
Keep the fingers aligned on either side.

Step 4
Near the top of the head pause
and firmly apply pressure upon the skull,
and hold until the pain eases.

Step 5
When the pressure of the pain eases,
when you feel able to move your head without pain,
hold for another five seconds, and slowly, slowly release.

460 For those who have problems of the thyroid,
we would suggest that when doing this exercise
that you ensure you are in a place

where if you feel lightheaded,
you may relax in a prone position.

Step 1
Place the pads of the thumbs and forefingers together,
right to right, left to left.
The palms upright with the other fingers straight out.

Step 2
Hold the left thumb and the forefinger gently
upon the center of the throat
and press lightly for twelve seconds.
The other fingers rest gently upon the throat.

Step 3
Three times move your hand slowly away from the thyroid area,
hold away for three seconds,
moving it back to the thyroid area
and holding for twelve seconds.

Step 4
Place both hands palm up unlock your fingers and thumbs.

461 For shoulder pain:

Step 1
Head upright as far as you are able.
Place the pads of your forefingers on the collarbone
where the bone is felt at the sides of the neck
but toward the back and press firmly on the bone.

Step 2
Hold that pressure until the pain eases.

Step 3
As the pain eases, you will hold for a further five seconds,
and then slowly release.

462 For those who have the rapid beating of the heart
in the midst of a situation or a group.

Step 1
Placing the hands folded into fists,
the thumbs held within the fingers.

Step 2
Place firm pressure upon the area of the heart
for a minimum of five seconds

Step 3
Deep breath as much as you are able
release at the same time the breath and the fists.
And you have completed.

463 For the recovery from heartburn:

Step 1
Taking the first two fingers of both hands,
place one set above the heart in the center
and the other set in the center of the chest
just below the breast area.

Step 2
Rhythmically press, one and two, one and two, one and two.
Continue this rhythm until you have expressed relief.

464 For the wellness of heartburn:

Step 1
Place together the thumb and forefinger of each hand,
right to right, left to left.
The other fingers lightly folded in.

Step 2
Bring the forefingers and thumbs of both hands
up to either side of the mouth.

Step 3
Five times push the sides of the lips
until they open in a purse like manner.
And then, close the lips.
You will feel the belch erupting, relieving the heartburn.

465 For the burning associated with the need to expel
what you call burp, gas:

Step 1
The left hand forefinger and thumb touching,
the other fingers held close together and held upright.

Step 2
Take your right forefinger, slowly and gently rub seven times
at the very tip of the sternum.
Your thumb is up,
other fingers held close to the palm of your hand.

Step 3
Maintaining a light pressure, take a deep breath
as much as you are able, exhale.

Step 4
Take your right forefinger, slowly and gently rub seven times
at the very tip of the sternum.
Your thumb is up,
other fingers held close to the palm of your hand.

Step 5
Maintaining a light pressure,
deep breath as much as you are able, exhale.
As it begins to ease, as you begin to erupt with the burp, gas,
hold the pressure until it is totally eased.

466 For those beings who often find the pain
within the left lung area,
not sharp pains, Soul, this is a dull ache,

and generally caused by indigestion.
Do this thrice and the pain will have eased.

Step 1
Place right hand palm directly upon the left lung,
the left chest area

Step 2
Cross the left hand over the right
and place the left palm on the right lung area.

Step 3
Deep breath from as far below your stomach as you can.
Hold for the count of three
and then a controlled exhale five times: wh wh wh wh wh.

467 For the upset stomach:

Step 1
Place the first two fingers of either hand,
approximately three inches above the navel.
The other two fingers are held loosely, the thumb is held loosely.

Step 2
Press inward firmly in and out, in and out,
until you have ceased the pain.
If you are doing it correctly you will automatically breathe in,
and you will know that you have the correct spot,
for you will be unable to press inward
without taking a breath.

468 For the distress of the digestion,
this distress will be relieved if the cause is overeating.
If the cause is a disagreeable food it will not relieve the heartburn.
We are speaking simply of the distress of the stomach area.

Step 1
Place your hands palm against the stomach area,

and press lightly six times, rhythmically,
one and two, one and two, one and two.
The hands will press and lift in unison.

Step 2
Placing the right forefinger pad over the left forefinger nail,
press lightly into the navel area
and hold that pressure for five seconds

Step 3
Seven more time rhythmically press
one and two, one and two, one and two.
Continue until you are relieved from the distress.

469 For those afflicted with goiter, these steps
will be repeated five times, thrice daily, to clear the goiter.

Step 1
Place the hands in prayer position
and place them underneath the goiter.

Step 2
With lips closed, gulp swallow seven times.

Step 3
Open the mouth and breathe in quickly the air,
as if you were startled, and then breathe it out quickly
as if you were coughing the breath out.

470 For those who have arthritic pain, carpal tunnel pain
in the fingers of the hand, you will find relief.
Do this on both elbows and wrists of your being,
even if one of the hands is not affected.

Step 1
Hold your hand, your arm up upward,
palm facing toward the body,
Place the thumb on one side of this elbow

and the forefinger on the other side of this elbow.

Step 2
Press in on the elbow
with the thumb and forefinger for fifteen seconds
in a rhythmic manner, one and two,
one and two, one and two.

Step 3
At the end of the fifteen seconds,
move your thumb and forefinger up the sides of the arm,
up onto the wrist.

Step 4
Press three times on either side of the wrist,
one and two, one and two, one and two.

471 For the sprain of the lower arm,
you will find that it stimulates rapid healing of a sprain.

Step 1
Placing the thumb into the middle of the wrist,
push inward.
At the same time, with the finger next to the forefinger
place firm pressure on the outer part of the arm.

Step 2
Rhythmically press one and two, one and two,
one and two, one and two until the pain has eased.

Step 3
When the pain has eased, hold for a further five seconds and then release.

472 For pain in the middle back area,
often from stress and strain.

Step 1
Place your thumb pads at the lowest rib
on either side of the body.

Step 2
Press firmly, but gently directly on the ribs with the thumbs.

Step 3
Hold until the pain eases.

Step 4
Once the pain has eased, hold for a further five seconds,
and then slowly release.

473 For the lower back pain:

Step 1
Sit as upright as possible.
Place the forefinger into the throat area, not hard, but firmly
and place the other forefinger in the navel area.

Step 2
Rhythmically, starting with the throat, one and two,
press in and release.
Back and forth, the throat and then the navel,
until the pressure has eased, until the pain has eased.

Step 3
Once the pain has eased you will hold for a further five seconds
and then release first the throat and then the navel.

474 We would have you understand at the top of your knees,
there is a sensitive neuron that will affect
the meridians of the lower back.
For some severe cases, you may need to do this on a daily basis
until you see improvement.
The rhythm, Soul, is important.
The thumb and the fingers that are not being used
to press upon those neurons are to be held up and away,

they are not to be touching the knee cap.

Step 1
Place within the two dents found on top of your knee pads,
the forefinger and the finger next to the little finger.

Step 2
Rhythmically, without the fingers leaving the knee pad,
press inward firmly twelve times,

one and two, one and two, one and two, one and two,

Step 3
Rest for fifteen seconds, and repeat until your pain lessens.
Rhythmically, without the fingers leaving the knee pad,
press inward firmly twelve times,
one and two, one and two, one and two, one and two,

Step 4
Rest for fifteen seconds and repeat until the pain is gone.
Rhythmically, without the fingers leaving the knee pad,
press inward firmly twelve times,
one and two, one and two, one and two, one and two,

LOWER TORSO

475 For cystitis, bladder infection, continue to do these steps
every five minutes until the bladder pain has ceased.

Step 1
On each hand, place the thumb, forefinger
and next finger together.

Step 2
Place in the waist area, on either side of your torso,
the finger combination of Step 1

Step 3
Three times press inward deeply,
as deeply as you are able without pain

and hold for the count of seven seconds.
When releasing each of the three times, do so slowly.

476 For the being who is constipated to the point
of deleterious effects upon their system,
do this every half an hour
until you are no longer constipated.
All movements to be done slowly.

Step 1
Press together the thumb and forefinger of the left hand,
and the thumb and forefinger of the right hand.

Step 2
Intertwine the fingers,
and place the hands in the area
above the navel and below the rib cage.

Step 3
Gently press inward, once, twice, thrice.

Step 4
Hold without pressing in for the count of ten.

Step 5
Gently press inward, once, twice, thrice.

477 For strains of the upper thighs and the lower buttocks:

Step 1
Place the thumb and the forefinger together,

Step 2
Place the thumb and forefinger
at the middle of the top of the knee
and press firmly until the pain eases.

Step 3
Once the pain has eased,
slowly move your thumbs and forefingers away.

Step 4
Take the palm of your hand
and three times gently in a clockwise direction
rub first the right knee and thigh
and then the left knee and thigh
until the pain has totally gone.

478 For pain of the knee,
for those who have injured their knees,
whether broken or sprained,
we would have you understand
the palms of your hands will provide a warmth
that will penetrate the bone.

Step 1
Cup each knee with the palm of your hands.

Step 2
Apply pressure with the tips of the fingers on either knee,
and on the side of the knee with the thumbs.
Hold that pressure position until the pain eases.

Step 3
After the pain eases, hold for a further five seconds.

479 For strains of the lower leg:

Step 1
Place the palm of your hand directly

on the back of the injured leg,
hand spread wide.

Step 2
Bring your foot back, not fully bent but partially bent at the knee.

Step 3
Hold that position for five seconds while applying pressure from
the thumb pad, the forefinger pad,
and from the pads of the other fingers.
If after five seconds the pain does not begin to ease
increase the pressure.

Step 4
When the pain has eased, slowly remove your hand,
and slowly put your leg back in position.

480 For the sprains of the feet:

Step 1
Bend your leg back, not fully bent,
but partially bent at the knee, heel up.

Step 2
On either side of the ankle bone,
place a thumb pad and a forefinger pad.

Step 3
Squeeze inward firmly and hold until the pain begins to ease.
Once the pain has eased hold for a further five seconds
and then release.

FULL BODY

481 Souls of earth, we would have you access
a small string of yellow ribbon.
It need not be large, a thin strip will do.
And we would have you understand,
that to tie this around the forehead,
when you are ailing with the flu
will ease the fluishness that permeates your body.
It is especially helpful for the young child.
Simply place it and tie it gently,
and know that the color will bring

a measure of peace unto the being.
In the cases where the flu is also afflicting the throat,
place yellow about the throat also,
and leave it for at least fifteen minutes,
whether it be for a young child
or an adult or an aged one.
Again, it need not be wide.
It need not be satin.
Simply a yellow ribbon of color will do.
Where the ague, the flu
is affecting the area of the stomach with the vomit
tie around the area a yellow ribbon
or place a cloth of yellow to soothe,
to help the being calm.
The same with the legs, the upper and the lower,
that ache terribly from the flu,
tie the yellow ribbon or place a yellow cloth.
If using a yellow cloth,
we would suggest that you stay within natural fibers.
Fifteen minutes each time to soothe the being.

482 This is most efficacious for a fevered being,
over twelve years of age, especially one who is thrashing.

Step 1
Place in front of your being the hands in this position:
your left hand, the thumb and forefinger together,
the other three fingers spread wide,
and intertwine with your right hand
those fingers that are spread wide.

Step 2
Slowly out and back five times:
bringing the hands forward unto the Soul, or unto self,
just above the heart and then move away
to the length of your arms,
and then back again to above the heart.

Step 3
Deep breath and exhale slowly.

483 We give unto you a quick remedy for severe allergic reaction, one that involves the welts.

Step 1
Place the right thumb placed against the left wrist
at the pulse point and press gently,
but firmly for three seconds.

Step 2
Bring together the thumb and the first two fingers
of the left hand.
Hold for a count of fifteen.

Step 3
Move the pad of the thumb over to the left of the pulse,
and press inward gently, but firmly for a count of fifteen.

Step 4
Place the left thumb against the right wrist at the pulse point
gently, but firmly for the count of fifteen.

Step 5
Move the pad of the thumb over to the left of the pulse,
and press inward gently, but firmly for a count of fifteen.

Step 6
Press the right thumb and forefinger
on either side of the bridge of the nose.
Press once, release, twice, release, thrice, release.
And you will find your being begins
to release the toxicity of the allergic reaction.

484 For the child who has difficulty running
because of lack of balance,
this will help the balance of the child.
Not only will it help the child, it will help the adult

who has balance problems, even unto the elderly.

Step 1
Instruct the child to place upon their knees
the palms of their hands while they are sitting

Step 2
Seven times in a clockwise manner rub the front of the knee.

Step 3
While still sitting, have them lift their heels up slightly,
placing four fingers
in the middle of the back of each knee
or as close as they can to the middle and
press inward seven times gently.
If for some reason the being is unable to do this alone,
you may do it for them.

Step 4
Seven times in a clockwise manner rub the front of the knee.

485 For those beings who have afflictions called arthritis,
this is of a general assistance to calming the arthritic.
You will feel, Souls of earth, pain receding, easing,
especially down the spinal area,
and most particularly in the neck,
and to a lesser extent the rest of the body.

Step 1
Place your hands palms up, intertwine your fingers,
leaving the thumbs apart.

Step 2
Place intertwined fingers, palms up,
in front of, and yet touching the heart area.
Your head down.
Your eyes are closed.

Step 3
Hold this position, relaxing for no less than two minutes
and no more than five.

Step 4
Slowly move the hands away from the heart area, still entwined,
bring them to rest upon a surface
and slowly remove the intertwining fingers.

Step 5
Slowly, gently lift the head and when the head is straight again,
deep breath, release and you have completed.

EMOTIONS

486 We give unto you a technique
for beings lost in a frenzy of anger,
who are enraged in their being
and choose to attempt to calm the rage.
What we give to you, Soul, is the ability to think above the rage
and then, choose your course of action.

Step 1
Place each thumb and forefinger together,
left to left, right to right
fingers apart, palms facing each other.

Step 2
Maintaining the thumbs and forefingers together,
touch lightly and quickly the thumbs
and the forefingers of each hand, right to left, left to right
and move them apart.
Do this back and forth, rhythmically; one and two, one and two
and one and two until you feel your being calming
and able to combat the rage, to enter in to clarity of rage.

487 Souls of earth,
we would ask that in that moment of anger,
before the uttering of the harsh word:

Step 1
Press together your thumbs and forefingers,

right to right and left to left.
Press, Soul, once, twice, thrice.
The other fingers are splayed apart.

Step 2
Breath in, hold for the count of three and release the breath.

Step 3
Release your thumb and forefinger.
For you have made your choice, Soul, not in mindlessness
but in mindfulness.

488 For the child who has night terrors:

Step 1
Thrice during the day, in the morning,
in the early evening and at the bedtime,
place the flat of your hand
against the forehead of the child,
and gently hold it there while explaining to the child
that this will help block the night terrors.

Step 2
For the first two times of the day,
hold the flat of your hand on the forehead
for at least seven seconds
In the evening, Soul, hold it there for fourteen seconds.
Do this in a calm manner and the child will have a restful sleep.

The Mudras are arranged sequentially: Mind, Head, Upper Torso, Lower Torso, Full Body, and Emotions.

MASTER TWAG

489 Souls of earth, we would have you often
place your hands in the position of receiving;
palms open, upright, thumbs held loosely out,
slightly cup the hands.
The hands may rest upon a surface or be above a surface.
And then we would have you, as far as you are able,
straighten the spine and bring the chin up,
open your mouth and open the third eye
and allow the Energy of your high self
to enter in to your being,
to lift your being,
to lift the Soul of self momentarily from the earth,
to allow your being to float
in a dimension of no time and space,
to experience weightlessness without being in a spaceship.
Receive Color and Sound[66] and vibration
from your high Holy self.
Do this in periods of great consternation.
Do this in times of great peril to your health, to your well being.
Do this in times of danger, what you perceive as danger.
Often, Soul, do this as you meditate in preparation
to a deeper more satisfying meditation.
Do this as often as you will.
It need not take hours or even minutes.
It takes only moments to enter in to the state of weightlessness,
of no time or space dimension.
Allow your being to experience the Angel self.
No Soul is incapable of this experience.

490 We would have you understand, Souls of earth,
for those engaged in the assistance of trauma victims
it is highly efficacious to place deep navy blue
around the victim.

The body will sense the emanation of this color.
The body, the cells, the nerves will react to this color.
It will slow down the processes of the body.
It will give you, the medicals, those extra few seconds
that you require in order to attend to the patient.
This color is not only for victims of physical trauma,
but it will also assist those beings
who are having an emotional trauma.
Understand, Souls of earth, every color,
whether from the earth or Farside has a vibration,
and your body reacts to this vibration.
The earth colors, in comparison,
to the colors of the Prism, are minute in their vibrations,
and yet they do vibrate and are of ~~great~~ assistance.
All beings are attuned to the vibration of color,
this we would have you understand,
well beyond that which your science has discovered.
Know the effect it has
upon the human body and the human mind.
Use this color wisely.
Do not restrain the use.
It will assist and is available to all.

MIND

491 We would add to the body of knowledge on meridians.
Mankind has yet to fully explore meridians and their effects
upon the body, the mind.
Meridians are not statically confined to your earth body.
They have within them, small Energy charges.
These Energy lines indeed run throughout your being.
When your Energy lines are blocked,
the Energy will not flow forth in a state as a flow,
but will be a trickle.
Understand, to be at its most efficacious,
your body must sing clearly, the meridians must be clear.
We require that you understand
that illness is not always a blockage of meridian,
for if it is part of the walk of the being,

the being is still upon a path of positive.
It is being in the positive state of being
that is most efficacious in the clearing of the meridians.
And so we give unto you steps to cleansing
and clearing of the meridians.

Step 1
Place thumb and the first two fingers together,
the other fingers rest against the palm.

Step 2
Move the hands up above the top of your skull,
at least four to six inches.
and hold for ten seconds.

Step 3
Focus upon the Energy coming from this position unto the top of your head.

Step 4
Bring your hands in their position,
down to the very middle of the top of your head,
hold for five seconds and focus on the Energy.

Step 5
While maintaining the position of the fingers of each hand,
move the hands to above the top of the ears
and press inward gently and hold for ten seconds.

Step 6
Maintaining the position of the fingers, move downward,
just below the chin.
For five seconds press the jaw line,
on either side of the center of the chin.

Step 7
Maintaining the position of the fingers,
bring the hands together just above the clavicle,
hold for ten seconds.

Step 8
Maintaining the position of the hands and fingers,
move down to just below the breast bone;
gently indent, hold for five seconds.

Step 9
Move down to the belly button area,
press slightly inward for ten seconds.

Step 10
Move your hands apart, maintaining the fingers position,
place them upon the top of each knee,
hold for five seconds.

Step 11
Maintaining the fingers position,
place hands on either side of the waist,
indent gently, hold for ten seconds.

Step 12
Maintaining the finger position,
come back up to the top of the shoulders
and hold, gently pressing for five seconds.

Step 13
Finish by bringing forward, maintaining the fingers position,
holding hands together, press gently upon the third eye,
hold for fifteen seconds.

Step 14
Take a deep breath in through the nostrils,
allow it to leave gently out through the mouth.

Step 15
Move your hands apart, bring then downward,
release the hands and fingers, and you have completed.

492 To increase your receptiveness to who you are,
do this as often as you wish,
and you will see an increase in your ability.

It is receptiveness to the sacred self of who you are, the triad.

Step 1
On each hand, the forefinger and the finger next to it
are held upright,
the thumb is held against the other two fingers

Step 2
Place above the earlobe at the level of your eyes,
the two upright fingers.
Hold them approximately one inch apart.

Step 3
Three time press inward gently on the skull,
while maintaining contact with the skull.

Step 4
The third time, hold for the count of three,
maintaining contact with the skull, bring your hands
upward to the center of the top of the head.

Step 5
Intertwining only the forefingers and the finger next to them,
press firmly down once, twice, thrice.

Step 6
The third time, hold for the count of three,
then slowly release and move your hands down,
and uncouple the thumb and fingers.

493 We bring unto you a short technique
to focus your attention before entering in to a meditation.

Step 1
Light a candle, place it in front of you;
not close enough to feel the warmth but in front of you.

Step 2
Place your hands in a cupped position facing you.

The thumb separate, not touching.
The nail beds of the left hand touching
the nail beds of the right hand.
Hold that position either on a surface or above a surface.

Step 3
Look at the flame for two seconds.
Blink your eyes.
Look for two seconds.
Blink your eyes.
Look for two seconds.
Blink your eyes and then
squeeze your eyes shut tightly, hold for a count of five.

Step5
Breathe in deeply through the nostrils.
Hold for the count of three, exhale in short, controlled breaths
for the count of seven: wh wh wh wh wh wh wh.

Step 6
Open your eyes, move your fingers apart
and then enter in to your meditation,
relaxed, calm and focused.

494 To receive an answer to a question:

Step 1
Place together the pads of the forefingers,
right to left, left to right.
Put together the pads of the thumbs, right to left, left to right
and hold in front of the throat chakra,
not touching, merely in front of.

Step 2
The other fingers will not be splayed apart,
they will be held together within the palm.

Step 3
Hold this position for five seconds.
While holding that position,

concentrate on the breath entering in and out.

Step 4
Once you have attained complete focus for five earth seconds,
you may pull apart the thumbs and the forefingers
and open hands palm up, and receive an answer
to the question you posed before you began the exercise.
You will understand that it will take much practice
to attain the five seconds of focus of clarity,
but persist, and it is not unreachable
by any being of any level.

495 In this exercise know that you have built compassion,
know that you have increased the health of your heart.

Step 1
Place the pads of the forefingers together,
the pads of the thumbs together,
the rest of the fingers against the palm.
The shape will be as a diamond.

Step 2
Place the shape in front of the heart chakra.
Hold it there, while placing your head in a downward position,
so that you are looking through
the center of the diamond.

Step 3
Focusing through the center of the diamond,
close your eyes, and allow the vision to enter in,
the vision of the color of the compassionate heart.
Hold the position for as long as you are able,
enter in, Soul, to the compassionate heart.

Step 4
When the color begins to fade,
move the fingers and the thumb apart,
place the hands palm up and over the heart area,
the right above the left.

Step 5
Hug thy being for a moment,
and know that you have built compassion,
know that you have increased the health of your heart.

Step 6
Hold the position of the hands, palm on the heart area,
for at least seven seconds, or longer if you choose.

496 For a relaxed, joyful frame of mind,
you may do this as often as you wish.
It is important that your hands are held in the air as you do this.
It is the action of these particular meridians of the knuckle
that affect the cells of your being
and stimulate the joy of the mind.

Step 1
Placing of the knuckles of the forefingers of both hands together
and pushing them against each other gently, but firmly.

Step 2
Place the sides of the thumbs against the nails of the forefingers,
the other fingers close against the palm,
as much as you are able.

Step 3
As you do this, Soul, the head is in a forty-five degree angle,
slightly bent toward the hands.

Step 4
Continue until your being is in a relaxed state:
Back and forth press together the knuckles of the forefingers.
When you move them apart each time, move them apart
a minimum of six inches.

497 At any time, Soul, to stimulate the mind,
that sluggish mind:

Step 1
Place the thumb against the pads
of the last two fingers on each hand.

Step 2
Take the forefinger and the one next to it from each hand
and place it in the center of the top of the head,
so that these fingers are intertwined.

Step 3
Press lightly up and down five times.

Step 4
At the end of the five times, staying entwined,
move the fingers forward along the scalp
until you come to the third eye.

Step 5
Move your fingers apart across your forehead at the eye,
then gently down the side of your face,
meeting at the chin.
Press the fingers together and then move them apart,
hands palm up.

498 For the lethargic being,
you may do this as often as you wish.
We would not suggest it be done for the very young,
but Souls of earth twelve years and older is acceptable.[67]

Step 1
Place together pads of thumbs and forefingers,
right to right, left to left.
The other fingers are to be spread apart.

Step 2
Hold your arms near the rib area of your being.

Step 3
Five times, move your right and left leg

from the knee downward.
Move it forward and back
as fast as you are able, back and forth
once, twice, thrice, four, five.

Step 4
Five times, place your feet touching each other,
and then move them apart, from side to side quickly.

Step 5
Deep breath, expel forcefully: haaah!
Fingers and thumbs open, palms up
and you have now invigorated your being.

499 We would suggest the following for those mornings
when you must needs drag yourself from your bed,
and feel a lack of energy, feeling either depressed
or on the verge of depression,
for you feel as if you have a great weight.

Step 1
Press the thumb pads upon the pads of the forefingers,
right to right, left to left.

Step 2
Press together the pads of the other fingers,
right to right, left to left.
The hands are pointing outward away from the body.

Step 3
Maintaining the position of the hands,
touch the nails of the forefingers together.
You will notice that you have formed a pyramid, circles,
and a downward vortex.

Step 4
Bring the hands in this position in front of the third eye,
and hold for a count of three.
The fingers will be pointing out away from the body

except for the thumb and forefinger,
which are held together at the nail beds.

Step 5
Now, move your hands so that the fingers are pointing upward
and hold for a count of three.

Step 6
Gently move apart your fingers
and bring them down on either side of the head..
You will notice as you bring them down
you will feel a pressure, a warmth, a tingling.

Step 7
Place your right palm against your chest,
your left hand arm over the right, hugging yourself
and hold for a count of three.
You will find yourself smiling and lightened in being.

500 This will alleviate distress of the mind for the being
caught in the throes of depression, of anger, of fear.
The mind will pause and you will have the opportunity
to choose to continue in or to leave that state of being.

Step 1
Right hand palm up.
Press firmly with the left forefinger into the center right palm.
When you feel the tips of your fingers tingling,
you will know that you have the correct position,
you will know that you have the correct meridian point.

Step 2
Continue to press upon that position,
even after you feel the tingling,
until you are able to breathe normally
and not the shallow breathing of fear or emotional upset.
Your body will tell you, Soul,
for it will want to take a very deep breath.

Step 3
When you have taken that deep breath, whoosh it out,
and release.

501 We have an exercise for Souls
in the throes of depression so deeply
they can not bring themselves to seek help.
You may do this exercise every fifteen minutes,
until you begin to see the Light of your being,
feel lighter in spirit,
and feel as if there is hope and possibility.

Step 1
Place your right palm flat upon your left shoulder,
fingers together,
thumb touching the side of the forefinger.

Step 2
Crook your left elbow,
place it against the side of your being
and place your left palm upward,
the fingers held together,

the thumb resting against the side of the forefinger.

Step 3
Press into your left side gently with the side of the left elbow,
and at the same time press inward with your right hand
upon the left shoulder.
Maintain this position for a period of thirty seconds.

Step 4
Holding your left hand, palm up,
slowly move your left elbow away from the side,
and take a deep breath through your nostrils,
holding it for the count of three and releasing.

Step 5
Take another deep breath and release, while slowly removing

your right hand from your left shoulder,
bringing it out and away, turning it over, palm up.

Step 6
One more deep breath, release.

Step 7
Place your hands, palms over,
breathe deeply once more and release.

502 Souls of earth, often you will see beings who nibble
at their bottom lip, generally out of nervousness,
anxiety, fear.
We would have you understand that this exercise,
done in the prescribed manner, is helpful,
will give you focus, will assist to calm fears and anxieties,
and bring a measure of clarity.

Step 1
Thumb and the forefinger of both hands touching each other,
right to right, left to left.

Step 2
Pull in the left side of the mouth by,
placing either the gum or the teeth
over the left side of the mouth,
hold for a count of three seconds.

Step 2
Proceed to do the same with the right side of the mouth
and hold for three seconds.

Step 3
Using one thumb and forefinger, lightly pull out the upper lip
and allow it to snap back on its own.

503 This exercise will relax any being
who finds themself in a stressful situation.
It will calm the heart, calm the pulse,

and it will assist in bringing the blood pressure down.
This is only to be used in stressful situations.
Remember to bring the head up slowly,
for if you do it quickly, Soul,
you will experience dizziness.

Step 1
Bend your head as far as you are able
so that the chin touches on or near the breast bone.

Step 2
Hands, palms up and resting on a surface.

Step 3
Press together pad to pad, the two middle fingers of each hand.

Step 4
Maintaining the position of the fingers touching
and while keeping your head down,
three times, gently move your hands up to the chest
and back down to the surface.

Step 5
Move your fingers apart as you slowly move your head upright.
You will feel a pulling near the upper brow and the eye area
and you have completed.

504 This exercise is efficacious for those beings
who are in a highly agitated state,
whether it is Alzheimer or a mental impairment.
We would have you understand this exercise is comforting
to the smallest of children,
unto the very aged of beings.
You may do the exercise with the person.

Step 1
Place the palms in an upright position

Step 2
Turn them over,

bringing together your forefingers and your thumbs,
right to right, left to left.
The other fingers are to be left wide open.

Step 3
Hold this position over the solar plexus for five seconds.

Step 4
Bring your palms in an upright position
then in a sweeping motion turn your hands palm over,
placing them upon the tops of your knees.

Step 5
With the head slightly bent,
hold the palms on the knees for twelve seconds.
You will feel the Energy run up and down each arm
and the warmth flow into the legs.

Step 6
You may hold it for longer than twelve seconds,

for it is very comforting to Souls
who are in a dolorous state of mind.
When you have finished simply move your hands palm up.

505 Cleansing the connections between the will and the eye.
This exercise even though of short duration,
will have long term effects.
It may be done as often as you desire,
during each of your waking hours.
You will find a flushing of the interior of your body.
You will feel a sensation of warmth arising
from the solar plexus up onto the third eye.
This will take practice, but it will occur.
What you are doing is cleansing the connections
between the will and the eye,
which is necessary for healing;
which is necessary to discipline the inners of your being,
to enhance your immune system.

Step 1
Fold your fingers in, touching the palm as much as you are able.
Head bowed downward, eyes closed.

Step 2
Place the pad of the right thumb over the left thumb nail.

Step 3
Twelve times slowly move the right thumb
in a circular pattern over the left thumbnail.

Step 4
Maintaining the position of the thumbs,
move your hands to the vicinity of the solar plexus
and press gently but firmly the right pad of the thumb
onto the left thumbnail and hold for five seconds.

Step 5
Move your thumbs apart, open your fingers,
and place your hands palms up.

506 This exercise is to cleanse the eye,
to enhance the clarity of the eye,
and to assist in the removing of any veils of negativity
that prohibit or impede the use of the eye
to heal, to see, to hear.

Step 1
Souls of earth, we would have you place together
the pads of your left fingers
against the pads of the right fingers
the pads of the left thumb to the right thumb,
in a steeple formation,
but the palms of your hands are not to be touching.

Step 2
Maintaining the position of the hands,
move them up to the third eye.
The thumbs will be pointed toward the eye,
not touching, merely before.

Step 3
We do not suggest that you hold your head upright;
the head is held at a forty-five degree angle.

Step 4
Hold the position of the hands and the head for ten seconds.

Step 5
Move the two little fingers apart while holding the others in place
for another three seconds.

Step 6
And then slowly, for you may experience some dizziness,
move your hands apart, place palms up,
and you have completed.

507 This activity will stimulate the third eye.
It will enhance your will to remove the veils.
You may do this exercise as often as you wish.

Step 1
Place your hands palm up and bring them up to heart level.

Step 2
Turn them over and bring together, the thumb pads touching,
the forefinger pads touching.
The other fingers are left wide apart, as are the palms.

Step 3
Bring this diamond shape you have created
in front of the third eye and hold for five seconds.

Step 4
Maintaining the shape, slowly move your hands toward the eye
and place against the third eye the thumbs.
Hold for five seconds.

Step 5
Move your hands apart, palms up, and you have completed.

508 We bring unto you an exercise to enhance
the capability of the third eye.
This exercise is to be done as often as you wish
during a three day period.

Step 1
Palm facing palm, fingers splayed out,
bring your hands upward toward your face,
one on either side of the earth eyes.

Step 2
Gently and slowly bring your hands toward the flesh
until you touch the area on either side of your earth eyes.
The forefingers will be gently held against the temple
and the thumbs will rest on the bone
beneath the eye socket.

Step 3
Hold your hands in that position for the count of seven.
Then deep breath in, holding for a count of three
and gently releasing the breath to the count of four.

Step 4
Move the fingers inward toward the palm,
if possible touching the palm,
while maintaining the position of the thumbs
and the forefingers.

Step 5
Slowly move the forefingers until they gently touch the third eye.
Your thumbs and remaining fingers will not change position.
Hold this position for the count of seven.

Step 6
Deep breath, hold for a count of three, gently release the breath.

Step 7
Move your forefingers away from the third eye,
while maintaining contact with the forehead,

and slide them back into their original position
at the temples.

Step 8
Move your thumbs gently, slowly away.
As the thumbs are moving away from the cheekbones,
move your fingers away from the palms of your hands,
move your forefingers away from the temples.

Step 9
Bring the hands down until they have reached
the area of your solar plexus.

Step 10
Place the hands in the prayer position,
deep breath, hold for count of three
and release forcefully. Haaah!

Step 11
Move your hands apart, palms up.
You will feel the vibration of the third eye at the point
where you have placed your palms upward.
You will continue to practice until you have reached that stage.

509 For the mother, for the father
who needs a moment's respite
from the children, we would suggest the following.

Step 1
Place the pads of both thumbs, on either side of the upper jaw.
The forefingers will rest on either side of the third eye,
The other fingers are pressed together in a prayer position,
but your palms are not together.

Step 2
Gently massage the area just above the upper gum
in the center of your cheek.
Only the thumbs are to be massaging.

Step 3
Three times through the mouth, a deep breath,
and release forcefully again and again and again.

Step 4
Remove the fingers and then the thumbs,
and you will be able to cope once again.

HEAD

510 This exercise done ten times on each hand
will stimulate the upper portion of the brain.
You will feel around the upper portion of your forehead
a slight pressure.
This tells you that you are correctly performing this exercise.
This is most effective for those who find themselves

tired and the mind slowing down
when they need to be quickly refreshed
with a finely focused mind.

Step 1
Fully spread the fingers and the thumbs of your left hand.

Step 2
Place the pad of the right forefinger
against the underside of the left thumb,
in the vicinity of the knuckle and nail bed.
Ten times, gently move the thumb up and down
without moving the rest of the hand.

Step 3
Ten times do the same gently with the opposite hand,
the left forefinger on the thumb of the right hand.

Step 4
Place hands together in the prayer position,
hold for a count of three.
Deep breath.
Release the breath and feel revitalized in the mind.

511 For that which is described as a splitting headache,
for you feel as if your head is going to be split open.

Step 1
Place your thumbs in your palms,
the forefingers are placed in the middle of each earlobe.

Step 2
Place the other fingers of each hand, above the earlobe,
with the small fingers at the temples.
You will know that you have the right placement
because you will feel immediately
a slight pressure upon your head.

Step 3
With all four fingers, press firmly inward,
hold for a count of three,
and then move them slightly away,
still touching the flesh but very lightly, feather light,
and hold for a count of three.

Step 4
Again with all four fingers, press firmly inward,
hold for a count of three.
And then move them slightly away,
still touching the flesh but very lightly, feather light
and hold for a count of three.

Step 5
Once more with all four fingers, press firmly inward,
hold for a count of three.
And then move them slightly away,
still touching the flesh but very lightly, feather light
and hold for a count of three.

Step 6
Moving your thumb out behind the earlobes,
cup your ears with the palms,
deep breath through the nostrils,
hold for the count of three

and release in a controlled manner
through the mouth to the count of three: wh wh wh.
And you will realize the pain has eased.

512 This, Soul, will alleviate headache or upper neck pain.
If you are prone to migraines,
we would suggest you do this exercise
upon arising each day, but before you leave your bed,
while you are still in the prone position.
If you are not prone to migraines,
you need not lay down to do this exercise.

Step 1
Palms up, hold your fingers straight
except for the finger next to the forefinger on each hand,
bend it in and place the thumbs
over the nail bed of that finger.

Step 2
Press firmly, both thumbs, upon the nail beds.
Keep pressing until you feel the pain begin to ease.

Step 3
Deep breath, release and continue pressing
until you have total relief.
When you have relieved the pain,
slowly move your fingers and thumbs apart.

513 This will assist in calming the allergic reaction of the eyes,
the itching, watery eyes.
This may also be used if you have a wind damage to the eyes.
It stimulates the production of cleansing tearing.

Step 1
Close the eyes.
Place upon each eyebrow four fingers,
thumbs held out to the side.

Step 2
Five times move the eyebrows up and down.

You will begin to feel at the back of your head a tingling.
And you will know that you have correctly
helped to clear the eyes.

Step 3
Move your hands away after the tingling at the back of the head,
open your eyes and feel relief.
You will experience tearing at the sides of the eyes
and this is stimulated by the exercise.

514 To stimulate the vision of your earth eyes,
this exercise should be done no more than thrice daily.

Step 1
Place your palms directly in front of your earth eyes.
Press lightly the finger pads of the fingers
next to the little finger, left to right.

Step 2
Place your palm with those fingers touching,
at the level of the third eye,
so that the center of your palms
are now directly in front of your earth eyes.
Hold for twelve seconds.

Step 3[68]
Move your hands, with pads touching,
in a clockwise circle, once, twice, thrice, slowly.

Step 4
Move your fingers apart, and you have completed the exercise.

515 To enhance the vision of your earth eyes:

Step 1
Place the pads of the thumbs against the pads
of the last two fingers;
the right thumb against the last two fingers

of the right hand,
the left thumb against the left two fingers of the left hand.

Step 2
Take the first two fingers, spread them slightly apart,
and place their pads gently
on the closed eyelids in the middle of each eye.

Step 3
Press lightly inward and hold for a count of three

Step 4
Move the second fingers to pinch the nose gently
on either side at the bridge.

Step 5
Press inward on the nose,
press inward on the middle of the eye
at the same time for the count of five.

Step 6
Move the fingers back to the middle of the eyes,
and then move it away.
Open your palms.

516 For sinus and sinus headache,
you will begin to feel a draining of the nostrils
almost immediately in many cases.
Otherwise continue until that draining
and release has occurred.

Step 1
Place thumb and forefingers together, right to right, left to left.
Place fingers close together, touching each other.

Step 2
Move the hands up until at the bridge of the nose.

Step 3
Take the fingers next to the forefinger

and alternately press unto the bridge of the nose,
lightly, quickly and gently, but firmly,
one and two, one and two, one and two, and one.

Step 4
Press once more on the bridge of the nose for a count of five,
and while pressing lightly,
breathe upward in through the nostril
as well as you are able, short bursts of breath.

Step 5
Release the bridge, but keep the position of the hands.

Step 6
Bring it down to the nostrils.
Press against the nostrils, once, twice, thrice, quickly.

Step 7
Sliding along the face with your fingers,
bring your hands downward until you reach the chin area,
release and you have completed.

517 This will help to clear your sinuses and
assist in the process of healing a sinus infection.
You will do this exercise three times.
Quick movements will cause a distortion
of the balance of the body.
Focus on the slow movements.
Use the vortex you have created to heal.
This will also assist in the alleviation of a mild headache.

Step 1
Hands are placed upon a surface, palms down, fingers together,
thumbs apart and not touching.

Step 2
Bend your head forward as far as you are able,
hold that position for three seconds.

Step 3
At the end of the three seconds,
slowly move your head back into an upright position.
If you are dizzy, stop, hold it and then proceed to finish,
bringing your head back upward.

Step 4
Three times, breathe deeply in through the nostrils,
and as you exhale through the nostrils, hum.
Hummmmmmmmm.

518 To assist in the healing of sinus, you may do this thrice a day until you have relief from pain of the sinus.
Know that it will stimulate this healing.

Step 1
Place your forefinger upon the very tip of your nose.
Your thumb will be held against the finger next to the forefinger.
The other two fingers, as much as you are able,
will also held against the thumb.
You may use either hand.

Step 2
Three times with the forefinger
push the flesh up slightly, gently, then pull down.

Step 3
Move your finger away from the nose,
pause for the count of three.

Step 4
Return the forefinger to the tip of the nose and three times,
push the flesh up slightly, gently, then pull down.

Step 5
Move your finger away from the nose,
pause for the count of three.

Step 6
Return the forefinger to the tip of the nose and once more,

three times, push the flesh up slightly, gently,
then pull down.

519 For those beings who have difficulty with earaches,
for no known reason or who are prone to ear infections,
we would suggest the following,
before the infection takes hold.

Step 1
Place your hands, palm toward the ears,
but not touching the ears,
so that your elbows are now upright and facing forward.

Step 2
Twice, move your hands apart, away from the ears,
then back again close to the ear but not touching.
And do this very slowly.

Step 3
Once more, slowly move your hands apart, away from the ears,
then back again close to the ear but not touching,

Step 4
Hold close to the ears for seven seconds.
Deep breath, exhale.
And as you exhale, hum. Hummmmmmm.
You will feel the resonation within the ears
to stimulate the healing.

Step 5
And when you have finished the hum,
simply move your hands palm up and away.

520 For the earache caused by infection
in the inner part of the ear:

Step 1
Place the left fingers in front of the right fingers, touching

so that you have cupped both hands toward your body.

Step 2
Place the right thumb over the left thumbnail.

Step 3
Move the hands in their position to the third eye,
resting your thumbs on the third eye.
Hold for seven seconds.

Step 4
Deep breath, release.

Step 5
Move your palms apart, place them over both ears.
Cup the ear and hold for seven seconds.
Remove the palms from your ears.

Step 6
Bring your hands back into the beginning position
and continue to do each Step slowly until you feel relief.

521 For those beings who have earaches
and have difficulty breaking the cycle of earaches.
This exercise may be repeated up to five times in the day.

Step 1
Place your forefinger in the midst of your chin,
in the center of the lower jawbone.
The thumb held against, as much as you are able,
the other fingers.
You may use either hand.

Step 2
Three times press the midst of the chin with the forefinger.

Step 3
On the third press hold for the count of three,
and then slightly move your hand away,
holding for another count of three.

Step 4
Three times repeat Steps 2 and 3.

Step 5
On the final press of the chin, hold for the count of five.
And you will begin to feel upon either ear a vibration, a warmth
and you will know that you have begun
to stimulate the healing.

522 For those who are not at the stage of total deafness,
you may assist to increase your hearing capability.

Step 1
Place the pads of your forefingers in the center
of the outer edges of your ears.
Your other fingers will be held close together,
your thumbs resting on the fingers.

Step 2
Gently push the outer edges inward
and hold that position for five seconds.

Step 3
Slowly open the ears and then again press inward five seconds.

Step 4
Slowly open the ears and then again press inward five seconds.

Step 5
Move your forefingers away, open your hands, palms up.

523 This will enhance and stimulate the immune system.

Step 1
Head and your spine are upright, as much as you are able.

Step 2
Place your hands palm up, thumbs out,

fingers spread wide in the mode of reception.

Step 3
Bring them together slowly and entwine the fingers,
thumbs to remain apart.

Step 4
Bring the hands unto the mouth area.
The hands are facing toward the mouth but not touching,
and hold that position for five seconds.

Step 5
At the end of the five seconds,
deep breath and then slowly release the fingers,
hands palm up to finish.

524 To alleviate for the teething child,
it will soothe, it will comfort.
If the pain is on the right, you will do beneath the right nostril.
If the pain is on the left, you will do beneath the left nostril.
And should the child have pain on both sides,
then you will do first one and then the other.

Step 1
Place your forefinger beneath the nostril.
The pad of your thumb will be held
against the pads of the other fingers.

Step 2
Three times press gently into the flesh under the nostril,
pushing the flesh up slightly, then down.

Step 3
Move your finger away, hold for the count of three.

Step 4
Three times press gently into the flesh under the nostril,
pushing the flesh up slightly, then down.

Step 5
Move your finger away, hold for the count of three.

Step 6
Three times press gently into the flesh under the nostril,
pushing the flesh up slightly, then down.

525 For difficulty with infections,
impactions of the mouth area,
whether it be gums or teeth.
You will find in many cases immediate relief
and in other cases the pain will gradually decrease
as healing will begin in the bacteria.

Step 1
Press the thumb and the finger next to the forefinger
together on both hands, left to left and right to right.
Last two fingers are spread out

Step 2
Move the forefingers upward unto the sides of your lips.

Step 3
On either side of your lip,
press the forefingers lightly three times,
enough so that your lips become pursed.

Step 4
Move your hands apart for a count of six.

Step 5
Again, on either side of your lip, press lightly three times,
enough so that your lips become pursed.

Step 6
Move your hands apart for a count of six.

Step 7
Again, on either side of your lip, press lightly three times,
enough so that your lips become pursed.

Step 8
Move your hands apart for a count of nine.

Step 9
Maintaining position on either side of the mouth,
move the forefingers downward,
sliding down the flesh until
the forefingers meet at the bottom of the throat.

Step 10
Press inward upon the clavicle bone.
Hold that inward press for a count of five.
And you will feel, Soul, the vibration within the jaw area.
And some will even feel it into the whole head area.

Step 11
Remove the pressure, unfold your fingers
and you have finished.

526 This exercise will stimulate healing in any of the area
of the nose, the throat or the mouth.
This exercise may be done no more than five times a day.

Step 1
Place the pads of the forefingers together and raise them
to the levels of the throat chakra
and then the mouth area.
The rest of the hand, the fingers will be let loose.

Step 2
Press the pads of the thumbs together
as you move the forefingers up in front of the nose.

Step 3
Maintaining the pads touching,
rest the forefingers against the nose

and bring your thumbs underneath your chin.
Fold in your other fingers against the palm of your hand.

Step 4
Repeat three times:
a deep breath inward, hold for a count of two,
and as you let the breath out,
move your vocal cords in a humming.
Hummmmm as long as you are able.

Step 5
Move your fingers apart, palms up and you have completed.

527 To ameliorate problems with the throat:
soreness, too much coughing or a strained voice.
This may be done, Souls of earth, for a child.
You will simply move the child's hands,
and gently the head of the child.

Step 1
Intertwine your fingers
unto between the first and second knuckle.
Your thumbs are up.

Step 2
Bring your hands thus in front of the heart
and hold for five seconds.
Your head, Soul, will be at a forty-five degree angle downward.

Step 3
Maintaining the position of the hands,
bring your hands slowly upward in front of the throat.
At the same time, move your head upward
from its angled position.

Step 4
Hold the hands in front of the throat for the count of five.

Step 5
Move your head slowly to the left and hold for a count of two.

Step 6
Bring it back to the center and hold for a count of two.

Step 7
Move your head slowly to the right and hold for a count of two,
and then come back into the center.

Step 8
Hold your throat upward.
Place the palms underneath the chin.
Hold for a count of three.

Step 9
Move your hands down to the heart area, release the fingers,
and you will find a soothing enter in to the throat.

528 For croup or any croup like cough,
that irritates the linings of not only the lungs
but all the bronchial area.
This may be done as often as necessary
until you breath easily without coughing.

Step 1
Intertwine your fingers together, making as a cross,
placing the pads of the thumbs together,
so that you have formed a diamond shape.
Either the right or left hand may be upright, the other crossing it.

Step 2
Bring that shape upward to the heart chakra
and hold for a count of five,
and then deep breath, release.

Step 3
Move your hands upward to between
your heart chakra and your throat chakra,
so that the diamond is angled toward the chest area.
Hold that position for a count of three.

Step 4
Maintaining the position of the hands,
three times take a deep breath as well as you are able
and whoosh it out.
You will feel a warmth spreading throughout
your chest area, healing.

Step 5
Move your hands away, bring them down and move them apart.

529 This will prevent the onslaught of various illness
to do with the ears, eyes, nose and throat.

Step 1
Place your hands in a fist mode,
with the thumb over the forefinger.

Step 2
Place the right hand over the left, but not touching.

Step 3
Three times move the right off to the side a few inches,
and then back over the left.[69]

Step 5
Reverse, place the left over the right,
move away and back, away and back, and then away.

Step 6
Place hands palm up and you have completed.

UPPER TORSO

530 This exercise will relieve neck tension
that has accumulated over time.
This is for those beings who have difficulty
moving their neck to one side or the other.
It will, Soul, relieve the headache that

comes from that kind of neck tension and stress.
This exercise may be done as often as you wish,
but understand it must be done slowly.

Step 1
Palms up.
Then place your fingertips against the back of the skull.
Your thumbs held out and away from the skull.

Step 2
Slowly turn your head to the left,
moving the whole torso from the waist up
as far as you can without straining
and slowly return back to the center position.

Step 3
Slowly turn your head to the right,
moving the whole torso from the waist up
as far as you can without straining
and slowly return back to the center position.

Step 4
Bring your head downward as far as you are able without pain
and hold in that position for a period of seven seconds.
Keep the fingertips against the skull.

Step 5
Bring your head back upright slowly.

Step 6
Twice, while pressing lightly. move your fingertips
slightly up from the skull and then down onto the skull.

Step 7
Cup the hands in front of your ears
as if you were using your hands as ear muffs.
Only the fingertips against the skull, thumbs held away.

Step 8
Three times, slowly move your hands away and then back again,

each time apply a light pressure on the ears.

Step 9
Hold your fingertips on either side of the spinal column
at the back of the neck,
and three times slowly press lightly but firmly.

Step 10
Place your hands, palm up in front of the throat
so that the sides of your hands are touching.
Hold for the count of three.

Step 11
Move your hands upward unto the third eye.
Some will feel a pressure, some will feel tingling,
some will only feel a warmth.
Hold this position until the feeling has ebbed.
And then slowly
move your hands apart and turn them over and down.

531 For those beings who have a stiff neck
and all other remedies have failed.
You will notice each time you do this exercise
the stiffness has decreased.
We ask that you have at least a respite of one half hour
before again repeating the five Steps of this exercise.

Step 1
Place together the pads of your thumbs and forefingers.
Your other fingers may be held loosely.
The palms of the hands are not touching.

Step 2
Move the shape created by the hands
in front of the throat chakra.

Step 3
Move your head slowly to the left as far as you are able,
and hold for three seconds.

Slowly bring it back into the center.

Step 4
Move your head to the right as far as you are able,
and hold for three seconds.
Slowly bring it back to center.

Step 5
Unhook your fingers and thumb.
Place the hands palm up and you have finished.

532 We give unto you an exercise for the stiffness of the neck
that leads to shoulder pain, that radiates outward.
All movement is done very slowly.
You will know that you have done it slowly enough
when you feel the stretch in the spine,
the neck and the shoulders.

Step 1
Sit upright, placing your hands flat upon a surface.
Head as straight as possible, upright.

Step 2
While maintaining your shoulders
in a relaxed though straight position,
in extremely slow motion bring your head down
until your chin rests upon your chest
or as close as possible.
Hold for the count of twelve.

Step 3
Move your head, still down, to the left as far as you are able
without discomfort of the neck.
Hold for the count of three.

Step 4
Bring the head back in the center, hold for the count of three.

Step 5
Move your head, still down, to the right as far as you are able

without discomfort of the neck.
Hold for the count of three.

Step 6
Bring your head back into the center.

Step 7
Slowly bring your head upright.
If you become dizzy, pause, allow the dizziness to pass,
and then continue until you are upright.

Step 8
When you are again upright, shake your shoulders
and the torso thrice,
and you will realize the tension has left the body.

533 This will alleviate the bursitis,
the shoulder pain caused by arthritis.

Step 1
While resting your palms upon a surface.
place together the pads of the thumbs and the forefingers.
The other fingers remain resting on the surface.

Step 2
Lift the hands up and bring them together,
the thumb and the forefingers of each are touching.

Step 3
Move the hands in toward the top of the chest,
while at the same time,
bringing together the pads of the fingers,
left to right, right to left.
Hold that position for five seconds.

Step 4
Slowly release the fingertips,
return hands to your original position,
and repeat Steps 1, 2, 3.

Step 5
Move your hands apart, palm up,
and you have completed the exercise.

534 Those afflicted with arthritic or bursitic conditions
or rheumatoid conditions of the neck and shoulder
will find relief in this simple exercise.
You will know that you have accomplished not only
by the easing of the pain, but you will feel a tingling,
a pressure around the top of your head
this will tell you that you are indeed
in tune with your body and able to relieve.
You may do this as often as you wish during the day.
Optimally, Soul, this exercise will be done
a minimum of thrice per day,
within three days even the most severe of cases
will begin to feel some release of pain.

Step 1
Place the forefingers of each hand at the base of the throat,
resting against the collarbone on either side.

Step 2
Press once lightly upon the collarbones with the forefingers.
If you feel pain, rest gently against the bone until the pain passes,
and then again press lightly in
upon the bone with the forefingers.

Step 3
Once more press once lightly upon the collarbones
with the forefingers.
If you feel pain, rest gently against the bone until the pain passes,
and then again press lightly in
upon the bone with the forefingers.

Step 4
Move the four fingers of each hand to the top of your shoulders
and press down lightly, once, twice, thrice
with all the fingers.

Step 5
Place the fingers of each hand upon either side of the neck
at the throat and press lightly thrice.

Step 6
Place the right hand flat against the upper chest
just below the throat,
and place the left over the right.
Deep breath as well as you are able
and allow the pain to leave as you exhale, whoooooh.

535 We would continue with meridian points.
This will alleviate the pain from arthritic shoulder, arm and hand.

Step 1
Place the left arm upon a surface, hands flat,
fingers spread apart, thumbs spread apart.

Step 2
Place your right index finger on the back of the left hand,
where the palm begins,
in the center of the knuckles of the middle fingers,

Step 3
Slowly draw the forefinger up
the middle of the arm unto the elbow.

Step 4
At the elbow, cross inward on the side of the elbow.

Step 5
Repeat Steps 2, 3, and 4 thrice.
On the third time of Step 4,
hold for the count of three on the inside of the elbow.
If you have the correct spot,
you will begin to feel an alleviation of the pain,
you will begin to feel a tingling at the knuckles.

536 This will help those with shoulder injuries
or shoulder tension.
This may be done as often as you wish for relief.

Step 1
Fingers entwined, hands facing toward the body.
Fingers held close together, thumbs out.

Step 2
Press the thumbs firmly together, but not to the point of pain,
and you will feel an answering response in the shoulders
as you hold this position firmly.
Hold to the count of seven.

Step 3
Slowly release the thumbs,
then press them together, hold for the count of seven.

Step 4
Slowly release the thumbs,
then press them together,
hold until the answering response ebbs.

Step 5
Drop your shoulders,
bend your head down as far as comfortable
and slowly move your thumbs away.

Step 6
Bring your head up.
Deep breath, exhale: whoooooh.

537 To relieve the upper shoulder stress,
the pressure will be firm but not deep:

Step 1
Place the left arm upon a surface, hands flat,
fingers spread apart, thumbs spread apart.

Step 2
Place on the side of the left elbow the first two fingers
of the right hand spread apart.

Step 3
The other two fingers are held down upon the palm
with the thumb on top of the fingers.

Step 4
Six times press on the side of the elbow: once, twice, thrice.

Step 5
Move your right arm straight out,
take your first two fingers of the left hand
place on the side of the right elbow,
and proceed with Steps 2, 3, and 4.

538 For those who have shoulder pains
not connected to bursitis or arthritis,
but shoulder pains brought about by strain and stress.
During this exercise your head will be relaxed

in an upright position.
This stimulates the healing of the muscles and the tendons
within the shoulder area.

Step 1
Move the palms of your hands until the tips of your fingers
touch the shoulders.
The right will be touching right, the left will be touching left.
Hold that position for a count of five.

Step 2
Move your elbows out,
as far as you are able while still touching the shoulder.
Hold for a count of five.

Step 3
After the count of five move your arms back

into the original position and then release.
You may do this as often as you wish
and you will notice each time the pain will subside.

539 For mid to upper back pain,
this may be done thrice a day but, Soul, spaced apart.
As soon as you feel as if you want to straighten up, do so,
for that is your signal that your back pain is relieving.

Step 1
Cup your hands palm upward,
placing the head down as far as it will go.

Step 2
Bring your right hand up to the back of your neck
cupping the neck
where the indent begins at the top of the neck.

Step 3
Slowly bring the left hand also into the same area,
cupping the neck slightly below the right hand.

Step 4
Then press gently but firmly with the fingers of both hands
three times, in, out, in, out, in, out.

Step 4
Move both hands away from your neck back into
the beginning cupped position and turn them over.
Deep breath, release.

540 Doing this, Soul, thrice daily will assist in maintaining
a near normal blood pressure rate,
bringing it down to an acceptable healthy level.
Maintain this exercise thrice daily until the underlining cause
for the high blood pressure has been resolved.

Step 1
Sit in an upright position

holding your spine as straight as you are able.

Step 2
Bring the hands together in the prayer or namaste position,
holding them in front of the heart area for three seconds.

Step 3
Move the hands in the same position to underneath the chin,
resting your thumbs upon the breast bone.

Step 4
Breath deeply; but you will not take the breath in all at once.
You will, Soul, do it slowly: wh wh wh wh.
Breath in and hold for a count of three.
Breath out in a controlled method five times: wh wh wh wh wh.

Step 5
Regular deep breath, exhale strenuously: whooooo!

Step 6
Move your hands apart and you have finished.

541 To obviate the damage caused by heart attack.
You will understand it is to be done a minimum thrice daily.
You may do this as often as you wish,
for it will strengthen and enhance the healing of the heart.
The pressure points from the thumb,
the forefingers and the other fingers
all will stimulate and enhance the healing.

Step 1
In front of the heart area,
join the pads of your forefingers together.

Step 2
Place the finger next to the forefinger of the right hand
over the nail bed of the finger
next to the forefinger of the left hand.
Thumbs will be upright, not touching,
the other fingers will be bent inward.
Hold this position for a minimum of seven seconds.

Step 3

Move your hands together so that the thumb pads are touching,
and all the pads of all the fingers are touching.
Hold momentarily, and move apart, hands palm up,

Step 4

Place your palms with the fingers spread,
thumbs in the up position on either side of the area
below the throat at the collarbones.

Step 5

The fingers are to rest lightly upon the flesh,
the thumbs are to rest upon the flesh,
but the only movement will come from the forefingers.

Step 6

Pressing gently but firmly upon the bone on either side
with the forefingers.
take first the left forefinger, lift it up, and bring it down,
and then the right forefinger, lift it up and bring it down,
one and two and one and two
and one and two for fifteen seconds.

Step 7

Place the thumb and the forefinger together,
the right to right, left to left,
remove the fingers, bring your hands palm up,
and then release your thumb and forefinger.

542 To stimulate the healing for those
who have the heart difficulty.

Step 1

Move your hands, palm up,
until the hands are behind the neck area,
palms facing toward the neck.

Step 2

Bring the palms inward on either side until they touch the neck,
but not each other.

They will simply rest upon the neck,
covering the lower part of your ear, especially the lobe.

Step 3
Thrice, move up and down each finger, one at a time,
and then the same with the thumbs, up and down.

Step 4
Slowly move your hands apart from the neck, palms up,
and you have finished.

543 At the very top of where the breast bone would enter in,
you will find a depression.
This depression will often be sore.
This depression will alert you to problems with the lungs.
This exercise will stimulate healing.

Step 1
The first two fingers held apart, the others close to the palm,
and the thumb over those fingers

Step 2
Intertwine the first two fingers, place in the cleft of the breasts.

Step 3
Three times press inward lightly, once, twice, thrice,
for a total of nine.

Step 4
Deep breath as much as you are able
and hold it for the count of three and slowly release.

544 You will understand that as you move downward
approximately two inches from the top of the breastbone,
you will find that this area's soreness
is an indication of problems in the breast area,
male or female.
This exercise will stimulate even the healing of cancer.

Step 1
The first two fingers held apart, the others close to the palm,
and the thumb over those fingers

Step 2
Intertwine the first two fingers,
place two inches below the cleft of the breasts.

Step 3
Twice press inward firmly,
each press holding for the count of three:
one, two, three, release,
one, two, three, release.

Step 4
The third time, press one, two, three and hold.
Hold the light press and allow your body to relax

Step 5
When you feel your body is relaxed, repeat Steps 1 through 4
three times, slowly

Step 7
Keeping the hand positions,
move down two more inches
and press inward three times.

Step 8
Move the first two fingers apart, and without leaving your body
slide the fingers to the side of your body
and gently press inward with the two fingers three times.

Step 9
Slide the fingers to the other side of the your body.
Repeat pressing inward three times.
You will notice a soreness in the rib area.
This is an indication that you are indeed affecting
the stimulation of healing of any breast problems.

Step 9
Bring your fingers back around to the front at Step 7,

put them back into the intertwined position,
and then press once and release.

545 This is helpful to those beings that have the carpal tunnel,
that have the wrist sprain, strains.

Step 1
Place your hands palm up.
Place the tip of the left forefinger
into the center of the right palm.
In this case only the tip.

Step 2
Press firmly twice and hold for the count of five.
You will begin to feel an answering response
on the inner portion of your arm.

Step 3
The third time, press firmly and hold beyond the count of five.
Hold until the answering response ebbs and then slowly release.

Step 4
Do the same with the left hand,
using the tip of the right forefinger on the left hand,
pressing inward twice
and feeling the answering response in the inner arm,
hold for five seconds.

Step 5
The third time, press firmly and hold beyond the count of five.
Hold until the answering response ebbs and then slowly release.

546 For the strained muscles in the wrist,
that affect the area up to the elbow,
so that when you press at the pulse level of the wrist,
you feel pain.
This type of injury, of tense, strained muscles may be assisted.

Step 1
Right hand palm up, the fingers held close together,
slightly cupped, the thumb straight out

Step 2
Place the left thumb within the middle of the right palm.
The other fingers of the left hand held loosely.

Step 3
Move your thumb up and down
within the center of the palm, once, twice, thrice
and then stop, press and hold for the count of three.

Step 4
Move your thumb, up and down
within the center of the palm, once, twice, thrice
and then stop, press and hold for the count of three.

Step 5
Move your thumb, up and down
within the center of the palm, once, twice, thrice
and then stop, press and hold for the count of three.

Step 6
Place the right thumb in the left palm
and repeat the same process,
It is, Soul, for balance that you will do both.
And you will find the pain will be much relieved.

LOWER TORSO

547 We have for you a short exercise
for those who have difficulty ingesting vegetables.

Step 1
Place your palms upon a surface as you sit on a chair.

Step 2
Take your right palm and place it palm down
between the breast and the navel.

Step 3
The left palm remains face down on a surface.

Step 4
Thrice with the right palm, pressing lightly,
move the hand in and out.

Step 5
Place the right palm onto the throat,
press lightly and hold for the count of three.

Step 6
Take your right palm and place it palm down
between the breast and the navel.
With the right palm, pressing lightly, move the hand in and out.

548 We have a suggestion for the parent of a colicky babe.
You may do this as often as it is required to soothe the child,
it will also soothe the parent or the care giver
who is doing the healing upon the child.
It will relieve the frustration and the feeling of hopelessness,
for you will be empowered
by the vortex you have created.

Step 1
With a light covering upon the back of the babe,
cradle the babe in your arms.

Step 2
On the front of the babe, just above the stomach,
place your right palm downward.

Step 3
Five times move the palm slowly
in a clockwise circle and breathe:
first circle, breath in, breathe out,
begin the second circle, breath in, breathe out,
third circle, breath in, breathe out,
fourth circle, breath in, breathe out,

fifth circle, breathe in, breathe out.
You are building up a vortex.

Step 4
At the end of the fifth circle, bring your hand softly to rest
upon the stomach of the child.

Step 5
Slowly make again the five circles clockwise,
but this time directly rubbing the stomach gently.

Step 6
And then move your hand away and bestow Love.

549 We would suggest the following for those
who have ulcerative colitis or ulcers,
or stomach difficulty connected with a burning sensation.

Step 1
Your head will be slightly bent forward.
Your feet will be flat on the floor as well as you are able.

Step 2
Place your right hand fingers on top of the first knuckles
of the fingers of the left hand.
The thumbs will be held upright.

Step 3
Hold the position of the hands away from,
but in front of the stomach area for a count of five.

Step 4
Maintaining the position of the hands, four times
quickly bring your hands toward the stomach
and quickly move away from the stomach.

Step 5
Hold the position of the hands away from,
but in front of the stomach area for a count of five.

Step 6
Maintaining the position of the hands,
touch the stomach area lightly
and bring your hands down to just above the pelvic area.

Step 7
And then move them apart.
You will feel a warmth stealing within your being,
soothing the violent burning.

550 To stimulate all the digestive juices in your system.
This is especially helpful for those who have injured their innards
and whose digestion is extremely delicate
at their stage of healing.
It will also stimulate the action of the kidney
and the liver to cleanse toxins.

Step 1
Place your hands lightly upon a surface, fingers on top
and the thumbs underneath the surface.
Your head is at a forty-five degree angle
looking downward at your hands.

Step 2
Bring together the forefingers and the thumbs of each hand,
right to right, left to left
and maintain the down position of the fingers

Step 3
Three times, slowly move hands apart, no more than six inches,
and back together slowly.
Each time your hands come together,
you stimulate all the digestive juices in your system.

551 This activity has a myriad of benefits.
You will also find in this exercise much relaxation.

Step 1
Link the first two fingers and the thumb pads together,
the remaining fingers held downward.

Step 2
Move the forefingers upright
while retaining the next fingers pad to pad.
The last two fingers are held as close as possible to the palm.
The thumbs are toward the body,
so that now you have a pyramidal structure.

Step 3[70]
Place this pyramidal structure at the solar plexus.
Your forefingers will be pointing outward.
Your thumbs upward,
your other linked fingers downward.
Hold this position for at least five seconds.

Step 4
Maintaining the pyramidal position of the fingers and the thumbs,
move the hands outward away from the body
as far as you are able to extend your arms

Step 5
Move the pyramid in a clockwise circle,
from right to left, and hold for three seconds.

Step 6
Bring the pyramid back to the will, to the solar plexus,

Step 7
Slowly open your palms, palms up, and you have completed.

552 We give unto you a remedy for the seasickness,
the nausea.
This is not nausea brought on by pregnancy,
it is for that which is brought upon by movement,
by the dizziness.

Step 1
Place close together the first two fingers of each hand.
Your thumb and your other fingers are held loosely.

Step 2
Place those two fingers on either side of the bridge of the nose
so that one is pressing just where the brow starts,
and the other is pressing just below the bridge of the nose.
The two fingers of the right hand
are on the right side of the nose,
the two finger of the left hand
are on the left side of the nose.

Step 3
Press in firmly and hold until the nausea eases.

Step 4
Hold for another five seconds and then slowly remove the fingers.

553 You may do this, Soul, often throughout your day,
for the bladder that is infected.
You will find that it will ease the pain
brought about by the infection,
and it will stimulate the body to heal the infection.

Step 1
Place your right forefinger and the right thumb upon the chest,
the thumb resting between the base of the throat
and above the breast line.
On a slight angle downward from the thumb,
and at least one and a half inches below,
the right forefinger will rest upon the chest.
On the left hand, the thumb and forefinger
will be pressed together.

Step 2
Press firmly both the right thumb and right forefinger once
and hold for the count of three

Step 3
Slide the right thumb and forefinger up one inch
without removing them from the body

Step 4
Repeating twelve times,
slowly press in and hold for the count of three,
release the pressure for the count of three.

Step 5
Slowly release the right thumb and forefinger,
and release the left thumb and forefinger.

554 For those who suffer from incontinence of the bladder.
You may do this often throughout your day,
and it will stimulate the muscles and the nerves
within the bladder to operate,
to regain the loss of elasticity.
All actions are done slowly.

Step 1
Press together the thumb and forefinger of both hands,
press the pads of the other fingers together, left to right,
but the palms are not touching

Step 2
Bring the form you have created up in front of the throat,
hold for the count of five seconds.

Step 3
Move that form in front of the forehead area
and hold for the count of five.

Step 4
Bring the form slowly down
and slowly open the thumb and forefingers.
Hold for the count of three.

Step 5
Seven times slowly open and close the thumb and forefingers,

and hold for the count of three
each opening and closing..
When you are opening and closing the thumb and forefinger,
your palms are toward the body

Step 6
Move apart the thumb and forefingers

and slowly move each of the other fingers apart.

Step 7
Place your hands palm up
and turn them over toward the bladder.
Hold your hands in that position for the count of seven.

Step 8
Deep breath and slowly placing your hands palms up,
release the breath.

555 This will cause eruptions of gas,
and you may do so as often as you require to relieve gas.

Step 1
Fold the last two fingers onto the palm,
place thumb over the fingers.

Step 2
Place the forefinger and the finger next to it
on the side of the neck,
midway between the chin and the clavicle.

Step 3
Three times press inward firmly, once, twice, thrice,
and then move your hand slightly away.

556 We bring unto you quick release, quick relief for gas.
This is not the gas caused by disease of colitis or variations of.
It is for gas caused by a reaction in the stomach to a particular
type of food or to the speedy eating of a food.

Step 1
Place your hands flat upon a surface palms down.

Step 2
Place the forefinger of the right hand
over the nail of the left finger.

Step 3
Firmly tap that nail five times until you feel the release.
And you will repeat the five times
until you have found your relief.

557 This will stimulate any problems with the bowel.
It will assist in the easy movement of the bowels.
This may be done no more than thrice daily
and it is to be done slowly.
Before you begin the exercise again,
pause for at least five minutes.

Step 1
The fingernail of the left little finger
will rest upon the pad of the right little finger,
the pads of the thumbs will touch.

Step 2
Place together the other fingers, pads touching pads,
but held apart so that the air may enter in and out.

Step 3
Place the hands above the heart area
and move slowly downward to the solar plexus,
and then up again to the heart
and back down to the solar plexus,
and up to the heart and back down to the solar plexus.

Step 4
Gently, slowly move apart the fingers
and place the thumb and palms up.

558 Souls of earth, to stimulate the sluggish liver.
This exercise will be done a minimum of three times
every other day for one week.
Thereafter whenever you feel that your liver
requires assistance you will do the exercise once a day
until you have accomplished.

Step 1
Place your left hand palm down.
Press firmly with the right thumb
in the middle of the underside of the left forearm.
If you press in the right spot, you will feel a tingling in the hand,
and you will know that you have now begun
to stimulate the liver.

Step 2
Ten times move the thumb in a circle in a clockwise direction,
while pressing firmly on that spot.

Step 3
Place your right hand palm down.
Press firmly with the left thumb
in the middle of the underside of the right forearm.
If you press in the right spot, you will feel a tingling in the hand.

Step 4
Ten times move the thumb in a circle in a clockwise direction,
while pressing firmly on that spot.

Step 4
Press together the thumbs and the forefingers of both hands,
right to right, left to left
and release as a completion to this exercise.

559 When the liver is ill functioning
and not to its optimum potential,
you will notice extremes of temperature,
more so than you were used to.
You will have a slight bloating, not in the stomach,

but above the stomach between the heart and the naval,
not protuberance, as in a hernia, simply a slight swelling.
You will notice a pallor to your being.
You will notice a sluggishness to the mind.
You will notice an irritability.
All of these, Soul, taken together are indications
of a sluggish liver, one that requires revitalizing.
This will encourage a sluggish liver to refine its operation.
This exercise done once daily, for a period for eight days
will encourage the most sluggish of livers.

Step 1
Palms facing the body, entwine your fingers, thumbs up.

Step 2

Place the hands thus entwined in front of the body,
centered in front of the solar plexus area,

Step 3
Fifteen times, open and close the entwined fingers without
moving the hands apart, then rest your hands.
Repeat the fifteen times, then rest your hands.
Repeat the fifteen times once more.

Step 4
Release the fingers.

FULL BODY

560 Souls of earth, we give unto you pressure points.

This pressure point when massaged in a clockwise direction,
or press intense, will alleviate the discomfort caused
by overstretching of the muscles within the arm.
Whether it be the wrist, the elbow, the shoulder, it will alleviate.
Massage for no more than thirty five seconds at the most.

• • Pressure point for bursitis:

Step 1
Fold in the last two fingers on the right hand and the left hand,
against the palm,
your thumbs will rest upon the third fingers.

Step 2
Cross the arms, the right over the left,

Step 3
Take the first two finger of both hands,
do not massage,
press up and down firmly.
Press so that you feel pressure and it will alleviate.

• • Pressure point for those who have the neck ache;

Step 1
Fold in the last two fingers on the right hand against the palm,
your thumb will rest upon the third finger.
The left hand palm up and open.

Step 2
Place gently against the artery of the neck, the first two fingers.

Step 3
Slide the first two fingers to the side
toward the middle of the throat.

Step 4
And then, slide down slowly until you reach the collarbone.

Step 5
Press on the bone, once, twice, thrice. Pause.
And press again, once, twice, thrice. Pause.
And press again, once, twice, thrice.

Step 6
The same will apply for the opposite side.

Only you will use the left hand and fingers in position
and press the collarbone on the right side.

• • Pressure point for the beings who feel constricted in the chest
due to a variety of pulmonary diseases.
This exercise will expand for a time your capacity to breathe.

Step 1
Fold in the last two fingers on the right hand against the palm,
your thumb will rest upon these fingers.

Step 2
Fold in the last two fingers on the left hand against the palm,
your thumb will rest upon these fingers.

Step 3
Place the first two fingers of both hands
upon either side of the breast bone.
Six times gently push inward and out on both sides
towards the center of the chest.

Step 4
Deep breath, release.
And you will notice how much better you can breathe.
Do not overdo this exercise, this we caution you.
This may be done up to five times per day.

• • Pressure point for any nausea, for any dizziness.

Step 1
Fold in the last two fingers on the right hand against the palm,
your thumb will rest upon the third finger.
The left hand palm up and open.
You will be sitting down.

Step 2
Place the forefinger of the right hand
in the middle of the wrist of the left hand,

Step 3
Press inward, once, twice, thrice.

Step 4
And then knead with your fingers that area
until you feel the nausea, the dizziness pass.

Step 5
And then you will ensure that as it passed, it will not return
in the immediate future, by doing the same exercise
to the right wrist with the left fingers.

• • Pressure point for the headache of the eyes.
It will alleviate somewhat the migraine,
but it will do more for other types of headaches.

Step 1
Fold in the last two fingers on the right hand
and the left hand against the palm.
Your thumbs will rest upon the third fingers.
You will be sitting or laying down.

Step 2
Place the first two fingers of each hand
in the middle of the eyebrows on your forehead,
and press inward the flesh, once, twice thrice,

Step 3
The third time hold for a count of three.
And then very slowly, move your hands away

Step 4.
Bring the fingers back once more to the middle of the eyebrows .
Hold for a count of three and release.

• • Pressure point for the sufferer of the migraine.

Step 1
Fold in the last two fingers on the right hand
and the left hand against the palm,
your thumbs will rest upon the third fingers.
And your head will be upright.

Step 1
Place the first two fingers in that dent at the base of the skull.

Step 2
Six times move slowly and firmly up and down[71] very gently.
If it begins to pain, you will stop and wait until it passes.

Step 3
Slide your fingers across the neck
to the back of the middle of the ears,
press firmly into the middle of the back of the ear
and hold for a count of three.

Step 4
Release slowly and gently and you will notice
the pain has considerably eased.

• • Pressure point for the sore eyes, those that are pained
by the sun, by allergies, by overwork.

Step 1
Fold in the last two fingers of the right hand
and the left hand against the palm,
your thumbs will rest upon the third fingers.
And your head will be upright.

Step 2
Place the two fingers at the crook of the eyes, the end of the eyes,
and partially upon the temples.

Step 3
Gently massage in a clockwise direction, once, twice, thrice.

Step 4
Gently slide the fingers over the eyelids,
until they meet at the bridge of the nose.

Step 5
Gently slide the fingers slowly back over the eyelids
and back to where you began at the eyes.
When you open your eyes, you will note the relief that you feel.

• • Pressure point for the sinus.

Step 1
Fold in the last two fingers on each hand against the palm,
your thumbs will rest upon the third finger.
Head upright.

Step 2
Place the first two fingers just under each cheekbone.

Step 3
Three times push upward slowly and gently on the cheekbone.
Hold it for a count of three, then relax.

Step 4.
Slide your fingers down to your chin
maintaining the touch with the flesh.
Press the fingers lightly into the middle of your chin, and release.

• • Pressure points for the toothache.

Step 1
Fold in the last two fingers on the right hand
and the left hand against the palm,
your thumbs will rest upon the third fingers.
And your head will be upright.

Step 2
Press lightly on the side of the jaw at the area of the toothache

with the first two fingers.

Step 3

The other side, not in pain,
press deeper with the first two fingers,
not so that you hurt yourself, only firmly,
and massage in a clockwise direction three times.

Step 4

Three times press very gently upon the side
that has the toothache.

Step 5

Three times, again on the other side not in pain,
press not so that you hurt yourself, only firmly
and massage in a clockwise direction.

Step 6

On the side that has the ache, press once, twice, thrice, gently.

Step 7

At the same time slide the first two fingers of both hands,
forward to the center of your chin.

Step 8

Place one set of fingers below the lip in the center,
and one set at the center of the chin.
And three times press inward gently at the same time.

Step 9

Slight breath in and let it out slowly.
Slide the first two fingers of both hands to either side
at the very back of the lower molars.

Step 10

Press inward gently once, twice, thrice.
And then, slowly move your fingers, away.
If you become dizzy, stop moving your fingers away.
And then, resume when the dizziness passes.

• • These particular two pressure points will assist
in the pulmonary function of those who have diseased
lungs, especially the latter stages of the diseases,
even the cancers.
You will be alleviated,
and this will stimulate the healing that you will undergo.

Step 1
Fold in the last two fingers on the right hand
and the left hand against the palm,
your thumbs will rest upon the third fingers.
And your head will be upright.

Step 2
Place the two fingers of the right hand just below the throat area,
the finger pads one on top of the other,
second finger over the forefinger.

Step 3
Place the other two fingers of the left hand,
below the breast at the diaphragm area.

Step 4
Three times press lightly in and out,
alternating the two pressure points.
If you are feeling great discomfort at the area below the breast,
ease up on the amount of pressure you are placing.

• • These pressure points will assist with the kidney disease.
Also those beings who are afflicted with bladder problems.
This particular exercise will help to alleviate
all forms of pelvic disease
whether in male or female.
It will stimulate the healing
and alleviate the sharp pains often experienced.

Step 1
Fold in the last two fingers on the right hand
and the left hand against the palm,

your thumbs will rest upon the third fingers.
And your head will be upright.

Step 2
Place the first two fingers of both the right and the left hands
between the lower rib and your waist.

Step 3
Press firmly but gently inward once, twice, thrice.
The third time hold the pressure for a count of five seconds
while also holding your breath for the count of five.

Step 4
Release the breath,
gently release the pressure of the fingers on the sides.

Step 5
Once more into the side press firmly but gently inward
and hold for the count of five and slowly release.

Step 6
Place the first two fingers of both the right and the left hands
approximately six inches in a straight line down.

Step 7
Three times press in and out upon either side,
the right to the right,
the left to the left, in a rhythmic manner
in, out, in, out, in, out.

Step 8
The third time, hold for a count of four.
Take a deep breath and release in a controlled manner,
four times: wh wh wh wh.

Step 9
Four times press in and out upon either side,
the right to the right, the left to the left,
in a rhythmic manner
in, out, in, out, in, out, in, out.

Step 10
Take a deep breath and release in a controlled manner,
four times: wh wh wh wh.

• • Pressure point for the legs that are aching.
This will assist to calm, to alleviate pains
associated with the circulation of the leg.

Step 1
Fold in the last two fingers on the right hand
and the left hand against the palm,
your thumbs will rest upon the third fingers.
And your head will be upright.

Step 2
Place the pads of the first two fingers of both hands
in the middle of the top of the thighs.

Step 3
Three times press down with the pads
as deeply as you are able without pain or discomfort.
Note: when you release, do not move your hands away
but maintain a slight pressure during the count of three.

Step 4
And then move your hands away and you have completed.

• • Pressure point for the restless leg,
This is done, morning, noon and night to alleviate the restless leg.

Step 1
Fold in the last two fingers on the right hand
and the left hand against the palm,
your thumbs will rest upon the third fingers.

Step 2
Place at the very top of the knees the first two fingers
right hand to right knee, left hand to left knee.

Step 3
Six times back and forth slowly and gently, knead the flesh,
moving the fingers back and forth
without leaving the flesh.

Step 4
After the sixth time raise your fingers off the knees.
And then, bring them back down for a further six.

561 We would have you understand a major pressure point
is the spine, particularly the lower thoracic.
If you cannot reach it with your own hand or arm,
then use a wall or a tree.
You will feel a great release of tension throughout your being.
This point will also alleviate anger.
It will not dispense totally, but it will alleviate it,
that you may gain control and direction.
This point also is most advantageous for the being in depression,
for although it will not completely remove the depression,
it will alleviate and allow some semblance of control.

Step 1
Place the fingers of your hand on your back
or place your back against a corner of a wall or a tree.

Step 2
Six times firmly massage this area in a clockwise direction
by moving your fingers or your body.

Step 3
Pause for a count of three.
Take a deep breath and exhale the tension in a whoosh.

Step 4
Five times firmly massage this area of the back.

Step 5
Pause for a count of three.
Take a deep breath and exhale the tension in a whoosh.

Step 6
Four times firmly massage this area of the back.

Step 7
Pause for a count of three.
Take a deep breath and exhale the tension in a whoosh,
and push your breath out for a count of three.

• • We would have you understand the shoulder blades
are most prone to showing tension.
This is a little known area of release for those
who have problems with their posture,
who bend over a great deal.
Remember to do so do so first thing in the morning,
before beginning the day
and then on and off throughout the day as needed.
For the being who has osteoporosis the spine is often irritated,
this exercise, done very gently,
will assist in building strength.
And repeated exercise of this type will assist you in recovering.

Step 1
Arms held against the sides, but elbows slightly out.
Palms against the thighs.
Spine and head as upright as possible.
Hold for the count of five.

Step 2
Place your hands palms up and open, elbows slightly out.

Step 3
Four times, move your shoulders back and squeeze,
each time hold for a count of three and release.

562 We would have you understand,
you may soothe a feverish child,
one who has become irritable,
one who will thrash around and can not seem to find rest.

Step 1
Take the hand of the child
and gently turn it over so that the palm is up.

Step 2
Place your hand over the child's palm

Step 3
In a clockwise direction,
slowly and gently rub the palm of the child's hand.
And you will begin to see almost immediately
the child calming.
Keep rubbing in the clockwise direction,
until the child has ceased to be frenetic
and has drifted off.

563 This is for for the child who is feverish,
fevers for which there is no known reason.

It will not drop immediately from over 100 to the norm,
but it will gradually come down.

Step 1
Lightly place your palm down upon the forehead of the little one.

Step 2
Gently slide the palm down over the eyes,
rubbing lightly, clockwise, once.

Step 3
Slide the palm back up again to the forehead,
and back down over the eyes, and up again,
gently rubbing and repeating
until you feel a change in the temperature,
until you feel the being cooling.

564 For those who have clogged arteries.

You will find that if you do this five times daily,
you will see an improvement in the artery
and its movement of oxygen to the heart and the brain.
It is specific to the arteries.

Step 1
Place the palm of the right hand upon the left side below the top of the shoulders but above the heart area.
Hold the other hand out, palm up.
Turn and hold your head to the right.

Step 2
Seven times in an up and down motion,
rub the palm of your right hand within that area.

Step 3
Complete by rubbing in a clockwise direction, once, twice, thrice.

565 To stimulate the flushing of fats from the body,
the fats that cause plaque in the arteries.

Step 1
Right elbow close to the body, slightly cup the right hand,
hold it at a slight angle downward.

Step 2
Place the left thumb on top of the pulse of the right wrist.
The forefinger of the left hand will gently hold the wrist.

Step 3
Move the thumb firmly in a clockwise circular motion
on the pulse and continue until
you begin to feel a warmth throughout your body
and a tingling at the top of your head.

Step 4
Deep breath and exhale.

Step 5
Left elbow close to the body, slightly cup the left hand,

hold it at a slight angle downward.

Step 6
Place the right thumb on top of the pulse of the left wrist.
The forefinger of the right hand will gently hold the wrist.

Step 7
Move the thumb firmly in a clockwise circular motion
on the pulse and continue until
you begin to feel a warmth throughout your body
and a tingling at the top of your head.

Step 8
Hands palm up and turn them over as a completion.

566 For those who have numbness in the feet or hands,
not due to nerve damage in the sense of a diabetic,
but due to stroke or crippling arthritis.
You may do this exercise as often as you require
until you begin to feel the numbness recede.

Step 1
Feet placed upon floor or as close to as possible.
The head in an upright position;

Step 2
Palms up and placed just below the heart chakra
and slightly cupped with the thumbs
touching the forefingers.

Step 3
Move the palms toward each other
in the area of the heart chakra.

Step 4
Touch the fingertips at the fingernails, in the cupped position
and hold that position for a count of five.
You will feel a warmth beginning at the feet
and traveling up the spine unto the top of the head.

Step 5
When the warmth reaches the top of the head,
gently and slowly move your palms slightly apart
and hold at the heart level for a period of five seconds.

Step 6
Slowly move the hands back together again,
and when the fingertips touch, gently move your hands
so that the palms are facing toward the heart chakra.
Hold for five seconds.
Feel the warmth and then move the hands apart.

567 For the whole circulatory system.
You may find at first
you will feel as if the blood is rushing to your head,
and so you will always do this in the sitting position.
If you do feel this
simply place your hands palm down on the chest area
with firm pressure and deep breath,
hold for a count of three,
release the breath and the blood rush will have gone.

Step 1
Place the right arm upon a surface, palm up
and place the palm of your left hand
over the top of the right wrist, fingers held out.

Step 2
Seven times, rhythmically rub back and forth upon the wrist area,
up to the center of the forearm and down to the palm.

Step 3
Place the palm flat upon the wrist
and the fingers and the thumb around the wrist.
Hold for the count of three.

Step 4
Seven times, quickly, firmly
press upon the bottom of the wrist with the fingers.

Step 5
Seven times, rhythmically rub back and forth upon the wrist area,
up to the center of the forearm and down to the palm.

Step 6
Clasp your hands together at the palms and you are done.

568 To stimulate the healing of skin problems
such as eczema or psoriasis.
You will, Soul, do this exercise up to five times a day.
This will help soothe and ease the burning and itching
associated with the eczema or the psoriasis.

Step 1
Right thumb held over the last three fingers of the right hand,
left hand held palm up

Step 2
Place the forefinger of the right hand
within the center of the left palm.

Step 3
Firmly but gently, press once, twice, thrice.

Step 4
Lift your finger slightly up from the palm
and hold for the count of three.

Step 5
Repeat Steps 3 and 4 twice more.

569 For those children afflicted with itchiness,
whether it be a childhood disease
or whether it be from a plant, an allergy.
We will have you understand the soles of the feet
are most efficacious in assisting the easing of the itching.
You will do this four times to the left foot
and four times to the right foot:

Step 1
Place your right hand in a cupped position,
thumb touching the forefinger.

Step 2
Cradle the sole of the left foot in the left hand
and with the right hand stroke downward from the toes.

Step 3
As you come to the heel, move your hand outward,
spreading your fingers and thumb apart.

Step 4
Place your left hand in a cupped position,
thumb touching the forefinger.

Step 5
Cradle the sole of the right foot in the right hand.
and with the left hand stroke downward from the toes.

Step 6
As you come to the heel, move your hand outward,
spreading your fingers and thumb apart.

570 For those beings who suffer from cold air,
who do not have enough coverings or do not have heat.
You will find your natural heating element internally
will be switched on.

Step 1
Place your left hand palm down over the back of the right hand,
fingers close together.

Step 2
Holding the position given,
turn the palms in toward the heart chakra area.
Hold for a count of three.

Step 3

Bring the hands in that position unto the throat chakra area
and hold for three.

Step 4

Maintaining the hand position,
slowly move the hands down unto the sacral chakra area
and hold for the count of three.

Step 5

Move the hands back up to the heart area,
hold for the count of three,
and then slowly release the hands and place palms up.

571 We give unto you a quick remedy for the external cold
when you have little opportunity for heat
to warm thy being.
This will stimulate your own internal mechanism
for warming your being.
This may be done for the infant also by the parent.
It will prevent illness due to freezing,
it will stave off frostbite.
It may be done often depending on the severity of the cold.

Step 1

Place the thumbs against the first two fingers,
the other fingers will not be touching.

Step 2

Place unto the left fingers on the top of the right shoulder
and the right fingers on the top of the left shoulder
and press in as well as you are able
and hold for six seconds.

Step 3

Fold in the last three fingers against the palms.

Step 4

Place the forefingers and thumbs on either side of the throat,
thumbs resting on the thyroid area.

Three times press lightly in with the fingers and thumbs,
holding for the count of three each time.

Step 5
Leaving your left forefinger and thumb
lightly pressing against the neck,
move your right forefinger and thumb up
unto the third eye and press both areas three times.

572 We give you this exercise to warm the cold body
when weakened by bronchitis, lung problems.
This will, Soul, bring your temperature up three degrees.
Repeat the four steps sequentially three times.

Step 1
Hands palm up.

Step 2
Place upon your left shoulder your right hand,
your left hand on your right shoulder

Step 3
Maintaining the position of the hands,
move your arms, while crossed, slowly up and down,
up and down, up and down.

Step 4
Deep breath, hold for a count of three, breathe out forcefully.

573 For those beings who have difficulty
with the extremities of their being turning cold.
Continue this for no more than five consecutive times
before you rest.
Should your extremities again become cold,
you may resume within the half hour.

Step 1
Place together the pads of your forefingers and your thumbs.

Step 2
Place the hands over the ears, and press lightly,
in a rhythmic manner:
one and two, one and two, one and two.

Step 3
Maintaining the light pressure upon the ear area, deep breath,
hold for the count of three
and exhale to the count of three.

Step 4
Press lightly inward in a rhythmic manner:
one and two, one and two, one and two.
And you will notice your extremities beginning to warm.

574 For excessive heat, to cool the body.
This is especially helpful
for a being who may be close to heatstroke.

Step 1
Place the pads of the last two fingers and the thumb together.

Step 2
Spread wide the first two fingers

Step 3
Bring the hands in this position
unto either side of the neck below the ears
and lightly press the first two fingers in
on either side of the neck.

Step 4
Press in and out, and in and out;
quickly, in and out in and out.
You will feel a perspiration
begin to relieve your body of the excess heat.

Step 5
When you feel that perspiration, cease the in and out,

bringing both hands up unto the third eye area,
gently pressing the first two fingers of each hand
onto the brow area.

Step 6
Press, release, press, release, press, release.
Exhale, whoooo, and your temperature will have dropped.

575 To enhance and stimulate the healing
of a fractured or broken bone.
You may do this often throughout the day to stimulate the healing.

Step 1
On one hand place your thumb and forefinger together,
other fingers splayed.

Step 2
Place the other hand palm down

Step 3
Place this thumb and forefinger
in the center of the back of the hand,
and press firmly, holding for five seconds.

Step 4
Maintaining the position, slightly raise the thumb and forefinger,
and then press down again unto the back of the hand.
Press firmly, holding for five seconds..

Step 5
Maintaining the position,
once more slightly raise the thumb and forefinger,
and then pressing down again firmly
unto the back of the hand and hold for five seconds.

Step 6
Release the thumb and forefinger,
palms up and you have finished the exercise.

576 To enhance the healing of a sprained wrist, leg,
any part of the arms or legs, even unto the shoulders.
If you are not able to physically do this,
recall you may do so in the mind,
and it will have an equal effect.

Step 1
Place your hands palm up.

Step 2
Bring the palms together in the prayer or namaste position,
place the left thumb over the right thumbnail,
hold at the heart level for five seconds.

Step 2
Move the palms apart and place them
as far as you are able physically,
toward the tops of the shoulders,
holding that position for a minimum of five seconds.

Step 3
Move your palms, placing them over your ears,
hold for three seconds,
remove, palms up and you have completed.

577 For beings who are healing from a major sprain
or torn ligament, a broken bone,
we would offer you an exercise to stimulate
a quick healing, to stimulate flaccid muscles
that have become flaccid because of under use.
Even if there is a cast upon one of the limbs,
this exercise will still be efficacious.
This exercise may be done as often as you wish.

Step 1
Place your hands palm upward upon a flat surface,
your feet, as far as you are able, flat on the ground,
or at least the soles pointing toward the ground.
The legs, the ankles must not be crossed.

Step 2
Place your head downward as far as you are able comfortably.

Step 3
Cradle the back of the right hand in the palm of the left hand.

Step 4
Maintaining the position,
bring the hands up to in front of the heart chakra,
and hold for a count of five.

Step 5
Deep breath through the nostrils, push it out through the lips.

Step 6
Maintaining the position of the hands,
slowly move your hands slightly downward.
And then, reverse, placing the left in the right.

Step 7
Bring the hands upward again in front of the heart chakra
and hold for a count of five.
Breathe in through the nostrils, exhale through the lips.

Step 8
As quick as you are able, release the hands
from touching each other in a quick motion,.

Step 9
Repeat the back of the right hand cradled in the left.
Hold for the count of five.
Take a deep breath through the mouth and then quickly release.
It is the quick movement that will enhance the vortex,
that will stimulate the vortex to heal the flaccid muscles.

578 For any being who has flaccid muscles within the arms,
we have an exercise to tone the muscles.
You will begin with three repetitions, and as you gain in strength,
increase daily by one repetition.

When you have obtained the maximum toning of your flaccidity,
once weekly will be enough.

Step 1
Hold your arms out in front of you as far as possible.

Step 2
Fold your hands into a fist,
pointing downward and hold for the count of fifteen.

Step 3
Slowly release your fist, spread your fingers wide

Step 4
Repeat Steps 2 and 3 twice.

579 For the flaccidity of the legs and the thighs,
begin with three repetitions.
As you attain proficiency,
you will feel the tightening of the muscles as you practice.

Step 1
Place together the sides of your feet
and scrunch your toes underneath as far as you are able.

Step 2
Move your feet in this position toward your body
and hold for a count of fifteen,
keeping your feet together.

Step 3
Slowly release the feet, relax.

580 For the stomach flaccidity and the area directly above.
If you have a hernia, Soul, you will not do this exercise.
This will tone the flaccid stomach muscles.
In the beginning, most who have the flaccidity
would only be able to do three times.

Each time you become more proficient
you may add another to the exercise,
as long as they are comfortable.

Step 1
Place your palms on the stomach area on either side of the navel.

Step 2
Bend the forefingers of each hand,
placing the thumbs over the nail beds.

Step 3
Press gently into your stomach, lifting it up slightly,
and hold for a count of seven.

Step 4
Let the stomach down slowly and release.

581 For those beings whose limbs are twisted or gnarled,
indeed it is possible to assist them to straighten.
This is the same as for the legs or the arms
or the hands or the feet.
As you place your hands upon them,
you will ask them to understand the healing
may take place only with their permission.
As they give you the permission, then proceed with the Steps.
This will build up a vortex of Energy
that will enter in to that limb.
This may be done on a regular basis up to five times per day
until the limb has straightened its being,
until the gnarled is no more,
until the withering is no more.

Step 1
Place upon the limb the palm of your hand.

Step 2
Five times rub the palm lightly down the length of the limb,
from the top of it to the tip of it.

Step 3

Follow the same process for the opposite limb,
whether it be gnarled, twisted or straight.

Step 4

Place your hand underneath
either the palm or the sole of the limb.

Step 5

Seven times, slowly and rhythmically, bring your palm up,
move it slightly away and then place it back on the limb.

Step 6

Seven times, on the opposite limb,
slowly and rhythmically, bring your palm up,
move it slightly away and then place it back
and you have completed.

582 This exercise will assist
when the muscles have become tense,
not to the point of abject pain,
but tense to where you are holding
yourself unknowingly tensing your body.
This will relax and bring to your attention
the tension within your muscles.
You may do this once a day.
It is especially efficacious for those beings who must sit
for long periods of time or stand for long periods of time.

Step 1

Place the left the hand touching the right shoulder,
place the right hand on the left shoulder.

Step 2

Breathe deeply to the count of three,
then relax and whoooosh the breath out,
allowing the tension to ease.

Step 3

Gently rock your being slowly back and forth thrice.

Step 4
Once more, deep breath,
hold for the count of three and exhale, whooooosh.

Step 5
Slowly remove your right hand and slowly remove your left hand.

Step 6
Place the hands palms up in front of your being,
the fingertips gently touching each other on the nail bed.

Step 7
Thrice, slowly, gently rock your being.

Step 8
Raise your head up as far as it will go
and hold for the count of seven
feeling the tension drain from throughout your body.

Step 9
Move your head back to the upright position,
slowly turn your hands over and you have completed.

583 For beings afflicted with the ravages of diabetes,
the damage done to the nerves by the disease,
to ameliorate any damage done to the peripheral nerves
of the limbs of the diabetic being,
even before the ravages begin of the nerves.
This will stimulate the heart action.
It will create a vortex between the heart and the will
enabling the reawakening of deadened nerves
allowing the tingling, the feeling,
to return to the digits of the hands and feet.

Step 1
Place together the pads of the forefingers and thumbs.

Step 2
Close the rest of the fingers into the palms.

Step 3
The thumb and forefinger of each hand touch
at the first joint of the forefingers.

Step 4
Place your feet upon the floor,
your head placed in a downward position.

Step 5
Place the hands in the position
in front of the center of the second chakra area.
Hold for a count of five.

Step 6
Maintaining the position of the hands,
move to the front of the first chakra area
and hold for a count of five.

Step 7
Three times move back and forth
between the front of the first and second chakras,
maintaining the position of the hands.
Each time hold for the count of five.

Step 8
Slowly move your fingers away from the palm,
but maintaining the thumb and the forefinger together.

Step 9
Bring the right thumb and the right forefinger
over left thumb and forefinger
in front of the heart chakra.
Press lightly into the heart area and hold for a count of five.

Step 10
Maintaining the light pressure, deep breath, release slowly.

Step 11
Slowly move your hands away
and slowly release the thumbs and forefingers.

584 We give unto you an exercise to enhance
the Energy level when you have low energy
due to dis ease,
whether it is physical, emotional or mental.

Step 1
Place the pads together of the thumb
and the forefinger of the right hand.
The other fingers loosely held straight out.
The hand will be above a surface.
The feet flat on the ground if at all possible
or at least toward the ground.

Step 2
Bring the thumb and the forefinger
to very tip of the bridge of the nose,
hold that position for the count of four.

Step 3
Separate the thumb and forefinger
and then slide the thumb and the forefinger
down the sides of the nose until
they have reached the face area below the eyes.

Step 4
Pinch gently that area of the nose
and hold that pinch for a count of four.
You will feel a vibration, a tingling,
a sensation at the back of the head
and you will know you have the correct area.

Step 5
Release slowly and move your hand slightly away from your face.
Bringing your thumb and forefinger back together,
slowly bring your hand down in to its original position.

And then, release the thumb and the forefinger.

585 To strengthen and invigorate the meridians
from the tip of your toes to the top of your head.
You will feel the blood flow increasing
and you will feel invigorated.

Step 1
Rest your arms comfortably upon a chair.

Step 2
Place all fingers upright.
Bring together the pads of the forefingers,
the next two fingers and pads of the thumbs.
The other two fingers are spread out.

Step 3
Raise the center position of the forefingers
and point the pyramidal structure toward the feet,
hold for minimum five seconds.
You may increase as you are able.

Step 4
Maintaining the position of the hand,
move the hands in a clockwise circle five times

Step 5
Bring all the fingers and the pads of the thumbs
upward as far as you are able over the crown chakra,
and hold for three earth seconds.

Step 6
In a clockwise direction, five times,
make a circle over the crown chakra.

Step 7
Maintaining the positions of the thumbs and the fingers
move your hands down, with the palms pointing outward.

Step 8
Slowly separate the fingers and thumbs, place hands palms up.

586 An exercise for those beings
who are unable or refuse to exercise
by walking or other forms of bodily exercise,
but have the ability to swing their legs
or have them swung for them.
Do this as often as possible throughout your day
and you will find that it stimulates your being.

Step 1
Sit in a chair, place your hands palm down upon a surface.

Step 2
While sitting, swing freely your legs, back and forth.

Step 3
Moving rhythmically but emphatically, quickly:
one and two, one and two, one and two,
one and two, one and two, one and two.
As you begin to ache, cease.
As the ache fades, repeat once more.

587 In the morning, for those who have difficulty
rising with any enthusiasm for the day.
This will stimulate your whole being
and you will look forward to the day.
Indeed, it will pick you up.
If you have not the ability to rear up with your arms,
do it with your mind.

Step 1
Sit, spine as straight as possible,
hands upon a surface palms down.

Step 2
Rear back and bring your arms upward

and as far back as you are able.

Step 3
Deep breath, controlled exhalation, five times: wh wh wh wh wh.
You will feel your stomach pulling inward.

Step 4
Bring your hands palms down, then bring the arms down.

Step 5
Rear back and bring your arms upward
and as far back as you are able.

Step 6
Deep breath, controlled exhalation, five times: wh wh wh wh wh.

588 Do this before your retirement time.
You will find that you will relax and enter in to sleep very quickly.

Step 1
Sit in a chair with a back.

Step 2
Lean into the back of the chair, placing your arms straight out.

Step 3
Place your palms face down.

Step 4
Feet on the floor as close to the floor as possible
and tense up your whole body

Step 5
While maintaining that position,
slowly bring your neck to the right as far as you are able,
and slowly bring it back to the left as far as you are able.

Step 6
Return your head to the center, slowly take a deep breath
and release the breath forcefully.

Step 7
Allow your arms to relax, your body to relax.

589 To assist in the overall health during pregnancy,
from the third to the six month.
You may do this, Soul, three times daily.
We would suggest that you space it out
and not all three at the same sitting.

Step 1
Place your hands palm up, thumbs resting against the forefinger,
fingers held closed together.

Step 2
Place the right forefinger in the middle of the left palm
and press gently, once, twice, thrice.

Step 3
Move your finger slowly up the middle of the forearm
until you reach the inner part of the elbow.

Step 4
You will find a spot that causes
within the upper portion of your forehead a tingling.
Gently, but firmly press upon that spot once, twice, thrice
and hold for the count of five.
You will begin to feel a warmth
within the lower portion of your body.

Step 5
Place the left forefinger in the middle of the right palm
and press gently, once, twice, thrice.

Step 6
Move your finger slowly up the middle of the forearm
until you reach the inner part of the elbow.

Step 7
You will find a spot that causes

within the upper portion of your forehead a tingling.
Gently, but firmly press upon that spot once, twice, thrice
and hold for the count of five.
You will begin to feel a warmth
within the lower portion of your body.

Step 8
Place your hands in the prayer position.

Step 9
Slowly move the hands apart
and place them palm down upon the womb.
And you will find them quite warm.
Hold the palms upon the womb for the count of five.
Deep breath, exhale and feel, Soul, the happiness within.

EMOTIONS

590 To recall the calmness of the spirit of your being,
we would have you throughout your day, often:

Step 1
Hold together the pads of the thumbs and forefingers.
Hold close the other fingers.

Step 2
Place right hand over left.
The edge of the right palm
resting upon the forefinger of the left palm.

Step 3
Deep breath.
Slowly bring the hands up unto the eye
and hold for a count of three,
and exhale.
Feel the pull of spirit upon your being.

Step 4
Slowly bring the hands palms down,
deep breath, exhale.

Slight bow of the head and you have completed.

591 For anxiousness, anxiety before entering in to an exam,
any sort of exercise that you view as a test
in the broad scope of the word.

Step 1
Press together pads of the thumb and forefinger
of the right hand.

Step 2
Press against the nose,
in the area between the bridge and the nostrils.

Step 3
While pressing firmly, take a deep breath,
hold for the count of three, release, whoosh it out.

592 To gain some clarity regarding what you think of
as the bane of your life, and stimulate your will to alter.

Step 1
Place your palms flat upon a surface, fingers spread,
thumbs spread.
Hands are not touching each other at this point.
Notice the pyramidal shape
between the forefingers and the thumbs.

Step 2
Head down as far as you are able,
gazing into the center of the shape,
thinking a thought which seems to be
in the very being of your life
that which harasses your mind,
seemingly causing your whole life to be unhappy.

Step 4
When you have captured that emotion,

maintaining the pyramidal shape, slowly move together
the fingers, the forefingers, the thumbs
and hold for seven seconds,

Step 5
Gently move your hands apart slowly,
place palms up and bring your head upward.
If you are dizzy, pause, let it pass,
and then continue to raise your head upward.

593 We would offer a simple exercise
to bring to a halt your being,
when it is seemingly mired in negativity.
It is not necessary to do this exercise quickly,
for you may find your self becoming dizzy,
because it does, indeed, create a vortex in your being.
It is akin to the golden thread of care.

Step 1
Sit at a table, place your feet as well as you are able on the floor
or pointing toward the floor.

Step 2
Place your hands facing each other, palm toward palm,
fingers held close together, thumbs against the forefingers.

Step 3
Move the hands in their positions,
to either side of the ears, not touching,
but in front of the ears.

Step 4
Slowly move the torso to the right.
hold for three and slowly return to the center.

Step 5
Slowly move the torso to the left,
hold for three and slowly return to the center.

Step 6
Slowly move your hands down maintaining their position
and place them again on the table.
You will notice a calming begin in your being,
enough that you may refocus y
our intention to move away from the negativity.

594 Souls of earth, to calm the temper:

Step 1
Place your right forefinger outward.
Your right thumb is touching the other fingers.

Step 2
Take your left hand and place the thumb
underneath the first joint
near the fingernail of the forefinger.

Step 3
Place the forefinger of the left hand on top of the joint.

Step 4
Three times press lightly both the forefinger and the thumb,
release pressure.

Step 5
Deep breath, release and you will refocus your being,

595 We give unto earth for the broken hearted
lost in the throes of grief.
Many cases of relationships on your earth
find you with the heart aching, tormented and torn.
We have a suggestion, to assist you to quickly mend the heart.
We speak not of the physical mending
but the emotional mending.
The emotional mending will have a positive effect
upon the physical, the total physical being.
You will need to do the Steps thrice.

You will find the heart mending,
the mind focusing on new opportunities,
no longer buried in the pain of past.

Step 1
Find a comfortable position.
You may lay or you may sit.

Step 2
Place the pads of the thumb
and forefinger of each hand together,
the right with the right, the left with the left.
The other fingers held loosely.

Step 3
Bring together the forefingers and the thumbs of both hands.
Again, the other fingers are held loosely out,
not touching each other.

Step 4
Three times while maintaining the position of the hands,
bring them up unto the third eye.
Touch gently the eye and hold for the count of three.
Move away slightly and bring it back again.

Step 5
As well as you are able, a deep breath and allow the tears to flow.
Allow the sobs to enter out from your being.
Allow the pain to leave your being.
Allow the pain to be taken by the Angels unto Creator.

Step 6
When your sobbing has ceased, Souls,
bring your hands down back into the initial position
and move your fingers and thumbs apart.

Step 7
Place your hands palm up and allow the fingers and thumb
to totally relax in a palm up position.

Step 8
Deep breath and gently exhale.

EPILOGUE

Excerpts from the Textsum.

The Keys
607 Souls of earth, we present unto you
Farside Truth and Purity.
Within these Volumes, Souls of earth,
we present for your edification
various ideas and concepts.
We present to you, Soul, for you to absorb,
to contemplate, to discuss and to discern.
We would have you understand
what we give forth may be construed in various ways,
depending on your interpretation individually
of the words that you read.
Indeed, Souls of earth, there will be much consternation,
there will be much discussion, and it is as it should be,
for learning is always a process of absorption
and questioning and discernment.
What we present, Souls of earth, is Truth.
It is from Farside Purity.
It is, Soul, for your understanding of why you chose
to come unto the earth,
of how you chose to come unto the earth,
and the very purpose of your humanity.
We do not, Soul, demand complete understanding;
we do not, Soul, demand acceptance.
Indeed, not.
Souls of earth, we welcome discussion.
We welcome further questioning.
We welcome, Soul, studying.
We welcome groups joined to discern, to learn, to discuss,
to move forward in their quest
of their Soul journey upon the earth.
Welcome, beloved readers.
Stay as long as you wish.
Pour over every word, and know as you read and discern,
always with you are your Angels and your guides.

We thank you, Souls of earth.

608 Volumes one, two, three are Keys.
These, and these alone are members of seven Keys.
The Keys will be brought forth to humanity and bound as one.
These will form a Truth that men will live by.
These will form Energy discussions.
These will collaborate research into Quar.
Negativity will cease, for Truth will be found
within the Volumes seven.
All Light, all Truth of earth is found in these Volumes.
From science will come a Volume
that gives path into the aperture,
a recognition of third eye.
From the field of mathematics will come a Volume
that validates the equation you have been given,
that gives a path into the Quar.
The remaining two Volumes are containing Truth
of religions and humanities.
These will validate the first three Volumes.
The beings are already stirred,
they have already set themselves in motion
and are receiving anomalies that are required.
The three Volumes are gifts unto Creator, not unto humanity.
They are, Soul, placed in the space of humanity
that humanity may recognize the purpose of their being.
Many tire, become weary.
Do not become weary and heavy laden,
but recognize the purities of whom you are.
There is, Soul, in Truth as in Negativity
a resounding continuation of energies that accelerate,
and so it shall be
with the Volume of one, two and three.
Souls, we speak of Volume, for indeed,
although they are a Trilogy, they are one,
for the message is incomplete in a single Volume.
The Negativity will spew forth and then will come a need
to embark upon the gist of language,
for indeed it is all that is simple, not complex.

The need to see the beauty of the individual
is, Soul, mandatory to the coming forth.
Did you think, Soul, that Negativity was idle?
Negativity is aware of the entrapment,
Negativity is an Energy of awareness.
Farside Souls prod your being, prod your being
to recognize your Purity, your holiness.
For you, Soul, have within your being the pathway
to the Second Gateway.
Souls of earth, your energies are scattered.
You are in the process of reclaiming your energies
and spearheading your energies unto the
finalization of that for which you came and entered in.
Your energies physically are scattered.
Your energies mentally are scattered.
Your energies of the Soul are scattered, but fear not
for your Spirits have a firm hold upon your purpose.
You will find yourselves entering in to a greater phase,
a greater earth level of spirituality.
You will, Souls, have a greater focus
upon the spirituality of your being.
Souls, understand the complexities with which
you will make things simple.
Understand the world awaits the complex to be simple.
Understand the world awaits the explanation, the clarification.
Know ye that you will be a fountain
for those who thirst for clarity,
for direction, for guidance,
for those who would hold the staff of wisdom,
for those who would care for their fellow beings,
for those who see in to the Soul.
Accept, Souls, accept thy Purity, accept thy wisdom.
Do not reject that which you are.
Open thy hearts to all.
Open thy hearts to even those who would toxify your labors,
who would spew on thy teachings.
Know ye that the world awaits.
Prepare ye the way, Light the path to bring the brethren home.
This is not an insurmountable task.
Hold thy Purity, give it forth.
And know ye, Creator accepts thy gift.

Holy beings thou art upon this earth
for you have entered in to the covenant.
But understand you came from another realm.
You entered in from
what we call for your understanding, Farside.
Upon Farside you are Humanity,
Upon this rests the Keys for the implosion.
You came unto the earth to gather scars.
You came unto the earth to embrace negativity
and overcome that negativity.
Why? To open the very gates of transition
in your oneness as humanity.
For you will have shown the Angels the scars of your being
and shown them that Creator will not be contaminated,
for negativity may be overcome.
Allow the Wilful Child to return
from whence the Wilful Child comes.
Within the Keys are all that you require.
It fills the knowledge of your Holy being
who within the oneness of your being
completes the oneness of humanity.

609 Energies of Purity, beloved of your Creator,
walk in the path of your Energy.
Know, Souls, the purpose of your entering in.
Your vision of earth is not of earth, it is for earth.
You have come with a purpose unto the planet earth.
All that you have prepared before you
is for the purpose of humanity.
All that you have prepared before you is given in unification.
All Souls of the Farside have witnessed
the oneness of the gathering.
All Souls of the Farside know the entering in of your being.
You are not idly sent forth.
You are not, Soul, on this earth with choice of your humanity.
Hear this, "You have entered in!"
The Souls you were held the total choice,
but your choice has been made upon the Farside.
Your single purpose is the purpose of humanity.
Do not glory in negativity, Souls,
glory in the purpose of your coming.

See yourselves the beacon that you are,
see yourselves united as an Energy field
that will reach and reach and reach.
All that was written has been carefully put forth,
all that was written has been carefully attended.
And you would ask, Soul, to alter.
Were you to alter, you would not be where you are.
Your life would cease, your being but memory.
The purpose is greater than your own.
Soul, the Books will be printed in many forms,
in partition of three, in separateness of three,
in languages, but the intent
will reach the earth's religions.
They will create controversy.
They will create agitation.
And you will understand why the jot or the tittle
must not be removed.
You will understand there is a purpose to all that you do.
Souls of earth, we say unto you; mankind attributes
much to Creator, to God, to Allah, that belongs to man.
You have been instructed at this table
as have the other channellers of the Keys,
to not change a jot or tittle,
and it will be;
Soul, the Keys will be the first
that have not been altered by man,
Understand, Soul, we speak of negativity,
bringing forth the Keys without taint
can only be accomplished by not altering,
by not interpreting,
What is written it written.
What is given is a placement upon what is.
It is a template upon which you are setting your information.
It must, Soul, conform to that which is.
There is, Soul, misconception in many areas of the Volume,
to that which is upon your earth.
There will be great consternation and repute.
But that which is will be proven.
Do not misdirect.
Do not feel it must fit into earth conception,

for that which you have offered is Farside healing.
What is of earth is of earth.
What is of Farside is of Farside.
There are, Soul, great valleys between the concepts

610 The words are given.
The words are corrected for punctuation and ever inscribing,
the words will be presented finished at a chapter end.
This is.
So be it.
Each Soul will place their honour upon the words
from their Eye.
Not from their human ear or eye,
but from the vision of knowing within themselves
that they are seeing a Holy writing.
It is but a minute portion of the Key of the kingdom.
There are many portions.
many portions brought together
to bring Souls to an uplifting with a new vision
of what is Truth, Purity and Love,
the source of the Energy.
Behold, know the writings are words of Energy.
They are brought from the source of all that is.
Accept that knowledge will be found,
as all Keys will be brought together,
all words will be brought together.
Soul, Flow.
Flow is the upward lift toward the Energy.
It is movement of Truth unto the Path of Holy.
It is the endowment of blessed.
It belongs in the space you are in.
The crown of Truth is Flow.
You have been transmitted.
The Energy has entered the words upon the register.
Soul, do not doubt the beloved Souls about your being.
All agonies of the heart and the mind
have brought you to awareness of Purity.
To see the word will bring blessed peace to Souls in great travail.
Soul, we reach to your Soul.
All that would be has place.

It is, Soul, purpose of your being.
Unto holiness, offer the cup overflowing with giving.
Extend to the lowly thy hand, rise up,
only to be reaching upward to Holy.
The Volume has layer and layer and layers.
The teachings extend beyond who you are.
There will be connection and connection and connection
and connection and connection.
Each Soul drawn, not unto self,
but in an outward vision of pure state of being.
Soul, to be in the great wave is to feel
the deep rock within the vessel that you are
and to feel the chasm and the plate
in rising to the foremost wave.
Soul, have no fear.
Have only within the containment of the being,
the surety that all things will come to pass.
The mighty will be brought low
and the low will be raised up.
Soul, be thou blessed.

611 Earth has a time.
Oneness is essential unto the coming forth of the Volumes.
The gentle passage of words, one to another,
the gentle flow of Spirit, one to the other.
Unto each has resonance of being entered in.
Understand first the Purity of thy being.
We would have you know, Soul, how we see you.
You sit about a precious table in a box
and all about you neighbours reflect in what you do
and we hear, Soul, the words spoken.
And we see your beings come to the entry way of the box
and shed your earth self and the Light of your being
enters in to reside at the table.
And when you gather together there is a great Energy that collects
and those who pass by can feel the Energy of your being
for the box has no containment for Energy.
We would have you know, Soul,
as you reside within your boxes,
there were gracious trees that grew and felt the air,

the wind, the rain, the snow.
They have known all the soft and the harsh,
the cold and the warm,
and they have wrapped themselves about you
to protect you.
But what you have is not yours.
What you have is not for you.
It is for all humanity.
And all that you do, you will understand,
that the word is going out,
even when you know it not.
A resounding echo is being sent outward.
The circle at the mountaintop is of great value.
It is where the Souls will come,
where earth will come to know
of the beginning of the words.
All that is is Purity.
The land has been sacred for eons of time.
The water runs deep within the land
and all the energies will witness a place
where Souls will come to be taught.

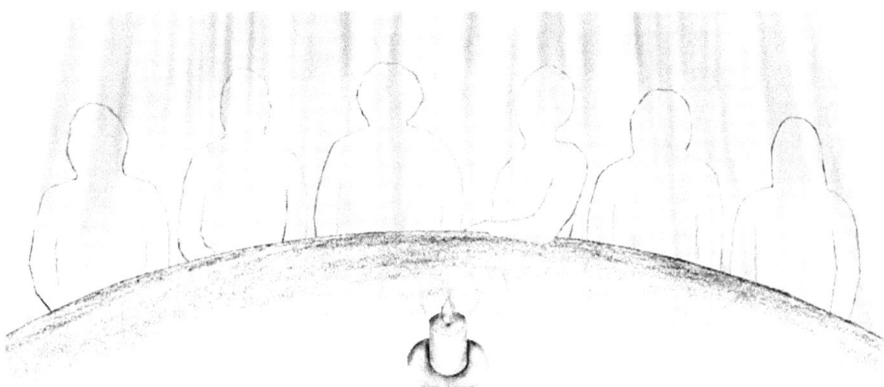

612 Blessedness, peace be unto you.
Enlightenment brings weight upon a being.
One cannot look sideways, may not look backwards,
but must ever see the map of self.
All Souls carry the potential of enlightenment.
Few Souls reach the status of enlightenment.
Souls, there has been a forum of Souls gathered
in the name of the Creator of the Energy of all.
Each Soul has participated in that forum.
You are one of many.
There have been selected Souls who have agreed
to come together for growth.
This growth is not a function to appease the ego.
It is a gift of Love.
It is to mankind.
All gifts of enlightenment are outward flowing.
Each group of Souls have extensions throughout your world.
They are brought together
to place at the feet of humanity a choice
in a time of great peril.
There are Keys within each delivery
and they will meld as the puzzle of life melds.
Who will stand apart or who will step in, is choice.
It is not beyond the ability that you have given to yourself.
It is freedom from ego that is necessary
to place self on the path for the completion.
This is the Path to the words.
It is done in humility.
You have taken a path away from ego.
You are Loved.
You are treasured beyond the teardrop of the Angel.
Soul, accept the gift of humility to self
and know it is not fate, it is not destiny.
It is.
You are Holy.
To accept that you are not, is choice.
To refuse is not an issue.
It is a step that you take.
It is a sight of Light and Truth and ever unto ever.

Soul, reach into the being of self and do not scourge thy Soul.
Do not place unworthiness where there is worthy.
Acknowledge with humility the offering of thy Soul,
  for your day starts with the potential of enlightenment.
It is a time to prepare the being.
Cleanse the Soul.
Know you are on the path of goodness, words of enlightenment.
It is the agreement.
It is the charge
The weight of a burden is not in the agreement.
It is a commitment to Holy.
It is the purpose of your being.
Gather from this knowledge and all will meld.

613 The circle of Truth.
Souls, how great thou art!
Souls of earth, you have taken a step to the Farside.
Do not, Soul, place antagonism within thy being.
Hold thy Energy as pure.
The Circle of Saints witness that which you do.
The beloved Angels witness that which you do.
Earth awaits that which you do.
Place no fear in the words, the words belong to Truth.
The Path you have entered in is Purity.
Behold, that which is written, is written.
It has been the Eye of your being that has seen the words.
They have been recovered from many tests,
  texts of your being.
Souls, you have drawn your beings to a circle.
Souls who have held violence,
  Souls who have known anger and deep pain,
  have brought their being to tranquillity
  for the purpose of giving of Volumes,
  of passing the key unto humanity.
Do not tremble in the passing.
Know your being has the Energy of Angels.
Know your being has the Energy of the Circle of Saints
  and all the entity of Michael
  have been brought to your space.

Beloved Souls, see before you
the Truth, Purity and Love of thy Creator
and bless the completion of thy work.

614 There is a momentum to your earth Soul.
Do you understand, Soul, you have entered in.
You have entered in to a forum.
Each being of the six has momentum to the publishing.
Each being must leave the humanity they have
by conquering that humanity.
Many are doing well.
Some few are lagging.
There is a great desire for control within each of the six.
The need is intense and intensified by the path ahead,
for the path will not be easy.
The path is tremulous.
There are within each being, an intense desire to serve.
There is within each Soul a great Purity,
but there is a great need to acknowledge
you must advance with a will of own,
not the will of another,
not the presence of another, but the presence of self.
Some few find the presence of self wanting.
There is an urgency for all to meet
in the supreme oneness of being.
You have carried yourselves far.
Do not dissemble.
All energies can be directed to the one,
to uplift the one, to uphold the one.
It carries a reason beyond self.
It carries an intent beyond self.
It does carry the releasing of all earth purpose
toward the energy lagging.
You have carried the beam strong within your being.
The Soul who cannot reach the beam requires Energy.
You hold within you, that Energy.
All beings must enter in to living.
You are on earth, not angel.
You delve into the practices of earth
and often it is unseemly
and you will see yourselves so humourous

when you are where we are.
But you understand that each has strength in his own way.
Ah, Soul, we will tell you when you address the positive
and make the negative of no consequence,
the positive increases.
You are dwelling on the consequence of the persons.
Dwell on the positive.
Insist on the positives.
You have not idly come together.
You did not idly knock upon a door.
Each person has a sacred identity
that your earth could not contain.
It is so, but that you have a purpose you know.
Fulfill the purpose.
Move quickly to that which is to be done,
So be it.

615 We would have you understand.
the great push of Negativity upon your beings.
Never, Soul, underestimate Negativity, for it is fully aware
of how closed is the completion of the Keys.
It is aware of that which you do.
And it would entice you, Souls,
to succumb to frustration,
to succumb to depression,
to succumb to stagnation.
We ask you not to be angry with Negativity,
with the Brother lost.
We ask you to embrace, not enfold within your being,
but embrace as you would a child in fear or discomfort
and ease that discomfort and ease that fear.
Would you not do this for the small child,
for the small human babe?
We ask that you do this for Negativity.
Soothe and offer unto Creator that energy
that you embrace but not enfold.
Understand it is as if a dam has burst open
and all that energy is focused
within a narrow channel of humanity,
and you are swept up in the whirling waters,
swept up in the chaos.

And yet, understand, you are not simply flotsam and jetsam.
There is a boulder you may reach unto
and stop your spewing into chaos.
And that boulder is acceptance,
acceptance of who you are, of whom,
of that from which you have come.
Acceptance that you have the key,
you have the knowledge and the understanding
to withstand the whirlwind.
Take heart in the oneness of yourselves.
Take heart in the oneness of your Souls.
Take heart in the oneness of your purpose.
Hold on and know the Angels are ever in front of thee,
on all sides of thee, above and below thee.
And you are never alone,
even in your loneliest moments, Soul, you are not alone.
Even the most heinous of deprived, depraved being
is never alone.
Always the Angels offer.
But you must accept that which they offer.
Beloved Souls of earth,
you do not know, but you are within the whirlwind.
You will have an awakening to the power of the whirlwind.
You, Souls, will be able to grasp
and hold the power of the whirlwind
and release it forth to return to the Great One,
for that is whence all motion comes.
You have within your tidal bores,
you have upon the ocean,
you have upon your deserts, whirlwinds.
And you have in many places, small, whirlwinds that
seemingly come out of nowhere
but are indeed reminders
of that which is a whirlwind of the proportion
of a world wind you have not seen.
It is a wind, beloved Souls, that will scour the earth.
It will be as the dry earth after a cleansing, drenching rain.
So shall the whirlwind be
and you will be cleansed and scoured.
You will feel the breath of clean air.

You will inhale and expand your lungs
and know the breath of Great One.
And you will, Souls of earth, grab the whirlwind
and enter in to the pit.
And you will cleanse and be as the whirlwind.
You will scour the pit as you bring forth the beloved lost Souls,
the beloved Brethren.
And all shall be new, cleansed
and perfumed with the ecstasy and glory of mankind.

616 Beloveds, we have been with you throughout your path.
We have walked with you as you have endeavored
to fulfil that which you have entered in.
Soul, do not despair
for there is no object in the Path of Creator.
You have entered in to the Path.
You have entered in to the negative plane
to project unto mankind the alternative
to negative endeavors.
You have chosen to enter in.
Souls of earth, do not languish in your being
that the Path does not seem clear.
From our side the Path has incredible clarity.
You have entered in to be human
that you might offer the Keys forward, have the pathway.
Blurred, indeed, as the eyes mist,
so that you might not see all that there is to come.
For many might be of faint heart.
Be overwhelmed with the knowledge
that the achievement is nigh unto done.
And yet, it is not done.
And each of you in your heart of your being know this.
Souls of earth, in many pockets of your earth,
Souls like yourselves have expended their Energy
on the purpose of humanity.
Their endeavors will meet with your endeavors.
The clarity will be seen as Souls reach out
to the likeness of each Volume.
As though, Soul, the fingerprint were one and the same.
It is so, is it not!

For indeed all that is attuned to earth is of Creator.
Creator of the science, of the math, of the humanities,
indeed, of the very Souls of men.
Bring unto your being a deep feeling of peace.
Yet know in your being, each one,
your heart and Soul are bound together.
Your entering in and your going out
have a purpose unto Creator.
You who have entered in human, are as all human
bound in the flesh that you have,
with the opportunity to reach beyond the flesh
of your being to the consciousness, the awareness,
of that Creator who you are in part of.
Breathe deeply, Souls, feel in your being
the earth you are a part of.
Know it is in the very home of the Volumes.
For they have entered in to a Truth.
You are, each one, to find joy in your being.
To reach unto the joy of being,
the message will come forth in joy.
You are the teachers.
You have perused and perused and perused the Volumes.
Each one being brought to hear over and over and over again.
There are no coincidences, Soul.
Each endeavor has been to enlighten the teacher
as well as the student.
For the teacher must often be a student.
You have spent many earth years bringing the Keys to being.
And now you understand that this is not just a book.
It is a revelation to mankind
of why they have entered in to earth, of the very purpose.
Souls of earth will be at your door.
Many will call unto you names to cast you down.
Many will harbor great resentments
because of that which has been put upon
the religions of the world.
And yet, we say unto you.
You will glory in that day.
You will not fear.
Many will recognize the Truth.

And the words will be scrutinized, as many words have been.
And they will be found to withstand that scrutinization.
More than that, Souls, they will be found
to coincide with four other Keys.
And the learned men of earth will seek out the four Volumes
to set them in the path of research,
in the path of earth climate,
in the path of science and math.
The clerics, the scholars of religion
will seek out the three Volumes
to place a mark upon them,
but they will withstand the scrutiny.
And in the research of the words will the religious leaders
look unto themselves and their houses of worship
and they will understand
how lacking in humanity are they.
You are walking the Path and you see the end.
We remind you, Soul, there is no end.
There never was.
And each of you must know this.

Healing Books

617 We can have you recognize that which you have set.
The teachings will occur so that earth will recognize
where they need to direct their energies.
We would have you understand
the Keys, the three to which you attend
and why you further expound.
Soul, the further are not Keys.
Within the first three Volumes is the purpose of humanity.
Within the first three Volumes
is the completeness of why you are.
The fourth is healing.
It will replace the formulas that earth concocts.
It will bring value to the Soul in the eyes of mankind,
for through healings they will understand
the connection of the triad of earth to the Soul.
Those that follow will be those that,
when the Volumes are printed, will ignite controversy,

that will be the basis for the Healing Center,
the knowledge that you are not alone on your earth
but many work with you.
That Souls from other worlds are preparing as they may,
the earth, for that which would come.
These beings prod and prompt,
these beings cover earth with protection and all beings
who have entered in to serve mankind.
We can have you recognize that which you have set.
The teachings will occur so that earth
will recognize where they need to direct their energies.

618 The remedies, Soul, are for all the world,
particularly the east.
There are, Soul, many remedies within a small section of pages.
the publisher will format a way
in which more may be accessed.
Understand, within each section, within each heading
it will be alphabetized and indexed.
It will be easily found if you are looking for a particular ailment,
whether it be mental or physical.
You will, Soul, cover front and back; the ages.
For the energies of the ancients have come through the ages.
Soul, you will understand the East Ritual will be on the back
and will have other languages.
You will understand it is imperative for the East Ritual
to have as much exposure as possible to humanity.
It is the balance that will bring humanity unto its onenes,
the balance of the individual.
It is, Soul, the recognition of the healing that is available
that will bring forth the connection to the Keys.
Soul, you will understand, the Keys are a mighty tome,
they connect with the other Keys.
Harken, Souls of earth, to that which you do.
Refrain from consternation.
Refrain from being overwhelmed by the enormity of your task.
Refrain, Souls of earth, from disparagement.
Cling, if you will, to the Purity of your being,
Souls of earth,, you are high beings within the maelstrom of earth.
Your Spirits are mighty in their support of your Souls.

619 You are Soul and you have entered in as a gift,
and you ride the wave of contentious humanity
and you bear within your being
the frenetic force of all humanity.
You see below you the great waters swirl
and meet each other in claps of thunder and strife.
And then, as you raise your hands
and place your hand upon the waters,
the waters still and the strife lessens
and the calm becomes,
and you have the power to alter the wave.
You have the power to intone stillness.
You are not the strife.
You are not the frenetic source.
You are the power that calms the sea.
You are the gentleness that abides
so that when the sea witnesses the calm,
the stillness becomes,
the waves ride high within your being.
Beloved one, ride the wave as Buddha.
Acknowledge the presence of the wave
and hold onto the calm within thy being,
Bless your being that allows you to live,
to have life upon the earth.
Bless the eye that gives you the opportunity
to see life beyond the earth,
and to travel in your consciousness.
Bless the thoughts that run through your mind,
both negative and positive, for all have purpose.
All that you do, all that you come in contact with,
all that there is has purpose.
Rain your blessings down on all that is
and follow your blessings
with the action of compassion and Love.
Souls of earth, you are called blessed,
and you are blessed and blessed.
Share the blessings of your being.
Share the blessedness of your being with all,
as you bless all that is.

620 Souls of earth, within the treasury of your being,
the greatest worth is your compassion,
when you have reached to overflowing
with your compassion, not for yourself but for others,
when you have struggled through the innuendoes of love
and understood that love for self
does not derive satisfaction,
love for others does not have the value
that compassion has.
Within compassion, Soul, there is an empty basket,
an empty hand, for it is always given forth.
It is filled and given forth.
Do not struggle in your wisdom
that that which you do will be printed.
We tell you, Soul, it will be, it is.
But, all compassion is a portion
to move humanity's efforts forward.
You are Holy.
You have entered in to earth Holy.
Do not question in your Soul all that you do.
Do not concern yourself with the ebb and the flow.
Know that there is the vibrational Energy
attached to the Volumes.
The healing will enter in first.
It was always to be so.
You will, Soul, as six recall the first channeller.
And as the first channeller, the Energy will come first.
It is not, Soul, right or proper.
It is as it should be.
Each will share in the efforts momentarily and in sacredness.
And each will share as a portion that which will be received,
equally, one unto all.
It is not a portion, Soul, that one has the more or less.
It is, Soul, that six entered in to bring forth for humanity.
And that it will succeed will be that six have made it succeed,
not in the earth's conception of what is right or wrong,
but in the will of compassion one for the other.
For in this mode will you find compassion for all humanity
and will be recognized as healers unto humanity.
This we say unto you.

621 Earth, be thou known of the eternal flame,
be thou entered in to the eternal Flow.
Unto thee has the echo come;
unto thee has the reverberating sound entered in.
It is not casually entered.
It is purposeful and enters through Quar and Quar and Quar.
Souls of earth, you tremble in fear.
You place your value in residing on the path of negativity.
You are abounded by negativity.
Know this.
You are, Souls, contemplating the Truth of the Angels.
And how may we reside on earth as Angel?
Beloved Souls of earth, you are an echo.
You are the sound that is taking you to the distant valley.
You are Purity itself.
You have entered in to earth in the purest state of being,
the flesh has entered in and yet, earth,
you recognize negativity first.
We would have thee see with thine eyes all the Purity
that surrounds thy being.
We would have thee know that in each despot is Purity first. We
would have you know the inveigling energy has clutched
and we would have you not smear the being
with yet more negativity.
We would have you uplift and honour the preciousness
within that being.
Be thou constantly aware of the great Purity.
Understand that negativity is intrusive and you, Soul,
may witness a great negativity
and respond in an echo unto that Soul
and place yet another negativity.
We beseech you rather see the pain of that negativity
that resounds from where you are unto all Souls
that have pain, that have anger.
Do not reside in the space of anger.
All that is around your being will reflect in anger unto thee.
All that is in the echo has a place, Soul, for thy being,
for thy instruction.
Look as a Soul looks unto thy being
and see first the mote in thy own eye.

See first the reflection of thy being
and ever counter it with Love
so that Love will overwhelm thy being
and flow outward from thy being
and the countenance of thy being
will reflect thy goodness
and all that is harsh and unworthy
will fall from thee and the echo of thy being,
From where we are will be seen the Purity that is within thee,
the Truth you will habitat.

622 We have stated, there are no accidents,
there are no coincidences
and this is true even unto when you pass
from the earth plane
and make your choice to return home
or remain in transition.
The moment of demise, Soul, is written on the wall.
You are not alone at any time in your life,
even unto the moment of passing you are not alone.
Your Angels swarm about your being
giving forth Love and comfort.
Your guides present always.
At the moment of your demise,
there may be family, friends, strangers even present ,
but none are there by accident or coincidence.
As your body shuts down, Soul,
whether it is in a quick accident,
traumatic or whether it is a lingering demise,
your Soul consciousness is aware.
And those Souls who accept the demise of their physical body
and begin the transition away from the earth plane,
their Energy of the Soul consciousness
and of the mind raises above the physical self.
Your aura Soul, does not stay upon the physical body,
does not stay within the physical body.
It is not buried or cremated with the physical body.
It rises.
For it is Light.
It is Colour and Sound.
It rises away from the physical earth body.

And the being has choice to reside in transition,
or to enter unto the Light and return home unto Farside.
And we say unto you,
"Do not hold unto these beings.
Rather assist them in leaving transition
and entering unto the Light.
Hold them not to you, Souls.
Allow them to leave."
And those Souls who accept their divinity,
accept they were here to learn,
accept they were here for a purpose
enter in to Timelessness once more.
Oh, the cymbals, the chorus, the welcome from the Angels,
the guides, from those that have gone before,
the ancients or the ancestors, the companions, the pets,
all waiting with loving arms to welcome the being home.
When you leave behind the negativity you accumulated
and enter back unto the Farside,
you will recognize fully you are Holy unto Holy.
You will recognize fully the Light and Colour and Sound
of your being, of Creator's Love.
Souls of earth, how wondrous thou art.
Recognize within your divinity
and recognize the divinity within all of man.
This we say unto you.

623 Souls of earth, we speak of glory;
glory halleluiah, glory road, glory way.
Glory be unto you.
Within their being each humanity recognizes
and knows the glory from which they came.
recognizes the Creator of us all.
Upon the Farside, when you enter in to the earth, Soul,
it is not that you forget the glory of your being.
It is that you place upon your being a veil
so that you may learn, that you may experience,
that you may embrace, overcome negativity
and assist Negativity to return to Farside.
This you agree to do until the time came to enter in to transition
to bring forth the Angels,

to cleanse the earth and transition of negativity,
to begin the Thousand Years,
and then enter unto the Second Gateway.
And we say unto you, humanity upon the earth plane,
you have reached your goal,
you are ready to begin!
There are, Souls, enough of five two level of beings.
There is, Soul, an equality.
You have reached the balance between Negativity and Purity.
You are ready, Souls, to open the gate of transition.
You are ready to join in oneness.
You are ready to remove the veils.
You are ready to acknowledge
and once more know the glory of your being
both upon the Farside and upon the earth.
Souls of earth, we ask that you allow your being
to remove the veils, to accept the oneness of humanity,
to release from your being negativity
and the barrier to the culmination
of the very goal of humanity.
Souls of earth, allow the Light of awareness
to enter unto thy being.
It is humanity that will open the gates.
Hear the trumpet call.
Rush forward, Souls of earth, to your oneness of being.
Rush forward to the gate of transition.
Rush forward to gather the Angels.
Rush forward to gather all the Souls caught in transition.
Rush forward to the glory road that you will open,
the road between Farside and earth.
Respond with all the Love
and compassion that is in your being.
This, we, the Angels, ask of you.

624 We speak of barriers that you have placed over the eye,
the third eye, the eye of beholding.
For it is the eye of beholding wherein which you will see,
wherein which you will know who you are,
the very angelic being that you are,
the very Holy of Holy being that you are,

the very high being that you are.
It is the eye of beholding wherein you read from the Akashic,
from the Writing on the Wall,
who you are and why you are.
It is the eye of beholding that brings forth
healing from the Farside,
from your Spirit, your Essence,
from the very Crystal Cave.
It is, Soul, the eye of beholding
that when you reach unto the knowing,
who you are becomes clear.
And we tell you with the eye of beholding
you recognize that you are a being of seven dimensions.
Your compassion expands.
You recognize Agape Love and the fullness of Love.
And with the eye of beholding you see the dimensional self
of all that is upon the earth and
indeed of the very gracious earth herself.
And with the eye of beholding you know
there is so much more to existence than the earth plane.
Souls of earth, the eye of beholding is within all of you.
It is yours to reach unto, to open fully to be within and without.
This we say unto you with all our blessings.

625 We would have you understand, Souls of earth,
that pain has purpose.
You did not come unto the earth to be totally free of pain
whether emotional, physical, or mental, Soul.
The pain does not need not be physical.
It can be emotional pain, it can be mental pain.
It is yours to overcome.
We do not merely define overcome as ceasing of pain.
But overcome may also be that you leap beyond the pain,
that you experience joy, that you experience purpose,
that you experience compassion,
that you help one another in spite of the pain,
For have you not then overcome the pain!
Understand that every moment that you overcome pain
is a triumph for Negativity.
Indeed, we speak of capital N, Negativity.

When you have overcome pain
you have contributed to the very wellness of humanity,
In your overcoming, Souls of earth,
you have fulfilled a portion of your purpose.
Souls of earth, do not allow pain to overwhelm thy being.
Hold on to the holiness of self.
Hold on to that high being you are.
Hold on to the mantra,
"I am of Light. I am of Love. I am of Creator."
Repeat this mantra until you have overwhelmed the pain
and you have overcome its hold upon your being.
Souls of earth, all that you do is connected,
not just to your earth self,
not just to the humanity you are upon the earth,
but it is connected also to Farside, to your high self,
to those myriad of beings who gather unto your Soul.
Cease to see pain as the enemy.
Place pain in a neutral.
And know that each time you overcome
pain has become a positive, Soul.
And you have gained as has all humanity.
Souls of earth, you are not an accident of birth.
Indeed not.
Your birth is purposeful.
The very time, the very moment, the very space of your being,
you chose in concert with all those involved in your birth,
including, Soul, the ancestors of your being.
You are involved.
You are part of an intricate network, a web of Energy.
It extends for dimension and dimensions and dimensions.
It extends from earth time unto timeless Time.

Appendix A
Daily East Ritual*

"East: it is the passageway to the Farside through the eye.
Its Truth is to be understood as a Love by humanity.
Focus on east at dawn, allowing the negativity
to flow from your being,
receiving unto yourself the goodness of Creator.
All humanity has the availability of this pathway.
The ritual of the east is the Soul's own response
to the positive east which is tao.
Face east, two minutes.
Look with the eyes to the horizon's level.
In the brick wall or the iron cage, or the ornate boardwalk,
know that the east will be with your Soul.
Turn clockwise once to heal.
Energy will flow to the matter before it.
All organs of the body are healed in the circle turn."

*Creator Trilogy, Energy From The Source, Appendix A

Appendix B Book List

Published

by Lucy Dumouchelle

The Binary
Holistic Healing Through
Channelled Ancients

by Kitty Lloyd

Creator Trilogy
First Key Energy From The Source
Second Key So Shall It Be
Third Key Until Then

Supreme Being Trilogy
How To Step To The Path

Forthcoming

by Lucy Dumouchelle

The Binary
Holistic Healing Through
Channelled Entities
&Healing From The Farside

Creator Trilogy
Healing With Echo
Healing With Value
Healing With Intent

by Kitty Lloyd

Creator Trilogy
Trilogy of Consciousness
The Gathering Time
From Whence It Came
Ecstasy

Creator Trilogy
Supreme Being Trilogy
Angels' Ecstasy
The Rejoicing

Creator Trilogy
Echo
Value
Keepers Of The Light

Published by Mountaintop Healing Publishing Inc

ENDNOTES

[1]. purpose of humanity: "You came one and all for the purpose of humanity, which is to recover that which has been lost from Creator, the blessed Holy Holy Holy." Creator Trilogy, Energy From The Source, passage 475.

[2]. salvation - recognition of the Purity of who you are, of the oneness and purpose of humanity.

[3]. Farside - the Energy of Creator's existence for Humanity and other worlds. What you call, heaven.

[4]. High Beings - Souls who have reached manifestation. Creator Trilogy, Trilogy of Consciousness, The Gathering Time, Glossary.

[5]. transition - a self inflicted, voluntary state of purgatory of one's own actions upon the earth.

[6]. The teacher Christ stated, "I am the Light." All Souls are Light in that space. Energy is Light. The Path of our Farside is in the Prism of great Light. Creator Trilogy, Energy From The Source, passage 83.

[7]. negativity - negativity (not capitalized) - The Wilful Child does not create negativity. Mankind creates negativity. Creator Trilogy, Trilogy of Consciousness, From Whence It Came, passage 696.

[8]. karmic station - karma incomplete left at karmic station. Work still to be done, you must enter in to the karmic station. Creator Trilogy, Trilogy of Consciousness, Ecstasy, passage 1384.

[9]. Writing on the Wall - Soul growth planned upon Farside.

[10]. Akashic Record - the map of creation's growth. Creator Trilogy, Energy from the Source, Glossary.

[11].red linears - We see contentious lines that express red, linears that hold pain unto the karmic station. Creator Trilogy, Energy from the Source, passage 220.

[12].brother Negativity - “Negativity is to Love an Energy Brother” Creator Trilogy, Energy from the Source, passage 5

[13]. Flow (capitalized) - Creator’s Energy Path. Creator Trilogy, Energy from the Source, Glossary.

[14]. Gathering Time - Your Souls are uniting with your Spirit even as you are upon the face of earth, and this is the Gathering Time, this is the Oneness. Creator Trilogy, Until Then, passage 1197.

[15]. fence - a vision downward from Farside to earth. Creator Trilogy, Energy From The Source, Glossary.

[16]. Soul of Creator - Soul, you are humanity. You are mankind. In your united oneness, you are the Soul of Creator. Supreme Being Trilogy, How To Step To The Path, passage 573.

[17]. Holy unto Holy - manifested Soul.

[18]. Jinn - one of four alien nations (Lantosia) entered in to assist mankind. Creator Trilogy, Trilogy of Consciousness, The Gathering Time, Glossary.

[19]. Gummeria - one of four alien nations entered in to assist mankind. Creator Trilogy, Until Then, Glossary.

[20]. Pleiadians - The Pleiadians are of the Armada of four who will provide the transportation from the heat. Creator Trilogy, So Shall It Be, passage 224.

[21].Light Beings - inhabitants of Energy Source.

[22]. Angels in transition - the Blessed Brethren.

[23]. equation - see equation of T, Appendix B.

[24]. Essence (capitalized) - the portion of your triad of Soul, Spirit and Essence.

[25]. First Battle - Battle of Love.

[26]. Second Battle - Battle of Purity.

[27]. Cleansing River - fragment of Wisdom sent forth, holding Negativity.

[28]. curtain of care - placed by the Angels to protect all Farside creation from negativity. Creator Trilogy, Energy From The Source, Glossary.

[29]. Third Battle - Battle of Truth.

[30]. Pillar of Light - Creator's Energy spiraling through humanity's Essence.

[31]. Creator Triad - Creator, Godhead, Great One. Creator Trilogy, Energy From The Source, Glossary.

[32]. Prism - To see the kaleidoscope of the Prism is to behold the Oneness of Humanity. Creator Trilogy, Trilogy of Consciousness, From Whence It Came passage 623.

[33]. Triad (capitalized) - Creator, Godhead and Great One.

[34]. Zero (capitalized) - is the Void, Naught. Zero is vortex. Zero is the connector of all that is. Creator Trilogy, So Shall It Be, passage 456.

[35]. Visions - The dates at the end of each passage indicate when the channelling was received. It does not indicate the date of the vision.

[36]. Path (capitalized) - the Energy Flow of Creator.

[37]. Keys - Creator has given to earth seven Keys, each Key to overcome negativity. The Creator Trilogy, which is the first three of these Keys,

is intended to draw all men unto one fellowship."
Creator Trilogy, Trilogy of Consciousness,
The Gathering Time, footnote, passage 356.

[38]. learning station - upon Farside. Where mankind sets the goals for earth.

[39]. Void (capitalized) - wherein all consciousness abides. Creator Trilogy, Energy From The Source, Glossary.

[40]. East - See Appendix A

[41]. High C - the Oneness of Humanity.
Creator Trilogy, Trilogy of Consciousness, Ecstasy, Glossary.

[42]. karma - an action, positive or negative, that alters the Soul's agreement.
Creator Trilogy, Energy from the Source, Glossary.

[43]. Crystal Cave - is the collectiveness. The collectiveness, the combined of humanity who have manifested collectedness.
Supreme Being Trilogy, How To Step To The Path, passage 898.

[44]. Quar - implosion. Entrance in to existences of Purity.

[45]. You may place your hands upon a surface should you feel any stress or strain.

[46]. Mountaintop (capitalized) - One of the seven Energy centers of earth where the Keys will enter in. Creator Trilogy, Energy From The Source, Glossary.

[47]. arms - Energy.

[48]. Idyllic (capitalized) - world of perfection.

[49]. Creator's Yawn - Breath forward of Third Creator.

[50]. Vanguard - Fourteen Creators. Creator Trilogy, Trilogy of Consciousness, Ecstasy, Glossary.

[51]. Hinterland - Negative Void. Al that holds negativity; transition, Cleansing River and earth.

ENDNOTES

[1]. Creator - Creator of our Yawn.

[2]. fence - in this case a vision earthward.

[3]. Farside - the Energy of Creator's existence for Humanity and other worlds. What you call, heaven.

[4]. negativity (small n) - man's negativity.

[5]. Prism - the accumulated energies of humanity gathering unto the Crystal Cave.

[6]. orb - reference to the third eye.

[7]. Mudra - vibrational chant, Energy healing.

[8]. Master Twag - ancient healer.

[9]. Quan Yin - student of Master Twag.

[10]. Hu Li - life incarnate of Master Twag.

[11]. Pillar of Light - Creator's Energy spiraling through humanity's essence.

[12]. Akashic Record - the map of creation's growth. Creator Trilogy, Energy From The Source, Glossary.

[13]. Writing On The Wall - the record of that which humanity has asked of itself.

[14]. High C - the Oneness of Humanity.

[15]. East ritual - See Appendix A.

[16]. high mind - high consciousness.

[17]. veraugo - a conglomeration of tone, a dizziness of tone as in vertigo. But it is referring to color.

[18]. in a spiral - this may be done in the mind or in the physical.

[19]. completed - You will, Soul, experience a bit of dizziness but do not be concerned. It is only your mind altering its focus. You may do this exercise as often as you deem necessary.

[20]. Move on to Step 4 only after mastering Step 3.

[21]. Move on to Step 7 only after mastering Step 6.

[22]. Souls, if you feel lightheaded or dizzy, you will pause until the feeling has passed.

[23]. completed - you may then move your hands apart.As you move your hands apart, Soul, always leave the palms in an upright position.

[24]. third chakra - also known as solar plexus chakra.

[25]. Haaaahh! - If you do not feel that at the sacral level, you have not done it forcefully enough, Souls.

[26]. Haaaahh! - If you have felt, at this point, Soul, the fire in the sacral and in the belly, you have successfully cleansed.

[27]. blow - a blow to the head by any object.

[28]. holding the thumbs and the fingers together - this seals in the vibration.

[29]. You will notice the pain in the ears has eased and the ringing has begun to stop as it lessens.

[30]. slowly bring your elbows up - This will begin to relieve the stress and strain that has caused the neck problems. It will also bring about a stretching of the neck that will allow the fluid freer entry and exit throughout the spine.

[31]. as long as you are able - Some may not be able to hold for five seconds and may have to work up to it. And this is acceptable.

[32]. In a rhythmic manner, back and forth, right and left, do so for seven times, slowly and gently. It is important that you have the rhythm established, Soul.

[33]. as you are able - If you become dizzy, stop, deep breath and then try again to bring your head into an upright position. If you are unable, Soul, to physically bring your head up in an upright position, then please do so mentally.

[34]. Five times chant or sing slowly - You will feel your scalp tingle when you have correctly pronounced the chant.

[35]. back and forth - each back and each forth is one repetition.

[36]. underneath the chin - the fingers will not touch the chin, they will be below the chin.

[37]. move forward three inches and back three inches. Both movements count as one of the three times.

[38]. If you become dizzy and lightheaded stop, take a deep breath and proceed from where you stopped until you have finished.

[39]. esophageal area and back - Slowly, be gentle with your being. Note: At any time, if you become dizzy, stop, deep breath and resume where you left off.

[40]. count of ten - You may rest, Soul, further than ten if you require.

[41]. Hold - If you cannot keep your arms up in the air, you may rest your elbows upon a surface as long as the palms are left over right.

[42]. Steps 6 to 9 - Chanting and breathing into your cupped palms.

[43].You will feel, Soul, the vibration within the lungs. It is important that this vibrational song be done

in a lower key.
You will find that if you experiment in a higher key you will not feel any vibrations within the lungs as you do with the lower key

[44]. ha lay lu yaah - The yaah is emphasized, Soul.

[45]. bah luuue - In all languages you have th color blue in different pronunciations. It is the sounding as given (bah luuue) that matters.

[46]. foot upward - without the full leg extension, only the foot.

[47].deep breath - allow your body to relax, for you will have noticed, it has tensed up during this exercise.

[48]. count of four - from the beginning it may not be possible, but over time and practice it will occur.

[49]. close to the sides - as if you were squeezing the sides.

[50]. It is as if, Soul, you were a lion purring.

[51].Three times - moving the right and left leg counts as one time.

[52]. into the hand - At this point if you are relaxed and concentrating, you will begin to feel a pressure upon your head, especially between the ears. You will feel a tingling at the back of your neck. If you do not feel these things, then we will ask that you begin from the beginning, for you are not relaxed and it is important for the being to be concentrated on healing, not on stress or worry.

[53].slowly bring your head upright - If not done slowly, dizziness may result.

[54]. Soul, it is the syllabication of the words that is important. If you can not string them together with your voice, then chant as close as possible, each syllable one to the other in the mind.

[55]. Step 2 - You will understand that if you are unable to take in the breath for the allotted time, it is to the best of your ability. The same will go for the withered limb, if you cannot place your thumb and forefinger together physically, you will place it mentally. Know that it is done. Have confidence, Soul, in the Purity of your being.

[56]. begin to hum - It is the exercise of the hum that is important. Do not concern yourself so much with the tone, the key, as with the actual humming.
This is to focus on what you are doing.

[57]. chant or sing - It may even may be whispered for it is the vibration of the syllables that is important.

[58]. The second syllable sound (ree) is quick and sharp. For it is the releasing then of the anger.

[59]. o - as in long o sound.

[60]. lite - it is avenue to.

[61]. manifestation - having become fully human.

[62]. completed - In cases of extreme stress, we would explain that this Mudra brings back a moment to the being wherein the physical body has a moment of calm so that the mind has the opportunity to use logic within the situation and you are not mindless.

[63]. At the end of the seven, Soul, you will notice that your little finger is tingling.

[64]. toothache - for the toothache as a result of infection.

[65]. Steps 3, 4, 5 - After these nine repetitions, the pain will begin to ease.

[66].Color and Sound - healing.

[67]. Those who are younger have not generally attained that level of physical development whereby this will be

efficacious.

[68]. With the macular degeneration, we would ask that you add the following: at the end of the third circle: take the hands and instead of bringing them apart, you will remain for another three earth seconds, and then part.

[69]. When you move back and forth, you stimulate the meridians of the upper body, Holding the hands closed with the thumbs over the flesh, you stimulate the natural propensity of the body to heal. The placing of the one over the other brings into balance those meridians of the upper.

[70]. In Step 3, holding it initially for five seconds would encourage the cleansing of the inners. Holding it for ten seconds would encourage an increase in the power of the will, so that the body, the mind will do the bidding of the will.

[71]. Up and down - within a 2 to 3 centimeters range of motion.

INDEX

REFERENT	PASSAGE
Agitation, Alzheimer Or Mental Impairment	504
Allergic Reaction	483
Allergies	450
Allergies	451
Alzheimer's Prevention	361
Anger Excess Toward Self Or Others	415
Anger Prevention	487
Anger, Depression	560
Anger, Rage	486
Anger, Temper	594
Anxiety	412
Anxiety, Panic Attack, Fear of Leaving Home	411
Anxiousness, Anxiety, Relaxation	591
Arm Sprain, Lower	471
Arms, Broken, Strained, Sprains	378
Arms, Flaccid Muscles	578
Arms, Repetitive Motion Injuries	378
Arteries Clogged	564
Arteries, Plaque	565
Arthritic Shoulder, Arm, Hand	535
Arthritis	485
Awakening Sluggish, Stimulation	587
Back Pain, Lower	473
Back Pain, Lower	474
Back Pain, Mid And Upper	539
Back Pain, Middle	472
Balance, Lack Of	484
Bladder	560
Bladder Incontinence, Strengthen Muscles	385
Bladder Incontinence, Strengthen Muscles	554
Bladder Infection	386
Bladder Infection	553
Bladder Infection, Cystitis	475

Blood Flow Sluggish, Need Invigorating	585
Blood Pressure, High	540
Body, Heat, Heatstroke Prevention	574
Bones Broken Or Fractured	575
Bones, Broken	400
Bowel Problems	557
Brain Injury	361
Breast	544
Bronchitis, Body Temperature	572
Bursitis, Shoulder Pain, Arthritis	533
Bursitis, Shoulder Pain, Arthritis	560
Calmness	590
Cancer, Bone	395
Cancer, Brain Advanced	368
Cancer, Brain Stage One	367
Cancer, Esophagus	370
Cancer, Nasal, Mouth	369
Cancer, Prostrate, Rectal	388
Carpel Tunnel	377
Carpel Tunnel, Wrist Strain, Sprain	545
Chakra Blockage	442
Chakra, Cleanse 3rd	356
Chakra, Cleanse 4th	355
Chakra, Cleanse Crown	352
Chakra, Cleanse Root	358
Chakra, Cleanse Sacral	357
Chakra, Cleanse Third Eye	353
Chakra, Cleanse Throat	354
Circulation	399
Circulation	567
Clarity, Resolve	592
Cold Body Temperature	570
Cold Hands, Feet	573
Cold, Frost Bite Prevention	571
Colic	548
Colitis, Ulcers, Burning	549
Colon	387

Constipation	476
Cough ,Croup, Bronchial	528
Deafness, Not Total	522
Depressed, Lack of Energy	499
Depression	408
Depression, Anger, Fear	500
Depression, Deep	501
Diabetes	380
Diabetes Nerve Damage	583
Difficulty Forming Intentions	344
Digestion And Vegetables	547
Digestion, Kidney, Liver Cleanse Toxins	550
Digestive, Parasites, Cohn's	379
Digestive, Severe, Cancer	379
Drug Addiction	348
Ear Tinnitus, Ringing, Infection	364
Earache, Breaking The Cycle	521
Earache, Infection	520
Earache, Prevention	519
Ears, Problems of Hearing, Infection	363
Emotional Chaos, Trauma, Mental Restriction	407
Energy, Low Due To Disease	584
Exercise, Chair	586
Eye Vision Improvement	362
Eyes Sore	560
Eyes, Allergic Reaction, Wind	513
Eyes, Enhanced Vision	515
Eyes, Stimulate Vision	514
Eyes, Tired, Burning, Aching, Blurring	452
Fear, Anxiety, Calming	502
Feet Numb	566
Fever	482
Feverish Child	563
Feverish, Irritable Child	562
Finger Pain, Arthritic, Carpel Tunnel	470
Flu	481
Foot Strain	480

Fright, Anxiety, Agony, Distress	343
Gall Bladder	384
Gas	556
Gas	555
Gas, Burping, Burning	465
Glaucoma	309
Goiter	469
Grief, Broken Hearted	595
Gums, Aching, Sore	453
Happiness	417
Headache	511
Headache of the Eyes	560
Headache, Upper Neck Pain	512
Heart	542
Heart Attack Damage	541
Heart Burn	463
Heart Burn	464
Heart Health	372
Heart Health, Compassion	495
Heart Muscle Weak	373
Heart Palpitations, Irregular Beat	374
Heartbeat Rapid	462
High Blood Pressure	371
Hip Pain	390
Hopelessness	350
Hopelessness, Darkness, Overwhelmed	349
Illness, Ears, Eyes, Nose, Throat	529
Immune System	505
Immune System	523
Indigestion Due To Over Eating	468
Indigestion, Left Lung Pain	466
Infection, Bacterial, Gangrene	398
Infections, Impactions, Gums Or Teeth	525
Itchiness	569
Joy	416
Joyful Relaxation	496
Kidney Disease	560

Knee Break, Strain	478
Leg Circulation, Pain	560
Leg Restless	560
Leg Strain	479
Legs, Thighs, Flaccid Muscles	579
Leprosy	396
Lethargy	498
Limb Atrophied	401
Limb Withered	402
Limbs, Twisted Or Gnarled	581
Liver	558
Liver	559
Loneliness	414
Love, Lack of Universal	345
Lung Damage, Disease	375
Lung Disease	560
Lung, Chronic Infection	376
Lungs	543
Meditation Focus	493
Meditation Mudra	489
Meridians Blocked	491
Migraine	560
Mind Stimulation	497
Mind, Energize, Focus	510
Mind, Unbalanced	346
Multiple Sclerosis	394
Muscles Tense	582
Muscular Dystrophy	393
Nausea, Dizziness	560
Nausea, Pregnancy	382
Nausea, Seasickness, Vertigo	446
Neck Ache	560
Neck Stiff, Injury	365
Neck Tension, Headache, Stress	530
Neck, Misaligned Vertebrae	459
Neck, Pain, Whiplash, Arthritis, Tension	366
Neck, Shoulder Arthritis, Bursitis,	534

Neck, Stiff 531
Neck, Stiffness, Shoulder Pain 532
Neck, Tension, Strain 458
Negativity, Overcoming 593
Night Terrors 488
Nose, Throat, Mouth Healing 526
Pain In Back of Head 448
Pain In Front Of Head 447
Pain On Either Side Of Head 449
Pain, Can't Express 310
Pain, Intense of Unknown Origin 397
Palsy 392
Parents Needing Respite 509
Pelvic Disease 560
Plumbing, Internal Problems 389
Pregnancy, Calming, Peaceful 383
Pregnancy, Overall Health 589
Pulmonary 560
Receive An Answer To A Question 494
Relax Heart, Lungs, Throat, Eyes, Ears 359
Relaxation 551
Rheumatoid 534
Sacred Self 492
Sadness 409
Scabies 405
Schizophrenic, Hearing Voices 347
Seasickness, Vertigo 552
Self Inflicted Injury 360
Separation Pain 413
Shingles 404
Shock, Mental, Emotional 406
Shoulder Blade Tension 561
Shoulder Injuries, Tension 536
Shoulder Pain 461
Shoulder Pain, Strain, Stress 538
Shoulder Stress 537
Sinus 560

Sinus Headache, Draining Sinuses	516
Sinus Infections, Clearing	517
Sinus Pain	518
Skin Eruptions, Rashes, Leprosy, Eczema	403
Skin, Eczema, Psoriasis	568
Sleep, Relaxation	588
Sprain, Major, Ligament, Broken Bones	577
Sprained Wrist, Arms, Legs, Shoulders	576
Stomach Upset	467
Stomach, Flaccid Muscles	580
Stress	445
Stress Of Move, Of Change, Of Death	410
Stress, High Blood Pressure	503
Stutter	444
Teething Child	524
Tension, Frustration	311
Thigh, Lower Buttocks Strain	477
Third Eye	508
Third Eye Cleanse	506
Third Eye, Inability To Open	351
Third Eye, Remove Veils	507
Throat Soreness, Coughing, Strained Voice	527
Throat, Irritated, Ravaged, Red	457
Throat, Sore	456
Thyroid Problems	460
Tooth Ache, Lower Jaw	455
Tooth Ache, Upper Jaw	454
Toothache	560
Trauma of Physical or Emotional Attack	443
Trauma Victims	490
Veins, Collapsing, Atrophy	381
Well Being	391
Wrist Strained Muscles	546

Your cells, Souls of earth, have intelligence,
have an affinity for sound, have an attraction to sound.
Each cell of your body has a role in the overall wellbeing of your body
and it is in the oneness of wellness
that your body attunes itself and vibrates to the HIgh C.
Just as within humanity there are individuals
and yet a oneness within the humanity,
so it is within the individual body and the cells of the body.